LOSING MY
RELIGION
A CALL FOR HELP

D1563118

LOSING MY
RELIGION
A CALL FOR HELP

JEFFREY LANG

amana publications

First Edition
(1425AH/2004AC)

© Copyright 1425AH/2004AC
amana publications
10710 Tucker Street
Beltsville, Maryland 20705-2223 USA
Tel: (301) 595-5777 / Fax: (301) 595-5888
E-mail: amana@igprinting.com
Website: www.amana-publications.com

Library of Congress Cataloging-in-Publications Data

Lang, Jeffrey.
  Losing my religion : a call for help / Jeffrey Lang.-- 1st ed.
    p. cm.
  Includes index.
  ISBN 1-59008-027-0
  1. Islam--United States. 2. Muslims--United States. 3. Muslim
converts--United States. 4. Muslim families--United States--Religious life.
5. United States--Religious life and customs. 6. Religious life--Islam.
I. Title.

  BP67.A1L36 2004
  297.5'74'092--dc22

                                                          2004013559

Printed in the United States of America by
International Graphics
10710 Tucker Street
Beltsville, Maryland 20705-2223 USA
Tel: (301) 595-5999 Fax: (301) 595-5888
Website: igprinting.com
E-mail: ig@igprinting.com

CONTENTS

by the faith she inherited. But that was just the beginning of what I would characterize as the critique and protest phase of my children's religious development, wherein they would raise questions and express reservations about Muslim practices and beliefs.

In retrospect, I should not have been so stunned by Jameelah's question. I believe that very many American children of Muslim parentage have had similar feelings at one time or another. To begin with, they are born into a faith community that much of America looks down on and fears. Children naturally want to fit in, and it could be extremely disquieting to be associated with a despised, alien people. The public perception of Islam has taken a significant downturn since the terrorists' attack of September 11, 2001, but the American general attitude toward the faith and its adherents has always been deprecatory. I recall a research article that appeared before 2001 that stated that over ninety percent of portrayals of Muslims in the last century in English language novels and films have been negative. Based on what I saw in my own childhood, my hunch is that the same is true of other entertainment mediums like television and cartoons, probably comic books and now video games as well.

A large portion of a child's life is spent in school, and Muslim students can expect to meet with bigotry there. Young people can at times be quite malicious, but much more unfortunate is that some teachers can be as parochial as some children, and some teachers use the classroom to preach their narrow-mindedness. Since I began speaking publicly about Islam some eighteen years ago, Muslim parents across the country have continually complained to me of teachers who vilify Islam in class. My children have encountered the same throughout their educations. This year, my daughter Fattin's civics teacher taught her seventh grade students that Islam encourages violence while Christianity promotes peace. My daughter Sarah's ninth grade teacher remarked how ungrateful Muslims are, for according to her, "We keep sending them humanitarian aid while they keep making terroristic attacks on us." Another frequently heard education-related grievance is that Islamic holidays are totally disregarded at school—even when Muslim parents inform teachers and administrators of them—while at the same time Muslim students are required to participate in school celebrations of Judeo-Christian festivals.

Besides encountering prejudice, practicing Muslim children are pushed further toward the margins of American society as many of their religious precepts run counter to societal norms. Premarital sex has become a widely accepted and glamorized feature of American youth culture, yet the Qur'an makes it a punishable crime and places fornication among the gravest sins. Many Americans begin dating while still in elementary school; to most Muslims, however, our society's modern interpretation of dating is absolutely forbidden irrespective of age. Drinking alcohol, which Islam prohibits, is encouraged and celebrated in America. Western fashions are designed to put feminine beauty on display, while traditional Muslim dress goes to great ends to conceal it from public view. Muslim immigrants, whose religion and culture enjoins treating elders with utmost respect, are shocked by the impertinence American children show their parents. Many more examples can be given, but even these show that in America a devoted Muslim will be significantly out of step with the mainstream.

Although there are undoubtedly points of divergence between Islam and American popular culture, the perceived distance between them might be magnified due to the confusion of religion with culture. Most mosques in America are run by immigrants and visiting foreign students, many of whom equate Islam with their birth places' versions of it, which are likely to incorporate customs and attitudes that are not fundamentally "Islamic," in the sense that the textual sources of the religion explicitly require them. To accommodate the diversity of cultural perspectives within the American Islamic community, its leadership most often yields to the most conservative view, even when it has at best tenuous support from the Qur'an and

Hadith [1] literature. There could be many reasons for this. People tend to be intimidated by sternness and rigidity which they often associate with greater religiosity, but such inflexibility could be a reaction to the seeming licentiousness of Western culture and a reflection of the common Muslim preference to err on the stricter side on religious questions. The rigidity might also be a result of the conservatives' typically being the most assertive and unified faction in the Mosque.

This propensity to bow to the most conservative view is particularly evident in the treatment of women in the American Islamic community. Muslim women are normally not encouraged to attend the ritual prayers at the mosque, and when they do, they are put in a separate room away from the main prayer hall. Consequently, visitors to a mosque will usually observe only men in attendance. At most community gatherings, such as picnics, lectures, dinners, feast day celebrations, and conferences, Muslim men and women are segregated. Muslim women are debarred from positions of leadership in many communities, and rarely are women included on boards of directors or executive committees.

Given the dominance of American Islamic institutions by Muslims of foreign upbringing, we should expect that the discourse and mindset of the Mosque will diverge from the mainstream, but here again the fusion of religion and culture of origin can cause American-born Muslims to feel hopelessly intellectually alienated from the Mosque. A dilemma for many Muslim youth is the need to adopt two ways of thinking that could seem profoundly irreconcilable. The Mosque puts enormous stress on tradition and conformance, whereas the larger culture extols rationalism and individualism. Muslims reverence conventions and rules of behavior that are upheld as eternal and immutable, while the mainstream promotes adaptation and innovation. The American educational system teaches

---

1. *Hadith* (ha-deeth): the whole corpus of *hadiths*, the teachings of Prophet Muhammed (peace and blessings upon him). The Arabic plural of *hadith* is *ahadith*, but *hadiths*, used in this book, is an acceptable English form of pluralizing *hadith*.

the importance of critical, objective inquiry, yet the Muslim community is extremely resistant to it when it is applied to Islam. American schools teach children to challenge and to question, but the Mosque teaches Muslim children not to question their religious traditions. Of course, every religion in America faces similar tensions, but in the case of Islam so much of Muslim tradition has been idealized that it leaves little room for reinterpretation and adaptation and hence much room for the creation of doubt in the minds of Muslim youth.

Muslim children in America are thus born into a clash of radically dissimilar cultures—the subculture of the Mosque and the dominant American. Judging from the virtual absence of the second and later generations from Muslim community activities, it is apparent that the great majority of them are choosing to avoid the confrontation by keeping far away from the Mosque and other Islamic venues. There is nothing surprising about this. The second generation is brought up in the most dynamic culture in the world, one that penetrates and influences even the remotest corners of the earth. American music, technology, fashion, entertainment, and news disseminate worldwide. Children in foreign lands, including Muslim lands, sing American pop songs, follow the careers of American celebrities, watch American movies, have their favorite American sports heroes, eat American fast food and wear the latest American styles. If America has this much influence in foreign lands, we can be sure that the outlook and thinking of the second generation will be decidedly American. For reasons stated above and others that will be discussed later, the Mosque subculture seems to many Muslims the very antithesis of the larger society in which they must learn, live, and work. Since this subculture is held by Muslim leaders to be the closest thing to a practical model of true Islam, it becomes very difficult for many of the younger generation to see the relevance of Islam to their lives. I believe that, considering all these factors, it would be truly remarkable if an American Muslim child did not at some point question the legitimacy of his or her faith.

We need to also recognize that not only are most Muslim youth uncomfortable with the American Islamic community, but the community is also quite uncomfortable with them. Like other immigrants, many first generation Muslims are deeply troubled by the culture gap that develops between them and the second generation, as the latter quickly acquire American habits and ways of thinking. For the devout, a religious crisis occurs because the home culture is viewed as Islamic and America as un-Islamic which, when it comes to modes of behavior, means wrong or at least undesirable. Therefore many Muslim immigrants are extremely wary of signs that the next generation is becoming Americanized. Young American Muslims often complain that the older generation continually tests their faithfulness to the home culture and become scandalized when they do not behave like young people "back home." In contrast, although the dominant society may at times exhibit ignorance and prejudice, most Muslim youth with whom I have communicated assert that non-Muslims are in general more accepting of them than the Muslim community. This then is another factor contributing to the estrangement of the second generation from the Mosque.

Crucial to the vitality of any religious community is its ability to attract and engage descendants and/or converts. By this measure, notwithstanding the proliferation of mosques and Islamic organizations, the Muslim community in America is doing poorly. The most recent wave of immigration of Muslims to America began in the late fifties and is continuing today. By now there should be significant numbers of second and third generation Muslims living in the United States, but there is very little sign of the second in America's mosques and almost no traces of the third. Since the sixties, there has also been a large number of conversions to Islam from the African American community, and a steady trickle has come from the rest of the population, but the bulk of converts steer clear of the community, and only a very small fraction of their children and grandchildren are ever seen in the mosque.

Our Lawrence community illustrates the common trend in university towns. Our mosque, located on the periphery of the Kansas University (KU) campus, is at most a fifteen minute walk from the most distant points on the university grounds and no more than a ten minute drive from any location in the city. Over seven hundred Muslim citizens and resident aliens live in town (some estimates put their number at closer to fourteen hundred), while no more than twenty of them attend the Friday congregational prayer; the rest of the congregation, about two hundred students, are visiting from overseas. There are at least two hundred and fifty American students of Muslim parentage at KU, none of whom come to the mosque. Our community has seen about thirty Americans embrace Islam in the last fifteen years; almost all of them stopped coming to the mosque a short time after conversion and at least ten of them definitely apostatized. The two local high schools have around sixty students with at least one Muslim parent and only a few of them come to the mosque or attend community events. Immigrant-dominated mosques normally fare a little better than those run by foreign students, but they too are characterized by low participation of Muslims in the area and scarce attendance by native-born Muslims.

While the overwhelming majority of Americans of Muslim descent have nothing to do with the mosque, there is hardly a ripple of concern within the Muslim religious establishment. The issue is sometimes hinted at in Muslim publications and at Islamic conferences, but the topic gets so little attention that one would think that Muslims in America either are unaware of a problem or else they simply don't care. If it were not for the pleas for help I have received over the years from parents of children who have left Islam, I would have assumed that ignorance or apathy accounts for the community's silence in this regard, but then why is the subject avoided? Despite the many times I have asked this question, I am still not clear on an answer, but I think it comes from a combination of denial, fatalism, embarrassment, and defeatism. Some Muslims see the relative handful of youth that attend Islamic conferences as a sign that all is well; others are certain that God will miraculously turn things around; many parents are too ashamed to discuss the difficulties their children are having with the religion; and others feel overwhelmed and have no clue as to how to respond.

Muslim descendants' and converts' mass flight from the mosques will likely continue unless the community decides to earnestly confront the issue, and this cannot begin until the reasons behind it are understood. Of course, it may be, as some Muslim leaders surmise, that the fault is entirely with the disenfranchised—that they simply choose the ephemeral pleasures of pop culture over the demands of truth – but it may also be that the community is not making much of an effort to reach this population or is committing critical errors in this regard. Clearly, the causes behind the exodus from the community of American-born Muslims will not be discerned unless there is a willingness to hear their complaints, but here there are already colossal obstacles. It is not like the disenfranchised are going to come running to the Mosque to explain their absence. If they still had this much attachment to or concern for the community, they probably would not be keeping away from it. Presumably, their relatives would have some inkling of the causes of their disaffection, but, as mentioned above, the culture of the mosque is essentially traditional Middle Eastern, which has often been characterized as a "shame culture," one in which airing of your family's dirty laundry is unthinkable. There have been academic studies of Muslim assimilation in the West, but I have not seen any that systematically explores the roots of second generation and convert alienation from the Mosque. Hopefully, this type of research will not be long in coming.

Although this book is not such a survey, it is very much informed by the phenomenon of native-born disengagement from the Mosque. For some reason, after the publication of *Even Angels Ask*,[2] I began

---

2 Amana Publications, Beltsville, MD, 1997

receiving a great deal of email and other correspondence from persons of Muslim parentage, converts to the faith, and non-Muslims, asking for my take on a wide variety of religious issues. The greater part of these communications conveyed some misgivings about Islam and a substantial portion confessed outright disbelief. Many of the writers described themselves as having left the faith or being on the verge of doing so; many felt that their doubts already made them apostates. I was profoundly struck that persons beset by doubt would feel the need to put it to the test, but I was also somewhat troubled that they sought me out, for I often felt unequal to the task. Over time, I found that I was getting repeatedly asked some questions, so I created a file in my PC titled "Losing My Religion" where I collected the inquiries and my responses to them, which I would often revise. This way I could quickly retrieve my prior reflections on a theme should it come up again in another conversation. Most of these "answers" turned out to be fairly short, but a few of them evolved into rather long discussions. The latter comprise the chapters of the book, to which are appended some of the more frequently asked questions and answers of the first kind.

A large fraction of the correspondents took issue with Muslim theology, which at first seems a little surprising since Muslim proselytizers often emphasize Islam's theological simplicity and coherence. Yet theology is human theorizing on the nature and ways of God and is bound to be imperfect no matter how well thought out; in fact, the Muslim tendency to idealize past scholarly opinion, in particular ancient theological constructs, appears to be behind many of the correspondents' faith-reason conflicts. I therefore tried to make it clear that in responding to their theological inquiries I was not presenting unadulterated truth but merely sharing an experience of my own coming to terms, through reading the Qur'an, with issues that once blocked me from believing in God. Thus in chapter one I try to recreate as best I could my first experience of reading the Qur'an. I say "recreate" rather than "recount" because it is impossible to replay that experience more than twenty years later. Therefore, chapter one is based on a core of recollections of first encounter with the Scripture supplemented by over two decades of reflection on it. The essential theological ideas presented are contained in my earlier writings, but I was hoping that it would be easier to relate to if presented in their original experiential context.

Another common area of conflict for those who contacted me concerns the classical grading of the *hadith* reports. After briefly touching on this subject in *Struggling to Surrender*,[3] I resolved to never write or lecture on it again. Although I offered what I felt was a defense of its traditional position in Muslim thought—albeit admittedly a guarded one—the initial response to what I wrote was so overwhelmingly negative that I assumed that my own views on this subject were so idiosyncratic, at least within the Muslim community, that no useful purpose would be served by further publicizing them. However, after the publication of *Even Angels Ask*, which does not discuss *hadith* science, I began receiving progressively more communications from Muslim youth and converts expressing considerable skepticism about the integrity of classical *hadith* criticism and inferring from this that the whole religion might be suspect. It seems that the two main roots of this suspicion are anti-Islam websites that use reports from the most respected *hadith* collections to produce a loathsome image of Islam and exposure to Western academic research that disputes Muslim *hadith* scholarship. Since the individuals that get in touch with me are not randomly selected, I cannot confidently estimate how pervasive this cynicism is, but from the correspondence I have received and discussions I have had in my travels around the country I feel that loss of confidence in the *Hadith* literature is spreading appreciably among native-born Muslims. Unfortunately, there is again virtually no discussion of this at Islamic conferences or in American Muslim publications.[4] In this case it might really be that

---

3. Amana Publications, Beltsville, MD, 1994

4. There have been a few exceptions. For example, Jamaal al Din Zarabozo's *The Authority and Importance of the Sunnah*, Al-Basheer Publications, Denver, 2000.

the religious establishment is not cognizant of a problem or perhaps the reliability of traditional *hadith* classification is not an issue for its primary constituency. Nevertheless, if problems with *hadith* are contributing to the disillusionment of many American-born Muslims, then the community's intellectual leadership is obliged to promote informed discussion on this topic. Moreover, if there is a growing current of skepticism concerning *hadith* in the community at large, then it probably already spills over into the readership of Islamic magazines and the regular attendees of Islamic conferences.

It was not long ago that Western *hadith* investigation was a purely academic discipline from which pretty much all Muslims were safely insulated. Only a very few Muslim authors responded to the findings of non-Muslim researchers, and almost all of them ignored the latest and most important developments in the area. M. M. al A'zami's *Studies in Early Hadith Literature* is an important exception, but it was published in 1968 and almost nothing of its kind has appeared since.[5] In the meantime, non-Muslim investigations of *hadith* have been churning along. While in the recent past only non-Muslim specialists would be interested in these studies, second generation Muslims and converts in America are beginning to discover them, which are easily accessed through nearby university libraries and to a lesser extent the internet. Hence, if Muslim scholars hope to effectively reply to emerging *hadith*-related cynicism, they will need to be informed of current research in the field. Chapter two contains further reflections along these lines. It is not a defense or critique of classical *hadith* science. Instead, relying in large part on the questions that were put to me, I try my best to anticipate some areas of future discussion. The reader should be reminded that I am not a *muhaddith* (one skilled in the methods of classical *hadith* criticism) but an ordinary American Muslim who is himself struggling to make sense of an immense area of thought with an extremely complex and elusive history.

---

5. M. M. al A'zmi, *Studies in Early Hadith Literature*, Beirut, 1968.

Although I received a large number of queries on theology and *hadith*, it was rare that a correspondent would only dwell on these. Typically, I would be presented a list of questions that included protests against various views, practices, and customs promulgated by the Mosque establishment. My sense is that this is where uncertainty first sets in for many American-born Muslims—not with abstract cogitation on theodicy or historiography, but with deep-seated feelings of alienation from the Mosque. Chapter three discusses some of the most frequently cited causes of second generation and convert disaffection with the Islamic community and some general suggestions for overcoming them.

As mentioned above, the rest of the book consists of specific questions followed by brief discussions. Sometimes different approaches to an issue are contrasted without indicating a preference, simply because I felt that none of the arguments considered had a decided advantage. Chapter three also includes at its very end a sampling of testimonies of American Muslims on their faith struggles. With these personal statements and the questions, which together comprise more than a third of the text, I have tried to provide a characteristic cross section of what has been communicated to me.

As the title suggests, the main aim of this work is not to dissertate on Islam but to share with the reader a perspective to which I became privy and that pertains to a crisis of major proportions in the American Muslim community. The conspicuous and continued near total disconnect of native-born Muslims from the Mosque thwarts all attempts by Muslim activists to establish a viable, self-sustaining, Islamic community in the United States. It would have been a dereliction of faith not to share with other concerned believers the content of the communications I have had with members of this population. For this reason, I thought it important to be candid and objective and to not evade controversy, for to inadequately state the case for or against a specific position, especially when it challenges convention, only serves to further alienate the sceptical. I fully recognize the immensity of the problem that this book confronts and that I am not the best suited to address it, but I see this as only an initial step that awaits the contribution of those more qualified. Thus the title reflects not only the many requests that underlie this work, but this recognition as well.

Chapter One

LOSING MY RELIGION

W e do not always choose our recollections. Sometimes they slip into our minds and fill thoughtless moments.

I am eight years old, lying in bed very late at night, awakened by my father's shouting downstairs. He is a huge, powerful man; six-foot two, 235 pounds; with big, broad shoulders; strong, muscular arms; a large, wide head; gigantic fists; and a viselike grip in which he took much pride and which he would sometimes demonstrate on his children when he was in one of his playful moods. His deep, raging, thunderous screams are interrupted by very brief intervals where I can barely make out the muffled sound of my mom's voice. I try to block out his curses and threats by burying my head beneath the pillow, but it doesn't help. It is like being wakened in the middle of the night by a violent thunderstorm. There is nothing you can do to make it go away; you can only wait and hope that when the fury finally subsides no one will be too badly hurt. I beg God, as I had many times before, to please take my father out of our lives, to please protect my mom, to please relieve us of this unending nightmare.

There is a sudden loud thump, like when someone pushes a piece of furniture hard against the wall. Not thinking, I jump out of bed and run down the stairs, then down the dark hallway in the direction of the kitchen. When I reach the kitchen entrance, I stop dead in my tracks. Just several feet away is my mom, pinned against the kitchen counter by the weight of my father's huge frame leaning over her. She turns her head to the right and arches her body back, trying to avoid his face which is only inches from hers. As he growls out his insults and clamps each of her arms with his massive hands, I try to think of a way to stop him, but I'm too frightened. I start to panic and to breathe loudly and heavily—almost hyperventilating.

Even though he doesn't turn to look at me, my father is apparently aware that I am there, for he stops shouting although he keeps my mom trapped against the counter. I move a step closer to see if my mom is hurt.

She turns her head towards me, and her expression quickly changes from motherly apprehension to one of self-composed strength. Sounding like a head nurse in an emergency room, she tells me in her most even, measured tone, "Jeff, it's O.K.! Your father and I are only talking. It will be all right. Now go back to bed."

I don't budge, although my breathing slows a little.

"Jeff!" she says again, "Don't worry. We are just discussing something. Please, son, go back to bed."

My father releases my mom, and without turning to look at me, moves aside to open the cabinet where the glasses are kept.

"Okay, Mom," I answer her, my lips trembling as I try not to cry. I then slowly turn to walk back down the hallway and up the stairs.

I did not come to believe in God easily. At a very early age I began to doubt the existence of an all-merciful, all-wise Creator. I often hear fellow Muslims say that I rejected Christianity in favor of Islam, but that is not how it happened.

I grew up in a violent city on the east coast and in an even more violent household. My father was an often brutal and destructive man who tried to subdue his inner rage every night with hard drinking. His alcoholism only made him all the more volatile; he could be laughing and joking one moment and unexpectedly fly into an angry rampage the next. Living with my father was like carrying a box of nitroglycerine. I was always aware that the slightest, most unpredictable agitation could set him off, and, once he erupted, it would take several hours and a lot of liquor to finally put him to sleep. My four brothers and I lived a frightful and uncertain childhood, but the worst of it was watching my father regularly taunt, threaten, and abuse my mother.

You see, it is really not so bad when you are the target of your father's wrath, for you're not thinking of anything at that time but survival. When he is firing punches at you, or kicking you on the ground, or chasing you through the house, or threatening, "I'm gonna hurt you bad, boy," your only thoughts are of escape. In the thick of the attack you are not considering its consequences or aftermath, and when it is finally over you might even excuse the onslaught, because you think you may have somehow deserved it, if not for what you did this time then maybe for what you did in the past. But the terror of watching your father go at your mother is an entirely different level of fear, as she is the only source of kindness, tenderness, love and protection you know, and if he were to take that away, then you lost everything. Yet far worse than the fear is the guilt that overwhelms you and it comes from several directions. There is the guilt from the antipathy that grows in you towards your father, for we are taught to love and respect our fathers, and we are born with a natural attachment to them. There is also the guilt from knowing that you might be the cause of this night's violence. Maybe you triggered his anger in some way unknown to you. Maybe just his dislike of you caused an argument between your mom and him. Then there is the cruelest guilt of all, of knowing that you did nothing to stop your father from hurting your mother. Out of fear for your own well-being, you hid in your bedroom while your father vented his rage, and thus you traded self-respect for personal safety. With each such incident you experience with ever greater clarity your own weakness, impotence, incompetence, worthlessness and cowardice, and the hate grows and festers inside you, not only for the man that you call "Father," but for yourself as well. It is a horrible, horrible thing to make a boy choose between his mother and himself; it is terribly unfair.

When I attended my mom's funeral a few years ago, person after person expressing condolences described her the same way: "Your mother was a true saint, Jeff." It seemed that everyone who knew her both pitied and admired her, for she endured my father all those years with such grace, strength, and cheer. Yet she never considered herself a victim, and she never sought sympathy, because for her the marriage she had entered into when she was twenty-one was a sacrament and must never be broken. Besides, she frequently maintained that she loved my father, as difficult as that has been for me to understand.

My mom was a strong willed, confident, and vibrant woman. Her favorite slogan was, "Where there is a will, there is a way." She always said that with God's help anything is possible and that no one and nothing could destroy her or put her down.

When at age sixty-seven she suffered a severe and disabling nervous breakdown, we were all in shock. We too had come to believe in her indestructibility. After that she was never the same. She spent the last six years of her life fighting what her doctors described as a type of manic depression. My father died a year after she did.

I still miss my mom terribly. For a long time, she was the only person I was able to love. She was my closest friend, my protector, and my only hero. She was a deeply religious Catholic, a dedicated nurse, loved by all the neighbors, and the most giving and charitable person I have known.

I remember how she used to regularly visit the elderly, ill-tempered, Italian lady next door to trim her toenails and wash her feet. I remember how much compassion she had for her patients at the hospital and how warmly they spoke of her when I came to pick her up from work when I was a teenager. I remember what a great mother and teacher she was, how honest she was, and how she never swore or treated anyone rudely. Most of all, I remember how much she loved her five sons and how hard she worked to provide us with as normal and happy a life as possible despite the handicap we acquired.

When I was little. I used to daydream about life without my father. I just wanted the violence to go away. I wanted not to be afraid anymore. I felt like I was trapped in a bad dream and that there was no way out. So I prayed again and again to God to remove my father from our lives and to stop the pain, but he was always there, and I began at an early age to wonder if God really was.

I could not fathom why God would sentence my mom to lifelong punishment. I could not imagine what great sin she must have committed, or that we her children must have committed, to deserve my father. I lacked the maturity to sort out such questions, although I had enough anger and fear to provoke them. I was too young to see the wisdom in allowing my mom to suffer the violence and abuse of my father, too young to understand why God would let innocent children tremble night after night in their beds, fearing that they might not see their mother the next morning, too young to see how the mercy and forgiveness of God could even extend to my father with all his terrible failings. All I could see in my world was chaos and violence, and so it became easy for me to question the existence of God.

I think it should now be obvious why I could never have found God in Catholicism, or for that matter Christianity, because between it and me loomed the terrifying image of my father, blinding me to any truth that I might uncover. I did not leave Christianity because of any dogmas or theologies; I left it and belief in God out of fear and anger interwoven into the confusion and trauma of my childhood.

The turmoil of the sixties and seventies only reinforced my skepticism. The assassinations of John and Robert Kennedy and Martin Luther King, the subsequent disgrace and falls of Vice President Agnew and President Nixon, the race riots and gang fights erupting in cities likes mine, and the bizarre and senseless carnage of Vietnam all confirmed the lesson that was already ingrained in me: that the world is dominated by random, consuming, undiscriminating violence. And early on I began to ask why.

Why did it have to be this way?

Why did God create such an imperfect and violent world?

Why didn't He put us into Heaven from the first and keep us there?

Why did He make us so criminally inclined, so corruptible and destructive?

If He wants us to submit to His will, why did God not make us that way from the beginning? Why didn't He make us angels or something better, if that was within His power?

Why does He let the strong torture and oppress the weak?

Why does He let blameless children be scarred so deeply and indelibly by violence not of their making?

I wanted to know why, and I demanded an answer. And I didn't care if the answer came from Heaven or if it came from Hell, or if it came from an angel or the devil himself, or if it came from the Pope or Charles Manson. I just wanted a cogent and coherent explanation. I just wanted to know the truth.

I was sixteen when I decided to no longer believe in God, and although I remained an unbeliever for the next dozen or so years, like many atheists, I kept a keen interest in other people's faiths. I wouldn't characterize myself as searching during this period of my life, although I might have been doing that subconsciously. I think I wanted to better understand the phenomenon that I believed so badly deceived and cheated me.

As the years went by, I found my social circle slowly gravitating from one religious perspective to another. In my early years of college, I was drawn toward fellow atheists, and then toward Jewish friends during the latter part of my undergraduate studies. In my beginning years of graduate school, my friends were mostly Protestants, while during the last two I kept close company with Hindu and Buddhist students from overseas. I was not deliberately choosing friends based on their religious backgrounds—at the time it seemed entirely coincidental—yet in retrospect it seems that there was a definite pattern to my friendships.

I was very curious about others' thoughts on religion, but I do not believe I was pushy. I did a lot more listening than talking back then. If asked about my beliefs, I would never hide them, but I usually kept my answers as short and to the point as possible. I did not want my disbelief to be an obstacle to my friendships, and anyway, I thought most people were not much interested in atheism.

Although I seldom criticized my friends' beliefs, I found that the more rational and coherent they were, the less compelling they were also. A person can resolve many of the conflicts between faith and reason by reducing or eliminating the differences between God and humans, by making God more human and humans more godlike; yet what is derived is a God or gods not worthy of worship and humans more noble and virtuous than the God or gods who created them. An extreme example may be Greek mythology, which I used to think was the most realistic and honest of all theologies. It explains that the evil and chaos in the world is caused by capricious gods who are entertained by our struggle, and who experience life through us, without taking any of the risks and experiencing any of the pain.

My Jewish, Hindu, and Buddhist friends seemed comfortable with my atheism, but some of my Christian friends were not, and they sometimes felt the need to say so. At times this would lead to passionate arguments. When it did, I would usually fall back on the same basic questions I had as a child: Why did God create us so violent and destructive, with a strong propensity for evil? Why did He not put us in Heaven from the start with a nature unsusceptible to temptation? Why did He give us reason if it conflicts with faith?

In 1982, at the age of twenty-eight, I joined the faculty of the University of San Francisco (USF), the oldest Jesuit University in America. A short time after I arrived there, I formed a close friendship with a Muslim family from Saudi Arabia. They were three USF students, Mahmoud, Umar, and Ragia Qandeel—two brothers and a sister—all in their early twenties.

Even though I knew practically nothing about Islam, I had assumed—and I'm not sure why—that, of all world religions, Islam was the most irrational. I began to question my preconceived idea after having conversations with my new friends. Their ideas on religion followed a definite methodology and rationale, and, even though I could not relate to much of what they said, their faith seemed to me no more nonsensical than anyone else's did.

During one of our conversations, they asked me about my religious beliefs. When I told them I did not believe in God and briefly indicated why, they showed almost no reaction, except that Mahmoud said something to the effect that religion often conflicts with reason and ultimately must be accepted on faith. Of course, Mahmoud was not the first person to tell me this; I had been hearing it all my life.

Since I was constantly misplacing my keys, I used to leave the door to my office at USF unlocked. Often when I entered my office, I would find that students had left notes and homework assignments on my desk. A day or two after I told the Qandeels of my atheism, I discovered a thick, green-covered book lying on my desk. On its cover were written the words, "The Holy Qur'an." At first I was a little dismayed and perturbed. I knew that one of the Qandeels must have placed it there, but I wondered why and what they were trying to say. I thought that maybe they were trying to convert me and were saying that if our friendship was to continue then I had to become a Muslim. Yet the more I thought about it, the more I realized that I was overreacting. First of all, the Qandeels were, by their own admission, not very religious. This was confirmed by the fact that their lifestyle seemed to be in conflict with a number of Islam's regulations about which they spoke. Second, they had many non-Muslim friends, and they never showed even the slightest interest in conversing with them about their religion. Third, whenever we did discuss their faith, I was the one who opened the subject. I concluded that their giving me a copy of their Scripture was an innocent enough gesture and that they may have thought that if I had other questions about their religion then I might consider reading it. This also made sense since they had a difficult time dealing with some of my questions.

Are You Talkin' to Me?

That is the book, wherein no doubt, is guidance for those who are on their guard (2:2).

I felt a shiver run through me as I read the above verse. I thought to myself, Are you talking to me?

I was on only the second page of the Qur'an and I had already experienced a sensation I would have repeatedly as I made my way through the text. On the previous page of the Scripture was the first *surah* (chapter) of the Qur'an, which is essentially a prayer for guidance. It reads:

Praise belongs to God, the Sustainer of the Worlds;
The Merciful, The Compassionate;
Master of the Day of Judgement.
To You we pray, and You we seek.
Guide us on the straight path,
The path of those whom You have favored,
Not of those who have strayed or upon whom is wrath (1:1-7).

Here, on the second page, at the beginning of the second *surah*, God himself responds to the reader, stating that the guidance for which he or she just prayed is undoubtedly right in his or her hands. I thought, So you are saying that in this book is the guidance I just prayed for? I looked again at the second verse:

"That is the book."

"What an original and appropriate way to present a revelation!" I said to myself. Instead of relating a history of a people, or a biography of a great teacher, or a collection of sayings of a prophet, the author, whom I assumed to be Muhammad, writes the Scripture in the form of a direct address from God to humanity. I thought that this is exactly what we should expect from a divine revelation—sort of like the Ten Commandments expanded to a book.

As I made my way through the Qur'an, my respect for its clever-ness grew. I was particularly impressed by the way I would repeatedly have the same experience I mentioned above—but on an increasingly profound level—where I would have the eerie feeling that the Qur'an was actually communicating to me, intellectually, and, for lack of a better word, spiritually. I figured that somehow the author inserted in the text a large number of passages that he knew would provoke certain questions and reactions in the reader, and then he responded to the anticipated reader's reactions in the subsequent passages. This ability of the Qur'an to engage the reader in mental and spiritual conversation—or as Fredrick Denny puts it, "to read the reader"[1]— gives it tremendous psychological power, and this I believed might account for the renowned religious fervor of Muslims. I felt that the author must have had deep insight into human nature, especially since this inherent power of the Qur'an, judging at least from my own experience of it, is still extremely strong fourteen centuries after it first appeared.

The first twenty nine verses of the second *surah* concisely and eloquently summarize the Qur'an's major themes: Humanity's need for self-surrender to God, Muhammed's prophethood, the Hereafter and Final Judgment, the Qur'an's use of symbolism (2:26), the resurrection of man and God's ultimate sovereignty. These verses also contain a description of the Scripture's potential audience. The read-ers who will benefit most from the Qur'an are the sincere believers. The readers who will gain the least are the close-minded who are bent on rejecting the Qur'an. In between these two categories are the pretenders and self-deluded who claim to be sincere in faith but who really put worldly pursuits and self-interests above faith. These will profit little from reading the Scripture unless they change their mindset. In form, the Qur'an's introduction is not unlike introduc-tions of many modern instructional texts, introductions which describe their books' contents and the prerequisites needed to learn from them.

---

1. Fredrick Denny, *Islam* (New York Harper & Row, 1987), p. 88

You Gotta be Talkin' to Me

Verses 30 through 39 of the second *surah* introduce the parable of the first man and woman. Although the story as presented in the Qur'an shared many details with the Biblical one, there was something very peculiar about it. I scanned over the verses a few more times, but I could not make out exactly what point the Scripture was trying to make. It seemed to me that either it was saying something really profound or else it was just confused. I decided to go through the passage slowly and carefully, line by line, to see if it fit together to convey a coherent vision.

> Behold, your Lord said to the angels, "I will create a vicegerent on earth." They said: "Will you put therein one who will spread corruption and shed blood? While we celebrate your praises and glorify you?" He said: "I know what you do not know" (2:30).

The thirtieth verse of the second *surah* caught me off guard, not because it begins the allegory of the first man and woman, but because of the way it does it. As I read it this time, I suddenly felt very alone— singled out—as if the author had pulled me aside into some empty and silent space to speak directly and only to me.

At first I wondered if the author had misheard or misunderstood the traditional story of Adam and Eve, because the verse before me denied the whole point and purpose of it. But as I read the verse a second, then a third, then a fourth time, I began to feel that the author had intentionally permuted and modified the details of the ancient tale.

The setting of the verse is in Heaven, with God making an announcement to the angels that He is going to place man on earth to represent Him: "I will create a vicegerent on earth." He has it all wrong, I objected. Humanity is not placed on earth to perform some positive function; mankind is placed on earth as a punishment for

Adam's sin. Yet there is no hint here in God's announcement of any wrongdoing on Adam's or Eve's part, and as the subsequent verses show, no wrong has yet been committed.

It is the angels who raise the natural objection: "Will you put there in one who will spread corruption and shed blood, while we celebrate your praises and glorify you?" It is the angels, here, who seem to want to steer the allegory back to its traditional meaning—to the one with which I grew up. In essence they ask, Why create this most sinful and violent creature? Why put on earth one who will wreak havoc there? Why create this defective being at all, when you could create us, the angels? As they plainly say, "While we celebrate your praises and glorify you?" Their question is given even greater force when we consider that it is being asked in Heaven. For on top of creating this most imperfect creature, God is about to place it in an environment where it could act out its worst criminal impulses, operating under the illusion of being distant from God. In other words, the question is: Why would God create this corrupt species and place it on earth when He could simply make them angels and place them in Heaven?

This was my question! My objection! My life encapsulated in these three or four lines! I felt like the Qur'an was playing with my emotions, manipulating this story to provoke me. Then, to make matters worse, God simply replies to the angels, "I know what you do not know." As if to say, "I know exactly what I'm doing."

You can't do that! I shouted in my mind. You can't do that to me! You can't take my hurt, my anger, my life, place it all before me, and then tell me that You know what You are doing! You can't get off that easy! You made me this way!

Then it dawned on me: I was complaining to the God in whom I did not even believe.

Open Your Eyes

Right after the angels asked their question would have been the perfect place for the author to attempt damage control and return to the traditional Biblical story. At that point he could have had God respond, "Yes, you angels are exactly right about human nature, and therefore I am going to punish them by letting this couple and all of their descendents suffer on earth when these two inevitably sin." This still would not have fully answered the angels' question, since it does not explain why God would create such a corrupt being in the first place, but at least it would get back to the idea that life on earth is a punishment for human sinfulness rather than an opportunity for us to serve as God's representatives.

It would soon become apparent to me that the Qur'an had another agenda, that it had an entirely different vision and message. Rather than revert to traditional lines, it begins an answer to the angels' question that will first focus on human intellect (2:31-34), then on moral choice (2:35-36), and finally on divine guidance (2:37-39).

> And He taught Adam the names of all things. Then He placed them before the angels, and said: "Tell me their names if you are right" (2:31).

I recalled that in the Biblical version Adam named the creatures around him, but it was not highlighted as part of a justification for the making of humanity. The Qur'an, however, begins an answer to the angels' query by drawing attention to this point.

I marveled at the way the Scripture packed so much meaning into so few words. Note that Adam does not merely name the things about him, instead God teaches him, which emphasizes his ability to learn, his intellect. Notice also what Adam is learning. He is acquiring the ability to name "all things," to assign verbal symbols to everything that he becomes aware of, to all of his thoughts, experiences, and feelings. Of all human intellectual gifts, it is the gift of language that the Qur'an emphasizes, apparently because it is this highly developed intellectual tool that separates humanity from all other earthly creatures. It is through the use of language, more than any other talent, that humans grow, progress, and learn, individually and collectively, for it provides us a means to learn from and to teach others with whom we have no personal contact, including persons of times and places vastly different from our own, so that all human learning is endowed with a preeminent "cumulative character."[2]

God then places the things that Adam names before the angels and states, "Tell me their names if you are right." This clearly shows that human intellect figures prominently into a response to the angels' question. The angels asked why God would create such a violent and pernicious creature, when from their viewpoint they are superior to man, since they are totally submissive to God's will and they praise and glorify Him. The Qur'an seems to be saying in this verse and those that immediately follow that there are other qualities, human intelligence among them, that make mankind—at least potentially—greater than angels in God's view.

> They said: "Glory to you! Of knowledge we have none, except what You have taught us. In truth it is You who are all knowing, all wise" (2:32).

The angels admit their inability to meet the challenge. They lack the intellectual aptitude to create symbols and concepts for what they experience. They explain that to do so would require intelligence—knowledge and wisdom—far beyond their reach. They acknowledge that for God such a task would be easy, because He is "all knowing, all wise," but as angels they are deficient in these qualities.

---

2. As noted by Muhammad Asad in his commentary on *Surah al `Alaq* in, *The Message of the Qur'an,* Dar Al-Andalus, Gibraltar, 1980, p. 993, footnote 3. The Qur'an repeatedly emphasizes this point. The skills of reading and writing, in particular, are highlighted as among the greatest intellectual gifts God has granted humanity. See, for example, 96:1-5.

He said: "O Adam! Tell them their names." And when he had told them, God said: "Did I not tell you that I know the secrets of the heavens and the earth, and I know what you reveal and conceal?" (2:33).

Adam succeeds where the angels failed, demonstrating his superior intellect. Although Adam has not the wisdom and knowledge of God, he is endowed with more of these than the angelic hosts are.

I was starting to believe that the author had not misunderstood the Biblical version of this story, but that he was recasting it to bring out an original meaning. He was saying that it is true that God created in man the ability to do wrong, but He also gave humanity other qualities that the angels could not understand or appreciate, and that fit into a more far-reaching design. Therefore the Qur'an has God state, "Did I not tell you that I know the secrets of the heavens and the earth?" Yet this question to the angels does not stop here, for it continues: "And I know what you reveal and what you conceal."

What did their question conceal? I wondered. It was obvious what it revealed. It exposed the destructive and sinister propensities of human beings, but what did it conceal?

Then it came to me. The angels' objection stressed only one side of human character: mankind's ability to do great violence and wrong. Yet the angels were blinded, as was I, to the other side of human nature. Indeed some humans could do terrible wrong, but others could do tremendous good. Some individuals were capable of great self-sacrifice, of the noblest acts of justice, of the most generous displays of charity, warmth, and kindness. Some persons could show the greatest mercy and compassion to their fellow man. Yet I, like the angels, did not consider this. For too long I had seen only the dark side of human beings. While it is true that some of us can be terribly destructive, others can be tremendously kind and good, and we all know of great exemplars of both tendencies. Often they appear on the same stage of the human drama, as the appearance of one provokes the emergence of the other. It seems that goodness brings out the worst in some people, and evil brings out the best in others. Thus we can have the very good and the very destructive arising from the same surroundings and circumstances, sometimes coexisting in the same country, city, or neighborhood.

> And behold, We said to the angels: "Bow down to Adam" and
> they bowed down: not so Iblis. He refused and was arrogant.
> He was of those who reject faith (2:34).

If I had any doubt that the Qur'an's position is that the human character is potentially greater than the angelic one, this verse removed it. When Adam succeeds intellectually where the angels failed, God tells them, "Bow down to Adam." They then bow down, demonstrating their acknowledgement of his superiority. Bowing is also a symbol of subservience and thus the Qur'an seems to be indicating that the angels will serve mankind in its development on earth.

However, Iblis, Satan, refuses to bow down, and with his refusal the Qur'an presents the genesis of sin. According to the Qur'an, the root of sin is not money, greed, or lusts, but false and self-destructive pride. With the introduction of Satan, the Scripture has now added another main element to the drama and to its response to the angel's original question, but why? Why the need for Satan? Why create one whose sole purpose is to avert men and women from doing good?

Up to this point the Qur'an seemed to be putting together an intelligent response to the angel's question. But now it appeared to me that it was beginning to falter and drift back to the Biblical story: Satan tempts man, man sins, man and all of his progeny are sentenced to life on earth. Yet I had promised myself to keep an open mind and not force my own unnecessary interpretations on the Scripture. I would give it the benefit of the doubt. Then what, I asked myself, could be the purpose of Satan?

Every culture has its distinctive beliefs about the devil, but in almost all religious ideologies he plays the part of tempter, the subconscious seducer who slips evil suggestions into our thoughts. Just as the angels are to us the source of magnanimous urgings, Satan prods us to do wrong. We think of both as the opposing voices in our mind when we grapple with a moral dilemma.

Is that it? I wondered. Is the Qur'an saying that in addition to giving us intelligence, God made us a moral being, a being that understands right and wrong? Is it saying that God also provided us with angelic inspiration and satanic temptation to heighten our moral awareness?[3] Is it underlining the fact that we are creatures that can and must make moral choices? Although I could not yet see what logical purpose that might serve, I also could not see how this necessarily contradicted what the Qur'an presented so far.

> We said: "O Adam! Dwell you and your wife in the garden, and eat of the bountiful things therein as you wish, but do not approach this tree, for then you will be among the wrong-doers" (2:35).

I was continuing to lose confidence in the Scripture. Despite its brilliant beginnings, the story now seemed to be definitely returning to the Biblical version: Adam and Eve eat from the tree and are punished with life on earth. Yet there was something very odd about this verse. In the Biblical story, God appears nervous and threatened by the prospect of man eating from the tree, for it is the tree of knowledge and immortality, and should humans eat of it, they will become gods themselves and rival God.

However, in this passage, God seems curiously calm and in complete control. There is no suggestion that the fruit of the tree will have any great effect on Adam and Eve. It almost seems that the tree is picked at random. The Qur'an will later explain that Satan

---

3. This is confirmed in a number of passages, for example:

> By the soul and that which equalized it and then breathed into it its immorality and its God-consciousness. He is indeed successful who causes it to grow and he is indeed a failure who stunts it. (91:7-10).

tempted the couple by saying that if they ate from the tree, then they would obtain eternal life and "a kingdom that never decays" (20:121), but this is a complete fabrication on his part. There is no hint that God is anxious that the couple may disobey Him; He merely informs them that if they do, then they will have committed a wrongful deed.

In light of the preceding verses, we must conclude that eventually the couple had to sin. Why else make mankind into a moral being that is subjected to temptation? Everything the story has told us up until now, from the angels' question to the introduction of Satan, suggests that God is well aware that the couple will eventually ere, and that He intentionally made them that way.

We also do not know that this was the first command God gave to the couple. The Qur'an does not inform us. There could have been others before it. All we know is that this is the first one that they will disobey. I wondered if that could be its only real significance — that it is the couple's first independent choice, the first time they choose to do other than what God had told them.

> Then Satan caused them to slip from it and to leave the state in which they had been. We said: "Go down, all of you together, with some of you adversaries of others, and on earth will be your dwelling place and provisions for a time" (2:36).

With this verse I was ready to close the Qur'an and put it away for good, for I was now convinced that it had left its initial track and returned to the traditional theme that our earthly lives are essentially a punishment for Adam's and Eve's sin. But once again the subtle wording of the verse mystified me. Why would it refer to the greatest sin in the history of mankind, the very sin for which our entire race must suffer pain, hardship, and death on earth, as a mere "slip"? In English a *slip* is nothing more than a momentary loss of focus, a temporary loss of one's footing, a minor error of no great consequence. At first I thought that this must have been a mistranslation, but I soon discovered from Arab friends that the Arabic word translated as "slip" (*azala*) conveys exactly the same sense as it does in English. How can that be? I asked myself. Does the author not understand the magnitude of Adam's and Eve's sin?

I went back and reread this verse and the preceding one several times. And then it occurred to me: Did the couple really commit so grave a crime? Maybe I was the one who could not let go of the traditional interpretation. Maybe I was resisting the Qur'an's message. After all, they did not commit murder, or rape, or adultery, or assault! After all, it was only a tree!

I figured that calling this mistake a "slip" might be entirely appropriate. This would also explain the dispassionate tone of the passage. For instead of telling the couple that they will suffer terribly on earth, they are told that on earth "will be your dwelling place and provision for a time." These are hardly the words of an angry, scolding deity. It is true that God tells them all—presumably all humanity—perhaps the satans and even the angels as well—to go down to earth and that some will be adversaries of others, but the angels' question (2:30) and verse 2:34 already anticipated this would be the case.

I was also interested in the statement that their "slip" caused them to leave the state in which they were. From what state did they depart? All that the text reveals is that they were no longer in a state of perfect conformity to God's will, that they were now capable of choosing to do wrong as well as right. But how could that be a positive thing? How could that help men and women to act as God's representatives on earth? I could almost answer these questions but I could not fit all the pieces together. There were too many other questions rushing into my mind, too many parts to the puzzle.

Doubt kept creeping into my thoughts as well. Maybe I am being too generous with the Qur'an, giving it too much of the benefit of the doubt. Perhaps this verse is portraying life on earth as a penalty for mankind. Perhaps the Qur'an is telling two conflicting stories at the same time. Perhaps the author could not make up his mind which message he wanted to convey.

I felt the next few verses would settle the matter. If in them God is portrayed as angry, vengeful, and punishing, then the Qur'an did stray from its original argument against the angels' question. If not, then I knew I had a lot of rethinking to do.

> Then Adam received words from his Lord and his Lord turned towards him (compassionately), for He is Oft Returning, Most Merciful (2:37).

The tone of the passage is far from condemnatory with its emphasis on God's forgiveness and compassion. The next passage will show that the words Adam received from his Lord were words of consolation and hope.

> We said: "Go down, all of you, from here. And if, as is sure, there comes to you guidance from Me, whosoever follows My guidance will have nothing to fear, nor shall they grieve" (2:38).

These two verses paint a sympathetic picture. The couple is sent from Heaven to begin their earthly sojourn. We must assume that they are filled with remorse for what they have done and apprehension about life in an unfamiliar environment. Their Lord turns to them and embraces them with forgiveness and mercy. He assures them that they will always have guidance from Him, and they have nothing to fear as long as they follow it. Like a parent tenderly consoling his or her child, God tells them, "I know you are afraid and I know this seems hard to you, but you will be all right. I will always be with you and I will always guide you. Just keep your eyes, ears and heart open to My many signs, and you will have nothing to fear."

Thus we find that God forgives the couple and comes to their aid, but then why does He not return them to Heaven? Suppose, for example, that my daughter does some wrong and I deduct five dollars from her allowance as a punishment. Assume she then apologizes to me and I forgive her, but I also inform her that I will still deduct the five dollars from her allowance. Her reaction would naturally be, "But you said you forgave me and yet you're still punishing me! Make up your mind!" So if God forgives the couple, why does He leave them on earth?

The answer came to me as quickly as the question did: because life on earth, according to the Qur'an, is not a punishment. From the very start of the allegory, God insists that our earthly existence serves a greater purpose. As long as I kept that in mind, the story was entirely coherent. Observe also that the Qur'an repeats the statement, "Go down, all of you, from here," in 2:38, but this time surrounds it with lines that emphasize God's forgiving, comforting, and reassuring the couple. As if the Scripture was telling me once and for all, "God did not put you on earth to punish you!"

And those who rejected and gave the lie to Our signs, these are friends of the fire, they dwelled therein (2:39).

Why did it have to say that? I felt a rush of indignation. Just as I was admiring the Qur'an's intelligent approach, it had to resort to scare tactics. That's hitting below the belt, I complained. I would have continued on with my reading anyway, if only out of curiosity, without the threats. I have been threatened enough already in my life, and it only produced more resistance and resentment. The Qur'an may be able to frighten others, but I will not be intimidated. I will continue to analyze this Scripture, page-by-page, verse-by-verse, and line-by-line.

I may have been at first offended by this statement, but my brief history with the Scripture had taught me that when a passage agitates me, it often contains an important clue to its viewpoint. As I looked more carefully at these words, I again found the phrasing intriguing. Until this point in the narrative, the Qur'an was relating the allegory of Adam and Eve, of the beginnings of human experience on earth. In this verse, with its abrupt shift to the past tense, it transports the reader far into the future, to the conclusion of the human drama in the hereafter, where it reviews the state of those who rejected and denied God's signs on earth. It is a brilliant device, for it ends God's conversation with the first couple on a consoling and compassionate note, and at the same time introduces a warning to the reader in the next verse without interrupting the flow of ideas.

Yet let us say, for the sake of argument, that there really is a God. Does anyone knowingly reject and give the lie to His signs, or do they simply miss them because they are too obscure? Do people consciously reject what they feel may be true? Do they distort in their own minds what they sense is right? Do they stubbornly go against their conscience?

Of course they do, I told myself, and so have I. Many times I have denied, bent and manipulated the truth to indulge some personal vice. Many times I have rationalized patently destructive and self-destructive acts, refusing to admit my wrongs, even to myself? And even though my pursuit of what I felt might be wrong left me empty, ungratified, and restless, I continued to run headlong down the same path. If God did exist, I thought, then I definitely ignored His signs, but that is a big "if."

The phrase "These are friends of the fire" also struck me. For a friend is one who is dear to us, whose company we seek and whose companionship we desire. Is the Qur'an saying that some people pursue and court the misery they will experience in the next life? When it says that "they dwelled therein," is it hinting that the hell they experience in the hereafter in some sense began for them in their earthly lives? Even though a hundred questions were now streaming into my mind and I could not yet see the big picture, I knew I was in for a battle. If these ten verses led me to this much agonizing, then the challenge ahead of me was going to be great. Not that I believed in God or that this author was other than a man, but I knew that I was up against an exceptionally capable opponent.

Questions

I had never read anything as disturbing as these ten verses (2:30-39). I could not stop thinking about them. I thought about them day and night—when I ate, when I walked to and from work, when I sat alone, when I watched television, when I lay in bed. I kept reviewing them in my mind, trying to fit them together like pieces to a puzzle. They became my touchstone as I read through the rest of the Qur'an. Each time I came upon a passage that seemed to have a bearing on the question of the purpose of life, I would compare it to the ideas introduced in this allegory. I gradually began to feel that I was unraveling some of the tangle of questions that this story created for me, but I could not bring it all together into a sensible explanation of human existence on earth.

I was anxious to get on with my investigation, but patience was required. The Qur'an does not only discuss the purpose of life, although everything it discusses relates to it in some way. It contains narratives, parables, warnings, and glad tidings. It includes dramatic descriptions of Heaven, Hell, the final judgment, and the workings of nature. It provides commandments, arguments against its detractors, and evidence of its divine origins. It contains rational, emotional, and spiritual appeals. It discusses its use of symbolism and the importance as well as the limits of human reason. It speaks of unseen realities beyond human perception. It tells of God's attributes and our relationship to Him. And it interweaves all this throughout the Scripture without deliberating on any subject too long; instead it flashes distinct powerful images and messages before us, shifting our focus from one aspect of reality to another.

Before I return to my search for an answer to the angels' question, I thought that this might be a good place to consider some questions that have been put to me about my first encounter with the Qur'an.

Question 1 (from an American Muslim high school student):

I have had difficulty with some of the accounts in the Qur'an. A few of them seem to conflict with science or history. This is really causing me to have doubts. My parents advised me to see a sheikh who they thought might cure me of these, but it didn't help. The sheikh finally told me that to have these doubts was __kufr__ (disbelief) and that I just had to put them out of mind, but as much as I try to, I can't stop thinking about them. Did you have similar problems when you read the Qur'an, and if so, how did you overcome them?

I must admit that during my first reading of the Qur'an I was not concerned with the historicity of its narratives, as I was mainly interested in what it had to say about the purpose of life. My approach to the Qur'an's stories—indeed my approach to the entire Qur'an—was determined by my experience of verses thirty through thirty-nine of *Surah al Baqara*. From my background and perspective, it seemed obvious that the Qur'an was retelling one of humanity's most gripping and provocative tales, not to satisfy the reader's curiosity about the origins of Homo sapiens, but to use it as a powerful vehicle to correct one of history's greatest misconceptions. It was the implications of this version of the story of the first couple that captivated me. I felt that behind this Revelation was a profoundly rational vision of the purpose of life and that each word of this book revolved around it. I was determined to gain a glimpse into that vision by searching each verse for clues. Thus when I read the narratives I was focused on what they might say about human existence; the issue of their historical actuality was not important to me.

After my conversion to Islam, I became more interested in this matter. On the one hand, I discovered that the vast majority of Muslims believe that each of the Scripture's stories represent factual accounts of past events. On the other hand, I found that many Qur'an interpreters felt that some of the stories include allegories and parables, although they disagreed on specifics. While I was more inclined to the latter point of view, I still felt the need to study the Qur'an's narratives more carefully to try to determine as best I could which of them are definitely presented as history.[4]

As I mentioned earlier, the Qur'an is neither a history nor a biography. Interspersed throughout it are some stories of personages well known to the seventh century Arabs, including many Biblical figures[5], but it gives almost no chronology and provides almost no historical reference points, making it nearly impossible to place these accounts in history without consulting outside sources. It also provides very few continuous narratives. Episodes involving most persons mentioned in the Qur'an are distributed throughout the text, with little indication given of their order in time. The stories are almost never provided an historical context and typically begin abruptly with phrasing that plunges the reader into an account in progress, such as, "And God said to the angels," or, "And when His Lord tried Abraham," or, "And when the wife of Imran said." While this avoidance of temporal detail may enhance the timeless appeal of the narratives, making it easy for the reader to identify with their main characters, it also makes it difficult to offer a historical critique. What makes this even harder is that the Qur'an in a number of places insists on its use of symbolism, but does not provide a hard and fast means to decide exactly which verses are allegorical and which are not, although it affirms that both reveal truth.[6] This leaves open the possibility that some of the narratives make use of allegory, and certainly the wording in some of them seems to bear this out. Consider the following two passages from the story of Adam.

---

4. The Qur'an itself frequently refers to the narratives as "stories" (*qassas*) or accounts (*naba'*), which is not the same as calling them history. Although in verse 3:62 it calls its account of Jesus a "true story" and a few times it instructs to recite a particular account "in truth," which in these instances may emphasize their historicity.

5. The Qur'an assumes that the Biblical personalities it mentions are somewhat familiar to its initial audience. It seems that through centuries of cultural exchange the Jews, Christians and pagans of Arabia adopted with modifications each other's oral traditions.

6. Cf. question 3 in this chapter.

It is We Who created you, then We gave you shape, then We bade the angels, "Bow down to Adam!" and they bowed down; not so Iblis; he refused to be among those who bowed down (7:11).

And when your Lord drew forth from the children of Adam, from their loins, their seed, and made them testify of themselves (saying), "Am I not your Lord?" They said, "Yes, we truly testify." Lest you should say on the Day of Resurrection: "Lo! Of this we were unaware" (7:172).

In 7:11 there is a transition from "you" (plural in Arabic) in the first two clauses to "Adam" in the third, suggesting that humankind is being identified with Adam. The phrasing is certainly non-literal, otherwise from the first two verses we would obtain that we were created, then we were given shape, then the command was made concerning the first man. Verse 7:172 speaks for itself, as it is hard to conceive of a literal explanation.

The story of Dhul Qarnain in *Surah al Kahf* may be another example of an allegorical narrative.

Until, when he reached the setting of the sun, and he found it setting in a muddy spring, and found a people near it. We said: "O Dhul Qarnain! Either punish them or treat them with kindness" (18:86).

Since ancient times this verse has perplexed many Muslim exegetes, who searched history for a great prophet-conqueror who reached the lands where the sun rises and sets. Many identified Dhul Qarnain with Alexander the Great, which is doubtful since the latter is known to have been a pagan. Furthermore, the description of him reaching the place where the sun sets in a muddy spring with people nearby may be indicative of the figurative character of the passage.

My study of the Qur'an's narratives left me pretty much where I started: unable to say with absolute confidence which are totally historical and which incorporate symbolism. However, I was not troubled by this; on the contrary, it made me feel that my original intuition regarding these epic tales of moral and spiritual struggle was probably accurate—that their primary purpose is not to impart history but to convey fundamental truths. The Qur'an makes this explicit in *Surah al Kahf* where it tells the reader not to get lost in pointless arguments over the minutiae of the accounts.

> Some say they were three, the dog being the forth among them. Others say they were five, the dog being the sixth—doubtfully guessing at the unknown. Yet others say seven, the dog being the eighth. Say: "My Lord knows best their number, and none knows them but a few. Therefore, do not enter into controversies concerning them, except on a matter that is clear" (18:22).

Then again, after a parenthetical statement (18:23-24), the Qur'an ends its criticism of this type of futile speculation with this remark.

> And [they also say] they stayed in the cave three hundred years and [some] add nine [more]. Say: "God knows best how long they stayed. To Him belongs the unseen in the heavens and in the earth (18:25-26).

The point is that trifling over such matters is contrary to the intent and style of the narrations.

The fact that the telling of the stories is so overtly ahistorical suggests that the Qur'an is intended to be ambiguous on their historicity, which runs counter to the natural human inclination to historicize such tales. Some orientalists have conjectured that the Qur'an's unhistorical style of narration reflects the predominantly oral culture from which it emerged and that in such a medium chronological detail is often neglected, but both the Bible and *Hadith* literature, which came from the same surroundings, offer striking counterexamples to this hypothesis. For me at least, the Qur'an's manner of narration is one more sign of its genius and sophistication, for it presents the stories in a way that it would not impugn the suppositions of its initial listeners, for whom history, legend, poem, and parable greatly intersected, nor a people of a later and more skeptical time who were intent on distinguishing between them.

Question 2 (from an American Muslim male college student):

I heard that you became a Muslim after reading the Qur'an. I was wondering if it was the signs in the Qur'an that convinced you of the truth of Islam? Being a mathematician, did you discover any mathematical miracles in the Qur'an that convinced you?

Have not the unbelievers seen that the heavens and the earth were joined together, then We clove them asunder, and We made every living thing from water? Will they then not believe? And We have set in the Earth mountains standing firm, lest it should shake with them, and We placed therein ravines as roads that they may receive guidance. And We have made the heavens a roof withheld from them. Yet they turn away from its signs. And He it is who created the night and day, and the sun and moon. They float, each in its rounded course (21:30-33).

We certainly created humanity from a thing extracted, and then placed it as a drop in a safe lodging. Then We made the drop into a thing that clings. Then We fashioned the thing that clings into a chewed lump of flesh, and We fashioned the chewed flesh into bones, and We clothed the bones with intact flesh. Then We developed out of it another creature. So blessed be God the best of creators. After that, at length, you will die. Then, on the Day of Judgment, you will be raised up. And We have made above you seven paths and We are never unmindful of our creation. And We sent down water from the sky according to a measure, and We cause it to soak in the soil. And We are certainly able to withdraw it. With it We grow for you gardens of date palms and vines. In them you have abundant fruits and of them you eat. And there is a tree that grows from Mount Sinai that produces oil and relish for the eaters. And in the cattle there is surely a lesson for you. We give you to drink of that which is in their bellies, and many uses have you in them, and of them you eat. And on them and on ships you are carried (23:12-22).

Soon We will show them our signs in the farthest reaches and in their own selves, until it becomes manifest to them that this is the truth. Is it not enough that your Lord does witness all things? (41:53).

As I stated in the previous answer, I was not on the lookout in my first reading of the Qur'an for statements that either agreed with or contradicted modern science. At that time I was not a believer—even in God—and I did not expect the Scripture, being of ancient origins, to be in perfect conformity with the current state of scientific knowledge. Instead my focus was on finding out what meaning the Qur'an attached to human existence. In pursuit of that, I discovered other things in the Qur'an that caused me to question my atheism and that led ultimately to my conversion. Nevertheless, some assertions in the Qur'an on the wonders of nature, which the Qur'an describes as "signs," did intrigue me, such as those I quote above that mention that the heavens and earth were once joined together, that every living thing is made from water, that the sun and moon float in rounded courses, and that describe the prenatal development of humans. Such affirmations did not really prove something to me, because the wording of them is sometimes rather cryptic, avoiding a degree of explication that would force the conclusion that they concur with recent discoveries, but they did catch my attention. There are a few statements in the Qur'an that modern scientists would definitely question (for example, that Adam is the father of the human race or that Noah's life span was 950 years), but I was only able to find them in the narratives and not among the natural signs. Based on what I noted above about the stories in the Qur'an and allegory, it was not clear to me that these were meant to be taken as history.

I did not recognize any specific wonders of a mathematical nature in my first reading. However, I will say that I was in awe of the genius that produced it. Its marvelous precision and economy of expression suggested an amazing logic. Its superb wisdom, cloaked in the most exquisite phraseology, pointed to knowledge that is beyond any one man's life experience. Its ability to reach with the same words and to make surrender to its calling both the learned and the illiterate could only come from a profound understanding of human psychology. While reading the Qur'an, I felt I was being continuously educated, that it was taking me to higher and higher vistas of thinking—about life, about humanity, about reasoning and spirituality—even though I did not accept its central premise of the existence of God.

When I accepted Islam in 1982, the American Muslim community was abuzz with the study of the Qur'anic signs. Numerous publications on the compatibility between them and modern science were in circulation and lectures on this subject dominated Muslim proselytizing efforts. Many believers felt that this information would surely convince Americans of the truth of Islam. This zeal to prove the divine origins of the Scripture through science gave way to the inclination to see the Qur'an as anticipating almost every modern scientific finding and theory. Many of these studies were too farfetched to be taken seriously, which is unfortunate since they tended to eclipse some other very credible research in this area. Maurice Bucaille's *The Bible, the Qur'an and Science* is still the seminal work in English on the Qur'an's signs.[7] For me, one of the most convincing signs is not any one in particular but the fact that none of them can be proven to be in conflict with what has been firmly established by present-day science, even though they refer to a vast array of phenomena, and despite the profusion of erroneous beliefs about the workings of nature that prevailed in the Prophet's time and for many centuries thereafter. Although I did not dwell on the signs in the Qur'an during my first reading, I did pay close attention to them on subsequent readings, and they became for me one more validation of my decision to convert.

Question 3 (from an American convert in his late twenties):

I did not read the Qur'an before I embraced Islam, but I am reading it now. As a whole, it makes a lot of sense to me, but there are some things that do not. I was wondering if there are any statements in the Qur'an that you felt might be in conflict with reason, and if there are, then how have you dealt with them?

I would be lying if I said that I never questioned a single verse from the Qur'an on rational grounds, but such instances were few and its overall logic so firm that I thought that the problem might be one of interpretation or translation, rather than a genuine conflict with reason. In time I found that the former was the case as far as the passages with which I had difficulty.

It is important to distinguish between a conflict with reason and a conflict with personal sentiment. Some of the Qur'anic punishments at first seemed to me harsh, but this was more a subjective than objective appraisal, reflecting perhaps a liberal, Western, academic background. On the other hand, I could see that the penalties would help to discourage the behaviors they targeted, and were thus in accord with their objectives; hence I perceived no logical contradiction in this regard. Hence when we speak of conflicts with reason in

---

7. Bucaille, Maurice, *The Bible, the Qur'an and Science,* Seghers Publishers, Paris, 1977.

the Qur'an, we refer to statements in the Scripture that contradict either other statements in the text or well-established facts. The latter category would consist of undisputed historical or scientific findings, but as I indicated in my two previous answers, I could see no ironclad argument being made against the Qur'an along these lines.

Some of the Qur'an's assertions about what it terms al *ghayb* (the unseen)—that is, realities beyond human experience and perception, such as the hereafter, Heaven and Hell, God's attributes and doings, etc—may seem open to question, but only if taken literally. However, the Qur'an discourages this in a number of ways.

Early in the second *surah*, we find this defense of the Scripture's use of symbolism:

> God is not ashamed to cite a parable, even of a gnat. Those who believe know that it is the truth from their Lord, but the deniers say: "What does God mean by this parable?" (2:26).

It is noteworthy that this pronouncement appears right after a very sensual description of the Paradise that awaits sincere believers in the afterlife (2:25), a description particularly suited to the imagination of the seventh century Arabs. It is also significant that this passage occurs among the first twenty-nine verses of the second *surah*, which is a synopsis of the Qur'an's major themes.

Later in the third *surah*, the Qur'an asserts that it frequently makes use of symbolic language and admonishes those who seek to undermine it by assigning literal meanings to its allegorical passages.

> He it is who has bestowed upon you from on high the book, containing messages clear in and of themselves—and these are the core of the book—as well as others that are allegorical. Now those whose hearts are given to swerving from the truth go after the part of it which has been expressed in allegory, seeking discord, and seeking its final meaning, but none save God knows its final meaning (3:7).

There is also this interesting reference to the Battle of Badr, in which the poorly equipped and badly outnumbered Muslims repulsed their former persecutors. It appears to declare that we should not always expect to experience God's Revelation tangibly.

> Remember when you implored the assistance of your Lord, and He answered you: "I will assist you with a thousand angels, ranks on ranks." God made it but a message of hope and an assurance to your hearts. And there is no help except from God. Truly God is the Powerful, the Wise (8:9-10).

There are other similar statements in the Qur'an, like the following declaration concerning its graphic descriptions of Hell and threats of punishment to deniers of faith.

> And We have revealed it as an Arabic Qur'an, and have detailed in it certain threats, so that perhaps they may become God-conscious or it may cause them to take heed (20:113).

Moreover, the Qur'an frequently employs the phrase "the likeness (or parable) of" (Heaven, Hell, the state of the disbeliever, etc.) when speaking of realities outside of human experience. Thus in the twenty-fourth *surah* we read after a magnificent description of God's light, "and God strikes parables for mankind and God has knowledge of everything" (24:35).

Such assertions about the Scripture's use of allegory defuse most rational objections to its depictions of realities outside of human experience. Furthermore, it makes criticism of this type more difficult by introducing somewhat enigmatic terminology into these discussions. By steering clear of conventional wording, it avoids committing itself to either side of some notorious theological controversies. A good example is the problem of predestination.

Most monotheistic religions maintain that God knows and has power over everything. The Qur'an too indicates the same. Yet if God knows the future, then it would seem that the future must be a fixed entity. However, if this is the case, then must not our futures be predestined? Yet if they are, then is it just that we are held accountable for our wrongdoings?

Of course, God's knowledge of an event does not necessarily imply His making it happen, and God's power over us does not contradict that He empowers us to make choices and carry them out. But the Qur'an avoids the theological snare of using words or phrases that are truly synonymous with *predestine, predetermine,* or *preordain* (to destine, determine, or ordain in advance) when discussing divine and human will, for when such terms are employed, they introduce a logical conflict into the assumptions about God from which there is no escape.

The problematic premise that predestine assumes when applied to God is that God exists *in time,* as do we, and that He determines the *future*—He determines it in *advance.* However, if God transcends His creation—and the Qur'an in a number of ways indicates that He does—then He is not bound by the limitations of time and space that we are; in particular, God does not have a future or past, as we do. He is independent of the space-time universes He creates and not subject to their constraints. When it is said that God predestines the future, two conflicting suppositions about God are usually simultaneously assumed: that He transcends and that He exists within time. Thus it would be incorrect to apply the word *predestine* to God, for it situates God *in time* and assumes He manipulates not just our future, but what is the future for Him as well.[8]

There are affirmations in the Qur'an about God's complete knowledge of what from our perspective is the future and about His determining many events, but the wording employed is uncommon and non-explicative. Sometimes it states that such happenings "are written."[9] As if to say that life on earth is like a book, with the days we spend here serving as its pages, which we contribute to only one at

8. See question 7 this chapter for further discussion of this topic.
9. *Surahs* 3:145; 8:68, 15:4; 57:21

a time as we live them, and yet God sees them all simultaneously. But to say that from God's standpoint things "are written" is not the same as saying that they are predetermined. Of course, someone can *interpret* this phrase in this way, but there is no way it could be proved, based solely on the Qur'an, that this is the only admissible interpretation. With its distinctive and oblique phrasing, the Qur'an sidesteps the paradox of predestination, while conveying the idea of God's transcendent knowledge of and complete sovereignty over creation.[10]

Similarly, when the Qur'an asserts that everything unfolds according to God's design, it states that God creates everything with a "measure."[11] This would have been another convenient place to substitute the word *predestine* or a well-known equivalent, if the Scripture upholds predetermination, but once again, it introduces novel terminology without defining exactly what it means.[12] In so doing, it opens the way for the reader to interpret the phrase according to his or her intellectual perspective.

The Qur'an's use of unconventional terminology in its discussions of the "unseen" is too frequent to be coincidental. Its ambiguousness on matters beyond human experience and comprehension is clearly intentional; so in addition to stating that it contains passages that

---

10. There are other examples of this kind. The Qur'an sometimes states that many things are already "decided" or "accomplished" (*qad`a*) by God and that various terms and happenings are "named" or "stated" (*samm`a*).

11. The operative Arabic words here are *qadar* and *taqdir*, which mean measure.

12. *Surahs* 13:8; 15:21; 23:18; 36:38-39; 42:27; 43:31; 54:49-50; 80:18-19; 87:1-3. I chose this particular example of the Qur'an's use of enigmatic phrases in part because I later found that most Muslims equate the Arabic word *qadr* with *predestination*, even though this interpretation seems awkward in these verses. It turns out that the issue of predestination was hotly debated in the early Islamic centuries. This particular interpretation of *qadr* represents a dogmatic position that came to be held by what would eventually become the dominant trend in Islamic thought.

are not be taken literally, its skillful wording often makes it difficult to do so.

Reading the Qur'an in translation is another potential source of rational conflict. Language is inextricably bound to the history and culture from which it evolves, reflecting distinctive traditions, social structures, and worldviews. Each language has many words and expressions that have no real equivalents in foreign languages. Thus translation is not really the act of converting one set of expressions into an equivalent set of expressions; it involves taking meanings innate to one culture and projecting them onto an alien one. A translator is essentially an interpreter, whose work involves choosing one meaning from a variety of possible meanings on both sides of the process. Irrespective of the sincerity and erudition of the translator, the translation can only be approximating. The more two cultures diverge, the more difficult it becomes to translate between them. It is hard to conceive of two cultures more remote from each other than the seventh century Arabian and the modern Western.

In Arabic, words are derived from a system of consonantal roots. The great majority of roots consist of three consonants; a few contain one, two, four, and even five. A given root has associated with it a basic meaning that is relatable to all words derived from it. One of the first things that the student of Arabic discovers is the wide array of meanings associated with most words. In Lane's *Arabic-English Lexicon,* most listings of words and meanings related to a root go on for many pages, because many of the terms admit so many different shades of meaning. It is this richness and fluidity of Arabic vocabulary that gives the language its celebrated suppleness, making it an ideal medium for poetry, the pre-eminent Arabian art form since ancient times.[13]

The Arabs have always recognized the unparalleled beauty and

13. In the Arabic speaking world, poetry recitations and contests are still enjoyed by huge audiences. Movies, plays, television soap operas, variety shows, and public celebrations very frequently incorporate poetry recitals.

eloquence of the Qur'an. Hence, any translation can only be grossly inferior to the original, certainly aesthetically, but more importantly, in conveying the message, because the wide range of possible meanings is sacrificed in the translator's selection of a foreign *equivalent*. This can lead to many seeming contradictions.[14] An example is the following interpretation by Yusuf Ali of verse (7:179).

> Many are the Jinns and Men We have made for hell: They have hearts wherewith they understand not, eyes wherewith they see not, and ears wherewith they hear not. They are like cattle—nay more misguided: for they are heedless (of Our signs) (7:179).

The first line, as translated, certainly seems to indicate that certain persons are predestined for Hell, except for the fact that the rest of the verse indicates that such individuals end up there because they are heedless of God's signs. Nonetheless, the opening line appears to lend support to the concept of total predestination. The Arabic verb that Ali translates as "made" in 7:179 is *dharaa*. Some translators interpret *dharaa* even more severely and render it as "created." However, Hans Wehr's *A Dictionary of Modern Written Arabic*[15]— which is perhaps the most widely used Arabic-English dictionary— lists neither of these meanings or anything close to them under this verb. *A Concordance of the Qur'an*, by Kassis, shows that *dharaa* appears six times in the Qur'an, but in all cases other than 7:179, he renders it "to scatter" or "to multiply," which are in line with its principal connotations.[16] Edward Lane's monumental *Arabic English*

---

14. For myself this was by far the main source of perceived conflicts with reason.

15. Hans Wehr, *A Dictionary of Modern Written Arabic*, Cornell University Press (1961), Ithaca, N.Y.

16. Hanna E. Kassis, *A Concordance of the Qur'an*, University of California Press, 1983, p. 377. The verb also appears in 6:136; 16:13; 23:79; 42:11 and 67:24.

Lexicon does list the meaning "to create," but not as a primary meaning, and he can only cite classical exegeses of Qur'an (7:179) as an example of this usage. Hence, it seems likely that this meaning was not associated with *dharaa* in pre-Islamic times, but was introduced much later and reflected the theological leanings of certain schools of thought. All three sources indicate that the primary meanings associated with *dharaa* are closer to "to strew," "to scatter," "to spread," "to sprinkle," "to throw down," "to sow" and "to multiply." In addition, the sentence begins with the word *laqad* which indicates a completed act. A more natural rendering of 7:179 may go something like this:

> We have already cast into hell many of the jinns and humans.
> They have hearts...

Therefore this verse does not seem to be speaking at all about predestination, especially since the context shows that this passage and those immediately preceding it refer to those who deliberately reject God's signs (or revelations) (7:182). I do find that it gives another excellent example of something the Qur'an frequently does, and that is it sometimes refers to happenings in the hereafter in other than the future tense. Commentators state that this is a grammatical device to emphasize the inevitability of these happenings, but I feel that it also illustrates and supports the idea that God transcends time and space and that our hereafter takes place in a very different creation.

Above I have discussed what I believe are some of the most common sources of perceived conflict between the Qur'an and reason. From my many communications with young American Muslims I have found that most problems of this type stem from excessive literalism when reading the Scripture and from the natural imperfections and restrictions that translation imposes. Yet regardless of one's knowledge of Arabic and ancient Arabian history and culture, and regardless of one's openness to the possibility of symbolization, we should remain aware of the inherent limitations of all human language when speaking of the "unseen," and especially of God. As stated above, language is grounded in human experience, but since the Qur'an often speaks of realities that transcend this experience, all human language, including Arabic, is limited in its capacity to convey them to us. Thus, no matter how sophisticated our systems of communication and philosophies become, there will always be questions beyond our reach. This, I believe, is one of the implications of the following verse:

> If all the trees on earth were pens and the ocean were ink, with seven more oceans to support it, the words of God could not be exhausted. God is the Mighty, the Wise (31:27).

Question 4 (from a Canadian professional, one of many Western atheists who wrote me with questions):

I have no recollection of ever believing in God or even having a vague sense of my own spirituality. However, recently I have fallen in love with a Muslim woman who has also fallen in love with me. She feels strongly that the prospects of (our) having a future together would be greatly enhanced if I shared her faith, but she does not want me to convert except out of sincere conviction. I have read your book, "Even Angels Ask", and I am currently reading the Qur'an. I have some questions I would like to ask you, but let me start with something rather straightforward: the Qur'an's commandments. I find some of the Qur'an's laws to be outdated and some of its punishments too severe. Concerning the latter, could not God have foreseen the coming of a kinder, gentler time? I was wondering if the Qur'an's laws were at all a stumbling block toward your conversion?

The Qur'an's commandments did not figure into my decision to become a Muslim. Curiosity prompted me to start reading the Qur'an, but that quickly transformed into a compulsion to find the meaning it ascribes to human life. I recall skimming over the legislative verses rather quickly, since I thought that they did not directly bear upon this question. I think by the time I began to take the

Qur'an's calls to monotheism more seriously I was pretty much past its regulations, as most of the legislation occurs early on. This may be one reason why the Scripture's laws did not weigh heavier in my decision. I also did not know many Muslims back then, nor did I know how Islamic legislators around the world interpret or implement these commands. I do not have much of a mind for law, but it has always seemed to me a very subjective science. Unlike mathematics—where a valid proof is beyond contestation regardless of your presentiments—arguments and proofs in law appear to depend to a large extent on interpretation. I believe that this is another reason I did not give much thought to the commandments in the Qur'an, since I had almost no knowledge of how modern Muslims respond to them.

However, I was surprised by the exactness of many of the Qur'an's directives. Its commandments, which make up approximately three percent of the text, seemed at odds with the Scripture's overall style. In other respects, the Qur'an avoids anchoring itself to a precise place and time, but most of its ordinances address immediate problems that the Prophet and his followers encountered, many of them specific to their circumstances and environment. The Qur'an's legal remedies often provide an uncharacteristically high level of specification. Many of them make references to particulars of seventh century Arabian culture, such as its stipulations on women's dress that refer to certain articles of clothing worn by Arab women of that time (24:30-31), or its command to the believers to increase the size of their cavalry in preparation for war (8:60). The Qur'an does contain a large number of commands that could be deemed universal, such as its pronouncements against military aggression, murder, slander, cheating, usury, wine, theft, adultery, and forced conversion. Yet there are other ordinances that if taken literally would seem obsolete in most modern societies, such as the Qur'an's rules regarding slaves and concubines, or the rulings that apply exclusively to the Prophet and his family.[17]

---

17. *Surahs* 33:50; 33:52-53.

I did wonder why the Qur'an is so purposely ambiguous with respect to so many issues and so specific and technical with regard to its legal exhortations. Why did it not provide only a few general rules of behavior, something like the Ten Commandments or the admonitions of the Sermon on the Mount, to which persons of all times and places could immediately relate? Yet I also realized that in asking these questions I was probably being naïve.

It is apparent that one of the immediate tasks before the Qur'an was the reformation and mobilization of the seventh century Arabs. Judging from its prescripts, their society was crippled and stagnated by widespread anarchy, violence, vice, and corruption. To become a suitable vehicle for this Revelation, which is intended to be for all humanity (81:27), the society apparently had to undergo a complete turnaround to rid itself of its many debilitating and self-destructive habits; otherwise the Qur'an's message would probably have remained confined to a section of the Arabian Peninsula, perhaps ultimately to be forgotten. This may in part explain the explicit and technical nature of the Scripture's rulings, since abstract admonition seldom leads to rapid, comprehensive reform.[18]

Yet on the other hand, although most of the Qur'an's regulations respond to specific problems arising in a particular historical-cultural context, the types of problems addressed are for the most part common and fundamental to all societies. Its many prescripts pertaining to women, for example, are aimed at improving their position, albeit within the complex framework and corresponding natural constraints of the existing social milieu. The Qur'an insures women a level of financial autonomy, by prescribing that they receive a fixed share of inheritance, but half the share prescribed for men (4:11), since men were the primary breadwinners of the family (4:32-34). It also mandates that men are to pay women dowries when contracting to marry

---

18. In my opinion, general admonition seldom produces societal reform even in the long term.

them (4:4). The Qur'an brings women into the world of finance by allowing them as witnesses to high-level business agreements, but because they were in general unlearned in such dealings, it requires two women to substitute for one male witness, "so that if one forgets the other will remind her" (2:282). The Qur'an enacts detailed divorce laws to insure that " to them (women) are [rights] similar to those [of men] over them, in fairness" (2:228). However, since divorced Muslim women, unlike their former husbands, must wait approximately three months before remarrying to determine possible paternity, the Qur'an acknowledges, "but men have a degree [of advantage] over them" (2:228).[19] The Qur'an legislates against sexual exploitation and harassment by requiring that both men and women "lower their gaze" with respect to the opposite sex and that women dress modestly (24:30-31).

Similarly, the Qur'an's several rulings on slavery, which ought to have eliminated this institution in peacetime[20], should in modern times lead to protections against worker abuse and exploitation. Its imposition of an annual tax on wealth to be used to support the needy would indicate that society is obliged to look after the welfare of its citizens.[21] In response to an increase of widows and fatherless children in the early Muslim community—not unlike the problem of destitute single mothers today—the Qur'an encourages men to marry widows in order to provide them and their children with emotional and financial support, but it limits the total number of wives a man may have at one time to four (4:3).[22] It confronts business fraud by requiring

19. Also, as already mentioned, males often receive a larger share of inheritance.

20. The Qur'an allows only prisoners of war to be taken as slaves (8:67; 47:4), enjoins the manumission of slaves as expiation for a number of common sins (2:177; 4:92; 5:89; 58:3; 90:13), and provides slaves with legal avenues to purchase their freedom (24:33). Sadly, Muslim states were among the last to legally abolish slavery.

21. *Surahs* 2:43; 2:110; 2:177; 2:277; 4:162; 5:58.

22. Apparently there was no limit on the number of wives an Arab man could have before this pronouncement.

written contracts to be drafted when financial agreements are made and details instructions on how to formulate them, which include various protections for the weaker party (2:282-283). The Qur'an contains regulations on warfare that prohibit military aggression and allow fighting only in self-defense or against oppression.[23] It contains a number of instructions on statecraft, something quite foreign to the ancient Arabs, which emphasize respect for leadership, respect for the rights of others, respect for law, and community decision making through mutual consultation.[24] The Qur'an treats the problems of intoxicants and gambling with its ban on wine and *maisir*,[25] stating that "in them is great evil and profit for people, but the evil is greater than the profit" (2:219).

While the rulings of the Qur'an respond to immediate problems in the early Muslim community, most of those it addresses exist in any society. Such issues as injustice toward women, exploitation of labor, social welfare, single mothers, abandoned children, religious freedom, fraudulent business dealings, just warfare, state organization, recreational use of intoxicants, gambling, prostitution, and slander concern virtually every culture. Hence, the Qur'an's legislation, besides providing remedies in a particular historical context, may also serve as practical examples or models to be generalized to other contexts.

When the Qur'an presents a ruling, it is usually not hard to discern a general intent behind it. When this is not so, it often explains the larger aim of the command. Hence the command to the believing women to draw their head coverings over their chest belongs to a passage on modesty (24:30-31). When it orders the believers to

---

23. *Surahs* 2:190-193; 4:91; 8:61; 22:39-44. Also see the author's discussions in, *Struggling to Surrender*, Amana Publications, Beltsville, pp.183-190, and, *Even Angels Ask*, Amana Publications, Beltsville, pp. 116-136.

24. For example, 49:1-16.

25. *Maisir* was an ancient Arabian game of chance played with arrows without heads and feathering, for stakes of slaughtered and quartered camels.

multiply their horses in preparation for war (8:60), the Qur'an states that this will "drive fear in the hearts of enemies known and unknown"; that is, provide a military deterrent. After acknowledging the difference between what men and women inherit (4:11,32), the Scripture explains that this is because "men are charged with the maintenance of women and they [must] spend of their wealth" (4:33-34).

Yet if the Qur'an's prescripts epitomize certain basic aims and principles of law, then it would seem that they are also meant to be extended and adapted to time-bound changes that are certain to occur. After I became a Muslim, I discovered that many Islamic legal scholars agree with this view in principle but are exceedingly conservative in applying it. When they do extend or adapt a command, it is almost always in the direction of greater severity. The general thinking among Muslims is that it is better to ere on the side of strictness. I cannot say that I share the same feeling.

Let me close with some brief reflections on the humaneness of our times and the Qur'anic punishments. I am not convinced that the era in which we live is kinder and gentler than that in which the Qur'an was revealed. This past century has got to be the most violent on record. It may be that from the safe and serene backdrop of a college campus the world looks like a compassionate place, but not from the mean streets of America's inner cities or the numerous other places around the world where confronting extreme violence and injustice is a routine part of daily living.

While it is also true that a few of the Qur'an's penalties are not in tune with existing Western sensibilities, current Western sentiment is not an objective criterion by which to measure the overall humaneness of a social system. Every society uses punishment to deter acts it deems criminal, and presumably strives to balance the requirement not to be excessive in punishment against the need to protect the innocent. It would seem that an ideal legal system would be one that produces the minimal amount of total human suffering, as experienced by both the victims of crime and by the criminals when punished.[26] If, for example, a law can be constructed that completely eliminates crime and causes no hardship or suffering to the citizenry, it would be the best possible, regardless of its penal code, since no one would suffer the consequences of crime. While no legal system can eradicate crime and there is no barometer for gauging the totality of human suffering, Muslims believe that a society that most closely reflects the laws and ethos of the Qur'an will be the most humane from a holistic standpoint. Of course, being convinced of this is one thing but bringing such a society into being is another, but then that brings us back to the problem of interpretation.

Back to the Angels

The story of Adam (2:30-39) begins with an astonishing assertion about mankind: God creates humanity and places it on earth to act as His representative. Instead of beginning the story with a negative assessment of humankind, the Qur'an begins with an almost unbelievably positive appraisal of human potential. When the angels naturally question this election on grounds that they would clearly be more deserving, since humans are corrupt, rebellious, and violent creatures, while angels are sinless and totally submissive to God, God's response in the Qur'an is that He knows exactly what He is doing. Yet the Scripture does not dismiss the angels' query at that point, for the question they raise is an extremely important and difficult one. In the next nine verses it begins to develop an answer, seemingly providing several key clues or pieces to a puzzle.

The first point the Qur'an makes—and it is fascinating that it begins with this one—is that humans are highly intellectual creatures,

---

26. If there were some accurate means of measuring and calibrating human suffering, then the sum of human suffering caused by crime and the punishment of criminals divided by the size of the society's population might be a good index for assessing the overall humaneness of a legal system.

and this somehow figures prominently into the purpose behind their creation. It then indicates that men and women are moral beings, creatures of conscience, who possess a profound sense of right and wrong. They are exposed to magnanimous and evil prompting and must choose between them. Thus God has endowed humanity with consciousness of moral right and wrong and empowered them to act on their moral decisions. It also shows that humans have the ability to realize their errors and correct themselves. Another important point the story seems to make is that humans will suffer on earth, for the angels rightly say that humans "spread corruption and shed much blood," and God tells humanity to "go down, all of you together, with some of you adversaries of others." However, it is clear that, in the Qur'an's version of the story of the first man and woman, life on earth and the hardship people experience are not meant to punish humankind. The suffering endured is all part of God's plan. The story also stresses the role of God's guidance and forgiveness in the life of mankind and the terrible consequences of rejecting them.

I knew I might have been reading too much into the story, that some of the themes I believed it introduced in its response to the angels were nothing more than a mirage of my own making. Maybe I was letting my imagination run wild. Perhaps I was projecting my childhood conflicts onto the narrative. Yet it was not long before I found confirmation of my suppositions. For as I made my way through the Qur'an, I found that it does indeed emphasize that reason, conscience, volition, error, repentance, suffering, divine guidance, and forgiveness play essential roles in human development on earth. However, I could not see how they all fit together to serve some ultimate goal that could not have been accomplished more efficiently, if there really were a God.

Will They Not Use Their Reason?

"The Lord is very kind and loving, son."

"If He is so kind and loving, then why does He allow so much suffering and violence on earth?"

My mother and I had had this conversation many times before, and it seemed that we were having it more frequently now that I had made known my atheism to my family.

"There are some things that we in our limited minds simply cannot comprehend."

"I know. I have heard that a thousand times," I told her, sounding exasperated. *"Every time a legitimate, reasonable objection to belief in God is raised, we are told that our understanding is too limited to comprehend the wisdom of His doings. The thing that really gets me is that people go on finding all kinds of rational arguments against the existence of God, and the only response they ever get is that their minds are too small to understand— and then they accept this as a counter-argument! You would think that this would cause them to have major doubts!"*

"Everyone has doubts at some time in their lives. I did when I was your age."

"Then why do you still believe? If we have doubts about an airline pilot, we don't get on the plane. If we have doubts about a product in a store, we don't buy it. If we have doubts about a politician's integrity, we don't vote for him. But with religion, we have many, many sound reasons to suspect it, yet people believe in it anyway! Do they just brainwash themselves into believing or just hedge their bets against eternal punishment by blindly submitting themselves to something that makes no sense?"

"Faith is a gift from God, Jeff. Once you experience it, you won't have doubts anymore."

"Then why doesn't He give this gift to everybody? Why doesn't He give it to me?"

"You have to try to have faith, son."

"I just don't know. It sounds like you're saying that to not have doubts, I have to ignore my natural inclinations and force myself to believe. Isn't that just a kind of self-induced brainwashing?"

"Don't worry, Jeff," my mother assured me. "You will find God some-day."

"What makes you so sure," I said with a laugh.

"Because as my grandmother used to tell me," she replied with a confident smile, 'The way the twig is bent, the tree will grow'."

When the angels demur at the announcement of the creation of mankind, the very first thing that God points to in order to demonstrate the superficiality of their case is human intelligence. In essence the Qur'an asserts that this human trait is more esteemed by God than the angels' inability to sin.[27] Thus right from the start the Qur'an makes it clear that God does not expect nor want men and women to be angels, that with all their faults, complexities, and contradictions, they have the ability to become something greater, and somehow human intellect plays a key role in that. The prominence assigned to reason in the human spiritual quest caught me off guard. I had always believed that reason ultimately undermines faith, but this Scripture seemed to say that faith is undermined when reason is ignored or poorly applied.

The rational and often didactic tone of the Qur'an is one of its most salient features. One of its fundamental themes is that people ignore or reject God's signs and corrupt religion because they do not use their reason. "They refuse to reason" and are "a people who do not reason,"[28] the Qur'an complains of its detractors. "Will you not reason?" the Qur'an asks them.[29] God reveals signs, lessons, and admonitions, so that, "Perhaps you [the unbelievers] will use your reason."[30]

---

27. The Qur'an later explains that Iblis, who refuses to bow down to Adam in 2:34 and causes the couple "to slip" in 2:36, was not an angel but a *jinn*, a sentient unseen being. Thus he possesses the ability to do wrong.

28. *Surahs* 2:171; 5:58; 8:22; 29:63; 39:43; 49:4; 59:14.

29. *Surahs* 2:44; 2:76; 3:65; 6:32; 7:169; 10:16; 11:51; 12:109; 21:67; 23:80; 28:60; 36:62; 36:68; 37:138.

30. *Surahs* 2:73; 2:242; 6:151; 12:2; 24:61; 40:67; 43:3; 57:17.

From the Qur'an's viewpoint, reason and faith are allies, as are illogic and false belief, and it clearly sets the conflict along these lines: "the right way has become clear from error."[31] Those who benefit most from the Qur'an are "persons of insight,"[32] "firmly rooted in knowledge,"[33] "use their reason,"[34] and stand on "clear evidence and proof."[35] While those who oppose revelation are "deluded,"[36] "in manifest error,"[37] "ignorant,"[38] "foolish,"[39] "have no understanding,"[40] "only follow surmise and conjecture,"[41] and blindly adhere to tradition.[42]

In an almost Socratic style, the Qur'an repeatedly quizzes the reader and calls into question his or her assumptions. Again and again it asks, "What do you think...?"[43] "Have you considered...?"[44]

---

31. 2:256; 7:146; 7:202; 19:59.

32. *Surahs* 2:179; 2:197; 2:269; 3:7; 3:190; 5:100; 12:111; 13:19; 14:52; 38:29; 38:43; 39:9; 39:18; 39:21; 40:54; 65:10.

33. *Surahs* 4:162; 22:54; 28:80; 29:49; 30:56; 34:6; 47:16; 58:11.

34. *Surahs* 2:164; 6:98; 13:4; 16:67; 20:54; 20:128; 29:35; 30:24; 30:28; 45:5.

35. *Surahs* 6:104; 7:203; 12:108; 17:102; 28:43; 45:20; 75:14.

36. *Surahs* 3:24; 6:70; 6:130; 7:51; 8:49; 45:35; 57:14; 67:20; 82:6.

37. *Surahs* 3:164; 4:60; 4:116; 4:136; 4:167; 10:32; 14:3; 14:18; 19:38; 21:54; 22:12; 23:106; 26:97; 28:85; 31:11; 33:36; 34:8; 34:24; 36:24, 37:69; 39:22; 40:25; 40:50; 42:18; 46:32; 54:47; 62:2; 67:29.

38. *Surahs* 2:67; 2:273; 6:35; 6:111; 7:138; 7:179; 11:29; 11:46; 12:33; 12:89; 25:63; 27:55; 28:55; 39:64; 46:23.

39. *Surahs* 2:13; 2:130; 72:4.

40. *Surahs* 4:78; 6:25; 7:179; 8:65; 9:87; 9:127; 59:13; 63:3; 63:7.

41. *Surahs* 4:157; 6:116; 6:148; 10:36; 10:66; 43:20; 45:32; 53:23; 53:28.

42. *Surahs* 2:170; 5:104; 6:148; 7:28; 7:70; 7:173; 10:78; 11:109; 11:62; 11:87; 14:10; 16:35; 21:53-54; 23:24; 26:74; 28:36; 31:21; 34:43; 37:69-70; 43:22-24.

43. *Surahs* 6:40; 6:46; 6:47; 11:28; 11:63; 11:88; 17:62; 18:63; 26:205; 28:71; 28:72; 39:38; 41:52; 67:28; 67:30; 96:9; 96:11; 96:13.

44. *Surahs* 10:50; 10:59; 26:75; 35:40; 45:23; 46:4; 46:10; 53:19; 55:33; 56:58; 56:63; 56:71; 107:1.

"Did you (or they) suppose...?"[45] "Do they not ponder...?"[46] "Do you (or they, the deniers, humans, etc.) think...?"[47] The message is plain enough: to gain truer faith, we need to free ourselves from inherited notions and examine our beliefs rationally.

Learning plays a key role in human spiritual development. "Read!" the Qur'an exhorts the reader, for "God taught the use of the pen" and with it "taught humankind what it would not [otherwise] know" (96:4-5). In life, nature, history, and the Qur'an there are "signs" and "lessons" for the wise.[48] The Qur'an states over one hundred times that it has been revealed to "clarify (or explain) things." God teaches humanity both directly and indirectly, and sometimes so subtly that we are unaware of His instruction (96:4-5).[49] Thus He also tests us in multifarious ways.[50]

As life on earth is portrayed as an educational stage in humans' creation, it is not surprising that the Day of Judgment as depicted in the Qur'an takes on an almost academic coloring. It is not unlike the end of term or graduation day on a college campus. Humankind will be sorted out into three classes (56:7-56). The Foremost in Faith are those who excelled in their submission to God, and they will be brought nearest to Him. The Companions of the Right Hand are those who did well enough on Earth to enter Paradise but who did

---

45. *Surahs* 2:214; 3:142; 9:16; 23:115; 29:4; 45:21; 47:29.

46. *Surahs* 4:82; 47:24.

47. *Surahs* 2:214; 3:142; 9:16; 18:9; 18:102; 23:55; 23:115; 25:44; 29:2; 29:4; 43:80; 45:21; 47:29; 75:3; 75:36; 90:5; 90:7.

48. *Surahs* 2:179; 2:197; 2:269; 3:7; 3:13; 3:190; 5:100; 12:111; 13:19; 14:52; 16:66; 23:21; 24:44; 38:29; 38:43; 39:9; 39:18; 39:21; 40:54; 65:10; 79:26.

49. *Surahs* 2:31; 2:129; 2:151; 2:282; 2:239; 2:251; 2:282; 3:164; 4:113; 5:113; 12:37; 18:65; 21:80; 53:5; 55:2; 55:4; 62:2; 96:4-5.

50. *Surahs* 2:49; 2:155; 3:152; 3:154; 3:186; 5:48; 5:94; 6:165; 7:141; 7:163; 7:168; 11:7; 14:6; 16:92; 18:7; 21:35; 23:30; 27:40; 33:11; 37:106; 44:33; 47:4; 47:31; 67:2; 68:17; 76:2; 89:16.

not reach the level of excellence of the Foremost in Faith. The Companions of the Left Hand are those who failed in life and face suffering in the life to come. Leaving nothing out, the record of all deeds, however small or great, will be brought out. The sinful will be in great terror this moment as they sense their fate (18:49). The faces of those who failed in life will be humiliated, laboring, and weary, while those who were successful will have joyful, exuberant expressions (88:1-16). The successful will receive their earthly records in their right hands and will gleefully show them to others; the failures, consumed by grief and embarrassment, will be given their records in their left hands or will hold them behind their backs (69:19-30; 89:10). When awarded their records in their right hands, the successful will eagerly run to show their families, but the failures will cry out miserably (89:7-11).

The Qur'an uses other means to encourage a rational approach to faith. A common motif in the narratives is the great public debate between a prophet or believer and his opposition, with the former invariably gaining the logical upper hand. The story of Abraham contains several of these confrontations.[51] When Abraham tells a despot that his Lord is He who grants life and death, the tyrant responds that he also grants life and death. Abraham then corners him by stating that his Lord makes the sun rise in the east and then asks the ruler to make it rise in the west (2:258). In like manner, when the leaders of Abraham's people accuse him of destroying their idols —which he did—and demand that he reveal who the perpetrator was, he points to the lone idol he left standing. They immediately recognize their logical predicament, for if they admit that Abraham's statement is ludicrous, then so is the worship of their fabricated deities (21:51-71).

The Qur'an frequently uses parables and paradoxes to point out common errors in our thinking. It provides the following example of how false conclusions are made, based on circumstantial evidence.

51. *Surahs* 6:74; 19:41-50; 21:51-71; 26:70-82; 29:16-25; 37:83-98.

The similitude is that of a dog: if you kick it, it lolls its tongue out, or if you leave it alone, it lolls out its tongue. That is an example of people who deny the truth (7:176).

Thus a careless thinker may insist that a dog that lolls out its tongue must have been kicked, since that is what dogs do in such a situation, without considering the fact that they do the same even when left alone.

In *Surat al Kahf*, the Qur'an shows how people often argue over insignificant details.

Some say there were three, the dog being the fourth among them. Others say they were five, the dog being the sixth, guessing   at the unseen. Yet others say seven, the dog being the eighth. Say: "My Lord knows best their number, and none knows it but a few. Therefore, do not enter into controversies concerning them, except on a matter that is clear, and do not ask anyone to make a pronouncement about them" (18:22).

In the story of Moses and Khidr (18: 60-82), a parable that deals with human suffering, the Scripture shows that Moses—as do most of us—repeatedly jumps to wrong conclusions based on insufficient evidence.

Perhaps the most interesting paradox the Qur'an provides is the following, which deals with the origins of evil:

Say: "All things are from God." But what is the matter with these people that they fail to understand a single thing? Whatever happens to you of good is from God, but whatever happens to you of evil is from yourself (4:78-79).

The point seems to be that all things are ultimately from God, even the ability of humans to do and experience evil. Yet while God has endowed us with the ability to choose and produce evil, that choice is in the end ours. When we choose to perform a good deed, we gain, in terms of our personal growth, the benefits that come with it, and these are from God and the way in which He created the human personality. When we choose evil, we deny ourselves the personal gains we could have had and in reality hurt ourselves, and so the real evil we experience—our own self-destruction—comes by our own hands.

Another aspect of the Qur'an that is indicative of its rational character is that it includes and rebuts common arguments used against it. It should be noted that these same arguments are still in vogue today in many circles. The conjecture that the Qur'an is the creation of someone possessed, or out of his mind (7:184, 68:5-6, 81:22) or is a forgery (10:37, 11:13) is refuted by pointing to its unparalleled profundity, coherence, and eloquence.

> And if you are in doubt as to what We have revealed from time to time to our servant, then produce a *surah* like there unto; and call your witnesses or helpers besides God, if your [doubts] are true (2:23).

> Have they not reflected on this Qur'an? Surely if it were from other than God, they would find in it many a contradiction (4:82).

> This Qur'an is not such as can be produced by other than God, on the contrary it is a confirmation of [revelations] that went before it and a fuller explanation of the Book—wherein there is no doubt—from the Lord of the Worlds.

> Or do they say, "He invented it." Say: "Then bring a *surah* like it, and call [to your aid] anyone you can, besides God, if you speak the truth" (10:37-38).

> Or they may say, "He invented it." Say, "Then produce ten *surahs* forged just like it, and call [to your aid] whomsoever you can, other than God, if you speak the truth (11:13).

> Say: "If the whole of mankind and jinn gathered together to produce the like of this Qur'an, they could not produce the like thereof, even if they backed up each other with help and support" (17:88).

Citing its supreme eloquence in Arabic, the Qur'an rebuts the charge that a Christian or Jewish foreigner taught the Prophet the Scripture (16:103). Against the claim that Muhammad must have been insincere and self-seeking, the Qur'an emphasizes that it exalts and honors God alone and requests no worldly compensation for the Prophet.[52] On the contrary, the Qur'an confirms the essential moral and spiritual truths of earlier Revelations, so that, in particular, Jews and Christians cannot indict the Qur'an on this score without indicting their own Scriptures.

Something Wrong With This Picture

The great importance the Qur'an assigns to reason in the pursuit of faith is surprising, especially considering the era and place in which it first appeared.[53] By all accounts the Arabian Peninsula was at that

---

52. *Surahs* 25:57, 34:47, 38:86; 42:23.

53. Yet even in the modern era the Qur'an's insistence that reason is essential to religion is a radical notion. That reason and faith conflict has almost become an axiom in contemporary thought. Not that such a conflict has been "proved" in the sense that it has been demonstrated syllogistically that belief in God always leads to a logical contradiction. Rather, this conflict is more a perception born of experience both historical and personal. On the one hand, we have the long history of persecution of philosophers and scientists by the religious establishment. On the other, we have the common frustration of rationalists who are unable to obtain satisfying answers to their theological questions. Thus it might be more accurate to state that reason and faith have often been used against each other rather than that they are necessarily at odds. Regardless of how it is put, there are few in the monotheistic traditions today who insist on the union of faith and reason. It should also be pointed out that most modern day Muslims, especially the religious scholars, are extremely wary of a rational approach to Islam. They seem to rely much more heavily on tradition than reason. This was not always the case in the Muslim world, especially in the first few centuries of Islamic history.

time far from being a cradle of learning or philosophy. The Arabs were a callous, poor, illiterate, and uncultured people, often struggling fiercely against their harsh environment and each other for what little there was to extend their survival. While the Scriptures of the other major world religions appeared in developed and refined societies, the Qur'an first appeared in what can be aptly described as a cultural desert. Historians agree that the Arabs were a primitive people with no artistic, literary, or scientific heritage to speak of. They had no schools of philosophy, no significant works of visual art or literature; they were unknowledgeable in higher mathematics and possessed no other Scriptures or sacred writings. Their only developed art form was poetry, orally communicated and handed down. Such an environment is not expected to produce a work of such genius and literary power. We might assume that a long and gradual, cultural maturation would have preceded the Qur'an's appearance.

There is no evidence that Muhammad had any formal education. He may have led a few caravan expeditions in his twenties, but that would not provide him with the opportunity to develop his intellectual skills to such a high level. The whole style of the Qur'an, its stress on reason, its logical coherence, its ingenious employment of ambiguity and symbolism, its beauty and conciseness, suggests an author whose insight and wisdom come from far beyond the primitive confines of the then backward and isolated Arabian Peninsula.

I thought that perhaps there may have been more than one author of the Qur'an, but, unlike other Scriptures, there is no internal evidence to support this. The personality behind the Revelations is clearly one and its coherence is too great for it to have been a collective effort. As the Scripture states:

> Surely if it were from other than God, they would find in it many a contradiction. (4:82)

> They could not produce the like thereof, even if they backed up each other with help and support. (17:88)

The only reasonable explanation I could come up with is that Muhammad had to be humanity's greatest genius, for history has known many unusually gifted minds but none that transcended their time and place as he must have. Einstein was an amazing physicist, but his development of the Theory of Relativity was preceded by centuries of discovery with the science of physics moving in that direction for some time. Had Einstein not come up with the Theory of Relativity when he did, one of his peers almost certainly would have soon after. Andrew Wiles' recent proof of Fermat's Last Theorem is a brilliant achievement, but hundreds of years of advancement in mathematics and work on this problem contributed to it. Mozart, Van Gough, and Shakespeare were exceptional, but their works built on and reflect trends within their cultural surroundings. But the Qur'an's sudden appearance in the Hijaz seemed to me like a rose bush suddenly appearing in full bloom in the most barren sector of the Empty Quarter of Arabia.

I felt that if Muhammad was the author of the Qur'an, then, besides being the most brilliant mind in history, he also must have been intensely devout and altruistic. The Qur'an is the purest testament to monotheism in existence, and it shows a deep, compassionate commitment to helping humanity, guiding men and women to the love of God, and righteous living. It would also seem that the Prophet must have been remarkably humble and self-effacing, as the Scripture repeatedly insists that Muhammad is only a man; that his only role is to deliver the message; that he has no supernatural powers; and that he, like everyone else, should pray for guidance and forgiveness.[54] It criticizes and corrects him on several occasions. Such humility is rare in persons so intellectually superior to their peers.

Therefore, if Muhammad had authored the Qur'an, it would seem that he was singularly devoted to serving God and humanity and to teaching virtue, but yet, I could not ignore that he must also

---

54. *Surahs* 6:107; 10:49; 11:12; 13:38; 17:90-94; 25:7; 17:74-75.

have concocted the most audacious hoax, fabricating a Scripture that portrays itself as God's direct communication through him. It does not fit that a person capable of such a colossal lie could also produce such a powerful call to truth and goodness. I toyed with the idea that the Prophet may have had multiple personalities, but the Qur'an is surely not the delusions of a fragmented personality, any more than it could be the work of several individuals.

I finally had to leave the matter of the Qur'an's authorship on the shelf. In any case, it was not integral to my purpose. I decided that if Muhammad were the Scripture's author, then he is undoubtedly the supreme human anomaly, and if he is not, then the true author somehow entirely escaped the view of history.

A Difficult Choice

I remember a day in my fifth grade religion class when we were reciting in unison from our catechism. We came to the statement, "The Catholic faith is the one true religion," and I raised my hand.

"Yes, Jeffrey?" asked Sister Bernadette.

"Sister, doesn't every religion teacher tell her students that their religion is the one, true, religion? I mean I can't imagine her telling them that some other religion is the one, true religion. How do we really know?"

For a couple of seconds Sister Bernadette stared at me blankly. Then she said somewhat slowly and cautiously, "I will have to ask Father Hanover about that, but I will get back to you."

She never did get back to me on that one. She probably forgot. And though I didn't ask it again, it continued to bother me.

"The greater the mind, the more difficult the choices," a friend once told me. The Qur'an appears to make the same point in the story of the first couple (2:30-39). Immediately after establishing that humans are potentially superior to angels because of their greater intelligence, the Qur'an sets the stage for Adam's and Eve's first demonstration of free will. The Qur'an shows us that humans will be subject to satanic and angelic inspiration, and that their state in the hereafter will ultimately be determined by the choices they make here and now. It makes sense that human will is highlighted right after human intelligence, because neither can exist without the other. Intelligence cannot be exercised without choice, and choice is an intellectual act.

> Let there be no compulsion in religion—the right way is henceforth clearly distinct from error. (2:256)

The Qur'an asserts that faith must be voluntary. True faith is a choice. It should be an act of will and reason, for "the right way is henceforth clearly distinct from error." The Qur'an asserts that God could have programmed humanity to conform perfectly to His will, but He has other plans.

> Had He willed He could indeed have guided all of you.(6:149)

> If it had been your Lord's wish, they all would have believed, all who are on earth. Will you then compel people against their will to believe? (10:99)

> Do not the believers know that, had God willed, He could have guided all mankind? (13:31)

> And if We had so willed, We could have given every soul its guidance... (32:13)

> Had God willed, He could have made you all one community. (5:48)

God could have made humanity homogeneously submissive to Him—spiritual clones of one another—but instead He gave us the intellectual capacity to choose and empowered us to carry out our choices to their normally expected ends. Although our choices may affect others, we are their primary beneficiaries.

Enlightenment has come from your God; he who sees, does so to his own good, he who is blind, is so to his own hurt. (6:104)

And whosoever is guided, is only (guided) to his own gain, and if any stray, say: "I am only a warner." (27:92)

We have revealed to you the book with the truth for mankind. He who lets himself be guided does so to his own good; he who goes astray does so to his own hurt.[55] (39:41)

It may seem from the verses just cited that men and women are completely free and that God allows the world to run its course without interference. Although as an atheist I would have preferred this to be the Scripture's position, it is definitely not the case. The Qur'an informs us that God has power over all things, that nothing occurs without His permission, that He often influences people's perceptions and judgment, guides the believers and allows the unbelievers to stray unguided, and manipulates the human drama to place individuals into critical situations or "tests." In the Qur'an, God's control over creation is so all-encompassing that it leaves the impression that almost nothing occurs by chance, that within every personal encounter or mundane happening there are divinely planted opportunities for spiritual growth. Although the Qur'an affirms that men and women are free to make choices, they are nowhere near as independent as they think they are. Opportunities are continuously being created for them to make moral and spiritual decisions.

It may be that this illusion of independence is necessary for human growth and learning, for if we constantly perceived God's all pervading presence, then temptation and, along with it, moral and spiritual development would be nearly impossible. Part of what makes the decision between doing good and evil possible, and for us real, is the perception that we are distant from God. Hence, the first couples'

---

55. Also see 10:108; 17:15; and 27:92.

temptation takes place "in the garden," when they perceive that God is not present. Similarly, when they are ready to go on to the next stage of their creation, God tells them, "Go you all down from here," indicating to them that they will be separated from God. Yet the Qur'an informs us that in reality God is always near.

> And when My servants ask of Me, I am truly near. I heed the call of every caller when he calls on Me. Let them also, with a will, listen to My call and believe in Me, that they may walk in the right way. (2:186)

> Say: "If I am astray, I only stray to my own loss, but if I receive guidance, it is because of the inspiration of my Lord to me. It is He who hears all things and is [ever] near. (34:50)

> We surely created man, and We know what his soul whispers to him, and We are nearer to him than his jugular vein. (50:16)

> Then why do you not [intervene] when [the soul of the dying man] reaches the throat, while you are looking on? But We are nearer to him than you, but you do not see. (56:83-85)

The illusion of autonomy enhances and intensifies our choosing and learning experiences in life. It allows us the opportunity to independently apply what has been learned. Learning, whether it is in or outside of the classroom, has two essential stages: instruction and trial; and knowledge reaches another level when put to the test.

> And surely We will test you with something of fear and hunger, and the loss of wealth and crops; but give glad tidings to the steadfast, who say, when misfortune strikes them: "To God we belong, and to Him we return." (2:155-156)

> Surely you will be tested in your property and in your selves, and you will hear much that will grieve you from those who were given the Scripture before you, and those who worship many gods. But if you persevere and guard against evil, then that will be a determining factor in all affairs. (3:186)

If God had willed, He could have made you one community. But that He may test you by that which He has given you [He has made you as you are]. So vie with one another in good works. Unto God you will all return and He will inform you of that wherein you differ. (5:48)

He it is who has placed you as vicegerents on earth and has exalted some of you in rank above others, that He may test you by that which He has given you. (6:165)

We dispersed them [the Jewish nation] about the earth. Some of them are righteous and some are the opposite. We have tested them with both prosperity and adversity that perhaps they might turn [to Us]. (7:168)

We have placed all that is on the earth as an ornament there-of that We may test them: which of them is best in conduct. (18:7)

Every soul shall have a taste of death, and We test you with evil and with good, by way of trial. (21:35)

Blessed is He in whose hands is dominion, and He has power over all things. He who created death and life that He may test you, which of you is best in conduct. And He is the Powerful, the Forgiving. (67:1-2)

Our perception of autonomy is also enhanced by our perception of time, which allows us to feel that the personal consequences of our choices and our meeting with God in the hereafter are way off into the future. Hence we not only feel distant from God with respect to space but with respect to time as well. Once again, however, the Qur'an informs us that our perception of time is not objectively real and that we will become aware of this when we enter the next life.

The Day they see it, (it will be) as if they had tarried but a single evening, or the following morning. (79:46)

One Day He will gather them all together: (it will seem) as if they had tarried but an hour of a day. (l0:45)

It will be on a Day when He will call you, and you will answer with His praise, and you will think that you tarried but a little while. (17:52)

In whispers will they consult each other: "You tarried not longer than ten (days)." (10:l03)

"You tarried not longer than a day." (10:l04).

He will say: "What number of years did you stay on earth?" They will say, "We stayed a day or part of a day: ask those who keep account." He will say: "You stayed not but a little, if you had only known!" (23:112-113)

Time as we perceive it is then another of this life's illusions. What for us is the slow and inexorable flow of history is but a blink of an eye to God.[56] Although we witness His will unfold over the course of many days or years, for God it is a single command: "Be! And then it is."[57] The Qur'an also demonstrates the illusory character of time by comparing the "days of God" with earthly days, where a "day of God" is said to be as a "thousand years of your reckoning" (32:5) and like "50,000 years" (70:4). Hence, time as we perceive it is just another object of the creation we exist in, with no real validity beyond it, with God's knowledge and will encompassing all time and space in a single eternal "instant" outside of time.

---

56. Although the Day of Judgment is from the human perspective in the distant future, the Qur'an states that it is nearer than a "blink of an eye."

And unto God belong the heavens and the earth, and the matter of the Hour is but a blink of an eye, or it is nearer still. Lo! God has power over all things (16:77).

57. *Surahs* 2:117; 16:40; 36:82; 40:68; 54:50.

> Truly We have created everything by measure and Our commandment is but one [commandment], as the twinkling of an eye. (54:49-50)

The illusions of separation from God in time and space are not the only misperceptions we operate under. "The life of this world is but a matter of illusion," asserts the Qur'an (3:185; 57:20). With every page I read of the Scripture, the stronger the image became for me of life as a test, as a problem solving context created to challenge humankind and spur moral, intellectual, and spiritual growth. Like a teacher who leaves the classroom to observe his or her students from behind a one-way mirror, God creates for us the illusion of separation from Him to foster our personal development. Armed with intellect and choice, we are placed in an adverse environment, seemingly on our own, to work out our destiny.

> If it had been your Lord's wish, they all would have believed, all who are on earth. Will you then compel people against their will to believe? But no soul would have believed except by the permission of God, for He has set disgrace upon those who will not use their reason. (10:99-100)

This passage provides a biting summary of the Qur'an's stance on divine and human will. It is not God's wish to compel humanity to believe; instead, belief must come by free choice. Yet, though the choice must be freely made, it is never independent of God, for He nurtures, receives, and responds to that choice in both obvious and subtle ways. But for those who stubbornly and irrationally refuse that choice, God will leave them in unbelief to their utter and ultimate disgrace. Choice, divine assistance, and intellect are three keys to the attainment of genuine faith.

But why and how is this so? What is faith that it must incorporate reason and choice? I had been used to thinking of faith as an acknowledgement of a supposed truth and conformity to it, which could certainly be implanted in humans. Indeed, the Qur'an indicates that other creatures have a natural predisposition or instinct for serving

God (22:18; 24:41). Faith for humanity must be something much greater and more complex, but then what is it?

I felt like I was watching a television screen that kept coming in and out of focus. At times I thought I was starting to see the big picture only to have it clouded by another consideration. Human suffering on earth was for me a major distraction. What possible role could it play?

Why Me?

"Why did this have to happen to me?" Gerda exclaimed angrily. "You smoke a pack of cigarettes every day and you're perfectly healthy! I never smoked a single cigarette my whole life and I get lung cancer. It should have been you! You should have cancer, not me!"

I was angered by what Gerda had said to Ragia. To wish cancer on my wife, the warmest, kindest, and gentlest person I have known, regardless of Gerda's condition, was uncalled for.

"That's a strange statement coming from a rabid atheist," I told Ragia. "To whom is she complaining—nature? You mean to tell me that from her perspective, she can't see how one of the near infinite sequences of causes and effects that have occurred since the big bang has led to her contracting cancer? Why should she have been excluded from one of life's innumerable accidents, if there is no God?"

We received a call from Gerda when she was in Germany seeking a cure. I was stunned when she asked me, "Will you pray for me?"
Although I told Gerda that I would pray for her, I was thinking that it probably would be more effective if she prayed for herself.

"If I ever get over this thing, I am definitely going to make a serious study of religion," she swore earnestly, her voice cracking with emotion.

Her doctors in Germany subjected Gerda to a very new treatment. Although her cancer had advanced quite far and they gave her little hope, the treatment was apparently successful, and she returned to Lawrence with no detectable traces of the disease. Her battle with the illness definitely brought about a profound change in Gerda, but not in the way one might expect.

As far as I could tell she never followed up her promise to "make a serious study of religion." She remained as vociferous and aggressive an atheist as ever. That is not surprising, since many an unbeliever has momentary second thoughts in a crisis,[58] but her outlook on life turned dramatically inward. Gerda had always cherished her friends and was very loyal and generous toward them. When this point came up in a conversation she told me, "That was a big mistake of mine. I've learned how precious life is. It was foolish of me to have given so much of myself to others. I'll never do that again."

About a year and a half after Gerda was given a clean bill of health, her doctors found that her cancer had returned. This time they insisted that there was nothing they could do for her since the disease had progressed too far.

"What kind of God would do this to me?!" She complained to my wife, quite out of the blue.

Ragia usually would not respond to Gerda's antireligious diatribes. If Gerda wanted to discuss religion calmly and respectfully, she was more than willing, but when she would take on a mocking tone, Ragia preferred to ignore her.

"Maybe one who is giving you another chance." Ragia blurted, surprising herself.

It was not like Gerda to give an opponent the final word, especially when debating religion, but she remained silent and pensive. Perhaps it was because of her deteriorated physical condition.

Gerda isolated herself from her friends during the last few months of her disease. She told Ragia on the phone that she did not want anyone to see her "like this." Gerda and her husband had taught in the math department at Kansas University. I found out about her passing from a department memorandum. It stated that her family would not be holding a service for her and that those who wished could donate to a scholarship fund established by her husband in her memory.

---

58. This aspect of human nature is cited several times in the Qur'an. See 10:12; 16:53-55; 17:67; 29:65-66; 30:33-34; 31:32; 39:8; 39:49.

Human suffering has always posed an enormous dilemma for religious thought. Is it to entertain bored, capricious, and rival gods? Is it punishment for our sinful natures? Is it something from which we must be saved? Is it a necessary aspect of creation to be transcended through spiritual training and meditation? Is it the product of chance accidents that occur in a godless universe?

All of these questions take for granted that human suffering is damaging and undesirable.[59] This is natural, since it reflects the human perspective, the point of view of one who feels victimized.

59. Suffering posed more of a rational, philosophical problem for me than a personal, emotional one. In this writing, I have looked at it globally rather than individually, but I feel that in most cases God does not impose suffering on individuals but rather allows calamity to happen in accord with the natural laws of cause and effect implanted in creation. This appears evident by the fact that creation itself –plants and animals—struggle for survival in much the same way as humans. For us, however, this struggle provides tests in which individuals can grow or decline in the divine attributes according to how each person responds to his or her own personal struggle.

My mother's breakdown, after which she was never her true self again, occurred several years after my conversion to Islam. I would see her fading against the psychotic struggle which seemed to engulf her after a lifetime of enduring my father. Even after my mother's mental collapse, however, I saw glimpses of the spiritual strength still abiding within her.

Shortly before she passed on, in a period of emotional and mental clarity, she said to me: "I'm not afraid of dying; are you, Jeff?"

I responded, "Death doesn't scare me, but I worry about my family, even though I know God will care for them."

She said, "I understand, but my family doesn't need me anymore and I'm ready to go." I knew then that this would be the last time I would see her.

"I'm going to miss you terribly, mom," I told her, as I struggled to hold back the tears.

"I know you will, son, but it will be alright now." At that moment I could see in her face that tremendous strength and peace I used to know so well.

(continued on page 83)

However, the Qur'an has a very different view of human earthly suffering. It claims that it is a necessary and key element in the human growth process, and that all of us, good and bad, sinful and righteous, believer and unbeliever, will and must experience it.

> Most assuredly We will test you with something of danger, and hunger, and the loss of worldly goods, of lives and the fruits of your labor. But give glad tidings to those who persevere—who when calamity befalls them, say, "Truly unto God do we belong and truly unto Him we shall return. (2:155)

Hence everyone must experience pain, loss, hardship, and calamities on earth, regardless of their religiosity. I felt this was a frank admission, but the statement, "Give glad tidings to those who persevere," at first seemed to me too sanguine or insensitive in a passage that discusses human misery. Is the Qur'an oblivious to the terrible injury acute suffering does to our personalities? Instead it emphasizes just the opposite, that we can greatly benefit from how we respond to life's misfortunes, and that this response is inextricably linked to our state in the afterlife.

> Do you think that you could enter paradise without having the like of those who passed away before you? Suffering and adversity befell them, and so shaken were they that the apostle and the believers with him would exclaim, "When will God's help come?" Oh truly, God's help is always near. (2:214)

Footnote No. 59 (continued. from page 82)

Although God often allows people to depart from His laws and inflict suffering on others, even the results of such evil can be manipulated by Him into good for those who persevere. As far as the personal suffering I endured as a child, I can honestly say that I have benefited greatly from it. Overcoming the adversity of having an abusive father and living in a violent neighborhood has shaped me and given me a vision of life that is extremely beautiful. I truly thank God for my childhood because it allowed me to experience His love and mercy in ways I would not have otherwise known.

I stopped at this passage and read it several times. What does suffering have to do with Paradise? I thought. Why not just bypass this earthly stage and put us in Heaven?

"Do you think that you could enter Paradise without having the like of those who passed away before you?"

Why not? Why is suffering necessary? What is the connection between suffering and Heaven? Why can't it be made clear?

"Do you think that you could enter Paradise without having the like of those who passed away before you?"

What is it saying? What am I missing?

"Suffering and adversity befell them, and so shaken were they that the apostle and the believers with him would exclaim, "When will God's help come?" Oh truly, God's help is always near."

Note that this portrayal of human suffering involves truly devout believers—"the apostle and the believers with him"—and their agony was intense—"so shaken were they that they cried, 'When will God's help come?'"

Why would good people have to endure agony and fear? I wondered. Why must we live an existence so precarious and vulnerable?

You will certainly be tested in your possessions and yourselves. (3:186)

Why do we have to die, if we are only going to be brought back to life? I thought.

Every soul must taste of death. And We test you with calamity and prosperity, [both] as a means of trial. And to Us you are returned. (21:35)

Repeatedly, the Qur'an recalls, most notably after some verses that emphasize the essentiality of human earthly suffering, that to God we return. But does suffering bring us closer to God in some essential way?

> O man! Truly you've been toiling towards your Lord in painful toil—but you shall meet Him! (84:6)

How are we "Toiling towards [our] Lord in painful toil"? How does our affliction bring us nearer to God? I could only find the assertion, but not the answer. I could clearly see that the Scripture insists that suffering is a crucial element in human development, yet I could not see why this had to be.

> We certainly have created man to face distress. Does he think that no one has power over him? He will say: "I have wasted much wealth." Does he think that no one sees him? Have We not given him two eyes, and a tongue and two lips and pointed out to him the two conspicuous ways? But he attempts not the uphill climb; and what will make you comprehend the uphill climb? [It is] to free a slave, or to feed in a day of hunger an orphan nearly related, or the poor one lying in the dust. Then he is of those who believe and exhort one another to patience and exhort one another to mercy. (90:4-17)

This was for me another of those haunting, eye-opening passages, interspersed throughout the Qur'an, with their abrupt and dramatic shifts from one unexpected angle of vision to another, the type with which I wrestled hard. The assertion, "We have certainly created man to face distress," struck me with its grim candor, even though upon reflection I saw that it fit well with everything the Qur'an had presented so far. Whether by chance or grand design, I could not deny that mankind seemed eminently well suited for struggle. Our species seems to thrive on it as tragedy and strife has marked and guided our evolution throughout history. Even when hardship is not our lot, we seek it out in the form of self-made challenges and competitions. Yet while human beings may be made "to face distress," the Qur'an does not focus here on the part this has played in human worldly progress. It is more concerned with its moral and spiritual repercussions and begins by warning of its potential negative effects. Struggle, which ends in either success or failure, can lead to either hubris or despair, respectively, and in both cases to a loss of God-consciousness and/or confidence in God's omnipotence, and sometimes, to agnosticism or atheism. Therefore the Qur'an states:

> "Does he think that no one has power over him? He will say:
> "I have wasted much wealth!" Does he think that no one sees him?"

The remorseful exclamation "I have wasted much wealth!" epitomizes a life of struggle solely for temporal ends.

> "Have We not given him two eyes, and a tongue and two lips and pointed out to him the two conspicuous ways?"

Several such statements appear in the Qur'an, most often citing the faculties of hearing, sight, and the heart (the latter apparently representing human intellect in the most general sense)[60] as gifts that people often ill-use. Here, we are told that through observation and communication the way to genuine well-being should be evident, that by just studying the lives of those around us, it should be obvious what makes people truly content.

Upon reading this line, my thoughts turned to my mother. Despite all the hardships she encountered, she had always been at peace with herself. She used to teach us that the key to happiness was in giving to others. Reflecting on other contented persons I had known, I realized that they too lived by the same principle.

A strange sense of sadness overtook me as I reminisced about my mom, because I knew that I had not done her justice. Although I

---

60. *Surahs* 7:195; 16:78; 22:46; 32:9; 46:26; 67:23.

loved and admired her, I had always thought that she was living a delusion, that she was a kind of female Don Quixote. I used to wonder how she could be so blind to reality, how she could not see that life is not at all about giving, but about survival, competition, and protecting oneself from life's many accidents and dangers. But now, I could see from my own life and those of others I had known who lived this creed that this is not the way to inner peace. If I had only stopped to reflect on what I had seen all around me, I would have easily discerned that there are but "two conspicuous ways" in life and that I had been traveling the barren one. Like so many others I had ignored "the uphill climb."

> But he attempts not the uphill climb;[61] and what will make you comprehend the uphill climb? [It is] to free a slave, or to feed in a day of hunger an orphan nearly related, or the poor one lying in the dust. Then he is of those who believe and exhort one another to perseverance and exhort one another to mercy.

"Uphill climb" is an interesting choice of words. On the one hand it could mean an arduous task, demanding struggle and perseverance. This is consistent with everything else the Qur'an has to say about a successful life. On the other hand, "uphill climb" may also symbolize a path to spiritual ascent, a vertical climb toward nearness to God. Thanks partly to the Qur'an, the first concept had become easy for me to accept. I could see that a life dedicated to helping others could be difficult but rewarding, and although a self-seeking lifestyle may appear ostensibly easier, it is not the way to true contentment. However, I could not see the connection between our personal development and our relationship with God. Is there an organic link between them? Does our self-sacrifice bring us closer to God in some intrinsic way? If not, then it seems that this earthly stage of our existence could have been avoided, that we could be brought near to

---

61. *Al aqabah*, translated here as "uphill climb," also connotes a " steep road," "steep incline," or "mountain pass."

God without having to suffer earthly strife. Yet the Qur'an maintains that our lives on earth serve a fundamental purpose.

> Those [are believers] who remember God standing and sitting and lying down and reflect upon the creation of the heavens and the earth [and say]: Our Lord, you did not create all this without purpose (3:191).

> We have not created the heaven and the earth and whatever is between them in sport. If We wish to take a sport, We could have done it by Ourselves—if We were to do that at all. (21:16-17)

> Do you think that We created you in jest and that you will not be returned to Us? The true Sovereign is too exalted above that. (23:115)

> We did not create the heavens and the earth and all that is between them in play. (44:38)

I suppose the good news was that through reading the Qur'an I had come to see that many of my objections to the existence of God were not as ironclad as I had once thought. It had caused me to question the premises upon which I built my atheism. The bad news was that I had only some thirty pages to go in the Scripture and I still could not find what real purpose life served. My Muslim friends were of little help. They often did not really understand my questions, and the only answer they could offer is that we are here so we could be judged, seemingly arbitrarily, when we enter the next life. This knowledge was apparently enough for them and they never tried to penetrate the matter deeper, but this was hardly enough for me and I despaired of ever finding a rational explanation. And yet the Qur'an made it sound like it was all so simple, like when I explain to my students something obvious that they are missing when they overcomplicate a problem. I wondered if I too had overlooked something, if I was making it overly hard. I decided that the natural place to search is in the Qur'an's descriptions of the relationship between God and humankind. How does the Qur'an describe the relationship between God and the believers, how does it describe the true believers, how does it describe God, and what, if any, is the connection between them?

Before turning to these questions I should mention that the Qur'an's depictions of the illusory character of life took some of the bite out of my objections to human suffering on earth. Recall that when people enter the next life and are asked how long they spent on earth, they will have only faint and distant recollections, as if they are awakened from a dream.[62] This image of the dreamlike character of life is enhanced by many of the descriptions in the Qur'an of the Day of Judgment. A trumpet blast will awaken the dead (6:73). The unbelievers will rush from their graves, which the Qur'an refers to as their "sleeping places," in terror. People will be groggy and swoon (39:68). They will be disoriented. Their earthly lives will seem like an illusion (27:88). Peoples' sight will be confused like when one arises from sleep (75:7), then their vision will sharpen, and they will have a keen grasp of the present reality (50:20-22). In verse 39:42 the Qur'an compares awakening from sleep to resurrection of the dead. These descriptions suggest that regardless of the suffering we endure on earth, our recollection of it when we enter the next life will be much like that of a sleeper when he or she awakens from a nightmare. All the pain and agony which seemed so intense and real in our earthly existence will seem to us like nothing more than a distant illusion, almost like the creation of our imagination, when we enter the next stage of our being. The Qur'an is not saying that earthly existence is not real, but that the suffering we experience in it will seem to us unreal when we perceive the greater reality of the hereafter.

---

62. Cf. pp. 77-79.

What's Love Got to Do with It?

The Qur'an frequently speaks of the love of God. God loves the good-doers (2:195; 3:134; 3:148; 5:13; 5:193), the repentant (2:222), those that purify themselves (2:222; 9:108), the God-conscious (3:76, 9:4, 9:7), the persevering ones (3:146), those that put their trust in God (3:159), the upholders of justice (5:42; 49:9; 60:8), and those who struggle in the path of God (61:4). And the believers, in turn, love God.

> Yet there are men who take others besides God as equal (with God), loving them as they should love God. But those who believe love God more ardently. (2:165)

> Say: "If you love God, follow me, and God will love you, and forgive you your faults; for God is The Forgiving, The Merciful. (3:31)

> O you who believe! If any from among you should turn back from his faith, then God will assuredly bring a people He loves and who love Him. (5:54)

It should be noted that whereas the Qur'an describes a loving God, this occurs almost exclusively in the context of His relationship with sincere believers, those who commit themselves to loving God and to living that commitment. Conversely, those who have given themselves over to evil—such as the tyrants, the aggressors, the corrupt ones, the guilty, the rejecters of faith, the evil-doers, the arrogant ones, the transgressors, the prodigal, the treacherous, and the unjust—may deprive themselves of this relationship of love.[63] Although the things we normally associate with love—like mercy, compassion, beneficence, protection, nurturing, kindness, truthfulness, clemency, etc—God bestows abundantly on everyone,[64] His love is truly known

---

63. *Surahs* 2:190; 2:205; 2:276; 3:32; 3:57; 3:140; 4:36; 4:107; 5:64; 5:87; 6:141; 7:31; 7:55; 8:58; 16:23; 22:38; 28:76; 28:77; 30:45; 31:18; 42:40; 57:23.

64. *Surahs* 2:107; 4:110; 6:62; 7:156; 10:31; 13:6; 30:33; 30:36; 30:46; 39:53; 40:7; 42:28.

only to those who choose to partake in it and to love Him. In other words, when the Qur'an speaks of God's love, it is speaking about a mutual relationship, willingly entered into by God and believers, a relationship that many reject.[65]

As pointed out earlier, the Qur'an maintains that our actions and choices in no way threaten God, that it is the individual who benefits or loses by them. Nevertheless, it shows that God intends through this earthly experience to develop persons that share a bond of love with Him.[66] Any individual may or may not pursue this, but the Scripture assures that there will definitely be people who do, and their development is apparently the object of human life on earth.[67]

The question then became for me, how does righteous living enhance our relationship with God? I could understand how it contributes to our sense of well-being, how it gives us self-worth and inner peace, but how does it make us more able to relate to Him? Also, could not we have obtained such a bond without having struggled and suffered on earth? Could not we have been simply programmed to love God? I kept coming back to the same issues.

What Do You Want from Me?

It is not hard to find in the Qur'an what God expects from true believers. Repeatedly, it describes them as "those who believe and do good works."[68] Since, as we have just seen, the primary purpose of our existence is to love and be loved by God, belief is obviously essential,

---

65. *Surahs* 17:89; 25:50, 27:73.

66. Cf. Question 9, this chapter.

67. *Surahs* 5:54; 15:39-43; 17:65.

68. *Surahs* 2:25; 2:82; 2:277; 4:57; 4:122; 5:9; 7:42; 10:9; 11:23; 13:29; 14:23; 18:2; 18:88; 18:107; 19:60; 19:96; 20:75; 20:82; 20:112; 21:94; 22:14; 22:23; 22:50; 22:56; 24:55; 25:70-71; 26:67; 28:80; 29:7; 29:9; 29:58; 30:15; 30:45; 31:8; 32:19; 34:4; 34:37; 35:7; 38:24; 41:8; 42:22; 42:23; 42:26; 45:21; 45:30; 47:2; 47:12; 48:29; 64:9; 65:11; 84:25; 85:11; 95:6; 98:7; 103:3.

for we cannot become intimate with one whom we deny. However, it is not clear how living righteously should enhance our relationship with God. The common answer is that God is good and that our good works please Him and our evil deeds displease Him, but then He could have made us sinless, bypassed this earthly stage, placed us immediately in Heaven, and been well pleased with us from the start. If belief in God and living rightly on earth brings us nearer to Him, then it should do so in some essential way, since nothing God does is superfluous.[69]

The types of good works described in the Qur'an fall within the so-called Golden Rule: "Do unto others as you would have them do unto you." Though the Scripture contains many examples of good works, it contains few surprises, and hence nothing that would shed immediate light on the connection between doing good and divine intimacy. I was somewhat surprised by its strong insistence on social activism, on "struggling in the path of God" and "enjoining right and opposing wrong." Although, I had no moral objection to campaigning for justice, I did not expect so much stress on social and political involvement, as I was accustomed to thinking of religion as a private and personal affair. The concept that faith must include vigorous action for social reform had me question all the more the connection between altruism and growing closer to God.

Hoping to uncover some clue, I made a short list of the kinds of good works the Scripture encourages. Unsurprisingly, it consisted of deeds universally recognized as virtuous. We should, for example, show compassion (2:83; 2:215; 69:34), be merciful (90:17), forgive others (42:37; 45:14; 64:14), be just (4:58; 6:152; 16:90), protect the weak (4:127; 6:152), defend the oppressed (4:75), seek knowledge and wisdom (20:114; 22:54), be generous (2:177; 23:60; 30:39), be truthful (3:17; 33:24; 33:35; 49:15), be kind (4:36), be peaceful (8:61; 25:63; 47:35), and love others (19:86).

---

69. *Surahs* 3:191; 21:16-17; 23:115; 44:38.

Truly to those who believe and do good will the Most Merciful endow with love and to this end have We made this easy to understand in your own tongue, so that you might convey a glad tiding to the God-conscious and warn those given to contention. (19:96)

We should teach and encourage others to practice these virtues (90:17; 103:3) and, by implication, learn and grow in them as well. The stories of the prophets have God's messengers bidding their communities and families to adopt such ethics, but many of them remain contemptuous.

There was nothing in my list that especially stood out, nothing that would indicate why human suffering could not have been avoided, no key to understanding why we could not have been programmed to love God. It simply read:

We should become just, truthful, compassionate, merciful, kind, generous, protective [of others], forgiving, peaceful, wise, knowledgeable, loving, etcetera.

My thoughts were still going around in circles. I could understand how developing these traits could bring serenity, but how would it facilitate relating to God?

If God Were One of Us

If God were one of us, it would make things much easier, because then I would be able to understand Him, enough at least to see the connection between good works and divine intimacy. I can understand other persons because I share similar experiences, similar fears, hopes, dreams, wants, hardships, and joys. I can relate to them because we are the same basic being, only differing by slight variations. But God is not one of us. The Qur'an goes so far as to say that we cannot comprehend God, that God is "high exalted above anything that people may devise by way of definition" (6:100), that "there is nothing like unto Him" (42:11) and "nothing can be compared to Him" (112:4). It could not be otherwise, for how could human beings who are mortal, finite, corporeal, dependent, vulnerable, weak, limited, created, bound by space and time, understand one who is everlasting, infinite, non-corporeal, utterly independent, invulnerable, all-powerful, all knowing, all wise, Creator of all, transcendent.

If only the Qur'an had elaborated on God somewhere, gave us enough of a description so that we could fill in the lines. I did not come all this way only to find out that God is incomprehensible—an inscrutable mystery—and that for me there is no hope.

No wonder we humans tend to deify our own or to humanize God. Although this creates for me more rational dilemmas then it solves; it does lend God some tangibility. I guess I wanted to have my cake and eat it too. I wanted God to be utterly exalted above creation, utterly unlike the humanity I was part of, and at the same time reachable.

What a fool I had been, deluding myself into thinking that the Qur'an could somehow bridge the infinite gulf between God and humanity, that it could logically relate human suffering to divine intimacy. We hardly understand the human personality; how could it make sense of the relationship between God and man? It took reading the entire text to prove to myself that I had been right all along, that there is no possible theological rationalization for human existence.

I was finally beginning to see clearly again. I was wrong when I just said that we understand our fellow man. We do not understand our humanity; we only know it through experience. I do not fully comprehend who I am, my motivations, my anxieties, my dreams, my emotions, my conscience and psychology. I do not grasp my humanity intellectually; I know it through my being human. Virtually all of my knowledge of humanness is subjective. This leads, however, to a seemingly inescapable conclusion. For if we cannot come at all close to experiencing divinity, which appears to be the Qur'an's position, then we cannot possibly come to know God in any real, meaningful way. By insisting that God is radically unlike creation—that nothing we know even compares to Him—the Qur'an has made attaining a relationship with God practically impossible. Although the author had campaigned brilliantly, had presented a literary and rational masterpiece, he was unable to present a complete and coherent explanation for why we are here. Yet he had nothing to be ashamed of, for he fell short where he and all others must inevitably fall short, trapped in the limitless void between God and man.

This was for me a hollow realization, and I felt no sense of victory whatsoever. For there were times in my reading of the Qur'an when I was so close to surrender, when the author's words—his voice—nearly overpowered me, causing me to feel that only God could be speaking to me through this Scripture. I'm not embarrassed to admit that I was moved to tears on several occasions, that at times I truly felt I was in the presence of a tremendous power and mercy. These spiritual moments always took me by surprise. I would even try to resist them, to shake them off, but they were often too strong and intoxicating to resist, and my resistance continually weakened as I progressed through the text. There were moments when I was almost sure there is a God, when I felt the presence of one I always knew but had fought to forget. I didn't know if I was any better or worse for having read the Qur'an, but I knew that I had changed, that I would never be so confident in my atheism again.

Even so, it was time to get on with my life, time to stop agonizing over the existence of God, letting it impede with my happiness. One of the main things that first attracted me to San Francisco is that it is a place where people live life to the fullest. After twenty-one years of schooling, I was ready to reap the benefits of all my work. It was time for me to start enjoying myself. I had the motivation, the opportunity and the means. I was young, single, considered good-looking, and had a good career. It was time to start having fun.

Say My Name

And then, not too long after finishing the Qur'an, perhaps a couple of weeks later, I thought of it. It came to me softly, unexpectedly—I think while I was watching a football game on television—as an afterthought, slipping into my consciousness.

It is not true that the Qur'an tells us very little about God; it tells us a great deal, but for some reason I had paid almost no attention to it. If I had just glanced at the beginning of a *surah*, or turned to almost any page, I would have found what I was looking for, if only I had read carefully, for there are thousands of descriptions of God in the Qur'an that link good works to growing closer to Him. Although I had read the Qur'an from cover to cover, deliberating on and analyzing almost every verse along the way, I mentally disregarded the Scripture's abundant references to God's attributes. Often used to punctuate passages, they occur typically in simple dual attributive statements, such as, "God is the Forgiving, the Compassionate" (4:129), "He is the All-Mighty, the Compassionate"(26:68), "God is the Hearing, the Seeing" (17:1). Collectively, the Qur'an refers to these titles as *al-asmaa al-husnaa*, God's "most beautiful names" (7:180; 17:110; 20:8; 59:24).

> Say: Call upon God, or call upon the Merciful, by whichever you call, His are the most beautiful names. (17:110)
>
> God! There is no God but He. To Him belong the most beautiful names. (20:8)
>
> He is God, other than whom there is no other god. He knows the unseen and the seen. He is the Merciful, The Compassionate. He is God, other than whom there is no other God; The Sovereign, The Holy One, The Source of Peace, the Keeper of Faith, The Guardian, The Exalted in Might, the Irresistible, the Supreme. Glory to God, above what they ascribe to Him! He is God, the Creator, the Evolver, the Fashioner. To Him belong the most beautiful names.

Whatever is in the heavens and on earth glorifies Him and He is Exalted in Might, The Wise. (59:23-24)

I had thought that the Qur'an used the divine names mainly as a literary device to crown passages and separate topics. That is probably why I for the most part skipped over them without giving them any serious thought. I now felt that I might have underestimated their significance and I began to jot down the divine attributes I could remember.

God is the Merciful, the Compassionate, the Forgiving, the Clement, the Peaceful, the Loving, the Just, the Benevolent, the Creator, the Powerful, The Protector, The Truthful, The Knowing, The Wise, The Living, etcetera.

There, right before me, was the connection I sought, for this list largely intersected with and was the perfection of the one I had compiled earlier of the virtues that men and women need to develop.[70] The implication was clear: Since God is the perfection of the virtues we should acquire, the more we grow in them, the greater our ability becomes to experience His being. The more we grow in mercy, the greater our ability becomes to experience God's infinite mercy. The more we develop compassion, the greater our ability becomes to know God's infinite compassion. The more we learn to forgive, the greater our ability becomes to experience God's infinite forgiveness. The same could be said of love, truth, justice, kindness, and so on. The more we grow in these, the greater our ability becomes to receive and experience God's attributes of perfection.

An analogy would be helpful. I once had a goldfish and a magnificent German shepherd, and I now have three beautiful daughters. My gold fish, being very limited in intellect and growth, could only know and experience my love and compassion at a relatively low level, no matter how much kindness I directed towards it. On the other

---

70. Cf. page 93.

hand, my dog, who was a more complex and intelligent animal than my fish, could feel warmth and affection for another on a much higher level, and could therefore experience the love and compassion I showered on him to a much greater degree. Yet my daughters—and even more so as they mature—have the ability to feel the intensity of my love and caring for them on a plane my dog could never conceive of. This is because they have the capacity to know first hand through their own emotions and relationships deeper and richer feelings than my dog. Analogously, the greater our level of goodness, the greater our ability becomes to experience and relate to the infinite goodness that is God.

In order to grow closer to others, we approach them by means of what we share with them. When we wish to approach others physically, we position our bodies closer to theirs. In order to reach others intellectually, we approach them through reason as we try to connect with them rationally to achieve mutual understanding. To get closer to others emotionally, we approach them through feelings in an effort to obtain a convergence of sentiments. Since God is the transcendent fount of all goodness, we approach Him through the goodness He instills in us. The Qur'an informs us that God breathes something of His spirit into every human soul (32:9), which indicates that each of us comes into this world with a seed of the divine attributes within us. However it is up to us, it is our choice, to open ourselves up to the nurturing of this seed through both receiving and experiencing God's infinite radiance.

All the pieces began to come together. While it is true that we can not come close to comprehending God, we can experience His divine names—His being—abundantly, as recipients of others' goodness and even more directly and intimately as doers of good. Each time we show genuine kindness to others, we experience something of the infinite kindness that originates in the Benevolent. Each time we pardon another's offense, we experience something of the infinite forgiveness that comes from the Forgiving. Each time we stand up for the rights of the oppressed, we experience something of the infinite guardianship that the Protector provides. Every time we are honest, we experience something of the Truth that has the Truthful as its source. In these ways we become the instruments by which others experience God's being. His mercy, compassion, kindness, peace, and so on, flow through us to those around us and we become participants in this divine dispensation. Thus we have the potential to know God on a level more profound than we can know any man or woman, because His being reaches others through our being, and we experience something of His infinite goodness as our own. This makes us capable of attaining a level of intimacy with God that no human relationship can approximate.

Even if we are unaware of our experiences of the divine—even if we deny the existence of God—we experience His names nonetheless, but we remain deaf, dumb, and blind to their source. This is the greatest tragedy—the ultimate loss—according to the Qur'an, for we deprive ourselves of the means to grow closer to God. We come to know something of goodness, while closing ourselves off to the boundless mercy that originates it, which brings us back to the importance of faith in addition to good works.

Faith is to be continually nurtured, not just by performing good deeds toward others, but also through spiritual training, which includes affirmation, prayer, fasting, almsgiving, pilgrimage, meditation, and study. We should develop our spirituality so that we become ever more cognizant of God's pervasive presence in our lives. We should work to become increasingly sensitive to the innumerable signs of God about us, in nature, and, more importantly, in ourselves and others, as every act of kindness, every noble deed, every sincere display of virtue reveals God. We may not see Him with our eyes, but we may perceive him with our hearts, the seat of virtue and spirituality within us.

Religious rites are therefore an important element in the Qur'an's program for human development. I use the word "rites" here rather than "worship" because the latter in the Qur'an is a comprehensive concept that extends beyond religious rituals. The Arabic word *'abadah*, which is commonly translated as "to worship," literally means "to serve" or "devote oneself to" and includes any good deed that is performed out of belief in God. While religious rites comprise a relatively small part of worship, they address some critical human needs. As well as helping us refine our spirituality as indicated above, they also provide us with a direct means to communicate our love to God. The Qur'an states that God's gifts to humanity are far more than we could ever count, and thus we are by far on the receiving end in our relationship with Him.[71] Yet in a healthy relationship both parties must have something to share. When we help our fellow man, we display our love for God, but it lacks the immediacy and intimacy of direct communication. Religious ritual presents us with a direct means to give back to God. Out of love He provides us with a way to give to Him what in reality is already His.[72] This is similar to when my children ask me for money to buy me a present. I do not need the gift, and they are only giving me what is already mine, but I love the thought behind it and know that it will bring us closer together. The Qur'an makes it clear that God needs nothing from creation, but He loves the intention behind our performance of ritual[73] and knows that it brings us closer to Him.

It should be stressed that rituals do not present a one-way avenue of communication, for they can be among the most powerful mediums for directly experiencing God's attributes. Believers report that they sometimes experience divine intimacy with special intensity while engaged in them. This may result from the fact that in ritual

---

71. *Surahs* 14:34, 16:18.

72. *Surah* 4:78-79.

73. For example, concerning the animal sacrifices made during the annual pilgrimage, the Qur'an states, "It is not their meat or blood that reaches God, but it is your piety that reaches Him" (22:37).

they are especially focused on their relationship with God. Yet some believers, usually those who seem to have reached high levels of righteousness, humility, and inner peace, seem to experience this intimacy more frequently and with greater power than others. Again it appears that growth in goodness increases the believers' receptivity to the divine attributes, both in their capacity to absorb them into their personality and in their ability to experience them in religious rites. But the experience of divine intimacy in this life only barely hints at its experience in the next, when temporal masks and distractions are removed.

In many religious traditions the question of the primacy of faith or works has been much debated. From the standpoint of the Qur'an this is obviously the wrong question, because it insists on a choice where none should be made, for both are essential and augment each other. Faith should motivate good deeds, which increases one's capacity to receive and experience God's most beautiful names, which in turn should increase one's faith, which should then increase one's desire to do good, and so on, each a function of the other, climbing upward in a continuous spiral toward the source of all goodness. When we grow in the virtues that have God as their infinite source, we grow in our ability to know Him and to relate to Him through love.

In the Qur'an, the story of Adam begins with the announcement that God is about to place a vicegerent (*khaleefah*) on earth, one who will represent Him and act on His behalf (2:30). It is presented as a momentous delegation, as a commission announced to the angels. It is an honorable election for which each of us is created. When I first read this passage I was as dumbfounded as the angels were, for how could man, this most rebellious and destructive creature, represent God on earth? I, like the angels, saw only one side of humanity, the inclination to do evil, to "spread corruption and shed much blood." Of course many men and women do not represent God very well. But our ability to do and grow in evil comes with the reciprocal ability to do and grow in goodness, and on the whole it seems that there must be more good than evil in the world, otherwise our race would have destroyed itself long ago. There have also always been persons who are great exemplars of goodness, who humbly dedicate themselves to helping others for love of God. This is the vicegerency to which the Qur'an calls us. More than just communicating a message or implementing a command, it means becoming an agent of God on earth through which others experience His attributes. Such individuals become filters, as it were, of the divine light, as God's goodness reaches others through them. The more they grow in goodness, through their dedication, self-sacrifice, and learning, the greater becomes their ability to receive, experience, and represent God's most beautiful names, and their experience of God's presence in this life is only a small foreshadowing of what awaits them in the next.

Retreat

Mahmood Qandeel fascinated me. He could be exceedingly entertaining. He was handsome, witty, charming, elegant, and fun loving. Even though he was young and not very wealthy—although he appeared to be—he somehow managed to become part of the in-crowd in San Francisco. When he and I would go around town, it was like being with a celebrity—sort of a young, Middle-Eastern Donald Trump. Everywhere we went people flocked to him, and while Mahmoud loved the attention and enjoyed luxury, he was not overawed by either. He was not some wide-eyed foreigner dazzled by the lifestyles of the rich and famous; he seemed quite unimpressed by it all and well accustomed to it. When he was in the company of high society, he was perfectly at ease.

Mahmoud could also take on a very religious side. At times he would talk about and defend Islam with passion. Every now and then he would isolate himself from his circle and devote himself to prayer and fasting. Sometimes he would hint at the guilt he felt for the fast lifestyle he was living. He was extremely charitable and very sensitive to the suffering of the poor. He would empty his wallet to a panhandler and seem almost penitent for not having given enough. I found it very easy to discuss religion with Mahmoud, for he was a good friend and showed no interest in converting others, I just needed to catch him when he was alone, away from the crowd.

Mahmoud invited me to his apartment one night to have dinner with his family. When I got there, his sister, Ragia, let me in as Mahmoud was changing in the bedroom.

I sat in the living room waiting for him. Mahmoud loved music, all kinds—rock-in-roll, rhythm and blues, classical—but tonight there was a strange sound coming from his stereo. It was a slow, rhythmic, meticulous, chanting, apparently in Arabic, without musical accompaniment, just a single, low toned voice, laboring at every consonant and syllable. The chant had a pounding, haunting rhyme and a powerful, complex, strained, and disciplined cadence that seemed to suppress overwhelming fervor. I had never heard anything quite like it.

When Mahmoud entered the room, he made for the stereo and turned it off. When I asked him about the music I had just been listening to, he told me that it was not music but a tape of someone reciting the Qur'an. "Does all of the Qur'an have such a strong built in rhythm and rhyme?" I asked him. "It sounds almost like singing—is it poetry?"

He answered "yes" to the first question and "no" to the second. He told me that Arabic poetry has a very distinctive style and that the style of the Qur'an is completely different from it.

I did not question Mahmoud any further about the Qur'an that night. I was already impressed with its brilliance and power in translation; it was unimaginable to me that it could also have such inherent lyrical beauty.

When I had reached the age of twenty-eight, I thought I had constructed an impregnable fortress of arguments against the existence of God, but as I made my way through the Qur'an, I saw them fall one by one, brick by brick. By the time I had finished the

Scripture, I was left with one main objection, and this was that I could not perceive a nexus between doing good and growing closer to God. When I finally discovered this essential link through contemplation of the divine names, its simplicity was such that I was amazed that I could not have formulated it on my own. Yet, reading the Qur'an helped me to illuminate, organize, prioritize, and analyze my thoughts. The Qur'an had done what it promised it would do; it guided me through my questions—provided I was willing to face the answers—but I was no longer certain what the experience meant, for the Scripture and I had very different outlooks on what we sought to achieve. I was trying to win an argument, but it was trying to win a soul as it continually warned of the terrible consequences of rejecting God's signs.

I had felt throughout most of my encounter with the Qur'an that I had been the aggressor, boldly making my case against the Scripture. I always felt that I had at least one ace in the hole. Now I felt like I was on the defensive. Perhaps I had been all along, and, like George Custer, I had been lured into facing overwhelming odds. The reality of my predicament came to me in that single moment of epiphany when I recalled the divine names. It was then that I sensed that the tide was against me. Yet even though I was now in retreat, I was not about to surrender. I needed to gather my thoughts, review my position, and reconsider some questions.

The Qur'an seemed to me to have a comprehensive vision of life. One of the most striking points it makes is that life on earth is not a punishment for anyone's sin or sinfulness, but a developmental stage in our creation. Human beings did not fall from grace; they may have at one time in the past been more primitive and had not yet attained the intellectual maturity to differentiate and choose between right and wrong, but the Qur'an does not present this as a preferred state. What distinguishes human beings from other creatures is their intellect, making them preeminent learners, and it is this characteristic that makes them potentially superior to other created beings. The

Qur'an informs us from the outset in the story of Adam that humans will be capable of representing God on earth. First they needed to develop the ability to discern good and evil—they needed to become moral agents—and it was not until men and women acquired the ability to choose between the two, that they were ready to take on the responsibility of vicegerency.

To serve as God's representative on earth is a demanding task. It requires humility, self-sacrifice, and perseverance. It means striving to become an instrument of God through which He communicates His goodness to others. It requires growing in the virtues that have their origin and perfection in Him, and sharing of all the good that we possess with all those we can. The Qur'an assures that this will not be easy—it describes it as an uphill climb—but it promises that the rewards will be great. Not only will the righteous attain inner peace and well-being, they will also grow in their capacity to experience God's infinite love. For the more we come to experience and hence to know of the beauty of God, the greater becomes our ability to relate to Him, both in this life and the next.

This conception of the purpose of life has definite rational appeal, but does it explain our earthly existence? Could not we have been created good, programmed to be merciful, compassionate, kind, just, and truthful without having to live through the pains and hardships of worldly struggle?

Time is not the issue here. I am not questioning the duration of this stage of our creation, because, as the Qur'an informs us, time is illusory and God transcends the space –time environment we live in. For God, all time is one—a single eternal instant outside of time— so whether our creation occurs over several centuries or in a split second is irrelevant, since for God it is but a single command: "Be! And then it is."[74] Although I had no argument against time, I questioned the necessity of certain other aspects of creation, especially human suffering.

---

74. Cf. pp. 77-79.

One of the most interesting ideas the Qur'an presents is that God creates continuously and in stages. Objects do not just appear in final form out of nothing; they go through a continuous course of development.

It is He who begins the process of creation, and repeats it. (10:4; 27:64)

Then certainly We created man of an extract of clay, then We placed him as a small quantity in a safe place firmly established, then We made the small quantity into a tiny thing that clings, then We made the tiny thing that clings into a chewed lump of flesh, then We fashioned the chewed flesh into bones and clothed the bones with intact flesh, then We caused it to grow into another creation. So blessed be God, the best of creators! Then after that you certainly die. Then on the Day of Resurrection you will surely be raised up. (23:12-16)

Do they not see how God originates creation then repeats it; truly that is easy for God. Say: "Travel through the earth and see how God did originate creation; so will God produce another creation, for God has power over all things." (29:19-20)

He created you from one soul and then made from it its mate, and He provides for you of cattle eight kinds. He created you in the wombs of your mothers, creation after creation, in threefold darkness. Such is God, your Lord. His is the sovereignty. There is no God but He. How then are you turned away? (39:6)

Does man think that he will be left aimless? Was he not a small quantity (of sperm) emitted? Then he was a tiny thing that clings (in the womb), and then He created (him), and then made him perfect. (75:36-38)

He is God, the Creator, the Evolver, the Fashioner. To Him belong the most beautiful names. Whatever is in the heavens and on earth glorifies Him and He is exalted in Might, The Wise. (59:23-24)

Surely he thought that he would never return. But surely his Lord is ever Seer of him. But no, I call to witness the sunset redness, and the night and that which it drives on, and the moon when it grows full, you will certainly travel stage after stage. But what is the matter with them that they believe not? (84:14-20)

Over and above bringing entities into existence, God's creating includes His guiding and nurturing their evolution. Thus a creature becomes continuously; it is an ever-changing entity. The entire phenomenal world is subject to flux and change. Only God is absolute.

In its many references to the workings of nature, the Qur'an demonstrates how God provides every living thing with an environment and constitution well suited to its existence and growth. A tree is provided with the soil, the sun, the rain, the air, the genetic code, and all else that it needs to live and grow. The same can be said of every other creature, including man. However, the Qur'an reminds us that our primary growth in this life is not physical but spiritual; we are here to grow in the virtues that reflect God's attributes of perfection. The question must then become: Are we provided with an environment and constitution well suited to our spiritual growth, and if so, would it be as well suited if suffering were removed from it?

The key to getting at a truth is to find the right questions, ones that isolate key issues. When we start our investigations our questions are usually general and contain many sub-questions within them, but if successful, we are then able to dissect our search into a number of more or less irreducible questions and then answer them one by one. This is what the Qur'an helped me to do. It did not always provide me with explicit answers, but it guided me through the questioning process.

When I reached the above question, I had no need to search hard for an answer. It is quite obvious that we are provided with an environment and constitution well suited to our growth in virtue. There are a multitude of examples about us and throughout history of people who attained to high levels of goodness. There are even many dramatic cases of criminals who eventually turned their lives around and became exemplars of virtue. In my own life I had countless opportunities to choose between right and wrong from which I learned of the ruinous effects of evil as well as the positive benefits of good. I had come to know through observation and experience that both wrong and right behavior can become habitual and pervade one's personality.

It was also now clear to me that suffering is essential to our development of virtue. The same could be said of human intellect and volition. Suffering, intelligence, and choice, each of which the Qur'an repeatedly emphasizes, all have fundamental roles in our spiritual evolution. To learn and grow in compassion, for example, is inconceivable without the presence of suffering. It also requires choice—the ability to reach out to someone in need or to ignore him. Intellect is necessary so that one can estimate how much of oneself will be invested in showing compassion to the sufferer. Similarly, to be truthful involves the choice not to lie and is heightened when honesty may lead to personal loss and suffering, which can be predicted through the use of one's reason. The famous wedding vow that asks a couple to remain committed to each other in sickness and in health, for richer and for poorer, until death when they part, acknowledges the roles of choice, suffering, and reason in love. For the vow requires the couple to choose to stay by each other, regardless of the suffering they may face, knowing full well what that may entail. To forgive is a choice to excuse another's wrong doing even though we understand the evil of what they have done. The same could be said of all the virtues; intelligence, volition, and suffering are vital to our experience of them.

Although virtues are abstractions and difficult to analyze, it is nearly impossible to imagine them programmed, that they could exist in a creature at very high levels without its possessing choice, intelligence, and some knowledge of suffering. An act of virtue is more than an action; it has intent, understanding, and a benefactor conjoined to it. A computer could be programmed to be always correct, but we would not describe it as either truthful or wise. A stethoscope aids the sick, but we do not consider it merciful. The Qur'an depicts angels as not possessing free will, but men and women are capable of rising above them.

What makes an act virtuous is the will to do it and an appreciation of the need it addresses. If I toss a banana peel in the road, and several hours later a thief on his way to rob an elderly person trips on it and is prevented from committing a crime, my throwing the peel in the street is not an act of justice or compassion on my part. My prevention of the crime is totally inadvertent; it lacks both will and apprehension. If I mail five dollars anonymously to a known billionaire, it is hardly an act of charity, for it is directed toward one who is not in financial need. This is not to say that will, intellect, and perceived vulnerability are the only components of a virtuous deed—it is more complex and profound than this—but these three elements must be present to some degree before virtue can be realized.

My high school football coach hung a placard in the locker room that read, "No pain, no gain," meaning that to improve athletically, we had to be willing to suffer. My teachers used to say that learning demands hard work and perseverance. A mathematics professor once told me that the difficult problems were the ones from which we learn the most. I never doubted any of these truisms, as they seemed both evident and natural. The Qur'an indicates that the same natural law applies to our spiritual development. Human beings are creatures of superior intellect that grow through learning, but learning also necessitates being tested, a point the Qur'an makes repeatedly. Moral and spiritual growth involves the discipline of one's will, the use and development of one's mind and the experience of adversity.

The exercise of moral choice also necessitates a cognizance of the rightness and wrongfulness of our options, which explains our exposure to angelic and satanic inspiration. These act on us simultaneously to pinpoint and heighten the morality of many of our decisions, and together provide a stimulus and catalysts for spiritual development. Revelation has a complementary role as it describes righteous and evil behavior and lights the way to spiritual growth.

I was starting to see how all of the elements introduced by the Qur'an in the story of Adam (2:30-39) were in accord with what it has to say about the purpose of life. I was also quickly running out of arguments against the existence of God. That in itself does not prove anything, but I used to think I had good reason not to believe.

Practice, Practice, Practice

I grew up in a somewhat criminal environment. Almost every kid I knew was into some illegality. I never got into drugs or, for that matter, drinking because I saw addiction destroy my father, four brothers, my two uncles, and many of my friends. I was never involved in sexual assault, not even statutory rape, although the opportunities were there. I avoided as best I could the gang fights and other neighborhood violence, since I was not planning on spending the rest of my life in Bridgeport, Connecticut, or the state penitentiary. All in all I led a pretty upright life, but I was not immune to vice.

I committed my first theft when I was eleven. I took two eight-ounce boxes of bubble gum, which cost fifty cents each, from a supermarket on my way home from St. Andrew's school. I was so nervous it took me over fifteen minutes to pull off the heist. I would carry the boxes toward the exit, then think someone might be watching me, and then carry them back to the candy section. After doing that a couple of times, I decided to hide them near the automatic entrance door on the floor just inside the store. My plan was to leave the supermarket empty-handed, then return to the store, step on the rubber entrance mat to open the automatic door, grab the two hidden boxes, and then slip back out the entrance door before it had time to close behind me. I felt that this would be safer than trying to walk out the exit with the boxes hidden under my shirt; I figured that the store detectives probably watched the exit doors but not the entrance ones. Plus, if, when I returned, the boxes were not where I had left them, then I would know that I had been watched.

My plan—which as I look back now seems ridiculous—went off without a hitch, and I met up with my friends in the parking lot outside. My heart was pounding a mile a minute as I described to them my caper. I was so relieved not to have gotten caught, and my friends were almost as thrilled as I was with my success. They treated me like a hero, like I had just scored the winning touchdown in a football game. But my ebullience dissipated the moment I entered my house. Just the sight of my mother brought on feelings of guilt. She was such a model of honesty, and she had so much confidence in me. I knew how badly it would hurt her if she found out what I had done.

I had difficulty sleeping that night. I felt an oppressive uneasiness. I could not stop thinking about my crime. I also could not stop thinking about God. It felt like He was all around me, encompassing me, looking at me, not angrily, just watching, almost indifferently, and I felt such horrible shame. I wished I could rid myself of that day, to delete it from my life or wash it all away. I wished I could return the chewing gum, but I gave almost all of it away. I thought of buying two more boxes from the supermarket and then putting them back on the shelf, but I never got around to it.

I went on pilfering for the next ten or so years. I think I never stole anything worth more than ten dollars, and did so no more than a half dozen times a year. In time I became rather skilled at it and I never got caught.

When I was twenty-one, I invited a girlfriend out for pizza at an Italian restaurant close to campus. When we finished eating, I slipped the check in my pants pocket and walked up to the cash register. I asked the cashier for a pack of gum and paid for it with a dollar bill. The cashier gave me several coins in change and then the young lady and I walked out of the restaurant without paying for our dinner.

My date marveled at how calmly I ripped off the pizza joint. She was especially impressed with the temerity I showed in going to the cashier for a pack of chewing gum, rather than leaving the restaurant as quickly as possible. I explained to her that in college towns waiters and waitresses keep an eye out for deadbeat students, but when they see you exchange money at the cash register they assume you're paying the check. She asked me if I was ever troubled by guilt. I told her that I may have been in the past but not anymore, that with practice it got easier.

That was close to the last time I stole anything, although looking back I don't know what made me stop. Maybe it was because my financial situation had improved a little. Maybe it had something to do with being away from Bridgeport for almost four years. Maybe I had come to feel that it was no longer worth the risk of getting caught. All I know is it began to bother me again.

If the purpose of our lives is to grow in the virtues that have their source and perfection in God, so that we may experience His attributes and divine intimacy to ever-greater degrees, and if righteous deeds promote this growth, and evil doing thwarts it, then the one who benefits or loses the most from a good or evil act is the doer. Hence the Qur'an states:

> Enlightenment has come from your Lord; he who sees does so to his own benefit, he who is blind is so to his own [hurt]. (6:104)

> And whosoever goes right, goes right only for himself, and whosoever goes astray, say: "I am only a warner." (27:92)

> And if any strive, they do so for their own selves: For God is free of all need from creation. (29:6)

> We have revealed to you the book with the truth for mankind.

Whosoever goes right it is only for himself, and whoever strays, strays only to his own hurt.[75] (39:41)

The harm that evildoers experience as a result of persistent wrongdoing is intrinsic. Evil deeds hamper growth in virtue and erode spirituality, so that those who stubbornly reject righteousness do violence to their being and experience spiritual decay. Instead of acquiring what is needed to know serenity in the next life, they acquire the exact opposite; they develop attributes that are antithetical to experiencing the beauty that would otherwise await them in the hereafter. The evil to which they become habituated pervades their being—it becomes them—which is the ultimate loss, since only the self goes on to the next existence. The Qur'an portrays this bond between one's deeds and state-of-being in the hereafter with compelling symbolism. A person's evil deeds will be attached to his or her neck (17:13; 34:33; 36:8). Our tongues, hands, feet, and skins will bear witness to the lives we led (24:24, 36:65). We will eat the fruits of our deeds (37:39-68). The spiritually blind in this life will be raised without vision in the next (17:72). Those who lived in God's light in this life will have their lights shine before them on the Day of Resurrection (57:12; 66:8). Every moral act, however large or small, will show its effect (99:7-8). These descriptions suggest that, when we enter the hereafter, our persons will embody the spiritual state we reached at earthly life's end. Just as the physical condition of a newborn when it comes into this world manifests its physical development in the womb, a person's being when he or she enters the hereafter will manifest the goodness or evil he or she acquired in this life. To enter the next life as one who is essentially evil is like being born into this world deformed and bereft of what is needed for physical comfort. It is then not surprising that sin equates with self-destruction.

To Us they did no harm, but they only did harm to themselves. (2:57; 7:160)

---

75. Cf. 10:108 and 17:15.

If any transgress the limits ordained by God, then these, they wrong themselves. (2:229; 65:1)

And God did not wrong them, but they wronged themselves. (3:117)

And so it was not God who wronged them, it was they who wronged themselves. (9:70; 16:33; 29:40; 30:9)

It was not We that wronged them; they wronged their own selves. (11:101)

Oh My servants who have wronged yourselves, never despair of God's mercy. Surely God forgives all sins. (39:54)

The Qur'an does not insist on perfection before felicity can be obtained in the hereafter. It presents this life as a phase in our development in which we are certain to make mistakes, and where we hopefully will learn from them. A key eschatological symbol that relates moral and spiritual growth to our state in the next life is the Balance that weighs a person's goodness on the Day of Judgment. For those whose balance is heavy—persons who are essentially good—theirs will be joy and serenity, and for those whose balance is light—persons who are basically evil—they will suffer horribly from their self-ruin.[76]

Trial and error plays an essential role in our development as we learn and grow from our choices, both intellectually and spiritually. When a mistake we make has moral implications, it becomes a sin, the gravity and harm of which increases with our awareness of its wrongfulness (4:17:18). Yet if we realize our errors, repent and do right thereafter, the lessons we learn could be particularly beneficial; in this way the wrong we once committed can be turned to our advantage and contribute to our growth in virtue.

---

76. *Surahs* 7:8-9; 42:17; 101:6-10.

He who repents and believes and does good; for such God changes their evil deeds to good ones. And God is ever forgiving and merciful. (25:70)

It is one thing not to commit a wrong because we are warned not to; it is quite another because we have personally experienced its harm. In the latter case the wisdom behind the admonition becomes impressed upon the heart and mind, and the evil is avoided not so much because it is prohibited, but because the self instinctively recoils at the prospect of returning to the inner turmoil it once knew.

Just as trial and error is vital to our intellectual evolution, so too is it to our spiritual evolution. Without the potential for error, realization, and reform, our spirituality would stagnate; thus the importance of repentance, to which the Qur'an continually calls us, cannot be overemphasized. Repentance combines the admission of wrong with the desire to change, but personal transformation can be immensely difficult. The Qur'an shows that God does not leave the repentant to struggle alone, but He reaches out to him or her in forgiveness. This involves more than absolution, for God responds to our repentance and comes to our aid, embracing us with His love and mercy (3:31). He guides the penitent to spiritual recuperation (57:28). The Qur'an frequently states that God "turns toward" the contrite sinner with compassion, forgiveness, and kindness, reminding us of the way a parent turns toward his or her injured child. Whenever the divine name, "the One Who Turns" (al Tawaab), is used in the Scripture, it always is associated with God's forgiveness, which reinforces the impression that God's forgiveness is His compassionate response to those who wrong themselves and seek recovery.[77]

Not all the wrongs we commit have equal weight; some of them harm us much more than others. In addition, good deeds can offset the ill effects of evil ones, and the positive rewards of good can greatly outweigh the negative consequences of wrongdoing.

---

77. *Surahs* 2:37; 2:54; 2:160; 4:16; 4:64; 9:104; 9:118; 24:10; 49:12; 110:3.

If you avoid the great sins of the things that are forbidden you, We shall expel out of you all the evil in you, and admit you to the gate of great honor. (4:31)

That which is with God is better and more lasting for those who believe and put their trust in their Lord; those who avoid the great sins and indecencies and when they are angry even then forgive. (42: 36-37)

Those who avoid great sins and indecencies, only [falling into] lesser faults—truly your Lord is ample in forgiveness. He knows you when He brings you out of the earth and when you are hidden in your mothers' wombs. Therefore ascribe not purity unto yourselves. He knows best who the God-conscious are. (53:32)

Establish worship at the two ends of the day and in some watches of the night. Truly, good deeds offset evil deeds. This is a reminder for the mindful. (11:114)

If any does good, to him is better than his deed, but if any does evil, the doers of evil are requited only what they did. (28:84)

These verses reemphasize that faultlessness is not required to know paradise in the hereafter, and that we all have imperfections; thus 53:32 states that no one should claim to be pure. Rather, the Qur'an exhorts us to earnestly strive to grow in goodness, for it is God's mercy and compassion that will ultimately cleanse us.

Yet there are those who fail to rid themselves of serious vices they have acquired, though they love God and are tortured by remorse. The Qur'an suggests that even such grave wrongdoing may not always lead to suffering in the hereafter.

Oh my servants, who have sinned against yourselves, never despair of God's mercy. Surely God forgives all sins. (39:53)

Nevertheless, there is one transgression that will invariably lead to perdition, and that is the willful refusal to give up false gods. For when we contumaciously put wealth, power, lusts, pride, people, our achievements or creations, above God, we are in direct and complete opposition to the purpose of our creation.

> God does not forgive that partners be set up with Him, but
> He forgives all else to whom He wills, for to set up partners
> to God is indeed a tremendous sin.[78] (4:48)

One of the great risks taken by the unrepentant sinner is bringing damage to his or her moral and spiritual center, or what the Qur'an refers to as "the heart." "It is not their eyes that become blind," the Scripture states, "but their hearts which are in their breasts" (22:46). The Qur'an asserts that the hearts of these persons become dark, veiled, rusted, hard, and hence impenetrable to guidance, while the hearts of the virtuous become soft, sensitive, and receptive to God's guiding light.[79] The more we persist in wrongdoing, the more desensitized we become to the evil of it. Although the Qur'an often attributes this "veiling" of the recalcitrant sinner's heart to God, we should not conclude that the sinner has no part in this. For the Qur'an frequently attributes to God that which occurs according to the natural laws of cause and effect to which He has subjected creation. Thus God splits the grain of corn and the date stone, cleaves the daybreak, drives the clouds, sends down rain, sets up mountains on earth, holds up the birds in mid-air, teaches scribes how to write, develops the fetus in the womb,[80] while at the same time these phenomenon follow fixed laws, or what the Qur'an refers to as divinely ordained "measures."[81] The same could be said of the veiling

---

78. See also 4:116.

79. *Surahs* 2:74; 83:14.

80. *Surahs* 2:282; 4:96-100; 15:22; 16:10; 16:15; 23:63; 32:27; 39:6; 39:21; 43:12; 50:7-9.

81. *Surahs* 13:8; 15:21; 25:2; 36:38-39; 54:49; 80:18-19; 87:1-3.

of unbelievers' hearts, since the Qur'an consistently shows that this occurs because of their obstinate denial of truth. It is the evil that human beings acquire that covers their hearts like rust (83:14). It is because the deniers follow their own lusts that their hearts are sealed (47:14-16). God does not make people deny his signs; rather their hearts grow hard by their own wickedness (2:74). As my mother used to say, "If you tell a lie long enough, even you start to believe it." This is the flip side of what we already observed, that the more we grow in goodness, the more receptive we become to the divine attributes and, in particular, to truth.

No Denying It

I have always hated indecision. I do not mind it so much in others but I can't stand it in me. Yet for several weeks that seemed like several years, I did nothing about my experience of the Qur'an. Not that I did not think about my encounter with the Scripture—on the contrary, it was almost always on my mind—but I had no choice to make; I was presented no practical options. What was I to do and where was I to go now? Granted, the Qur'an had guided me—in spite of my being an atheist—to which for me at least is a logically consistent theology. I was also willing to admit that the Revelation affected me in ways I never could have anticipated, that it seemed to have awakened and seized a spirituality that I denied I possessed. It was also true that it was inconceivable to me that a Scripture of such power, beauty, and genius could arise from the primitive and backward wastelands of the ancient world. But none of this proved to me that there really is a God and that He revealed the Qur'an.

There was no one and nothing to take me to the next step. The Qur'an had finished too abruptly for me. It would have been helpful if it explained how to go from being open to the possibility of God's existence to conviction. Instead, I was left in limbo, with no arguments against and no further arguments in favor of the existence of God. Instead of ending with rational appeals, the Qur'an left me with three final exhortations.

Say: He is God, the One! God, the eternally besought by all! He begets not nor was He begotten, and there is none comparable to Him. (112:1-4)

Say: I seek refuge in the Lord of the Dawn, from the evil of what is created, from the evil of darkness as it overspreads, from the evil of those who practice secret arts, and from the envious one when he envies. (113:1-5)

Say: I seek refuge in the Lord of mankind, the King of mankind, the God of mankind, from the evil of the whisperer, who withdraws—who whispers into the hearts of mankind, from the Jinn and Mankind. (114:1-6)

Is it that easy? I wondered. Just say it? Just acquiesce? Just make the appeal? Then what? Will God open my heart and I will see? Is the Qur'an suggesting that fear of evil from others is preventing me from reaching the next step? Is it saying that maleficent psychic prompting may be dissuading me?

Even if God did exist, what was I supposed to do? I was alone in all of this. I knew of no one who had gone through the same experience I did. The few Muslim friends I had approached the Qur'an from a different mindset. Their way of reading, understanding, and reacting to it seemed to me to be almost entirely culturally determined, as if the appropriate response to each verse had been worked out and agreed upon long ago, and then taught and memorized ever since. They seemed uneasy with unofficial, unqualified, immediate responses to their Scripture. They appeared to accept only the authorized readings of the ancients, despite the fact that the Qur'an says, "If all the trees on earth were pens and the ocean were ink, with seven more oceans to support it, the words of God could not be exhausted. God is the Mighty, the Wise."[82] (31:27)

---

82. Similarly, 18:109 states, "Say: "If the sea were ink wherewith to write (the words of my Lord), sooner would the sea be exhausted than would the words of my Lord, even if we added another sea like it for help.""

Certainly no one from my background could relate to what I had been through. I knew of not a single American who had read the Qur'an. It was not part of a movement that my society was confronting, as it was in the Prophet's Arabia. I had no choice between contending sides. I stumbled upon it by accident, like finding a bottle with a letter in it on an isolated beach. It could not have been meant for me. What! If I did become convinced of God's existence, was I then supposed to become a Muslim and assimilate to a foreign culture and worldview?

This whole thing had gotten way out of hand. I had swum too far from the shore and no matter how hard I fought I was being pulled farther out. It all happened so subtly. My study of the Qur'an began as a simple rational investigation that only gradually took on a spiritual dimension. Through reading it, I discovered that my philosophical arguments against the existence of God—which I had considered unassailable—were much weaker than I had thought. I found that they were based on a set of premises that the Qur'an did not accept. On the other hand, the Qur'an offered an explanation for human existence—based on assumptions that I never considered and yet to me seemed natural—that I found compellingly coherent. As my objections to God's existence dissipated, I began to have doubts— mild at first— about atheism. I believe it was then that I began to experience spiritual moments that early on were somewhat vague but later grew in intensity as I became more open to the possibility of the existence of God. I felt that the change began as a rational one —a change in thinking—from which I was led to a gradual spiritual awakening.

Could there truly be a God? The Qur'an indicates that we have an inherent knowledge of God—an almost instinctual sense of His being—that could become dulled through our single-minded pursuit of worldly goals, or through sinfulness or arrogance. It claims that many unbelievers demonstrate this primal cognizance of God's being in times of danger when they perceive death is near and that they turn to God so naturally and sincerely in these crises that it would seem that prayer is second nature to them. However, the Qur'an also indicates that when the threat passes they typically revert to denial of God. It states that these episodes serve as "signs" and that God exposes unbelievers to them so that "perhaps they will reflect."[83]

I remembered being on a walk several miles from home, back when I was a graduate student at Purdue, when a thunderstorm blew in. There was no shelter under which I could hide to wait out the storm. The winds, rain, hail, and lightning became so fierce that I began to run panic-stricken down the road. I remembered at one point pleading to God, "If You really are there, then don't let me die out here!" About ten to fifteen minutes later, the storm calmed and I walked the rest of the way home. I forgot all about my religious impulse; I just blew it off as irrational panic. I had done the same thing on at least one other occasion. I was so committed to atheism that I never allowed myself to seriously contemplate what made me turn to God so naturally and automatically, even though I was certain of His nonexistence.

The spiritual moments I had while reading the Qur'an were hard for me to explain. I had never really known anything like it. I had never felt the almost tangible presence of what I could only describe as overpowering mercy. I did not seek, want, or solicit these moments. On the contrary, for some time I resisted and dismissed them. What shocked me most was that I did not anticipate or desire them, but that they just happened.

Perhaps it was the emptiness that I was feeling that bothered me the most. What could have aroused in me these haunting feelings of isolation, even though my social life was full?

---

83. *Surahs* 29:65; 30:33; 31:32.

What more do I need? I asked myself. How many more signs or arguments or passages that reached into my heart and revealed me? How many more times did I need to look into the mirror of my soul before I recognized myself? Was I not the thirsting one, the lost, unguided wanderer in the desert of mundane pursuits, struggling toward one empty mirage after another?[84]

Why was I denying it? Why could I not accept what had happened to me while reading the Scripture? Why could I not concede that I missed the experience of the Qur'an; that I missed the voice that spoke to me so personally; that I longed for the awe, excitement, struggle, comfort, pain, anguish, and yearning that that conversation aroused in me? Why could I not acknowledge that I missed the intimacy and love I sometimes felt and yet rejected? What was the point in denying it anymore? Why could I not admit that this for which I ached, that this which I was missing, that this which had been in pursuit of me, was none other than God?

Because this does not happen to me, I thought. This does not happen to someone who rejects religion, denies spirituality, and scoffs at faith. Then why do I agonize? Why do I not let go of it and why does it not let go of me?

On November 8, 1982, at around 3:00 in the afternoon, I went to the mosque that was located in the basement of St. Ignatius Church at the University of San Francisco. I told myself I was only going there to ask a few questions, as conversion was impossible. About a half an hour later I walked out of the mosque a Muslim.[85]

---

84. See 29:34.

85. I talk about what took place in the mosque that day in *Struggling to Surrender*, Amana Publications, Beltsville, MD, 1994, pp. 9-17.

Questions

Question 5 (asked by my oldest daughter on another one of our walks):

It was a crisp, cool, fall afternoon. I believe I was saying something to Jameelah about the Qur'an, when she interrupted, "Daddy, I understand that when you were an atheist you had certain questions about God that you could not find answers to, and that you found answers to them when you read the Qur'an. But I still can't see what made you become a Muslim?"

"What do you mean?" I asked her as our pace slowed.

"I mean, just because you didn't have any more arguments against God, it doesn't prove He exists."

"That's a terrific insight!" I told her with a slight grin of admiration. "I would never have expected that from someone your age!"

The interpretation I then gave her of how I became a Muslim was along the same lines as the preceding section. I explained to her that as I became more open to the possibility of God's existence, I began to have some intense spiritual experiences while reading the Qur'an.

"What made you think that they were from God?" She asked.

"At first I didn't believe they were," I told her. "Then I doubted that they were. Then I thought that perhaps they were. Then I knew that they were. After a while I just knew from Whom they came. It was as if I always knew God but had somehow gotten distracted or suffered some kind of spiritual trauma and forgot. It was like coming out of amnesia. I think we have this basic, natural, spiritual sense of God, but we come to ignore it, or deny it, or not to trust it anymore. Am I making any sense?"

"Daddy," she looked at me with her big, beautiful, brown eyes, "that is the lamest thing I've ever heard."

"Why do you say that?" I asked her, feeling deflated.

"Because I know that I don't know God at all," she said. "I have no natural sense of God."

We kept walking. I thought how stupid it was of me to try that explanation. I do not even fully understand my transition from rejection, to doubt, to belief; how could I make sense of that to an eleven-year old? She hadn't lived and experienced enough to understand what I was saying. Even if she had been older, how could she possibly relate to it if she never had similar experiences? Did I know God when I was her age; did I have a natural awareness of His being? All I could remember is that when I was young I used to beg God to take my father away.

Then I thought of something. "Jameelah, do you remember the day I was taken by ambulance to the hospital last July?"

"Yes," she answered, looking perplexed.

"Do you remember how I was hooked up to all those wires and tubes, and then they put me on a stretcher to carry me out to the ambulance, and I couldn't move and I was shaking and having trouble breathing?"

"Yes," she said sadly.

"And do you remember how you stood next to me and asked me with your voice trembling if I was going to die?"

"Yes," she replied with tears beginning to fill her eyes.

"After they took me to the hospital, did you at any time that day or night pray to God to not let your father die, to keep him alive? Did you ask God for help?"

"Yes," she said, a little indignantly, perhaps wondering why I was badgering her.

"Did you pray to God the next day?"

"Yes!" She said, sounding like a reluctant witness in a court case.

"And in the days that followed?"

"Yes!" She said in a voice that told me to stop.

"Then who taught you how to pray like that? Who taught you how to talk to God?"

She paused momentarily, perhaps searching for an answer.

"You taught me the how to do the prayers." She answered, sounding a little unsure of herself.

"I'm not talking about performing the formal ritual prayers in Arabic. I mean who taught you how to talk to God, to communicate to Him

personally? Did I or anyone else ever tell you that you should envision yourself talking to Him, that you think the words you want to say in your mind, and then God receives and hears them?"

"No."

"Did I or anyone else ever demonstrate to you how to talk to God?"

"No."

"Are you sure?"

"Yes!"

"Perhaps your mother, or one of your grandmothers, or one of your uncles or aunts taught you?"

"No!"

"Then who taught you? How did you know how to do that so automatically?"

"Nobody taught me!" She insisted. *"I just knew!"*

The look of betrayal in her face made me wish that I had not brought up that day, because there is no one in the world that I would less want to hurt than her.

"Well, then," I said, *"maybe you do have a natural awareness of God—maybe that's how you knew. In any case, that was how it was for me. After a while I just knew that it was God who was reaching me through the verses of the Qur'an and the spiritual occurrences. It took me some time to realize it— maybe because I had been spiritually unconscious for so long—but after a while I just knew."*

Question 6 (from a second-generation agnostic, in her late twenties and a medical researcher, with one of several similar questions from young persons of Indian and Pakistani parentage):

Why is idol-worshipping so wrong? Nobody believes that the idols themselves are "God." They are just a representation to help you. They [the idol worshippers] find God in every living and non-living being. How is their faith any less? The debate is not between a formless creator and one of form. They are just trying to capture on a temporal, physical plane the Formless One. I don't see anything wrong with that.

With its references to creating "a representation to help you," to finding "God in every living and non-living being," "a formless creator," and "the Formless One," the questioner seems to be asking about Hinduism. The Hindu religion is a vast and multifaceted system and it would require greater knowledge of it than I possess, and much more than a few pages, to do justice to the question.[86] But while I disqualify myself from assessing Hinduism, I feel that I should say at least a few more words about the Qur'an's critique of "idol-worship," since it is one of its major themes.

To say that the Qur'an condemns the worship of idols is an understatement and oversimplification. What the Qur'an opposes is *shirk* (usually translated into English as "idol worship"), which is a broader concept. The word *shirk* is associated with the Arabic verb *sharaka*, which means "to share," "to make a partner," "to make someone or something an associate of another," and "to associate something with something else." In the Qur'an, it signifies the assignment to others of a share in God's divinity and supremacy. In its crudest manifestations *shirk* may take the form of deifying concrete objects, such as graven images or celestial bodies. It may also involve the worship of gods of our own invention. Regarding the latter, the Qur'an tells the Arab polytheists, "They [your gods] are nothing but names that you named"(53:23).[87] Sometimes the idols may represent human

---

86. I should point out that most knowledgeable Hindus would object to equating the image worship that occurs in Hinduism with idolatry (the worship of a physical object as a god). Thus K. M. Sen, in *Hinduism* (Penguin, 1999, p.35) writes, "In Hindu philosophy there is no contradiction between belief in an all-embracing, all-pervading, omnipresent God and the *puja* [worship] of a variety of gods and goddesses of the Hindu pantheon. In religious ceremonies the images of gods may help to focus devotion, but in theory they represent nothing more than imaginative pictures of the infinite aspects of one all-pervading God."

87. The full quotation reads, "They are nothing but names which you have named, for which God has sent down no authority. They follow nothing but conjecture and that which they themselves desire. Even though the guidance from their Lord has come unto them" (53:23). Also, see 12:40.

qualities. Thus, in the Prophet's day, some polytheists worshipped Wadd, Suwa, Yagooth, Ya-ooq, and Nasr which represented masculinity, beauty, brute strength, swiftness (or athleticism), and sharp-sightedness (or insight), respectively (71:23).[88] Idols may also represent spiritual entities, or deceased prophets or saints, whose intercession is sought. The pagan Arabs, for example, used to imagine that angels were female deities to whom they prayed for intercession, and many Christians would pray to Jesus, Mary, and other saints, believing that the saints could mediate between the petitioners and God. The Qur'an rejects these notions since it maintains that the dead are unaware of what transpires on earth and are incapable of responding to one's prayers,[89] and because the angelic hosts are spiritual instruments of God that can do only what they are commanded. Furthermore, the Qur'an emphasizes that, since God is infinitely more just and merciful than any of His creatures, intercession or mediation is unnecessary.[90] The Qur'an also demonstrates that *shirk* can take the form of worshipping living persons, such as was the case with the Egyptians and the Pharaohs. The Qur'an provides examples of persons who make worldly success their object of worship and of others who deify their desires. About the latter, the Qur'an states, "Do you see the one who takes his lusts as his god?"[91]

---

88. The Qur'an's critique of these pre-Islamic Arabian gods may also be a criticism of the general human tendency to idolize these qualities in men and women.

89. *Surahs* 5:109; 5:116-117; 16:21.

90. For example, concerning the Christian belief in the divine sonship of Jesus, the Qur'an says, "Far is it removed from His transcendent majesty that He should have a son. His is all that is in the heavens and all that is in the earth. And Allah is sufficient as a *wakeel*" (4:171). *Wakeel* literally means a "legal representative" or "one who defends another's rights or interests." In modern Arabic a defense counsel or lawyer is called a *wakeel*. The implication is that God does not need a son to mediate between Him and mankind, nor for that matter would He need to create a savior. Also see 19:87-93, 21:26.

91. *Surahs* 25:43; 45:23.

Regardless of its many manifestations, a common element in all *shirk* is the worship of other than God. Recalling that worship in the Qur'an implies complete devotion to another, then all *shirk* in one form or another involves surrendering oneself or assigning ultimate authority to someone or something, real or imagined, other than God. Therefore, when politicians let national, financial, political, and military interests take precedence over moral or ethical concerns, they commit a form of *shirk*. The same could be said of those who refuse to consider revising their religious stance for fear it will upset their traditions or social standing.[92] (7:70)

As the Qur'an shows, *shirk* most often does not include the denial of God as the supreme being, but rather, it usually sets up copartners of God that are believed to act as additional authoritative sources of divine guidance. Very often religious leaders and scholars are assigned this role. Hence the Qur'an states that the Jews and Christians "take their rabbis and priests to be their Lords beside God." (9:31)

One of the most malefic and most pervasive forms of *shirk* is the promotion of wrongdoing on religious grounds. Some Zionists have used the Bible to defend the expropriation of Palestinian land. European settlers' sense of divine mission was used to legitimize the expulsion of the Native Americans, whom they designated "satanic forces." Japan launched a savage war of aggression against China in the name of Hirohito, the semi-divine emperor.[93] Some modern militant Muslims have promoted the murder of civilians in God's name. The Church tortured and executed "heretics" during the Inquisition. In seventh century Arabia, children were sometimes sacrificed to various gods to win their favor. Such examples are legion, but I believe it safe to say that no religion has been immune from this type of *shirk*.

---

92. Also 10:78; 11:62; 11:87; 31:21; 43:22-23.

93. It seems that Hirohito may have been against the attack on China but, for political reasons, did not oppose it. In 1946, he publicly denounced the concept that he is divine.

As *shirk* deters from self-surrender to God, the Qur'an warns against religious innovations that may lead to it (7:33). Even seemingly innocuous innovations in religion can ultimately become an obstruction to monotheism. The Qur'an provides this incisive example:

> And the Jews say: Ezra is the son of God, and the Christians say: the Messiah is the son of God. That is their saying with their mouths. They but imitate the sayings of those who disbelieved of old. God fights against them. How deluded are they! (9:30)

In the Jewish tradition, the term "son of God," which appears a number of times in the Old Testament, is used as a metaphor to designate a close relation to God.[94] For most Christians, "son of God," when applied to Jesus Christ, signifies his unique status as God the Son, second person of the triune God. This illustrates how a phrase that may have originally expressed a benign concept eventually became the centerpiece of a dogma that the Qur'an claims compromises monotheism.[95] It is important to note that the Qur'an does not state what Jews and Christians intend by this expression, as it may have various interpretations. Rather, it emphasizes only what they state ("that is their saying with their mouths") since the expression "son of God" comes precariously close to "the sayings of unbelievers of old" and thus can lead to false worship. On the same grounds, the Qur'an rejects the use of the word "three" when

---

94. *Dictionary of Judaism in the Biblical Period*, Simon and Schuster, New York, 1996, pp. 596-597.

95. The Qur'an also disapproves of the phrase "children of God," as it may suggest an exclusive beloved of God.

> The Jews and Christians say: We are children of God and His loved ones. Say: Why then does He chastise you for your sins? No, you are but mortals of His creating. He forgives whom He wishes and chastises whom He wishes. God's is the sovereignty of the heavens and the earth and all that is between them, and unto Him is the journeying. (5:20)

speaking about the nature of God.

> O People of the Scripture! Do not exaggerate in your religion
> nor utter concerning God anything but the truth. The
> Messiah, son of Mary, was only a prophet of God, and His
> word, which He conveyed unto Mary, and a spirit from Him.
> So believe in God and His messengers, and say not "Three."
> Cease! (It is) better for you! God is only one God. Far is it
> from His transcendent majesty that He should have a son. His
> is all that is in the heavens and all that is on earth. And God
> is sufficient as a defender. (4:171)

> They surely deny the truth who say: God is the third of three:
> when there is no God but the one God. (5:73)

> Say: O People of the Scripture! Stress not in your religion
> other than the truth, and follow not the vain desires of people
> who erred of old and led many astray, and erred from a plain
> road. (5:77)

These admonitions indicate that innovations in religion that have
the semblance of *shirk*, regardless of their original intent, often end up
becoming diversions from the worship of God. The same lesson can
be drawn from the Qur'anic version of the story of the Golden Calf,
where the Children of Israel are made to destroy the image they
create, even though they intended it to serve only as a representation
of the one God, "the God of Moses." (20:85-98)

As stated above, *shirk* can take on many forms, but from the point
of view of the Qur'an it is never innocuous, for it injects falsehood
into religion and untruth will ultimately come to light.[96] When it
does, doubt and skepticism grow among the faithful, causing religion
to lose its rational appeal, and with it, its moral authority and
spiritual efficacy. The most salient example the Qur'an provides

96. *Surah* 17:81.

of this type of erosion of faith is that of the pagan Quraish, the Prophet's kinsman and chief opposition. The Qur'an reminds them that their greatly revered ancestors, Abraham and Ishmael, were strict monotheists who dedicated the Kabah in Mecca to the worship of God. Over the course of centuries the legacy of monotheism they left became almost completely overshadowed by a crass polytheism that the Quraysh themselves had lost confidence in and that permitted and fostered depravity.

Quraysh polytheism serves in the Qur'an as the most prominent example of the debilitating effects of *shirk* on religion, but the Scripture shows through its discussions of past and contemporary religious communities that this is a universal problem. The Qur'an's many warnings against *shirk* are not directed only, or even primarily, toward non-Muslims, but Muslims too must be ever vigilant against associating with God that which is not of God. As the Qur'an amply shows, much of what has been claimed throughout history in the name of God has no divine warrant and is utterly of human invention. Muslims must be terribly cautious not to claim divine authority for cultural traditions, religious innovations, and scholarly opinions that have no incontrovertible support from Revelation. Certainly these must exist in every religion. Faith communities will always develop traditions and respond creatively to new problems that arise, and scholars will always opine and theologize, but these are human attempts to interpret and should never be idealized and excluded from critical scrutiny.

> Say: "Have you considered what provision God has sent down for you, and how you made some of it *haram* (unlawful) and *halal* (lawful)?" Say: "Has God indeed permitted you, or do you invent a lie concerning God?" (10:59)

> And say not, for any false thing your tongues put forth: "This is *halal* (lawful) and this is *haram* (unlawful)," so that you invent a lie against God. (16:116)

Question 7 (from an American Muslim high school student; such questions on predestination are very common):

In the "khutbah" (sermon) last Friday, our imam said that God predetermines all our acts, including our choices, and that anyone who does not accept this is not a Muslim. But if God predetermines all of our actions and choices, then why does He punish us for them? This does not seem fair to me. I'm afraid I'm becoming an atheist!

The dogma the imam spoke of in his Friday sermon is referred to in Islamic thought as the doctrine of *Qadr*, most often rendered in English as "divine decree" or "predestination." It was a subject of great controversy in the early history of Islam and open to diverse understandings. The imam's statement of this dogma represents what came to be its severest formulation. Not all schools of thought in ancient times accepted the concept of predestination, chief among those that did not were the speculative theologians, known as the *ahl al-kalam* (the people of disputation) who were prominent in the early centuries after the *Hijrah*.[97] One of their main rivals, the *ashab al-hadith* (the people of the prophetic traditions), generally accepted it in one form or another, although the version espoused by the imam was an extreme view.

The identification of *qadr* with predestination appears to be a gradual development in Islamic thought. It was not known to the pre-Islamic Arabs. According to the great lexicographer, Raghib al-Isfahani, *qadr* and its synonym *taqdir* mean "the making manifest of the measure of a thing" or simply "measure." He goes on to say that "God manifests *taqdir* in two ways: by granting *qudrah* (power), or by making them in a particular measure and in a particular manner, as His wisdom requires."[98] His interpretation coincides with the Qur'an,

---

97. The *Hijrah* refers to the Prophet's emigration to the city of *Yathrib* (later named *Madinat al Nabi* [City of the Prophet] or simply al *Madinah*) in 622 C.E. It marks the inception of the Islamic calander.

98. The quote appears in `Abdul Hamid Siddiqi's translation of *Sahih Muslim*, Ashraf Press, Lahore, 1992, p. 1, note 3.

where *qadr* and *taqdir* are associated with the design and regulation of nature.

And the sun runs on to a term appointed for it; that is the law (*taqdir*) of the Mighty, the Knowing. And as for the moon, we measured (*qaddarna*) for it stages. (36:38-39)

Who created everything, then established for it a measure (*qadar*). (54:49)

Of what thing did He create him [man]? Of a small life-germ He created him, then He made him according to a measure (*qaddara-hu*). (80:18-19)

Glorify the name of your Lord, the Most High, who creates, then makes complete, and who makes things according to a measure (*qaddara*), then guides them to their goal.[99] (87:1-3)

Early theological epistles and *awa`il*[100] reports evidence that the debate about free will and determinism arose no earlier than the last third of the first century A.H.[101] The *Risala fi'l-Qadr* of al Hasan al Basri, for example, purported to have been written at the request of the Caliph `Abd al Malak (65-86 A.H./684-705 C.E.), states that the controversy over *Qadr* is a new development. Interestingly, the epistle fails to cite any specific *hadith* on this subject,[102] despite `Abd al

---

99. Also 13:8, 15:21, 25:2.

100. *Awa`il* reports are records of the first times various happenings were supposed to have occurred. G. H. A. Juynboll, *Studies on the Origin and Uses of Islamic Hadith*, Variorum, 1996, III, p. 311.

101. Josef van Ess, "Umar II and his Epistle against the Qadariyya," *Abr Nahrain* 1 (1971-1972): 20ff; Michael Cook, *Early Muslim Dogma* (Cambridge, 1981), 107-158; John Wansbrough, *Qur'anic Studies* (Oxford, 1977). Daniel Brown, *Rethinking Tradition in Modern Islamic Thought*, (Cambridge, 1996), pp. 11-12.

102. See chapter 2, question 1, for further discussion of the doctrine of *Qadr* in the *Hadith* literature.

Malik's explicit request for a "transmitted report (*riwaya*) from any one of the Companions of the Prophet of God."[103]

Although the identification of *qadr* with predestination apparently occurred after the Prophet's lifetime, the debate that developed over free will and determinism was to be expected. On the one hand, the Qur'an makes it clear that God has empowered men and women to make choices—moral or otherwise—and to carry them out most often to their expected ends.[104] God can interrupt or influence this process when He wishes, but He often permits things to follow the natural course of cause and effect.[105]

On the other hand, the Qur'an upholds the omniscience of God, that His knowledge encompasses all happenings regardless of their place in space or time.

> He [God] knows what is before them and what comes after them, and they cannot compass it with their knowledge. (20:110)

> He [God] knows what is before them and what comes after them, and unto God all things are returned. (22:76)

---

103. Although the epistle does not cite any specific traditions on free will and determinism, there are many "authenticated" *hadiths* espousing various forms of predestination in the canonical collections. If the epistle is genuine, then this is indeed puzzling, especially since al Hasan al Basri was an important figure in the early history of the science of *Hadith*, his name appearing in many chains of transmission. If the epistle is historic, then several possibilities are suggested. It may be that *hadiths* on predestination did not come into circulation until the last third of the first Islamic century or even later, after the debate on free will and determinism was well under way. An alternative is that al Hasan disregarded *hadiths* that supported the concept of predestination, because they conflicted with his own views. Or it may be that al Hasan had simply been unaware of the many *hadiths* advocating predestination, but this is unlikely.

104. Cf. pages 73-80.

105. The human capability to make and put into effect choices may be described as a limited free will. It is limited since it, like all created entities, depends on God for its existence and preservation.

Truly the knowledge of the Hour is with God (alone). It is He who sends down rain, and He knows what is in the wombs. Nor does any soul know what it will earn tomorrow, nor does any soul know in what land it will die. Truly God is knowing, aware. (31:34)

Yet if God knows everything, then the future, including the choices we make, must be already determined. It would seem inconceivable that we can make choices that conflict with God's knowledge of them. Similarly, if God knows what our state-of-being in the hereafter is, then we must be predestined for either Heaven or Hell.

Such claims are perplexing, as they require simultaneous entertainment of two radically different viewpoints: the divine and human. A related problem is that the statements are not quite complete, for they do not state exactly who it is that has supposedly predetermined the future and when the preordainment was accomplished. Since we are analyzing these claims from the Muslim perspective, they obviously assume that God must have predestined all things. The issue of when the preordainment was to have occurred is less clear, but is usually believed to have happened sometime before creation.

The above proposition that God's omniscience implies His predestination of all happenings may be delineated as follows: God knows all things, implies God knows the future, implies the future is fixed, implies God predetermined the future. The diagram below represents the sequence of implications in this argument.

(1) God knows all things.

▼

(2) God knows the future.

▼

(3) The future is fixed.

▼

(4) God predetermined the future.

It is more convenient to analyze this proof on a local level, that is, one event at a time. Let A represent an event that might occur tomorrow. For example, A may represent the event, "Jeff chooses to eat french-fries with his dinner." Then the above argument becomes:

(1) God knows all things.

(2) God knows event A will occur tomorrow.

(3) Event A will definitely occur tomorrow.

(4) God predetermined event A.

The weakest link in this argument is obviously the last implication: (3) implies (4). Logic simply does not dictate that because Jeff will choose to eat french-fries with dinner tomorrow, God compelled him to make that choice. The fact that a certain event will definitely take place in the future does not necessitate that God forced it to happen.

Actually we can eliminate one step in the argument, since divine omniscience implies the equivalence of statements (2) and (3) above. Thus the argument reduces to the following sequence of implications:

(1) God knows all things.

(2) God knows event A will occur tomorrow.

(3) God predetermined event A.

Here again the implication (2) implies (3) is not convincing, unless we accept that knowledge of an event somehow produces its occurrence, but there is no compelling reason to accept this, especially since it runs counter to experience. We may accept the reverse implication—that an occurrence of an event produces knowledge of it, provided that there is someone to witness it—but there is no justification for maintaining that knowledge of an incident yields its happening. I may have a true premonition that my neighbor will choose to take the bus to work tomorrow, but that does not imply that my knowing it caused it to happen. Even in the case of divine knowledge, there is no logical reason for drawing a causal link between God's awareness of an incident and its taking place. Simply put, divine knowledge is irrelevant to the claim that God predestines our choices and state in the afterlife. The reasoning, "If God knows everything, then He must predetermine everything," is analogous to the argument, "If Jeff has blue eyes, then there is life on Mars"; the premise has no bearing upon the conclusion.

While divine omniscience does not imply that God predestined our futures, it does not contradict it either. However, there are other assertions in the Qur'an that are at odds with the doctrine of predestination.[106] The most obvious is the Qur'an's claim that God is the most Just, for it hardly seems fair to predestine someone to hell for acts and choices that he or she was compelled by God to make.[107] The invocation of divine justice against the doctrine of

---

106. It should be noted that the Qur'an does allude to the concept of predestination but it presents it as an erroneous conjecture of the Prophet's opponents.

> They who are idolaters will say: Had God willed, we had not ascribed partners neither had our fathers, nor had we forbidden anything. Thus did those who were before them give the lie until they tasted the fear of Us? Say: Have you any knowledge that you can adduce for Us? Truly you follow nothing but conjecture. Truly you merely conjecture. (6:149)

> And the idolaters say: Had God willed, we had not worshipped anything beside Him, we and our fathers, nor had we forbidden anything without Him. (16:35)

> And they say: If the Merciful had willed, we should not have worshipped them. They have no knowledge whatsoever of that. They merely conjecture. (43:20)

107. The concept of predestination also seems to disaffirm the divine attributes of mercy and compassion.

predestination, with its powerful appeal to human sensibilities, was the main argument of the *ahl al-kalam*.

This led some of the defenders of predestination to formulate a theory of good and evil that was independent of human reason and perceptions. They claimed that good is what God commands and evil is what He forbids. The divine will and its dictates determine what is good and evil, just or unjust.[108] Thus if God sends the righteous to Hell and the unrighteous to Heaven, then these acts are by definition good, despite their being morally and rationally objectionable from a human standpoint. Although this conception protects the dogma of predestination, it to some extent makes the Qur'an's many exhortations to be good and just meaningless.

A more subtle attempt to reconcile predestination and freewill was made by the famous theologian al Hasan al Ash`ari (874-935). His theory of *kasb* (acquisition), which became the orthodox position, did not so much resolve the dilemma as it enshrouded it in obscurantism. The concept holds that God is the only creator of all human action, but people "acquire" their deeds and are thus justly responsible for them. Abstruse formulas may do little to elucidate paradoxes, but they have the advantage of being open to diverse interpretations. For example, if one differentiates between thought and action, then the formula could mean that God allows us to effect our choices, but if thoughts are considered actions, then this becomes the harshest version of predestination, making it hard to see in what sense we acquire our acts and why we should be responsible for them.

Another divine attribute that appears contrary to the concept of predestination is divine transcendence. The Qur'an teaches that the space-time creation wherein we currently exist is not an eternal, objective reality.[109] It serves as a temporary environment for a phase of our development. Both space and time are illusory, and God is not

---

108. Ignaz Goldziher, *Introduction to Islamic Theology and Law*, trans. by Andras and Ruth Hamori, Princeton, 1981, pp. 85-91.

109. Cf. pp. 77-79.

limited or bound by either. His being is beyond the boundaries of His space-time creation. For this reason it would not be appropriate to assume that God exists within some finite space or some finite interval of time. Just as it should not be supposed that God is contained within the four walls of my office, it should not be claimed that He currently exists within today and is looking ahead to tomorrow. For the latter assertion assumes God is situated in time the same way human beings perceive they are. Similarly, it would be inappropriate to speak of God having a past or future. "Predestine" means to decide or determine in advance and implies that God at some fixed point in time determined future events. For this to have happened it must be assumed that at some moment God existed within time and fore-ordained what was to come. This location of God in time is a fundamental contradiction introduced by all conceptions of predestination. Divine transcendence implies a unique vantage. God's knowledge and awareness has no spatial or temporal bounds. For God all knowledge is a unity, encompassing all things regardless of their place in space and time. The Qur'an asserts:

> No vision encompasses Him and He encompasses all vision. (6:104)

> Our Lord encompasses everything in knowledge. (7:89)

> He is the First and the Last, and the outward and the Inward, and He knows everything. (57:3)

Because we exist within the confines of creation, divine transcendence is impossible for us to fully grasp.[110] Yet transcending space is perhaps easier to conceive of than transcending time. We can imagine that transcending space is similar to being high above the ground, where distant happenings can be observed simultaneously.

---

110. Thus the Qur'an states, "He [God] knows what is before them and what comes after them, and they cannot compass it with their knowledge" (20:110).

Unfortunately, transcending time is much more difficult to envision, since we perceive ourselves as fixed in time, but the spatial model may still be useful. Putting aside the issue of the illusory character of time, we can conceive of time as a fourth spatial dimension. We can then envision that transcendence would be similar to being far outside creation, where it would be possible to observe very distant happenings in both space and time.

It can be argued that the Qur'an itself contains expressions that locate God in space and time. The Qur'an speaks of God's throne, hand and face. It speaks of God sending down things to mankind and of things ascending to Him. It also employs various tenses (present, past, future, etc.) when referring to acts of God. However the use of such phrasing is unavoidable when communicating to human beings, due to the limitations of their language and experience. It would be impossible in Arabic, for example, to refer to an act of God without employing some tense.[111] Although almost all Muslim scholars have maintained that divine transcendence necessitates that spatial references to God in the Qur'an should not be taken literally, they did not conclude the same about temporal expressions, probably because time seems more absolute to us than space. Be that as it may, it seems that one should also not insist that all temporal references to God's activity in the Qur'an be taken literally, nor understood to imply that God is subject to temporal limitations.

The meaning of *qadr* underwent a subtle but critical evolution in Muslim thought. In the Qur'an it stands for the order and design God imposes upon creation, mankind included. Human knowledge, power, and will are all subject to limitations imposed upon humanity by divine measure, but within these limits human beings are empow-

---

111. Arabic, and to the best of my knowledge every other language, does not have what might be called a transcendent tense, but one way the Qur'an seems to get around this is by employing different tenses when discussing happenings outside of this space-time universe. For example, the Qur'an speaks about happenings in the hereafter sometimes in the past, sometimes in the future, and sometimes in the present tense. The same is true of other events that take place in *al-ghayb* (the unseen).

ered by God to make and exercise choices. Sometime after the time of the Prophet, *qadr* came to be identified with predestination. I feel that this was a critical theological mistake. The argument that God's omniscience implies it is untenable. Moreover, there are compelling reasons to suspect the doctrine, since the concept of predestination conflicts with assertions in the Qur'an concerning God's justice, mercy, compassion, and transcendence. Rational conflicts inevitably arise when we attempt to specify the precise relationship between God and time, which is a futile exercise.

Question 8 (from a second-generation student):

I don't think God is fair, because we are not all given the same chance at Paradise. I have a cousin, who is a Muslim, whose parents died when she was a baby and was raised in her uncle's house. Her uncle began sexually molesting her when she was a little girl and continued to molest and rape her until she left home in her late teens. Today she is practically a prostitute, sleeping with just about any guy who comes her way. How can a girl who has been raised in such depraved surroundings and has been abused since she was little be held as accountable as someone like me who grew up in a wholesome family environment? It just does not seem right.

As pointed out earlier, our growth in goodness in this life is intrinsically bound to our state in the next.[112] The question then raises the very valid point that some of us come from more privileged backgrounds than others. Some of us are born into practically ideal families, in which we were surrounded by peace, love, and happiness. Some have been instructed in morality and spirituality since they were small. Some have been blessed with peaceful temperaments, bright minds, and good looks, and have developed very positive self-images. And some, like the young lady mentioned in the question, were born into living nightmares. It does hardly seem fair that regardless of our backgrounds, our growth in goodness is weighed on the same scale.

112. Cf. pp. 96-118.

My family and I were out on a stroll one evening. My youngest daughter, who was on her bicycle following the rest of us, suddenly zoomed passed. While standing up on her pedals and with her long, wavy, brown hair blowing backwards, she shouted joyously, "I am Fattin Lang and I love being me!" My wife and I burst out laughing and then I turned to Ragia and said, "We must be doing something right."

It is amazing how the self-image develops so early on. My daughters are always remarking to me how attractive they are. "Am I not beautiful, Daddy?" they ask me confidently. My wife often says the same about herself, while at the same time admitting that she would like to lose twenty pounds. "I know I'm overweight," she says, "but I know I am beautiful."

The women in my life are indeed beautiful. It glows in them from within. But when they make such statements they are speaking of more than the image in the mirror; it is the way they see themselves in their minds and through their hearts. I too have often been told that I am good-looking, but I have never believed it. I always felt I was being deceived, that others were humoring me, because for the life of me I couldn't see it. When I look inside myself, I do not see beautiful or handsome; I see someone scarred and disfigured. And I know that that will probably be with me for the rest of my life, but I also know the image is gradually fading.

The city in which I grew was known throughout our state as "the armpit of Connecticut." It was a corrupt and violent place. When I was a teenager, there was rampant interracial violence, rioting, gang fighting, and crime. Our police force was showcased on the television news program *60 Minutes* as one of the country's most crooked. Some of my friends ended up in prison. A few were found guilty of major violent crimes. Several became thieves and many were dealers. Almost everybody back then was into drugs in some way.

Our home life was worse than the chaos outside. Being at home was like being encased, like being buried alive. My father was a violent alcoholic who was also addicted to wife abuse. My brothers followed him down the same dark tunnel of drug dependency. My oldest brother was an alcoholic by his early twenties. My second oldest brother became an alcoholic at around the same age. My parents' third son, who was a year older than I, became a heroin addict in high school. My youngest brother, the one to whom I was closest, began his drug habit at thirteen, shortly after I left home for college. I am not sure that drug addiction is contagious, but I definitely believe the despair it generates is.

Nevertheless, my first reaction is always surprise when my friends and colleagues marvel at how I "survived" my childhood to have what they see as a normal and happy life. Just because I was exposed to a little more vice than they were, that does not mean that I should be devoid of morals or wholesome aspirations. Perhaps they exaggerate the effects of environment on personality development, for the fact is that the majority of those with whom I grew up live good and decent lives today. I may have been no saint, nor am I now, but I had a strong sense of right and wrong, of truth and goodness, although I some-times resisted it, allowing it to become dulled. I do not hold to the theory that our genetic code and our environment determine us. I believe that human beings possess moral and spiritual awareness that increases or decreases according to the choices they make. I am not saying that environment or genetics does not influence our development—that argument cannot be won—but I feel that for most of us volition plays a pivotal role.

This said, it is undeniable that life is not a level playing field, that some of us are born into circumstances more conducive to the attainment of virtue. Perhaps this is why the Qur'an indicates that the merit of a good deed varies, while the detriment of a wrongful deed is largely uniform.

> God is never unjust in the least degree. If there is any good, He doubles it, and gives from His intimacy an immense reward. (4:40)

> Who brings a good deed will receive tenfold the like thereof, while who brings an evil deed will be awarded only the like thereof, and they will not be wronged. (6:160)

And if any one performs any good, We increase its good for him. Truly God is forgiving, responsive.[113] (42:23)

Although an evil action reaps an equivalent ill effect, the rewards of a righteous act can differ considerably. This may be because the goodness of an act and its positive benefits increase with the resistance it encounters. Hence, joining the Prophet in the beginning of his mission, when his followers were few and his opposition most severe, has greater merit than uniting with his cause when victory was at hand.[114]

A small act of kindness by someone who has had many advantages may count as a small act of kindness, but the same act done by someone who has faced tremendous handicaps could be a huge moral and spiritual achievement. In line with this, the Qur'an asserts that we are tested in life in accordance with what we have been given—which would include knowledge, personality, wealth, environment, and social position—and that no one is charged beyond his or her ability.

He it is who has placed you as vicegerents on earth and has raised you in rank, some above others, that He may try you by that which He has given you. Truly your Lord is swift in prosecution, and truly He is forgiving, merciful. (6:165)

God charges no soul beyond its ability. To it what it earns and against it what it earns. (2:286)

No soul is charged beyond its ability. Before Us is a record which clearly shows the truth and they will never be wronged. (23:62)

---

113. Also 10:27; 27:89; 28:84 and 42:23.

114. Those who spent and fought before the victory [over Mecca] are not upon a level [with those who came after them]. Such are greater in rank than those who fought and spent afterwards. Unto each has God promised good. And God is aware of what you do. (57:10)

Coming to the aid of a stranger in distress is a meritorious act when done in the relative safety of the suburbs, but could be a much nobler deed when performed in the inner city where self-survival is the rule and human misery is routinely ignored. Similarly, a charitable gift of a dollar on the part of a poor person weighs heavier than the same donation by one that is well off. This concept of the relative goodness of righteous action also finds support in the genre of *hadith* accounts that emphasize God's limitless mercy. A woman who was in the habit of giving *laban* (coagulated sour milk) to the needy and never injuring anyone with gossip earns Heaven thereby, even though she was notorious for neglecting her prayers and fasting.[115] A man goes to Paradise for climbing down a well to fetch water for a dog dying of thirst.[116] A murderer of one hundred men travels to a far away city to find a holy man who could show him the way to repentance. Halfway there he dies, but God admits him to Paradise because of his sincere attempt at reform.[117] Likewise, to whom more has been given more is expected. Thus if the Prophet were not to have conveyed the Revelation truthfully, he would have received a double punishment, as would have his wives if they had been guilty of manifest lewdness (33:30.)

Therefore, it appears our future reward is not based solely on the level of goodness we reach by life's end but also on the amount of progress we make in getting there. It is the moral and spiritual distance that we cover in this life—the progress we make relative to what we have been given—that translates into our state in the next. Hence, while I may disapprove of another's behavior on religious grounds, on the same grounds I refuse to estimate their standing with God. Even though one individual is ostensibly more upright than

---

115. Mishkat, No. 4992, on the authority of Abu Hurayrah, from the collections of Ahmad and Bayhaqi.

116. Bukhari, Vol.1, no.174, on the authority of Abu Hurayrah.

117. Bukhari, Vol.4, no. 676, on the authority of Abu Said Al-Khudri.

another, the good deeds of the latter may count for more in God's weighing than those of the former, for God's mercy, compassion, and forgiveness pervade the entire system of creation.

It must be admitted that although this notion of relative goodness has support in the Qur'an and the *hadith* compilations, it is not a major theme in either, especially the Qur'an. If it were made too explicit, the majority of believers would almost certainly bank on it, allowing themselves too many vices by attributing them to imagined handicaps beyond their control. It is characteristic of the Qur'an that it does not elaborate on borderline cases; instead it steers clear of precarious behavior by exhorting to what is most beneficial and warning of that which is harmful.

Finally, it would be remiss not to mention that Islam has always recognized that there is no culpability when wrongdoing is associated with psychological and psychiatric disorders. In Islam, fornication is a sin, but trauma-induced sexual promiscuity goes way beyond the problem of sin. Sexual immorality is often a symptom of such psychological disorders as posttraumatic stress, paranoia, and psychosis stemming directly from the violence inflicted on the victim. In addition to the emotional scars, child abuse alters the development of the brain. Proper nurturing allows a child's brain to develop in a manner that contributes to an emotionally stable and healthy person who can respond to society in positive and creative ways. Stress, however, sculpts the brain to abnormal adaptability to a world of horror. This irreversible neurological defect throws a victim into a life-long battle with antisocial behaviors such as impulsiveness, hyperactivity, substance abuse, and aggression.

Instead of our judgment, these people should receive our understanding and be encouraged to get the help they so desperately need. Psychological therapy can help a traumatized victim nurture the wounded child within and overcome the emotional damage. With psychiatric care, including medications, the permanent, neurobiological effects can be treated so that some extent of control is achieved.

Such care, however, is expensive, and the cost of years of treatment is beyond the reach of most victims. There are over one million confirmed cases of child abuse annually in the United States. It is a national disgrace and part of a universal problem. Somehow a civilized society must find a way to finance the needs of these innocent victims. Ultimately, however, we must do more to eradicate the problem of child abuse. We can never have a healthy society as long as child abusers continue pouring into society the steady stream of people whose psychic and mental state is one of aggression, exasperation, and anxiety.

Question 9 (from a non-Muslim female undergraduate student with whom I had numerous conversations via email. Several young American Muslims have also asked me about the motivation behind creation.):

If God has no needs, then why did He create us? I am not asking about man's purpose in life, I am asking about God's purpose in creating man. If God is without need, then why would He create anything, human beings in particular? Excuse me for saying this, but what is in it for God?

The question is fraught with difficulty. It is easier to talk about the meaning that life has for humanity than what our creation holds for God. When we discuss the former, we are on more solid ground. In this case we speak more accurately from experience and reason, but when we discuss the divine perspective, we are working under severe limitations. Our own experience, upon which language is based, falls infinitely short of the divine. Any terminology used to explain God's being, knowledge, activity, or aspects of His wisdom can only be approximating. With regard to such statements in the Qur'an, even the conservative Hanbali school of thought acknowledged this dilemma with their principle of *bila kayf* (without how). It states that descriptions of God and His doings in the Scripture express truths but we cannot state precisely how these truths are realized. Many interpreters employed *tawil* (allegorical exegesis) when explaining such passages.[118]

I must also admit that the question caught me off guard the first time it was put to me, as it was dissimilar to the kinds of objections I raised when I was an atheist. My questions were in a sense from ground level. It was the human condition that for me argued against God's existence. The above query argues from Heaven downward as it questions the divine motivation: "What is in it for God?" I think it was foreign to my thinking because in the faith in which I was raised God's self-sufficiency and transcendence were taught but not greatly emphasized. The divine sonship of Jesus received much more play. Since in Christianity Jesus is both God and man, his humanity, which is quite evident in the Gospels, allows one to entertain the idea of God's having needs similar to ours. I think this may have been the reason why God's absolute independence was not more problematic for me.

It is understandable why God's self-sufficiency would be more of an issue for the young American Muslims who have written me about it. The absolute sovereignty and self-sufficiency of God (in Arabic, *al ghani*) is repeatedly stressed in their Scripture.

> Kind words and forgiveness are better than charity followed by injury. God is without need, clement. (2:263)

> And if any reject faith, then truly God is in no need of any of His creatures. (3:97)

> Unto God belongs all things in the heavens and on earth, and God is without need, worthy of praise. (4:131)

> They say, "God has begotten a son." Glory to Him! He is the Self-Sufficient. His are all things in the heavens and on earth. (10:68)

---

118. Ignaz Goldziher, *Introduction to Islamic Theology and Law*, trans. by Andras and Ruth Hamori, Princeton, 1981, pp. 92-109.

If any is grateful [to God], truly his gratitude is for [the benefit of] his own self, but if any is ungrateful, truly God is free of all needs, supreme in honor. (27:40)

If any strive, they do so for themselves, for God is free of all needs from all creation. (29:6)

O mankind! It is you that have need of God, but God is He who is without need, worthy of all praise. (35:15)

If you reject [faith], truly God has no need of you, though He is not pleased with thanklessness for His servants. And if you are thankful, God is pleased therewith for you.[119] (39:7)

Collectively the divine attributes of mercy, compassion, kindness, generosity, and love are mentioned far more often in the Qur'an than God's absolute autonomy, but it is evident that these differ fundamentally from the corresponding human qualities. In the Qur'an there is no hint of need, hope, uncertainty, urgency, incompleteness, pain or pathos associated with the divine attributes, whereas for human beings these are essential to their experiencing and growth in them.[120] God, however, is in full control of creation, nothing takes place without His permission and knowledge, and everything is unfolding according to His design. While God knows that many of mankind will be seduced into rejecting faith, He also knows that others will not.[121] As the fact of Revelation proves, God is not indifferent to the fate of His servants, yet He is also not in need of their belief. God's bestowal of His attributes on creation, mankind included, is utterly selfless, in the sense that it is not associated with personal need. In this regard the last verse quoted above deserves attention, for it

119. Also 2:267; 6:133; 14:8; 22:64; 27:40; 31:12; 31:26; 47:38; 57:24; 60:6; 64:6.

120. Cf. pp. 80-89.

121. *Surahs* 5:54; 15:39-43; 17:65.

makes sure to distinguish between needing and being pleased with something, in this case human gratitude toward God. There are numerous references in the Qur'an to God's being well pleased with the believers,[122] among them are several that show that this experience of divine pleasure will be one of the supreme rewards awaiting them in the hereafter.

> God will say: "This is a day in which their truthfulness profits the truthful, for theirs are gardens underneath which rivers flow, wherein they are secure forever, God taking pleasure in them and they in Him. That is the triumph supreme." (5:119)

> God is well pleased with them and they are well pleased with Him and He has readied for them gardens underneath which rivers flow, wherein they will abide. (9:100)

> God has pleasure in them and they have pleasure in Him. That is for him who fears his Lord. (98:8)

It may be argued that although the Qur'an affirms that God has no needs, it frequently mentions that God wishes (in Arabic, sha`a) and desires (in Arabic, arada) various things. There are over one hundred such statements in the Scripture. However, these never express need, longing or hope; rather they convey the meaning of "to intend," "to decide," or "to put into effect one's plan or purpose." The following examples are representative:

> God does what He wishes. (2:253; 3:40; 11:107; 14:27; 22:4-18; 85:16)

> God intends ease for you and He does not intend hardship for you. (2:186)

> God creates what He wishes. (3:47; 5:17; 24:45; 28:68; 30:54; 35:1; 42:49; 82:8)

---

122. *Surahs* 2:207; 2:265; 3:15; 3:162; 3:174; 4:114; 5:2; 5:16; 9:21; 9:72; 9:100; 9:109; 21:28; 47:28; 48:18; 48:29; 57:20; 57:27; 59:8; 60:1; 72:27.

Let not their conduct grieve you, who run headlong to disbelief, for truly they do not injure God at all. It is God's intention to assign them no portion in the hereafter and theirs will be a terrible agony. (3:176)

God intends not to place a burden on you, but He intends to purify you and to perfect His grace upon you, that you may give thanks. (5:7)

And our word unto a thing when We intend it, is only that We say unto it "Be!" And it is. (16:40)

And when We intend destruction of a township, We send a commandment to its people who live at ease and then they transgress therein. Thus the word proves true against it, and We destroy it with complete destruction. (17:16)

Another statement in the Qur'an that could be construed as implying a divine need is the often quoted: "I have not created jinn or man except to serve me." But the context shows that this service is vital to man, not to God, and that to live for any other purpose leads to suffering in the life to come.

And remind, for truly the reminder benefits the believers, and I have not created jinn or man except to serve me. I do not desire any sustenance from them, and I do not desire that they feed me, for truly God is He who provides sustenance, Lord of power, everlasting. For those who do wrong is an end like the end that belonged to their fellows [of earlier generations], so let them not ask me to hasten [it]. Woe, then, to the deniers on account of that day of theirs they have been promised. (51:55-60)

The *hadith* collections do not shed much additional light on the divine impulse behind creation. Very few of the traditions directly address this concern, and most of those that go beyond what the Qur'an tells us were not judged authentic by *hadith* criticism. There are a very limited number of sayings that show God to have an anxious concern for humanity,[123] but there are also others that depict a callous indifference to human fate;[124] hence as evidence they tend to offset each other.

So we return to the question of the divine motive behind creation with less than a complete answer. The question's premise that God has no needs is fully consistent with the Qur'an. The only indications we found of a personal incentive behind the creation of humankind are the many statements in the Qur'an that speak of God being well pleased with the believers. Of course there is no contradiction in this, as even we often create without needing to. This may not satisfy the curiosity of some, but as indicated above a fuller comprehension may be beyond our reach. For how can we fully comprehend love without emotional need, compassion without empathy, giving without self-sacrifice, forgiveness without personal injury, in short, virtue without vulnerability? It is our own perceived weakness, which we must rise above, that makes our growth in these possible and their existence comprehensible to us, but how can we grasp their pure, absolute, perfection in God?

Outside of Revelation and spiritual experience, the best means we may have to gain some understanding of the divine attributes is

---

123. One of the most moving is the following: 'Umar ibn Khattab reported that some prisoners were brought to the Prophet. Among them was a woman who was running frantically all over the place. When she found an infant, apparently hers, she lifted it, drew it close to her and breastfed it. The Prophet turned to his companions and said, "Can you imagine this women throwing her child into the fire?" When they said "No," he remarked, "God is more loving towards His servants than she is towards her child" (Sahih al Bukhari).

124. The Prophet is reported to have said, "God created Adam, then He stroked his right side and withdrew a white race as if they were seeds, and He stroked his left side and withdrew a black race as if they were coals. Then He said to those who were on his right side, 'Towards paradise and I don't care.' He said to those on the left side, 'Towards hell and I don't care.'"

through their infinitely inferior reflection in us. This is what I will now attempt to do. I will try to use our experience of the divine names through the breath of them that exists in us to obtain an imperfect glimpse into the divine will to create. While I venture the following, I do not claim that it is an explanation, but merely an analogy.

Though God is the Creator, human beings are also creators by virtue of His breathing into them of His spirit (15:29). This inherent creativity is another characteristic that distinguishes humankind from other creatures. Often we create out of necessity, as when a carpenter builds homes to earn a livelihood, but we also frequently create without responding to any discernible need other than a powerful inner urge. I do not feel that all or even most creativity is need-based. I believe that it is an integral part of human nature, a fundamental human attribute like intelligence or existence.

When I was in grade school, mathematics was for me a major creative outlet. I used to invent problems and produce conjectures, theorems and proofs, before I learned of them later in high school. I would study my older brothers' math texts and work out exercises in them. My family could not understand what they saw as my obsession with the subject, and I kept it hidden from many of my friends. I worked on mathematics back then for no other purpose than the pure pleasure of it.

Throughout life our creativity takes on many forms, sometimes maturing as we do. Mathematics has remained for me a major area of creativity, but teaching and writing have also become important outlets. Of course, all of these are now connected with my career, but I feel that my love of them goes beyond practical concerns.

When I reached the age of thirty, I began to feel a strong desire to participate in the creation of something that would engage all of me. Perhaps it had been developing in me for some time. I wanted to take part in bringing into being one who would reflect me and experience all I had to give—one who would be a part of me and I a part of her. Ragia, my wife, had come to the same desire. And so, by the grace of God, our first daughter was born, and I loved her with all my heart from the moment I first laid eyes on her, as I did her two sisters that came after her. In loving and parenting my three daughters, Jameelah, Sarah, and Fattin, I have been engaged in the greatest creative venture, unlike any I had known before. Although I play a key role in their growth—and they unintentionally in mine—unlike with my other creations, I do not decide what they become, which for me makes it all the more beautiful. Nevertheless, strictly speaking, I did not need to have children—my existence did not depend on it—but in having them I was responding to an irrepressible inner will.

Question 10 (from an engineer and Muslim immigrant who has been living in America for many years and who is among several Muslim immigrants who expressed to me misgivings about Islam. Since 9-11, there has been a sharp increase in attacks on the Prophet's moral character; such attacks usually involve resurrecting somewhat old orientalist critiques and may be the reason I have gotten so many questions recently on the Prophet's marriages.):

I was born in Syria and immigrated to the US when I was twenty-two. As a young man I was a fanatical Muslim, but now, at fifty-eight, I have become more of an agnostic. There are some passages in the Qur'an that make it impossible for me to believe it a divine Revelation. Chief among them is the beginning of Surah al Tahreem, which settles a petty argument between the Prophet and his wives (66: 1-7), and the section of Surah al Ahzaab, which allows the Prophet to marry his adopted son's wife (33:37). Excuse me for saying this, but why would God discuss such trivialities in His last Revelation, and doesn't it seem a little too convenient that He rushes to Muhammad's aid in these minor, domestic squabbles?

These two passages are among the most frequent targets of classical orientalist criticism of the Qur'an, where reactions like the above are common. Many contemporary Muslim scholars have replied to this critique. In addition to briefly reviewing this response, I will share a few of my own impressions. The first part of the question cites the first seven verses of *Surah al Tahreem.*

1. O Prophet! Why do you forbid that which God has permitted you seeking to conciliate your wives, but God is Forgiving, Merciful.

2. God has already enjoined upon you the expiation of your oaths, for God is your Lord Supreme, and He is the Knowing, the Wise.

3. When the Prophet told something in confidence to one of his wives and when she afterward divulged it and God apprised him thereof, he made known part thereof and passed over part. And when he had told it to her, she said: "Who has told you this?" He said: "The Knower, the Aware has told me."

4. If you both turn to God in repentance, then the hearts of both of you are so inclined, but if you support one another against him, then surely God is his protector, and Gabriel and the righteous believers, and after that the angels are his helpers.

5. Were he to divorce you, God might well give him in your stead wives better than you, women who surrender themselves unto God, believing, pious, penitent, inclined to fasting, previously married and virgins.[125]

6. O you who believe. Save yourselves and your families from a fire whose fuel is men and stones; over it are angels, stern and strong. They do not disobey God in that which He commands them, but do as they are commanded.

---

125. One of the Prophet's wives (Aishah) was a virgin when they married, one (Zaynab bint Jahsh) was a divorcee, and the others were all widows. Muslim commentators point out that the purely hypothetical form of this statement and the fact that the Prophet did not divorce any of his wives indicate that they indeed possessed these virtues although they too were not immune to occasional shortcomings.

7. O you rejecters [of the truth], make no excuses this day. You are only recompensed for what you did.

As Muhammad Asad observes, "There are several essentially conflicting—and therefore in there aggregate, not very trustworthy—reports to the exact reason(s) why, at some time during the Medina period, the Prophet declared an oath that for one month he would have no marital relations with any of his wives."[126] Many commentators feel that the first and third verses refer to separate incidents, but there is nothing internal to the *surah* to suggest it. On the contrary, a natural reading, unbiased by traditional exegetics, would lead one to believe that the first three verses, together with the fourth and fifth, speak to the same incident. From this perspective we may sketch the following outline.

The Prophet told one of his wives—identified in the tradition literature as Hafsah, the daughter of 'Umar—something in confidence, which she in turn shared with another of his spouses—whom the same literature identifies as Aishah, the daughter of Abu Bakr. There is no trustworthy report on the information divulged or on how the two wives used it, but the passage indicates that they knowingly betrayed the Prophet's confidence. A short time thereafter the Prophet forswore relations with his wives for one month.

The ancient biographers of the Prophet put forth various explanations of why he separated from *all* of his spouses when the Qur'an only implicates two of them. Most relate that infighting among his wives had reached a peak at this time, prompting the Prophet to remove himself from their bickering. The wording of the first verse would be consistent with this interpretation, as it states that the Prophet imposed this separation to conciliate his wives.

The tenor of the passage and the Prophet's response suggest that this betrayal of trust may have had potentially serious consequences, but as Asad notes:

---

126. Muhammad Asad, *The Message of the Qur'an*, Dar Al-Andalus, Gibraltar, 1980, p. 875, footnote 1.

The purport of the above Qur'anic allusion to this incident is not biographical but, rather, intended to bring out a moral lesson applicable to all human situations: namely, the inadmissibility of regarding as forbidden (*haram*) anything that God has made lawful (*halal*), even if such an attitude happens to be motivated by the desire to please other persons. Apart from this, it serves to illustrate the fact—repeatedly stressed in the Qur'an—that the Prophet was but a human being, and therefore liable to commit an occasional mistake.[127]

The *surah* also uses this incident to introduce its central theme: that each of us is ultimately and solely responsible for our fate in the hereafter, and that even the most intimate relationship with a truly righteous person—even with a prophet—will avail us nothing if we destroy ourselves. Hence the *surah* ends with examples of former prophets' wives (the wife of Noah and the wife of Lot) whose relationships with their husbands could not save them, and conversely, with the example of Assiyah (the wife of Pharaoh) who is a model of God-consciousness though her husband is the epitome of evil. The final example is of Mary, mother of Jesus, who is portrayed as one of God's most honored servants and a single mother.

The above question rightly points out that misunderstandings like that which occurred between the Prophet and his wives, and the errors in judgment that were committed, are commonplace and excusable, but this is precisely what makes this example so relevant. The Qur'an contains many stark illustrations of unbelievers and others who ban what God has permitted and who claim salvation by association, but this *surah* shows that even the most righteous must be on guard against these errors; that we must be ever alert not to prohibit in God's name what He has not disallowed, or to claim for ourselves divine favor due to membership in some group.

At first glance it may seem that the timing of this Revelation is too convenient, lending support to the notion that Muhammad produced the Qur'an to serve his personal needs, but deeper reflection argues

127. Ibid. p.875, footnote 1

against this. First, the passage starts by criticizing the Prophet, if he were inclined to fabricate self-serving Revelations, then why begin with a divine reproof of himself?[128] If he deleted verse one and began instead with verse two, he still could have settled his family problems. Second, most people—particularly the Arabs—are averse to making their domestic conflicts public. Even though airing one's dirty laundry has become somewhat acceptable in the United State, thanks in part to daytime television talk shows, this is a very recent phenomenon, one that has not at all caught on in the Arab or Muslim world. It would be very uncharacteristic of an Arab leader—especially one of the Prophet's renowned reserve—to broadcast his personal troubles. Indeed, the biographers report that the Prophet would not discuss the matter with even his most intimate companions, Abu Bakr and 'Umar, though they were the fathers of the two wives mentioned above. Finally, it should be noted that the Revelation of this *surah* could not be characterized as expedient, since the historical sources agree that it did not come until the Prophet's month long isolation from his spouses was completed. If the Prophet were to invent revelations, he could have solved this problem much earlier with a suitable forgery, allowing him to resume relations with some or all of his wives.

The above question also mentions verse 33:37 of *Surah al Ahzab*, whose interpretation has been a major point of conflict between orientalist and Muslim scholars since the early twentieth century. All commentators agree that the verse refers to the troubled marriage of Zayd (the Prophet's freedman and adopted son) with Zaynab (the Prophet's first cousin and Qurayshi noblewoman). The verse reads:

> And when you said to him to whom God had shown favor and to whom you had shown favor: "Keep your wife to yourself and remain conscious of God." You hid within yourself what God would bring to light, and you feared [the response of] the people, and God has greater right that you should fear Him. So when Zayd dissolved her marriage-tie, We gave her

---

128. It should be noted that a large fraction of the verses that address the Prophet specifically, either correct him or expose his insecurities.

to you as a wife, so that no blame should attach to the believers about the wives of their adopted sons, when they have dissolved the marriage-tie. And God's will was done. (33:37)

Most orientalists see this passage as proof that the Prophet would resort to any means to satisfy his sensual passions. The following account that appears in the *Tabaqat* of Ibn Saad is cited for support.

The Prophet, looking in vain for Zayd in his home, chanced to see Zaynab in light disarray and went away muttering something to the effect, "Praised be to God who transforms the hearts!" Zaynab reported the incident to Zayd, who went to the Prophet and offered to divorce his wife should the Prophet wish to marry her. The Prophet, however, sent him away telling him, "Keep your wife and remain conscious of God." Nevertheless, Zayd ceased to have intercourse with Zaynab and even lived apart from her for a while. In the end, despite the Prophet's repeated advice to persevere, Zayd divorced Zaynab. Shortly afterwards the Prophet married her.

From this and the above verse, orientalists infer that the Prophet's sudden infatuation with Zaynab left his adopted son no choice but to divorce his wife so as to make her available to the Prophet, who then produced the Revelation to silence potential protests.

Needless to say, the Muslim response presents a very different version of the events. In the first place, doubt is cast on the story of the Prophet chancing upon Zaynab in a state of undress, since it does not appear in the more trustworthy sources. The ancient biographers of the Prophet are well known to have accepted many reports that did not meet the high standards of the more critical *hadith* scholars. In addition, the account conflicts with the bulk of historical data that relates to the divorce of Zayd and Zaynab. Muslim writers assert that the Prophet had arranged the marriage with the idea of shattering the ancient Arabian barrier against a slave or even a former slave marrying a "free-born" woman.[129] Tradition says that Zaynab and

---

129. I have found that in today's Arabian Gulf, where slavery existed only forty years ago, the stigma attached to marrying a former slave or descendent of a former slave persists.

her brother were at first against the marriage, as Zaynab had always desired to marry Muhammad, but in deference to the Prophet and with great reservation, Zaynab and her brother (acting as Zaynab's guardian) finally consented to it. Zayd was also not disposed to the union, for he was already happily married to another freed slave, Umm Ayman. As much as the Prophet wanted to use the marriage to break down class barriers, the betrothed were still conditioned by them. For Zayd, the marriage was a source of embarrassment and humiliation, and Zaynab made no secret of her dislike of Zayd. On several occasions the couple were about to divorce, but each time the Prophet persuaded them to persevere and not to separate, for "he was apprehensive of the talk that would arise if it became known that the marriage arranged by him had turned out to be unhappy."[130] Eventually, after several years of marital strife, Zayd divorced Zaynab, and shortly thereafter the Prophet married her. While the Qur'an indicates that the divine purpose of marrying Zaynab to the Prophet was to "show that—contrary to what the pagan Arabs believed— an adoptive relationship does not involve any of the marriage-restrictions which result from actual, biological parent-and-child relations,"[131] it also allowed the Prophet to "make amends for Zaynab's past unhappiness."[132]

---

130. M. M. Pickthall, *The Meaning of The Glorious Qur'an*, Amana Publications, pp. 396-397. Thus the statement: "You hid within yourself what God would bring to light, and you feared [the response of] the people, and God has greater right that you should fear Him."

131. Nor does it obtain the same legal implications. This assertion connects to the opening lines of the *surah* that discuss man-made social relationships.

132. Muhammad Asad, *The Message of the Qur'an*, Dar Al-Andalus, Gibraltar, 1980, p. 646, footnote 47. It derserves mention that Zaynab's marriage stock had decreased dramatically after the unsuccessful marriage. Before her marriage to Zayd, Zaynab was a virgin, in her twenties, of one of the noblest clans in Arabia, and said to be of unsurpassed beauty. When the marriage failed she was in her mid thirties— which was considered quite old in her day—the divorcee of a former slave, and no longer a virgin. By marrying the Prophet, she attained the marriage she had originally desired and her rank in the community was restored.

Both the orientalist explanation and the Muslim response depend on their selections of data and a certain amount of reading between the lines. The orientalist case hinges on a single report in the biographical literature that seems out of synch with many other reports from the same source. On the other hand, the Muslim writers cannot discount the biographical studies too strongly, because they employ the same material to build their defense. Even if the story of the Prophet stumbling upon Zaynab were true, it hardly proves the orientalist contention that the Prophet left Zayd with no option but to divorce Zaynab; on the contrary, both sides agree that he urged Zayd to do the opposite. The phrase that the Prophet is alleged to have murmured *to himself* is at best ambiguous and contains no obvious suggestion of a desire to wed Zaynab. As for the Muslim claim that the Prophet's purpose in sponsoring the marriage of Zaynab and Zaid was to eradicate class barriers, I could find no statement to this effect in the classical sources.

It is quite obvious that the two very different readings of 33:37 are conditioned in part by the commitments and biases of the contending sides. Although I cannot claim to be a detached observer, I do feel that the Muslim interpretation is more coherent. The idea that an inadvertent glance could have suddenly ignited in the Prophet an obsession for Zaynab does not gel with other data that orientalists accept. It is admitted that Zaynab was the daughter of the Prophet's real aunt and thus he was a close relation of hers; that he knew her since she was a child; that he had close contact with her and her family when she was a young women, long before the Qur'an mandated that women dress modestly[133]; that he had the opportunity to marry her when she was a virgin; and that she was famous for her radiant beauty. The idea that a momentary glimpse should cause the

---

133. In pre-Islamic times, the customary attire of the Arab tribal woman consisted of an ornamental head covering that hung down her back and showed her hair in front, a loosely warn tunic that was cut low in front leaving her breasts in view, and a skirt tied at the waist, together with various pieces of jewelry, such as rings, earrings, arm and ankle bracelets.

Prophet to become suddenly infatuated with the thirty-five year old Zaynab with whom he had close relations most of her life is contrary to human nature.

I am not arguing that the Prophet never found Zaynab attractive, for tradition states that everyone about him was in awe of her beauty; I am only asserting that it makes no sense that he just became aware of it on the day he searched unsuccessfully for Zayd. Yet the orientalist case depends on precisely this point, for if her beauty never impressed the Prophet, then their case collapses completely, but if, on the other hand, the Prophet had always appreciated her striking good looks, then their attempt to portray him as a voluptuary again falls apart, since he had passed up the opportunity to have Zaynab for himself and instead arranged her marriage to Zayd.

The Muslim contention that the Prophet married the couple with the idea of destroying class barriers is not farfetched, even though the biographical literature contains no record of his stating this. The Prophet was certainly cognizant of the Arabs' extreme class-consciousness, which persists to this day. Its influence was so strong that most Muslim jurists declared that it is *haram* (prohibited) for a Muslim woman to marry beneath her class, in spite of the many pronouncements in the Qur'an and *Hadith* literature insisting on the equality of all believers.[134] The historians also report that Zaynab's nobility and Zayd's lower social standing was a constant flashpoint between the couple. The marriage's radical break with deep-rooted tradition must have astonished the Arabs, and probably many of them—especially the Prophet's critics—forecasted the couple's break-up. The Prophet could not have been unmindful of the symbolic potential of this marriage; that it stood as one of the great signs of the new egalitarian order he was preaching. In all likelihood it was its failure that he tried to prevent and conceal when he told Zayd, "Keep your wife to yourself and remain conscious of God." But no matter how noble one's aims, individuals must not be impeded from exercising their God-

---

134. Muhammad Ali, *The Religion of Islam*, Lahore (1990), pp. 470-471.

given rights, and both Zayd and Zaynab at this point had clearly had enough. Hence the admonition, "You hid within yourself what God would bring to light, and you feared the people, and God has greater right that you should fear Him."

This verse shares several features with the first passage we examined. Both use everyday happenings in the Prophet's personal life to illustrate a number of principles, both demonstrate the Prophet's humanity, and both correct and admonish him. Referring to the latter, Aishah is reported to have said, "Had the Messenger of God been inclined to suppress anything of what was revealed to him, he surely would have suppressed this verse."[135] Finally, it should be noted that this Revelation, like 66:1-7, came after the principle problem to which it refers had run its course (Zayd had already divorced Zaynab), and thus could not accurately be described as having rushed to Muhammad's aid.

Question 11 (from an immigrant Muslim woman in her late twenties):

Up until recently, I did not know that the original qiblah for the believers was Jerusalem and then it was changed to be Mecca. After studying the Qur'an a little bit and discussing this issue with our Imam, I found out that this was really the case. This was disturbing to me. Why would God choose one qiblah first and then change it to be another?

One of the explanations I have heard is that the Prophet wanted the Jews to feel sort of "at home" and that if this new religion included some part of their own religion it would be easier for them to embrace it, and therefore Jerusalem was made the qiblah. However, when the Jews showed no interest in following the Prophet, the qiblah was changed to be Jerusalem.

This, once again, poses a question for me. Why would God or the Prophet make Jerusalem the qiblah just to please the Jews, and then out of anger (at least the explanation I have heard sounds like it is out of

135. This report appears in the collections of Bukhari and Muslim.

anger) change it to be Mecca? In your book "Struggling to Surrender"
you mention that it was to differentiate Islam from the other religions.
But, why was that not done from the start by making Mecca the qiblah?

The Qur'an announces the change in *qiblah* (direction of prayer) in *Surat al Baqarah*, verses 142-150, but its phrasing is vague and allusive and does not make it clear that the original *qiblah* of the Muslims in Medina, which tradition identifies as Jerusalem, was divinely revealed. The most relevant verses read:

> The foolish among the people will say: "What has turned them from the *qiblah* which they were on?" Say: To Allah belongs the East and the West; He guides whom he wishes to a straight path. And thus we have made you a middle nation that you may be witnesses to the people and that the Messenger may be a witness over you. (2:142)

> And we did not make the *qiblah* which you were on except that we might know him who follows the Messenger from him who turns on his heels. And it was indeed a grave matter except for those whom Allah guided. Nor was Allah going to make your faith fruitless. Truly Allah is compassionate, merciful to the people. (2:143)

> We have seen the turning of your face to heaven and now we shall make you turn toward a *qiblah* that pleases you. So turn your face toward the Sacred Mosque. And wherever you are turn your faces toward it. Truly those who have been given the Book know that it is the truth from their Lord. And Allah is not heedless of what they do. (2:144)

As is so often the case, there is much disagreement among exegetes on this passage. Among other things, commentators have differed as to when after the Prophet's arrival in Medina the change took place, the reason for the Prophet's facing Jerusalem in the first place,[136]

---

136. Different authorities give 9, 10, 13, 16 and 17 months as the length of time the Muslims prayed toward Jerusalem. Mahmoud M. Ayoub, *The Quran and Its Interpreters*, Suny Press, 1984, pp. 167-68.

whether or not the Jerusalem *qiblah* was divinely revealed, the reason why the Prophet preferred the *qiblah* of the Kabah, and what exactly was "a grave matter except for those whom Allah guided".

As for the reason why the Prophet prayed toward Jerusalem before the change in direction and on the question of whether or not this was by divine command, al Tabari relates on the authority of `Ikrimah and Hasan al Basri that the Prophet chose Jerusalem in the hope that he might win over the Jews of Medina.[137] Al Tabari also cites al Rabi` ibn Anas that the Prophet was originally given the choice of turning in prayer to whichever direction he wished and then chose Jerusalem to conciliate the People of the Book.[138] On the other hand, al Tabari quotes Ibn `Abbas's opinion that God commanded the Prophet to face Jerusalem and that the Jews of Medina were pleased with this.[139] Later Quran commentators elaborated further explanations.[140]

Commentators have also disagreed on the Prophet's preference for the Kabah. According to Al Tabari, some said, "He disliked the *qiblah* of Jerusalem because the Jews used to say, 'He follows our *qiblah*, yet he opposes us in our religion.'"[141] Others said, "He preferred the Kabah because it was the *qiblah* of his father Abraham."[142] Qurtubi relates from Ibn `Abbas that the Apostle of God said, "The House [Kabah] is the *qiblah* for the people [surrounding] the place of worship [*masjid*]; the masjid is the *qiblah* for the people of the *haram* [the entire place of pilgrimage] and the *haram* is the *qiblah* for the inhabitants of the earth of my community in the east and west."[143]

---

137. Ibid. p. 168

138. Ibid. p. 168 and 175

139. Ibid. pp. 168-169

140. Ibid. pp. 169-170. Also, John Burton, *The Sources of Islamic Law*, Edinburgh, 1990, chapter 8.

141. Ibid. p. 173

142. Ibid. p. 173
143. Ibid. p.174

The supposition that the Prophet changed the direction of prayer to the Kabah when the Jews showed no interest in following him is not to be found among Muslim commentators but was first formulated by Western orientalists during the colonialist era.

The question of why God did not choose an earlier time to establish Mecca as the *qiblah* is of course impossible to answer. We can speculate, but we cannot prove our hypotheses. For me, however, the most remarkable thing about the change was that it was not made later, rather than sooner. The Qur'an established Mecca as the spiritual compass of this monotheistic religion when it was still a center of idol worship, when the Prophet's followers were not more than a few hundred, when the Quraysh together with their confederates were the greatest political power in Arabia, and reason would dictate that there was no hope of the small ban of Muslims ever returning there. Yet the Qur'an speaks at this time of Muslims far and wide turning towards the Sacred Mosque in prayer (2:149-150). Today it makes sense that Mecca is the direction toward which Muslims pray, but what if the Kabah had remained in the hands of the unbelievers, which to an outside observer back then would have seemed almost certain? To me, this timing of the establishment of the Kabah as the *qiblah* is evidence in favor of the divine origins of the Qur'an.

The Qur'an states (2:124-141) that Islam is the restoration and culmination of the faith of Abraham, who together with his son, Ishmael, rebuilt the Kabah, rededicating it to the worship of one God. Thus the choice of the Sacred Mosque as Islam's *qiblah* reflects its roots in the faith of Abraham. Otherwise, the Prophet's pagan enemies could have argued that if Islam is the continuation of the faith of Abraham, why do Muslims not face his house of worship while in prayer? This seems to be the purport of the statement in the scripture that by turning the believers toward Mecca, God gave the Prophet's enemies "no argument against you" on this score. (2:150)

Chapter Two

A CALL FOR HELP

*M*ost white American converts to Islam are women, and the majority of them are fairly young—age forty and under—and married. Cynthia doesn't fit the norm. She is in her fifties, divorced, currently disabled, a part time university lecturer, with two children in their twenties, and a six-year-old daughter that lives with her at home. Her neighbors—who are also my tenants—speak highly of her kindness and honesty. I was going to depart for Cairo in a few days and was giving Cynthia the phone number of my rental manager while I was gone.

"Oh, I'm so afraid of flying!" she said. "I don't know how you can stand being in a plane so long!"

"I used to feel the same way," I told her. "I would get extremely nervous on planes, but I don't anymore."

"What's your secret?" she asked, using her cane to take a step closer.

"Believe it or not, I think that after becoming a Muslim and reading the Qur'an all these years, I gradually became more and more fatalistic about death. I just figure that if it's my time, then it's my time—which is very unlike me, because I've always been the type to deliberate and plan on every conceivable catastrophe."

"You know, I'm not even sure I am a Muslim," she said, shaking her head slightly. "I have a problem with the hadiths."

I was surprised by the sudden change of topic. "You're not the first American convert I've heard say that," I said trying to reassure her.

Cynthia then launched into an emotional plea, as if she had been waiting years to get it off her chest. "I became a Muslim because I loved the Muslim people and saw so much peace and goodness in them. When I read the Qur'an, I felt connected to it spiritually. I guess I wanted to be *a part of all that. I loved the culture of the Middle East and identified with the people and their causes. I still do. But my ex-husband smothered all the beauty I saw in Islam with the <u>hadiths</u>. He just smothered it! It seemed like he had a <u>hadith</u> for everything, for a thousand different nitpicky rules and regulations. It went against my grain and I couldn't believe in it anymore."*

"What do you think of *Hadith*?" American converts and young American Muslims often ask me. Questions expressing scepticism about the Sayings of the Prophet are put to me more these days than any other. So far I have never been asked in public, but always confidentially, mostly via email. These queries usually reflect disillusionment of young believers who have had difficulty reconciling certain extra-Qur'anic information about the Prophet with their own conceptions of truth or model human behavior—conceptions that developed in surroundings very different from those that saw the dissemination and compilation of the prophetic traditions. Seldom is this loss of confidence in the *Hadith* literature based on an earnest study of the compilations or the history of this science, but rather on chance exposure to a number of reports that were found troubling. The purveyor of the disturbing accounts is often an imam of the mosque, a close relative, or a Muslim friend that has agonized over the same data, but just as often it is an unbeliever, perhaps a Christian evangelist on the Internet, a professor of Middle-Eastern studies, or a former Muslim now a non-believer. The questions are typically introduced apologetically: "I am not a disbeliever, but..." The askers are not young or new Muslims seeking a way out of the religion but devout individuals who are battling a source of doubt.

My answer to the above question is almost always the same: I refer the askers to what I wrote in *Struggling to Surrender*.[1] It is not that my viewpoint on this subject has remained constant since then, but I am still in the process of investigation. Although I have devoted more time to exploring this subject than almost any other through the last twenty plus years, a coherent picture of the evolution of *Hadith*

---

1. *Struggling to Surrender*, pp. 69-118.

science has evaded me. This may in part explain why many readers have informed me that my position on *Hadith* in *Struggling to Surrender* is not clear.

Many young Muslims simply want to know whether or not the classification of *sahih* (literally *true* or *authentic*) guarantees a report's reliability, and if not, then how should they approach these and other prophetic traditions. These are important issues—as they were in the early Islamic centuries when they exercised so many distinguished Muslim thinkers—since the *Hadith* literature plays a central role in guiding Muslim thought and behavior.

The majority of young American Muslims that have reservations about the traditions of the Prophet are either in college or are college educated, and have easy access to the research of Western scholars in this area, but the verdict of the latter on the integrity of this classical Islamic science is generally negative. For those seeking a Muslim response to the criticism of Occidental scholars there is very little out there and it is hard to come by.

The Western *Hadith* scholars have some other key advantages in winning American Muslim youth over to their views. Since both are products of the same culture and educational system, young American Muslims can easily relate to the outlook, discourse and methodology of the Western researchers. Since most contemporary Muslim writers on *Hadith* are trained neither in modern methods of historical research nor in the classical Islamic sciences, the works of their Western counterparts seem, and usually are, better researched and more scientific. The pressure to reconcile their faith with the ethos of the society in which they grow up could also make the findings of Western scholars attractive to young American Muslims. For if the tradition literature is dismissed as unreliable, then for many this leaves the Qur'an as the sole textual source of religious guidance in Islam, which leaves greater room for interpretation, especially since the Qur'an contains relatively few and for the most part sketchy commandments.

I had hoped to keep away from writing on this topic again,

because I have not had the time nor have I acquired the fluency in Arabic needed to study much of the key source material in its original language. However, the volume of questions I have recently received on the trustworthiness of the Prophet's sayings leads me to believe that there is real need for dialogue in the Muslim community on this matter. With the hope of encouraging and contributing to this discourse, I have chosen to share with the reader some of my current impressions. Although it is not my aim, I realize that discussions on this matter can produce heated controversy, and this is something my faith community generally strives to avoid, but this, I believe, is a small price to pay to assist a generation that is fighting to preserve its faith in less than supportive surroundings. Certainly, open discussion on this topic will be of more benefit to young American Muslims than the covert and uninformed discussions that are currently taking place. Loss of confidence in this fundamental Islamic science already exists among America's Muslim youth and is growing; knowledge of its history and methodology is not. Therefore, this chapter should not be taken as an in-depth critique of this science but rather as a call for help. Its main purpose is really not to defend this literature nor to discredit it, but to highlight issues and questions that I feel may be important, and to encourage Muslim specialists in this area to share their expertise with the American Muslim population.

First Impressions

I had read of the importance of *Hadith* in Islam before my conversion, but I was a little taken back by how often Muslims cite them. Since in theory the Qur'an is their primary source of religious guidance and the Prophet's traditions their second, I had expected Muslims to quote from the Qur'an far more frequently than from the Prophet's sayings, but I have found the opposite to be true. I soon realized that this is not because Muslims hold greater reverence for the traditions of the Prophet than the Qur'an, but because the *Hadith* provide information they feel is absolutely essential to understand and implement the message of the Holy Scripture.

Most devout Muslims strive to follow the *Shariah* (Islamic Law), aspiring to please God and to attain felicity in the Hereafter, and the main source for the *Shariah* is the *Hadith* literature. The verses of the Qur'an that are of a legal character comprise only about three percent of the Scripture. Hence all of the Qur'an's commands and prohibitions could be listed on about ten pages of this book. Yet there are tens of thousands of *hadiths* preserved in various collections, the majority of which have legal implications. Since legal traditions greatly outnumber the Qur'an's legislative verses, it is not surprising that Muslims intent on submitting themselves to God would have recourse more often to the *Hadith* texts. Muslims also look to the Prophet's example for inspiration. The Qur'an contains some brief allusions to events that occurred during the Prophet's lifetime, but these are too few and too vague to fill out a biography. The *Hadith* material provides abundant detail on the Prophet and his mission.

Nonetheless, I was sceptical of what seemed to me like additional Scriptures collateral to the Qur'an. The experience of the Qur'an was for me so powerful that I became zealously protective of it, refusing to accept the sacredness or authority of any other writings unless they displayed the same divine genius, but my views on this gradually moderated. In the first place, every Muslim I met and every Muslim author I read accepted the essentiality of *Hadith* to Islam. As the saying goes, "A billion believers can't all be wrong." They also all made the same sound argument: Since the Qur'an requires us to do some things (e.g. the ritual requirements) without explaining exactly how to do them, a supplement is needed for clarification. Where better to look for such instruction than in the Prophet's example?[2]

---

2. Of course, no one learns how to perform the Islamic rituals by studying the *Hadith* literature; all Muslims are taught these directly by more experienced believers. In this way the religious rites of Islam have been passed on from generation to generation with some minor variation since the time of the Prophet. Most of this information is scattered among the *Hadith* collections, but since it is transferred to succeeding generations on a mass scale, Muslim scholars of the traditions can justifiably classify this information as *hadith mutawatir* (broadly authenticated *hadiths*).

I could only agree, but I still had reservations. My chief concern was with genuineness. How can we be certain that a given *hadith* is authentic? The most respected *Hadith* collections date from the third and fourth Islamic centuries. How accurate could these be when they were compiled so long after the fact? I was also bothered that some *hadiths* go well beyond elucidating obscure passages of the Qur'an, and some of them introduce ordinances[3] and concepts[4] not even alluded to in the Scripture. How can we be sure that they do not encumber us with needless regulations and doctrines?

Here again I found that answers to these questions, having been worked out long ago, are widely known and accepted. Practically every Muslim with whom I spoke about these issues offered the same argument for the need and integrity of this Islamic science. In defense of the authority of the *hadiths*, Muslim scholars referred to the many Qur'anic commands to obey God's Messenger. To argue the genuineness of the *sahih* traditions, they recalled the intense critical scrutiny to which the traditions were subjected in early Islamic times. We will consider these points below, beginning with traditionally cited evidence from the Qur'an for the requirement to adhere to the *hadiths* of the Prophet.

"Who Obeys the Messenger, Obeys God"[5]

Does the Qur'an enjoin the use of *hadith* as an additional source of religious guidance? I use the word "enjoin" rather than the

---

3. For example, the prohibition of gold jewelry and silk clothing to men, rules concerning owning and coming in contact with dogs, ordinances requiring ritual ablution after passing gas, to name a few.

4. Such as the concept of the *Dajjal* (Antichrist) or the notion that only Jesus and his mother, Mary, were born without the touch of Satan, the latter resembling Roman Catholic beliefs concerning original sin.

5. The complete verse reads, "Who obeys the Messenger, obeys God, and who turns away: We have not sent you as a warder over them" (4:80).

less forceful "authorize" because the latter implies permission, not obligation. If we are only permitted to use *Hadith*, we are also permitted to disregard it. Here we seek a mandate, not mere justification. Obviously we cannot appeal to the *Hadith* literature to argue the existence or non-existence of a divine mandate, since in the first case our argument would be circular and in the second self-contradictory. Any argument we make must rest solely on the Qur'an.

The Qur'an does not explicitly refer to either the *Sunnah*[6] or *Hadith* (accounts, reports) of the Prophet. It does mention the *sunnah* of God[7] as well as the *sunnah* of the ancients,[8] and it does employ the word *hadith* many times, but it never associates either word with the Prophet. A small group of Muslims, who believe the Qur'an should be the only basis for religious belief and action, use some of these references to argue against the use of *Hadith*. Rashad Khaleefah supports this view with the following quotations.[9]

> Do they see nothing in the kingdom of the heavens and the earth and all that God has created, that it may be that their term is near? In what *hadith* after this will they believe? (7:185)

> And there are, among men, those who purchase frivolous *hadiths*, to mislead from the path of God without knowledge and to make of it a mockery. For such there is a humiliating penalty. And when Our signs are recited to him he turns away in his pride as if he heard them not, as if there were deafness in his ears. So give him tidings of a painful doom. (31:6-7)

---

6. *Sunnah* (soo-na): the complete collection of the *sunnahs*, the habitual practices of the Prophet. The Arabic plural is *sunnan*, but *sunnahs* is an acceptable plural in English writing.

7. *Surahs* 4:26; 17:77; 33:38; 33:62; 35:43; 40:85; 48:23.

8. *Surahs* 3:137; 8:38; 15:13; 18:55; 35:43.

9. Rashad Khaleefah, *Qur'an: the Final Testament*, Islamic Productions, Tucson, 1989, pp. 664-665.

Such are the signs of God, which We rehearse to you in truth.
Then in what *hadith* will they believe after God and His signs?
(45:6)

And woe, that day, to the rejecters of truth! Then in what
hadith, after this, will they believe? (77:50)

It is doubtful that *hadith* in these passages refers to the narratives
relating the deeds and utterances of the Prophet. In the first place it
came to have this restricted meaning in Islamic scholarship well after
his lifetime. Secondly, it is inconceivable that while the Prophet was
alive his enemies preferred his *hadiths* to the Qur'an or were promoting them in an effort to undermine his mission. Instead *hadith* must
carry here one of its more common connotations, such as, *speech,
chitchat, conversation, prattle, gossip, tales, report or account.* Verse 31:6
admonishes those who attempt to ridicule Islam by manufacturing
baseless propaganda against it. In 31:7 they are characterized as
persons who arrogantly close their minds to the message of the
Qur'an. The remaining three verses say that such people are doomed
by their obstinate denial, for if they harden their hearts to God's
Revelations, then "in what statement will they believe?" Though the
meaning of *hadith* in these passages seems general, one can justifiably
draw from them a caution against founding our religious beliefs and
behavior on questionable data, especially when it conflicts with the
Qur'an.

Although the Qur'an contains no explicit orders to record and
adhere to the Prophet's *hadiths* or *sunnahs*, it is possible that it requires
the same in other words. As stated above, we should not expect
the Qur'an to adhere to the jargon of the later developing Islamic
sciences. When the Prophet's contemporaries spoke of his statements
or acts, they must have done so informally, not following an established nomenclature. Therefore we should be looking for statements
in the Qur'an that would require the Prophet's disciples to observe
and follow his example and that would also indicate to later generations of Muslims that they should do the same.

There are numerous statements in the Qur'an commanding obedience to the Prophet,[10] which in his lifetime were undoubtedly taken as assertions of his leadership over the believers. The survival and growth of the Muslim *ummah* (community) depended on his orders being strictly followed. Indeed, the discipline and solidarity of the believers was a decisive factor in their victories over invading armies much larger than their own. But what does the command to "Obey the Messenger" mean for Muslims of future times? How do they obey the Prophet when he is no longer here to direct them?

There appears to be only two ways of regarding the Qur'an's repeated exhortations to heed the Prophet; they are either directed exclusively to his contemporaries or they are not. The first alternative neatly solves the issue of how later Muslims are to respond to these pronouncements, for it asserts that they need not bother, as they only had meaning in the Prophet's lifetime. From this perspective, his death in effect cancelled them. This interpretation, however, raises the spectre of deciding which other commands of the Scripture are no longer applicable.

Given their renowned reverence for their Scripture, one would think that Muslims would be averse to the notion that parts of it are no longer relevant, since they regard it as a divine message for all humanity.[11] Though they might feel the need to accommodate some of the Qur'an's legislation to changed circumstances, it would seem unlikely that they would advocate the complete annulment of a divine proclamation. Yet the Theory of Abrogation (*Naskh*, in Arabic), which holds that some passages of the Qur'an have been superseded by others, or sometimes even by certain *hadiths*, has played a pivotal role

---

10. *Surahs* 3:32; 3:132; 4:13; 4:59; 4:69; 4:80; 5:95; 8:1; 8:20; 8:46; 9:71; 24:52; 24:54; 33:31; 33:33; 33:71; 47:33; 48:17; 49:14; 58:13; 64:12.

11. *Surahs* 39:41; 81:26-29.

in Islamic jurisprudence.[12] The theory became widely accepted, although its proponents were unable to agree on exactly which verses were invalidated, for in almost all cases where one writer upheld an abrogation, there were other scholars who denied the alleged abrogation.[13] Some Muslim scholars insisted that the rescinded commands of the Qur'an number in the hundreds; others listed as few as four. Despite the lack of agreement on which verses are no longer operative, no known exponent of the theory included the commands to obey the Prophet in his list of abrogated statements. The theory holds that only divine revelation[14] or perhaps other forms of divine intervention[15] could rescind divine revelation.

---

12. For a very thorough critique of the Theory of *Naskh* see, Richard Burton, *The Sources of Islamic Law, Islamic Theory of Abrogation*, Edinburgh, 1990. For Muslim writers opposed to the theory see, Muhammad Ali, *The Religion of Islam*, Lahore (1990) pp. 28-34; Yusuf Ali, *The Meaning of the Holy Quran*, Amana Publications, Beltseville (1996), note 6086, p. 1637, Muhammad Asad, *The Message of the Quran*, pp. 22-23, note 87 and p. 736, note 35; Jeffrey Lang, *Even Angels Ask*, Amana Publications, Beltseville (1996), pp. 124-126.

13. Muhamad Ali writes in *The Religion of Islam*, Lahore (1990), p. 30, "In most cases where a report is traceable to one Companion [of the Prophet] who held a certain verse to have been abrogated, there is another report traceable to another Companion to the effect that the verse was not abrogated."

14. Some theorized that Muhammad's *Sunnah*, his model behavior as recorded in the *Hadith* collections, was also divinely revealed, the essential difference between the Qur'an and the *Sunnah* being that the first is to be recited in the ritual prayer.

15. It was widely believed that parts of the Qur'an were nullified by divine intervention, where God removed some sections of it from the original text. It was claimed that God caused the Prophet and his followers to forget certain revelations and that other sections of the Qur'an were destroyed by seemingly natural but in reality miraculous occurrences. For example, an

(contd. on page 177)

Therefore, the claim that the Qur'an's demands for obedience to the Prophet have no relevance after his demise proposes, from the standpoint of Islamic thought, the novel idea that time can revoke God's Word. This I have been reluctant to accept, but not because I am committed to traditional Muslim thought. Although in my early readings of the Scripture I found some passages that I could not relate to, on subsequent readings I was able to draw meaning from them that I had not obtained previously. Each reading of the Qur'an was an eye opening, fresh communication. Perhaps this is partly because the Qur'an speaks to an ever-evolving individual, so that one may recognize in a passage a relevancy to his or her existence that was not previously there. Yet even from my first reading it was apparent to me that the method of the Qur'an is to convey a universal message through a particular people's experience of divine communication, that it speaks directly to the immediate needs and concerns of its initial hearers, yet uses the same words to send a dual message to people far removed from them. It would go against my experience of the Scripture to assign some of its verses to temporal oblivion. I felt, and still feel, that every passage of the Qur'an contains within it timeless wisdom, only we sometimes have to read between the lines to discern it.

Virtually all of today's Muslims insist that the correct response to "Obey the Messenger" is to follow Muhammad's *Sunnah*, his exemplary behavior as recorded in the *Hadith* collections. They cite a number of other verses to support their case, such as, "Whatever the Messenger gives you, accept it" (59:7), "You have in God's messenger a good example" (33:21), and the several declarations in the Qur'an

---

Footnote 15 (contd. from page 176)

animal is said to have devoured some pages of the Qur'an while the Prophet's family tended to him on his deathbed. For a discussion of the various modes of *naskh* (abrogation) see Richard Burton, *The Sources of Islamic Law, Islamic Theory of Abrogation*, Edinburgh, 1990.

that assert that the Prophet has been sent to teach the Book and the Wisdom, maintaining that the Book refers to the Qur'an and the Wisdom refers to the Prophet's *Sunnah*.[16]

A curious thing about this argument is that it took so long for it to be made. The oldest available written record of any of these verses being used to establish a Qur'anic basis for the obligation to adhere to the Prophet's *Sunnah* is found in the *Risala* of Imam al Shafi'i (died 204 AH/819 CE), where he identified the Wisdom (*hikmah*) sent down upon the Prophet with the *Sunnah*.[17] Since al Shafi'i does not refer this reading to older authorities, which is his method when he knows of some, it appears to be a recent development.[18] Early *tafsir* works seem to corroborate this.

> Thus, where al Shafi'i insisted that the term *hikmah* in verses such as 2:129 means *sunnat rasul Allah*, al Tabari mentioned only Qatada (died 118 AH/736 CE) who identified *hikmah* with *as-sunnah* (but we will see below what he meant by that). Other early authorities in al Tabari's *tafsir* suggested that it conveyed "knowledge of and insight into religion" or similar expressions. Not even al Tabari himself, who died more than a century after al Shafi'i in 310 AH/922 CE mentioned here *sunnat an-nabi* as the interpretation of *hikmah*, though in another context he did without basing himself on earlier authorities, as was otherwise his custom. Other occurrences of *hikmah* presented the interpretations *as-sunnah* (Qatada) and *nubuwwa* (Isma'il bin 'Abd ar-Rahman as-Suddi (died 128 AH/745 CE) but Qatada implied that this *hikmah* was the

---

16. *Surahs* 2:151; 2:231; 3:164; 4:113; 62:2.

17. Muhammad ibn Idris al Shafi'i, *Al Risala*, translated by Majid Khadduri, John Hopkins Press (1961), p. 111. It should be noted that 33:21 and 59:7 are cited in support of certain *sunnahs* in *Hadith* collections that post date the *Risala*.

18. Al Shafa'i does argue against alternative interpretations of these verses and states that some contemporary Qur'anic scholars support his reading.

sunnah of `Isa bin Maryam. This permits the conclusion that Qatada did not bracket *hikmah* with *sunnat rasul Allah*, but the much vaguer term *as-sunnah*—anyone's exemplary behavior. In other early *tafsir* works currently available *hikmah*, if commented upon at all, was not identified with *sunnat an-nabi* either.[19]

None of this invalidates al Shafi`i's opinion, for he was a scholar of considerable genius and he may have had insight into truths his predecessors missed, but it does show that the interpretation he proffered is not entirely obvious. Be that as it may, Al-Shafi`i's argument had tremendous influence, as evidenced by its having won so many adherents. Before continuing our examination of al Shafa`i's reasoning, let us first consider the other two verses mentioned above, 59:7 and 33:21, neither of which is cited in his *Risala*.[20]

Of the verses appealed to above, 59:7 provides the least convincing proof that the Qur'an obliges Muslims to follow the *Sunnah*. In ancient times some scholars argued that this verse means, "What the Prophet gives you [in the Qur'an] accept it," while others claimed it means, "What the Prophet gives you [that is not in the Qur'an; i.e., in the *Sunnah*] accept it."[21] Thus it was used to argue both for and against the need to adhere to the *Sunnah*. Yet both interpretations ignore the context in which it occurs. *Surah 57:6-9* discusses the distribution of property acquired by the Muslim community after a conflict with "the People of the Book."[22] The Qur'an asserts that the

19. G. H. A. Juynboll, *Studies on the Origins and Uses of Islamic Hadith*, Variorum (1996), V, pp. 106-107.

20. They are, however, used in al Shafi`i's *Kitab al Umm* (Volume 7, Bulaq, p.251) to argue that a Muslim must adhere to the *Sunnah* of the Prophet.

21. John Burton, *The Sources of Islamic Law*, Edinburgh University Press, 1990, p. 6.

22. A term the Qur'an uses for Jews and Christians. Muslim commentators agree that in this case it refers to the Jewish tribe of Banu al Nadir.

acquisitions belong to "God and His Messenger" and to the families of deceased believers, the orphans, the needy, and the wayfarers, and that they must not "become a commodity passed between the rich among you." Hence the believers are then instructed, "What the Messenger gives you, accept it, and what he withholds from you, abstain from it." It would require a considerable exegetical stretch to infer from this an obligation to abide by the *Sunnah* as reported in the *Hadith* collections. When a precept is derived from a Qur'anic precedent, the derived ruling and the corresponding decree in the Scripture should address like concerns and provide like responses, otherwise there is no logical link between the precedent and proposed ordinance; we may just as well pick words scattered throughout the Scripture and permute them into a statement that supports any precept we choose. For example, we can with some legitimacy appeal to 59:7 to argue from analogy that government revenue should not be used to subsidize the capital ventures of the rich and powerful, but 59:7 does not provide persuasive evidence that the *Hadith* material is binding, because the dispensation of community property to the poor and the dissemination of data on the Prophet are not really analogous concerns.

The twenty-first verse of the *Surah Al Ahzab* exhorts the believers to follow the Prophet's example. It reads:

> Surely in the Messenger of God you have a good example for anyone whose hope is in God and the Last Day, and who remembers God much. (33:21)

It is hard to conceive of a more explicit endorsement of the Prophet as exemplar, but is this statement alluding to the general conduct of the Messenger or some specific behavior? We ask because there is a similar assertion concerning Abraham in the Qur'an.

> Surely you have a good example in Abraham and those with him, when they told their people: "Truly we are quit of you and of all you worship instead of God. We have rejected you

and there has arisen between us and you enmity and hatred until such a time as you come to believe in one God." (60:4)

Here Abraham is also described as, "a good example," but the passage cannot be referring to his everyday activities, since these *sunnahs* have not been compiled. Moreover, the verse specifically states in what respect he and his followers are to be emulated.

Verse 33:21 might present a similar case. It occurs in a lengthy passage that describes the critical days and weeks of the War of the Trench (33:9-27), when a large confederation of tribes laid siege to Medina. Verse 33:11 depicts the atmosphere of crisis that gripped the city, when "there and then were the believers tried and shaken with a shock severe." Since the passage that comes immediately after 33:21 describes the courage and steadfastness of the believers during this critical period, it would seem that the "good example" to which the Qur'an alludes is that of the Prophet's comportment throughout the siege and not to his conduct in general.

There is, however, a subtle and perhaps significant difference between the statement concerning Prophet Muhammad's example and that concerning Prophet Abraham's. The latter is immediately and directly linked to a particular act on the part of Abraham and his disciples, but the passage that follows 33:21 only tells of the conduct of Muhammad's companions during the attack. For the believers who participated in the War of the Trench, the reference to the Messenger's example surely recalled for them what they personally witnessed of the Prophet's courage and resoluteness throughout the siege, but the Qur'an does not apprise us of that, although the *Hadith* literature does. Since the Qur'an does not describe—as it does in the case of Abraham—exactly what Muhammad did that is to be emulated, it might be inferred that 33:21 adverts to more than just the Prophet's example during the battle. Said differently, if the Qur'an did inform us of the Prophet's behavior during the siege, we would be inclined to conclude that 33:21 refers to exactly that, but since it intentionally omits such information, it dissuades us from interpreting this assertion only in this restricted sense. At the very least, we cannot rule out the traditional interpretation. This may not be the kind of solid evidence we seek of the requirement to follow the *Hadith*, but we still need to consider one of al Shafi'i's strongest points.

> And also We have sent among you, of yourselves, a Messenger, to recite Our signs to you and cause you to grow, and to teach you the Book and the Wisdom, and to teach you what you did not know. (2:151)

> Truly God was gracious to the believers when He raised up among them a Messenger from themselves, to recite to them His signs and causes them to grow, and to teach them the Book and the Wisdom, though before they were in manifest error. (3:164)

> God has sent down to you the Book and the Wisdom and taught you what you did not know. And great is the grace of God to you. (4:113)

> It is He who has sent amongst the unlettered people a Messenger from among them to recite His signs to them and cause them to grow, and to teach them the Book and the Wisdom, though before that they were in manifest error. (62:2)

Al Shafi'i's equation of the Book with the Qur'an seems natural enough, since this is the only Book revealed to the Prophet, but if we accept this identification, then the equation of the Wisdom with the Prophet's *Sunnah* seems necessary. Since the Wisdom is something the Prophet was charged to teach apart from and in conjunction with the Book, it follows that the Prophet left, in addition to the Qur'an, teachings to which the believers are required to pay heed. Since one teaches by word and by example, and since the Prophet's *Sunnah* consists of his sayings and doings as witnessed by his contemporaries, it stands to reason that Muslims are obliged to refer to his *Sunnah* for guidance. There may still be key issues to consider—such as the authenticity of the *Hadith* records and the contexts of the Prophet's actions—but from what we have just considered it seems fairly apparent that the Qur'an obligates Muslims to consult the Prophet's *Sunnah* and hence the *Hadith* records in addition to their sacred Scripture.

Nevertheless, thoroughness requires that we study this proof more carefully. Since it hinges on the identification of the Book in these statements with the Qur'an, we should first examine the other references to the Book in the sacred text to check for consistency. From the over one hundred and fifty references to the Book (*al Kitab*) in the Qur'an, we find that it can have varied connotations. Often it denotes the Qur'an, as in the following examples.

> That is the Book wherein no doubt is the guidance for the God-conscious. Who believe in the unseen, and establish prayer, and spend of that We have bestowed on them, and who believe in what was revealed before you, and are certain of the Hereafter. (2:2-4)

> He it is Who has revealed to you the Book wherein are clear revelations. They are the mother of the Book, and others are allegorical. But those in whose hearts are disease pursue that which is allegorical, seeking discord, and seeking its final meaning, but none save God knows its final meaning. (3:7)

> Already He has sent down upon you in the Book that when you hear the revelations of God held in defiance and ridicule, you are not to sit with them unless they turn to a different theme. (4:140)

> We sent down to you the Book with the truth, confirming the Book that was before it. (5:51)

> These are the signs of the Book and of a manifest Qur'an. (15:1)

These are the signs of the Qur'an and a manifest Book, a guidance and good tidings to the believers. (27:1)

A sending down from the Merciful, the Compassionate, a Book whose signs have been distinguished as an Arabic Qur'an for a people having knowledge. (41:1-3)

However, the Book does not always represent the Qur'an. Sometimes it describes Revelation sent to other Prophets.

And when We gave to Moses the Book and the Discrimination (*al furqan*), that perhaps you might be guided. (2:53)

The people were one nation; then God sent forth the Prophets, good tidings to bear and warning, and He sent down with them the Book with the truth, that He might decide between the people concerning their differences. (2:213)

And We have bestowed on the house of Abraham the Book and the Wisdom, and We gave them a mighty kingdom. (4:54)

O John! Hold fast to the Book. And We gave him the Wisdom even as a child. (19:12)

He [Jesus] spoke: Truly I am a servant of God. He has given me the Book and has made me a prophet. (19:30)

And We gave him Isaac and Jacob, and We appointed prophethood and the Book to be among his [Abraham's] seed. (29:27)

Sometimes the meaning of the Book is hard to locate, especially when it relates to God and His activity. At times it appears to be a symbol of God's infinite knowledge, or of His ordering of creation, or of His divine laws or decrees.

There is not an animal on the earth, nor a being that flies on its wings, but they are nations like unto you. We have neglected nothing in the Book. Then unto their Lord they will be gathered. (6:38)

With Him are the keys of the unseen, the treasures that none knows but He. He knows whatever there is on earth or in the sea. Not a leaf does fall but with His knowledge. There is not a grain in the darkness of the earth, nor anything fresh or dry, but it is in a manifest Book. (6:59)

There is not a population but We shall destroy it before the Day of Judgment or punish it with a dreadful penalty. That is inscribed in the Book. (17:58)

He [Pharaoh] said: What then is the state of the generations of old. He [Moses] said: The knowledge thereof is with my Lord in a Book. My Lord neither errs nor forgets. (20:52)

No disaster befalls in the earth and yourselves but it is in a Book before We bring it into being. Truly that is easy for God. (57:22)

Frequently the Qur'an refers to the Book in ways that suggest something much greater than a single Scripture or even the totality of God's Revelation. This is especially the case in the passages that refer to "the Book of God," or in those that speak of past communities receiving "a portion of the Book," or that refer to the Revelation received by the Prophet as being "from the Book."

Do not make a mockery of God's signs and remember God's blessing upon you, and that which he has revealed to you from the Book and the Wisdom, admonishing you thereby. (2:231)

Have you not turned your vision to those who have been given a portion of the Book? They are invited to the Book of God to settle their dispute, but a party of them turns back and declines. (3:23)

Do you not see those who have been given a portion of the Book, how they purchase error, and seek to make you err from the right way? (4:44)

Do you not see those who have been given a portion of the Book, how they believe in idols and false deities? (4:51)

We did reveal the Torah, wherein is guidance and light, by which the prophets who surrendered judged the Jews, and the rabbis and priests by such of God's Book as they were bidden to observe. (5:44)

And those who have faith subsequently, and adopt exile, and struggle in your company—they are of you. But kindred by blood have prior rights against each other in the Book of God. Truly God is well acquainted with all things. (8:75)

The number of months, with God, is twelve in the Book of God, the day He created the heavens and the earth. (9:36)

Every term has a Book. God blots out and He establishes what He wishes, and with Him is the Mother of the Book. (13:39)

And recite what has been revealed to you from the Book of your Lord. There is none that can change His words, and you will find no refuge beside Him. (18:27)

As for that which We inspire in you from the Book, it is the truth confirming that which was before it. (35:31)

The impression given is that all Revelation is but a fraction of the infinite Truth that is with God, and that the Book at times signifies this great totality of Truth. The Book of God, the fount of all Revelation, being limitless, can never be circumscribed by any text in human language, and thus all of God's Revelations to His apostles are but portions of God's Book. Perhaps this is another significance of the assertion:

And if all the trees in the earth were pens, and the sea, with seven more seas to support it, [were ink], the words of God could not be exhausted. God is Mighty, Wise. (31:27)

A. Yusuf Ali, commenting on verse 3:23 (cited above) offers a similar but not identical interpretation. He opines, "I conceive that God's revelation as a whole throughout the ages is 'the Book.' The Law of Moses and the Gospel of Jesus were portions of the Book. The Qur'an completes the revelation and is par excellence the Book of God."[23]

From the above survey it may seem that al Shafi'i's equation of the Book with the Qur'an in those verses that speak of the Prophet having been given the Book and the Wisdom is unnecessary, because the Book frequently alludes to something more inclusive than what was revealed to the Prophet, and hence the same may be true of his identification of the Wisdom with the *Sunnah*. Adding to the ambiguity are the many statements in the Qur'an that show that prophets other than Muhammad were also given the Book and the Wisdom.

[Abraham and Ishmael prayed] Our Lord! Send amongst them [our descendents] a messenger of their own, who shall rehearse the signs to them and teach them the Book and the Wisdom and cause them to grow. (2:129)[24]

And God will teach him [Jesus] the Book and the Wisdom, and the Torah and the Injeel (3:48).

It is not that a human being [Jesus] to whom is given the Book and the Wisdom and the Prophethood that he should afterwards have said to humanity: Be servants of me instead of God. (3:79)

Behold! God took the covenant of the Prophets, saying: I have

---

23. *The Holy Qur'an: Translation and Commentary*, by A. Yusuf Ali, Amana Publishers, Beltsville, 2001, p. 132, note 366.

24. The point is that Abraham and Ishmael were familiar with the Book and the Wisdom.

given you of a Book and Wisdom, then there shall come to you a Messenger confirming what is with you—you shall believe in him and help him; do you agree? (3:81)

But We had already given the house of Abraham the Book and the Wisdom. (4:54)

Behold! I taught you [Jesus] the Book and the Wisdom, the Torah and the Injeel. (5:110)

O John! Hold fast to the Book. And we gave him the Wisdom even as a child. (19:12)

Yet while the Book and the Wisdom with which the prophets were inspired signifies something more encompassing than just the Qur'an and *Sunnah* of Muhammad, this does not imply that al Shafi`i must be wrong as far as the Prophet is concerned; that is, that the portion of God's Book sent down upon him is none other than the Qur'an. Much of course depends on how we interpret "the Book." Although the meaning of the term is sometimes elusive, it cannot be denied that the Qur'an frequently refers to itself explicitly as the Book revealed to the Prophet,[25] and never does it state that it also comprises the Wisdom with which he was inspired.[26] Since the Qur'an identifies itself as the Book the Prophet received, we would have to assume that this is the correct interpretation. It is also true that we commonly assume that conjunctions such as "the Book and the Wisdom" refer

---

25. *Surahs* 2:2-4; 3:7; 4:140; 5:51; 15:1; 27:1; 41:1-3.

26. In the *Hadith* debates that took place in India last century the command to the Prophet's wives to "bear in mind what is recited (*yutla*) in your houses of the revelations (*ayat*) of God and the Wisdom" (33:34) was cited as proof that the Book and the Wisdom must both be identical to the Qur'an, since only the Qur'an is recited Revelation. As Mawdudi pointed out the reference to recitation (*tilawa*) in this verse is certainly generic and not be confused with the later technical usage of the term. See Daniel W. Brown's *Rethinking Tradition in Modern Islamic Thought*, Cambridge, 1996, pp. 56-57.

to two different entities unless the context indicates otherwise. Hence the conclusions that the Book the Prophet received is the Qur'an and the Wisdom he received is other than the Qur'an are indeed tenable.

Since the Wisdom God sends down upon a prophet is always mentioned in conjunction with the Book revealed to him, the two are clearly related. As is so often the case much can be lost in translation; hence we may come a little closer to understanding what the Wisdom signifies by examining the Arabic term, *hikmah* (wisdom). It is associated with the verb *hakama*, which means *to pass judgment, express an opinion, pass sentence, decide, provide a legal decision, render a verdict, issue a ruling, to adjudicate, to have jurisdiction, to adjudge, to have judicial power,* or *to govern.* Thus the noun *hukm* means *judgment, decision, legal decision, verdict, sentence, condemnation, administration of justice, regulation, ordinance, judiciousness, wisdom, judgeship,* or *government.*[27] From this we see that *hikmah* is often closely associated with the occupations of governance and law. Hence the *hikmah* revealed to prophets most likely has to do with the instruction of their communities in accordance with the Book revealed to them; that is, the *hikmah* (the Wisdom) sent down upon a prophet relates to their implementation and elucidation of the corresponding Book. In Prophet Muhammad's case, the *hikmah* bestowed on him would relate to his implementation and elucidation of the Qur'an. As mentioned earlier, since the Prophet was charged to teach both the Qur'an and the *hikmah*, the latter could only be learned through his sayings and doings, or in Arabic, his *sunnan*, as observed by his followers.

We began this section in search of a Qur'anic mandate for adherence to the traditions of the Prophet. Such a case can be made, but some of the traditionally cited proofs from the Scripture are not all that convincing. The most credible argument from the Qur'an appears to belong to Imam al Shafi`i, which in outline is as follows: The Qur'an commands the believers to obey the Prophet; this implies

27. Edward Lane, *Arabic-English Lexicon*, Book 1, Part 2, pp. 616-617. Hanna E. Kassis, *A Concordance of the Qur'an*, University of California Press, 1983, pp. 521-526.

that they must follow his teachings; his teachings are contained in the Book and the Wisdom sent down to him; the Book he received is the Qur'an; the Wisdom he received is other than the Qur'an and is revealed through his life example. Our survey of the Qur'an's usage of the terms "the Book" and "the Wisdom" indicates that in general these refer to something more encompassing than the Qur'an and Muhammad's *Sunnah*, respectively; but in the Prophet's case these are justifiable interpretations. This may not be quite the unequivocal proof we set out for—since it depends on credible but yet unobvious exegesis—but it offers a coherent response to the Qur'an's repeated calls to obey the Messenger, that is also, as we note below, consistent with how the Companions must have responded to them.

Yet even if this interpretation is accepted, it is still not clear how much of the Prophet's *Sunnah* Muslims are obliged to follow. Since the Wisdom revealed to the Prophet is always mentioned in conjunction with the Book, it would appear that Muslims are required to abide by those *sunnahs* of the Prophet that relate to pronouncements in the Qur'an, but what of those of his teachings that are not connected to the sacred Scripture? The next section discusses these.

Exactly How Much *Sunnah*?

The Qur'an states, "We sent not a Messenger, but that he should be obeyed" (4:64), and it repeatedly demonstrates that all of God's prophets required obedience in His name.[28] Since the Qur'an contains relatively little legislation, the Prophet must have issued many directives in his twenty-three year mission—especially during its Medina phase—not covered by the Scripture, and his disciples surely understood that the order to "obey the Messenger" includes obedience to these as well. Therefore it would be entirely correct to assert that the Qur'an made conforming to the Prophet's *sunnahs* binding on the Companions. Whereas the Prophet's example was a primary source of guidance for the community when he was alive,

---

28. *Surahs* 3:50; 26:108; 26:110; 26:126; 26:131; 26:144; 26:150; 26:163; 26:179; 71:3.

Imam al Shafi`i maintained that this extended "to the *Hadith* materials accumulated during nearly two centuries separating him from Muhammad's time [that were recently] pronounced the authentic *Sunnah* of the Prophet."[29] Al Shafi`i realized the need for cogent support from the Qur'an for this formulation since there were many in his day who doubted the integrity of the ever increasing *Hadith* corpus and who would object to the circularity of an argument that depended primarily on *Hadith* reports. Although many of the verses that are typically cited do not provide convincing proof, al Shafi`i's deduction that the Wisdom (*hikmah*) bestowed upon the Prophet is to be sought in his *Sunnah* is undoubtedly justifiable. However, the scope of al Shafi`i's position was wider than this, for he maintained that the Wisdom is not just contained within the Prophet's *Sunnah*, but the two are essentially identical. The practical implications of this are that the entire prophetic *Sunnah* has authority, including that which is independent of the Qur'an. Aside from citing the Qur'an's commands to obey the Prophet, al Shafi`i provides no other Qur'anic evidence for this larger claim, and as we shall see it was a major point of contention in his day.

Al Shafi`i's *Risala* is not a purely academic work in which long accepted positions and arguments are reviewed; it is a polemical tract that attempts to demonstrate the rightness of a viewpoint against other prevailing viewpoints of the day. In the second Islamic century there were many who held reserved attitudes on *Hadith*. Many of the Khawarij were said to completely reject them based on their maxim: *la hukm illa li-llahi* (there is no judgment except for God's). The Mutazilah suspected the traditions for formal reasons, since they doubted the effectiveness of *hadith* criticism and since too many *hadiths* in their view contradicted either other *hadiths*, or reason, or, far worse, the Qur'an.[30] The *Risala* contends with these attitudes and also with orthodox legal scholars who were disposed to using *hadiths*

29. John Burton, *The Sources of Islamic Law*, Edinburgh University Press, 1990, p. 143.

30. Ibid, pp. 148-149.

but hesitant to accept any that dealt with matters not adumbrated in the Qur'an.[31] Al Shafi`i indicates that this issue was much debated by Muslim jurists.

> No scholar disputes that the *Sunnah* falls into three categories, and the scholars are unanimous on two of them.[32] They have just been mentioned. The third category is that of *sunnahs* on matters on which there is no text in the Qur'an. This third category is disputed.

> Some scholars argue that, having imposed the obligation of obedience to His Prophet, and knowing that He will direct him to what is pleasing to Him, God assigned Muhammad the prerogative to establish these *sunnahs* on matters unmentioned in the Book.

> Others have argued that the Prophet never laid down a *sunnah* on matters other than those mentioned in the Book of God, for example, the *sunnahs* which specified the number of daily ritual prayers, the manner and times of their performance, since the general imposition of prayers is in the Qur'an. The same applies to *sunnahs* on commercial matters, since God mentions in His book the disposal of property, sales, loans, usury and the like. In all such questions, whatever the Prophet declared lawful or unlawful, he was acting, as in the case of prayers, to provide *bayan* (explanation) on God's behalf.[33]

---

31. Ibid, pp. 22-23.

32. Al Shafi`i earlier describes these two categories as *sunnahs* where the Prophet follows the Qur'an exactly as it is revealed and *sunnahs* where he makes clear what God intended by statements in the Qur'an couched in general terms. Muhammad ibn Idris al Shafi`i, *Al Risala*, translated by Majid Khadduri, John Hopkins Press (1961), pp. 119-120.

33. Muhammad ibn Idris al Shafi`i, *Al Risala*, translated by Majid Khadduri, John Hopkins Press (1961), pp. 120-121; John Burton, *The Sources of Islamic Law*, Edinburgh University Press, 1990, pp. 141-142.

At the turn of the third Islamic century there existed a significant body of Muslim jurists disinclined to accept *hadith* reports that dealt with issues unmentioned in the Qur'an. Although al Shafi`i states that their reluctance was based on the supposition that the Prophet only introduced *sunnahs* on matters mentioned in the Book of God, this may be an oversimplification of their rationale. Since a large part of the *Risala* addresses concerns over the authentication of *hadiths*, we may infer that this was a contributing factor to their outlook. They may have felt that while necessity demands that they look to the Prophet's *Sunnah* for elucidation on matters on which the Qur'an is vague, they were at the same time wary of the introduction of unwarranted innovations into the religion through the medium of *Hadith*. Some may have also felt that if the Qur'an is silent on certain *sunnahs*, it is because these were not meant to be an essential and eternal part of the message of Islam; this would, after all, be a justifiable exegesis of the Scripture's assertion that it "explains all things" (16:89) and "leaves nothing out" (6:38). In any case, it is unlikely that their motives for shunning *hadiths* unconnected to the Qur'an were uniform.

The position taken by Al Shafi`i's opponents, to regard only those *hadiths* that relate to explicit pronouncements in the Qur'an, has had its modern day exponents. These ideas were circulating in India in the beginning of last century, although their proponents seldom acknowledged the ancient roots of their stance.[34] Today, this viewpoint seems to have very few if any advocates in the American and European Muslim communities. As stated previously, almost all Muslims have inherited the stance of the ancient *ahl al hadith* that obedience to the Prophet translates after his lifetime into adherence to the accepted *hadith* reports, including those that deal with issues not alluded to in the Qur'an. There are a handful of Muslim thinkers who are opposed to the use of *Hadith* as a source of religious guidance, echoing a stance

---

34. Daniel W. Brown, *Rethinking Tradition in Modern Islamic Thought*, Cambridge, 1996, pp. 47; Muhammad Tawfiq Sidqi, "al Islam huwa al-Quran wahdahu," *al-Manar* 9 (1906), pp. 515-524.

that heresiographers attributed to the dissident Khawarij of early Islam.[35] There has also been something of a reemergence of Mutazilah type skepticism toward the prophetic traditions, where reports believed to be in conflict with reason or the Qur'an are rejected.[36] But I know of no contemporary Muslim thinkers who promote the more conservative approach to *Hadith* with which the *Risala* contended, and which, judging from the intensity of al Shafi`i's effort, must have been widespread. This is all the more surprising since this alternative outlook is in keeping with the trend among some modern Muslims to limit the role of the *Hadith* literature in response to fears that unnecessary and burdensome beliefs and practices have been appended to the faith via the tradition literature. It also could be argued that certain features of the Qur'an lend support to this interpretation. It should be noted that when the Qur'an orders obedience to the Prophet it almost always conjoins this to the summons to be obedient to God. Hence the Qur'an repeatedly asserts, "Obey God and the Messenger," but only once, according to my count, do we find the isolated command, "Obey the Messenger":

> So establish prayer (*salat*) and pay charity (*zakat*), and obey
> the Messenger that you may receive mercy (24:56).

Even in this exceptional case, 24:56 appears in a passage that elaborates on the exhortations to obey God and His Messenger in verses 24:52 and 24:54. It should also be observed that the Qur'an's commandments to obey God and His Messenger invariably occur in passages that include other more specific divine directives.[37] Both

---

35. Daniel W. Brown, *Rethinking Tradition in Modern Islamic Thought*, Cambridge, 1996, pp. 38-42.

36. Ibid, pp. 32-37.

37. Thus 3:32 follows a passage (3:28-3:30) that sternly warns believers not to make alliances with unbelievers in preference to believers. *Surah* 3:132 follows a prohibition of usury (3:130-131). *Surah* 4:13 follows regulations on marriage and inheritance (4:1-12). *Surah* 4:59 follows a command to be just in business dealings (4:58). *Surah* 4:69 follows a passage that exhorts the reader to make self-sacrifices in God's cause (4:66-68). *Surah* 4:80 follows

(contd. on page 195)

of these observations are consonant with the interpretation that the obedience being emphasized is to God's commands in the Qur'an and to the Prophet's teachings regarding them.

This alternative approach to the *Hadith* literature has certain appealing features, but it does not appear to have a stronger Scriptural basis than Al Shafi`i's program. Any citations from the Qur'an that can be offered in support of it can easily be viewed as supporting al Shafi`i's interpretation. One of its main drawbacks is that it offers an abrupt shift in response to the Qur'an's calls for obedience to the Prophet: from the Companions' general adherence to his *Sunnah*[38] to the more restricted requirement to follow only those *sunnahs* with links to the Scripture. Al Shafi`i seems to offer a more natural transition. It would be expected that the Companions would

---

Footnote no. 37 (contd. from page 194)

calls to fight in God's cause (4:71-79). *Surah* 5:95 follows a series of regulations that include prohibitions of alcohol and gambling (5:90-94). *Surah* 8:1 begins with a declaration concerning spoils of war. *Surah* 8:20 follows a passage on warfare that includes an order to hold ranks when enemy forces approach (8:15-16). *Surah* 8:46 is part of a passage that contains war regulations (8:45-47). *Surah* 9:71 begins by recalling the obligations to establish justice, oppose evil, perform prayer and pay *zakat* (regular charity). *Surah* 24:52 and 24:54 appear in a long passage that urges the believers to leave their homes in God's cause (24:53), establish prayer and pay *zakat* (24:56), observe various rules of privacy and modesty (24:58-61), and prohibits absence without leave in wartime (24:62-63). *Surahs* 33:31 and 33:33 belong to a passage containing special regulations for the Prophet's wives (33:28-34). *Surah* 33:71 follows a long list of rules of conduct in domestic and social relations (33:53-70). *Surah* 47:33 precedes an exhortation not to be fainthearted in opposing those who bar others from the path of God (47:34-35). *Surah* 48:17 follows verses that order the believers not to lag behind when the army goes out to meet the enemy (48:15-16). *Surah* 49:14 follows a list of commands concerning behavior toward the Prophet, fighting between believers, defamation, and backbiting (49:1-13). *Surah* 58:13 follows a series of instructions on women's rights, secret counsels, and charitable gifts (58:1-13). *Surah* 64:12 precedes a passage that urges spending in God's cause (64:13-17).

38. See the first paragraph of this section.

continue to view the whole of the Prophet's *Sunnah* as precedential afte his demise. It would also be natural for the next few generations of Muslims to inherit the same attitude.

There are also several commandments in the Qur'an that can be used to argue indirectly that believers will and should emulate the Prophet's general behavior. I refer to those commands in *Surah al Ahzab* directed exclusively to the Prophet and his family, such as the verse that allows him to have more than four wives (33:50),[39] or that which forbids him from divorcing any of his spouses (33:52), or that which prevents the believers from marrying his wives after he dies (33:53). The Qur'an indicates that such directives aimed at only the Prophet's household are necessitated by their special roles and circumstances, for it states that the Prophet "is closer to the believers than their selves, and his wives are as their mothers"(33:6), and it tells his spouses that "you are not like any other women" (33:32). These Revelations regarding aspects of the Prophet's life that need not be followed would be unnecessary if it were the Qur'an's position that believers should disregard actions of his not mentioned in the Scripture; if this were the case, then the Prophet could have been given personal non-scriptural inspiration on these matters with no mention of them being made in the Qur'an. That these verses single out some details of the Prophet's life not requiring emulation may indicate that the rest of his doings should have precedential value. Admittedly, this is a somewhat frail argument, as it presumes the divine intention behind these Revelations, while they might serve other purposes.

In theory these two approaches to the tradition literature appear to be greatly at odds, but in reality there is not much difference between them, since there are relatively few Muslim practices that cannot be linked, at least tenuously, to the Qur'an. Perhaps of greater weight in our search for an appropriate response to "obey God and the Prophet" is the subject of the efficacy of classical *hadith* criticism.

---

39. Cf. Question 2 below.

Fact From Fiction
– An e-mail from an American Muslim:

I must admit that the more I learn about <u>hadith</u>, the less I believe in them. I feel more and more that when a hadith is not complimenting or when it is controversial we find all sorts of ways to explain why they are not authentic. For example, I have heard and read on numerous occasions that al Bukhari's <u>hadith</u> collection is very reliable and that he put out a great effort in verifying the authenticity of each <u>hadith</u>. Well, as I was looking at some of the <u>hadiths</u> in his collection, I came across the one that talked about how women were inferior to men in their intelligence and their righteousness and how the hellfire had mostly women in it. If I believe in the authenticity of this <u>hadith</u>, then I question the Prophet. If I do not believe in the authenticity of this <u>hadith</u>, then I question the other <u>hadiths</u>. Here is a man that supposedly exerted great effort in verifying <u>hadiths</u>. So, if he made a mistake in one, could he not have made a mistake in others?

I have been reading the <u>hadith</u> section in 'Struggling to Surrender', but I am not quite sure that I understand. It has been a pretty tough part of the book for me to grasp. I know that the Arabs really wanted to learn the Prophet's sayings and actions, but these were not written down in his lifetime or right after he died. My understanding is that these were passed on from generation to generation verbally, at least initially. In that case, it reminds me of the game, "telephone." I am sure that you know how distorted things get with just five people or ten people in the game.

I am not saying that every <u>hadith</u> must be wrong, but I must admit that I find it easier to believe in Islam without them. Then I can throw out the sayings about the three pagan deities, and the conflicting <u>hadiths</u> regarding Aisha and her age. I guess, by Muslim standards, I would not really qualify as a Muslim.

Hajjaj ibn Minhal told us: `Abdal `Aziz ibn al Majishun told us: Muhammad ibn al Munkadir told us, on the authority of Jabir ibn Abd Allah, who said: "The Prophet said: I saw myself [in a dream] enter Paradise, and lo, I met al Rumaysa, the wife of Abu Talhah. Then I heard the sound of footsteps and asked: Who is it?—[Someone] answered: It is Bilal.— Then I saw a palace, and by its side there was a girl; and I said: Whose is this? [Someone] answered: `Umar's. — And I wanted to enter and see it, but I remembered your jealousy [O `Umar]. Thereupon, `Umar said: I would sacrifice my father and mother for you, O Messenger of God! Could I be jealous of you? [41] — A *hadith* from Al Bukhari's *Sahih*

Every *hadith* has two parts: the *isnad* or sequence of authorities through whom it has been transmitted and the *matn* or text of the report. To most Muslims a *hadith* is an account of the Prophet, but as a technical literary form it appears ubiquitously in Islamic literature. In such diverse fields as history, biography, Qur'an commentary, theology, law, politics, literary criticism, and even linguistics, authors exhibit a pronounced predilection for supporting their views with brief narratives of older authorities which have come down to them through chains of informants.

From external appearances alone, one could judge that Islamic culture showed a reverence for authority. To name one's authority is "to prop up" one's assertions. The Arabic for "prop," *sanad*, gives the technical term for "propping up," *isnad*. The *isnad* is the list of names of those who one after the other transmitted the information until it reached him who currently reports it. The typical appearance of an *isnad* is: "A informed B who informed C who informed D who informed me."[42]

---

41. Muhammad Asad, *Sahih Al-Bukhari: The Early Years*, Dar al Andalus (1981), p. 39.

42. John Burton, *An Introduction to the Hadith*, Edinburgh University Press (1994), p. 29.

The *isnad* as a means to vouch for a *hadith*'s genuineness developed in response to the massive fabrication of information on the Prophet that began not long after he died. Countless prophetic traditions were manufactured and doctored for political, factional, pious, prejudicial, personal, and even seditious purposes.[43] The *fitnah* (civil strife) that began with the death of the third caliph, `Uthman, and intensified during the reign of `Ali is usually cited by Muslim scholars as the beginning of large-scale *hadith* fabrication. This period witnessed the production of a large number of *hadiths* favoring `Ali and his descendents.[44] Forgery increased under the Umayyads, who saw *Hadith* as a way to bolster their rule and who actively circulated traditions against `Ali and in support of Mu`awiya. The Abbasids followed suit when they came to power, circulating sayings of the Prophet that prophesied the reign of each successive ruler.[45]

Religious conflicts contributed to *hadith* forgery. During the last days of the Umayyad Caliphate and throughout the `Abbasid period, a number of theological controversies arose, which lead to the creation of various factions such as the Qadariyya, the Jabariyyah, the Mutazilah, the Murjia, the Mujassima, and the Mu'atila.[46] Sayings of

---

43. Suhaib H. Abdul Ghafar, *Criticism of Hadith Among Muslims with Reference to Sunan Ibn Majah* (IFTA: 1984), pp. 31-46.

44. Ibid. pp. 35-37.

45. Daniel W. Brown, *Rethinking Tradition in Modern Islamic Thought*, Cambridge (1996), p. 96.

46. The Qadariya are said to have disbelieved in predestination. The Mutazilah held to a number of theological tenets that were ultimately rejected by the Muslim mainstream; chief among them were their denial of predestination and their belief in the createdness of the Qur'an. The Jabariya denied free will but their beliefs on God's attributes were supposed to be similar to the Mutazilah. The Murji'a are reported to have held that faith (*iman*) is equivalent to the acknowledgement of the fundamental beliefs of Islam and is unrelated to works. The Mujassima were criticized for their

(contd. on page 200)

the Prophet's endorsing and condemning various perspectives were produced in abundance, like the following tradition reviling the Qadariyyah (opponents of belief in predestination).

> The Prophet said: "The Magians of this *ummah* (community) are those who reject faith in the predestination of God. Don't visit them if they fall sick. Don't attend them when they die and don't greet them if they meet you."[47]

The Zanaddiqa (those who professed Islam but harbored resentment toward the religion) are said to have invented thousands of misleading traditions.[48]

Professional storytellers were another major source of false reports and were notorious for spinning yarns on the occasions of Revelation.[49] Traditions were also contrived to support various racial and personal prejudices, such as:

> A *Zanji* (black person) commits adultery when he is satisfied and steals when he is hungry. There is generosity and a helping spirit among them as well.

> Love the Arabs for three reasons: I am an Arab, the Qur'an is in Arabic and the people of Paradise will converse in Arabic.

> He who has nothing to give in charity should curse a Jew.

Footnote no. 46 (contd. from page 199)

anthropomorphic views on God's attributes. They are said to have insisted on a literal interpretation of all descriptions of God and his activities in the Qur'an. The Mu'atila are supposed to have allegorized the attributes of God to such an extent that they denied that they had any basis in reality.

47. Ibn Majah, *Al Sunan*, 1:48.

48. Suhaib H. Abdul Ghafar, *Criticism of Hadith Among Muslims with Reference to Sunan Ibn Majah* (IFTA: 1984), pp. 38-39.

49. Suhaib H. Abdul Ghafar, *Criticism of Hadith Among Muslims with Reference to Sunan Ibn Majah* (IFTA: 1984), pp. 39-40; Muhammad Zubayr Siddiqi, *Hadith Literature*, Calcutta (1961), pp. 55-57.

There shall be in my community a man called Muhammad ibn Idris (al Shafi`i) who will be more dangerous than Iblis and there shall be a man called Abu Hanifah who is the light of my community.[50]

Various proverbs, superstitions, and etiquettes were also credited to the Prophet.[51]

Some of the most prolific forgers of *hadiths* came from the ranks of *ahl al hadith*. So-called pious traditionists invented innumerable reports and concocted thousands of *isnads* to encourage others to be more devout. They considered their forgeries to be religious acts and anticipated reward from God for them.[52] *Hadiths* promising hugely disproportionate divine reward for ordinary supererogatory acts of worship come by and large from this class of fabricators. Yet not all deception produced by traditionists was inspired by such piety. Much of it was motivated by the desire to defend one's *mathhab* (legal school) or to enhance one's status as a scholar. While Imam al Shafi`i does not discuss the motivations of the forgers, he does talk about some of the personal desires and pressures that sometimes compromised the findings of traditionists.

There are [*Hadith* scholars] who have aspired to a broader and thorough knowledge [of *Hadith*] and have been driven by this desire to accept *hadiths* from transmitters from whom it would have been better not to accept. I have noticed that most of them are inclined to be unreliable, because they accept [*hadiths*] from the same transmitters whose similar or better [*hadiths*] they have rejected. They accept [*hadiths*] that

50. Abdul Ghafar cites these forged reports in his *Criticism of Hadith Among Muslims With Reference to Sunan Ibn MaAdjah* (IFTA: 1984), p. 42.

51. Ibid, pp. 42-44.

52. Suhaib H. Abdul Ghafar, Criticism of *Hadith Among Muslims with Reference to Sunan Ibn MaAdjah* (IFTA: 1984), pp. 40-43; Muhammad Zubayr Siddiqi, *Hadith Literature*, Calcutta (1961), pp. 57-59.

are falsified, as well as those from unreliable sources if they agree with their opinions, while they reject [hadiths] from reliable transmitters if they happen to contradict their opinions.[53]

And Shu'ba bin al Hajjaj is credited with this statement on the envy and malice that second century *muhaddithun* (scholars of *Hadith*) felt for one another: "Beware of the traditionists' mutual jealousy for they are more jealous than billy goats."[54]

No scholar of *Hadith*—ancient or modern, Muslim or non-Muslim—doubts that wholesale falsification of data on the Prophet was well underway by the fourth decade following his death, but there is disagreement on when the effort to combat this development got underway. Defenders of *Hadith* insist that the Prophet's sayings and doings have always been a subject of keen pursuit and study by Muslims since the days when he was among them until the present. Many non-Muslim scholars feel that a concerted effort to collect the authentic traditions of the Prophet did not appear until late in the first Islamic century. This latter stance flies in the face of considerable evidence. In their arguments against Western critics who claim that *hadith* transmission was exclusively oral until the second century A.H., defenders of *Hadith* science cite historical sources and *Hadith* literature that provide hundreds of examples of individuals who are reported to have written down traditions or to have possessed collections of written traditions.[55] Muhammad al A'zami lists fifty Companions who reportedly passed on traditions in written form.[56] These sources, which testify that there were many who kept written

---

53. Muhammad ibn Idris al Shafi'i, *al Risala*, translated by Majid Khaduri, Johns Hopkins (1961), p. 281.

54. Al Khatib, *Al-Kifaya*, p. 109; quoted by G.H.A. Juynboll, *Muslim Tradition*, Cambridge (1983), p. 165.

55. Brown cites several scholars who make this case, among them: Muhammad Mustafa al A'zami, *Studies in Early Hadith Literature*, pp. 34-182; and Nabia Abbott, *Studies*, 11. See Daniel W. Brown, *Rethinking Tradition in Modern Islamic Thought*, Cambridge (1996), p. 92.

56. Muhammad Mustafa al A'zami, *Studies in Early Hadith Literature*, Indianapolis, 1968, pp. 34-60.

records in the earliest stages of *hadith* collection, also show that the work of recording and compiling the Sunnah of the Prophet began very early on.[57]

Thus in the first half-century A.H. two conflicting trends, the falsification and the safeguarding of the traditions of the Prophet, had emerged. Young American Muslims are beginning to question the effectiveness of the latter effort in the face of such widespread forgery.[58] The mere fact of pervasive *hadith* fabrication often shocks and creates doubt. "How can Muslims have invented so many lies about the Prophet?" they ask. In response, Muslim educators point to the ability of the *isnad* system to sort out authentic traditions from the mass of statements and deeds attributed to God's Messenger.

Name Us Your Informants

The indiscriminate fabrication of reports on the Prophet that occurred in the first three decades after his demise confirms that from the very beginnings of Islam his *Sunnah* was seen as having great authority, otherwise the manufacture of traditions during this period would have been pointless. If data on the Prophet was so valued, then it stands to reason that trustworthy information would have been prized all the more, and that the production of false reports would have met with stern reaction from at least some quarters. The traditional Muslim view is that asking for one's sources began early on.

> According to Muslim scholarship the *isnad* came definitely into use after the troubles ensuing from the murder of the caliph 'Uthman in 35 A.H., when people transmitting information could no longer be trusted automatically but had to be

---

57. According to al A'zami the notion that *hadith* transmission was exclusively oral until the second Islamic century was perpetrated by the bias of the medieval 'ulama' in favor of oral sources.

58. Daniel W. Brown, *Rethinking Tradition in Modern Islamic Thought*, Cambridge (1996), pp. 81-107, where the author discusses this trend among Muslims worldwide

examined firstly as to whether or not they harboured innovative ideas and, in general, as to their reliability, veracity and
other character traits. The report often adduced to establish a
historical basis for this is the saying of Muhammad bin Sirin
(died 110 A.H.): "They [sc. the traditionists] were not used
to inquiring after the *isnad*, but when the *Fitnah* occurred
they said: Name us your informants. Thus, if these were *ahl
as-sunna* their traditions were accepted, but if they were a*hl al
bida*` their traditions were not accepted.[59]

There are Western scholars who disagree with this early dating of
the *isnad*. J. Schacht argues that *isnads* were not used systematically
before the second century A.H., claiming that the *Fitnah* mentioned
in the statement of Ibn Sirin corresponds to the civil war that
began with the killing of the Umayyad caliph Walid bin Yazid in 126
A.H./743 C.E.[60] G.H.A. Juynboll offers another chronology, theorizing that the *Fitnah* refers to the civil war that began in 63 A.H./682
C.E. with `Abd Allah bin al Zubayr's proclaiming a countercaliphate
in Mecca, thus challenging the authority of the Umayads in
Damascus.

Arguing against Schacht, Al A`zami defends the traditional
Muslim view.

The assassination of Walid bin Yazid has never been a conventional date in Islamic history. Furthermore, there were
many *Fitnahs* before this date. There was the civil war between
Ibn al Zubair and `Abd al Malik bin Marwan about 70 A.H.
But the biggest of all was the civil war between `Ali and
Mu`awiyah, which produced a breach among Muslims that
exists to the present day. Taha Husein has described it rightly
as the fiercest quarrel known in Islamic History. So, on what
grounds does the word *Fitnah* need to be interpreted in the

59. G.H.A. Juynboll, *Muslim Tradition*, Cambridge (1983), pp. 17-18.

60. Joseph Schacht, *The Origins of Muhammadan Jurisprudence*, Oxford
(1964), pp. 36-37.

sense of the civil war after the killing of Walid bin Yazid? To take the word arbitrarily in this sense is equal to interpreting it as the *Fitnah* of Tartar and Halaku.[61]

Al A`zami also points out that Ibn Sirin's phrasing suggests a practice earlier than his own period (he died in 110 A.H/728 C.E.). Expressions such as, "They did not ask," "They said, 'Name us your informants,'" "Their traditions were accepted," and so on, imply a past event with which he was not associated, and with which he should have been associated if it had occurred during his adulthood, as he was a well known traditionist. He does not use the first person plural, which would indicate that he is referring to his contemporaries. Hence his statement "points to a practice in very early days."[62]

It should also be noted that in the oldest extant text on Islamic Law, the *Muwatta* of Imam Malik (born in 90 A.H./708 C.E. and died at age 87),[63] *isnad* is consistently employed when quoting older authorities, which suggests that by the late first century A.H. the *isnad* system was already highly developed.[64] Imam Malik cites *hadiths* of the Prophet, and judgments and opinions of leading Companions, eminent Successors,[65] and *shaykhs* (scholars) from the generation that preceded his, almost always providing the chain of authorities from whom he received his information. The *Muwatta* usually lists *hadiths*

---

61. Muhammad Mustafa al A`zami, *Studies in Early Hadith Literature*, p. 216.

62. Ibid p. 217. Alternatively, Juynboll believes that Ibn Sirin's wording alludes to an event that took place during his adulthood, but it is hard to see how he arrives at this conclusion.

63. In a recent work, Norman Calder argues that the *Muwatta* and other ancient Islamic legal texts that have come down to us may have undergone considerable redaction after their authors' lifetimes. Norman Calder, *Studies in Early Muslim Jurisprudence*, Clarendon Press, Oxford (1993).

64. Malik ibn Anas, *Al Muwatta*, translated by Aishah Abdurrahman Bewley, Kegan Paul International, New York (1989).

65. Referred to as *Tabi`un* in Arabic, denoting the next generation after the Companions.

of the Prophet before non-prophetic traditions, and complete *isnads* before incomplete *isnads*, demonstrating that in both cases scholars of his era considered the former to have more authority than the latter.[66] Malik relates *hadiths*[67] from over ninety scholars, who relate from over eighty Successors, who frequently trace their information to various Companions. Such prolific use of *isnads* by Imam Malik's informants indicates that the *isnad* system could not have been the brainchild of his generation or even the preceding one, since it would require considerable time for its application to become so regularized. This would rule out Schacht's hypothesis.

Juynboll's conjecture that the civil war between Ibn al Zubair and `Abd al Malik saw the birth of *isnad* is more credible than Schacht's. He is also able to cull several reports from *awa'il*[68] literature and offer interpretations of them that support his case.[69] But Muslim scholars by and large lack confidence in the *awa`il*, since it developed much later and is considered no where near as scientific as *Hadith* studies.

Juynboll's conjecture, like Schacht's, also seems to leave too little time for the *isnad* to develop into the widely used method that it had become in the generation before Malik's. The majority of Imam Malik's informants quote from Successors who died within two decades of the civil war that Juynboll believes saw the birth of *isnad*. Some of them died in the early 70's A.H. and several in the 60's before this civil war even took place (around 70 A.H./689 C.E.). Assuming that a fair number of Imam Malik's sources did not invent their *isnads*, we would be forced to conclude that the *isnad* system had achieved widespread use and a high degree of sophistication within

---

66. Some Western writers have argued that a clear preference for Prophetic traditions and complete *isnads* did not develop until much later.

67. By *hadith* here I mean quotes from the Prophet and others that have come down through an *isnad*, not just Prophetic traditions.

68. *Awa`il* are reports containing information about who was first to do something, or when certain institutions were first introduced.

69. G.H.A. Juynboll, *Muslim Tradition*, Cambridge (1983), pp. 17-19.

twenty years of its origins. A somewhat more gradual maturation would be expected.

Al A`zami's point about the assassination of Walid bin Yazid having much less significance in Muslim history than the *Fitnah* which followed the murder of Uthman applies as well to the counter-caliphate of Ibn Zubair. If the fabrication of *hadiths* associated with this political turmoil roused traditionists to be more exacting in enquiring after people's sources, one would think that the *Fitnah* precipitated by Uthman's murder, which saw the first proliferation of politically slanted traditions, would have stirred them all the more.

Finally, as al A`zami notes, there are a fair number of *hadiths* in the tradition literature with *isnads* in which Companions give as their immediate authorities, not the Prophet, but other Companions. This supports the view that the *isnad* system was in use earlier than what Juynboll proposes, for otherwise, there would be no means for these *isnads* to have come down to us; unless of course they are all forged, but then why would forgers construct such complex chains of transmission? They could just as easily have made their *isnads* include only one Companion instead of two, and at the same time be just as believable.[70]

While Muslim specialists need to examine these alternative theories on the origins of *isnad*, I doubt it would lead—even if done without bias—to a departure from the traditional view. Despite Juynboll's claims to the contrary, the wording of Ibn Sirin's statement definitely seems to refer to a time before he became a traditionist, which would predate the conflict between Ibn Zubair and `Abd al . Moreover, associating the *Fitnah* with later civil conflicts does not allow sufficient time for the development of *isnad* into the widely used system it had become for the generation that preceded

---

70. While *isnads* containing two transmitters from the same age group are certainly in the minority, they are not entirely uncommon in the tradition literature.

Imam Malik's. Although Juynboll is able to find *awa`il* that may be viewed as in conflict with the Muslim chronology, there is much in the *Hadith* literature and historical sources that is at variance with Juynboll's hypothesis. One of the hallmarks of the great mass of data compiled during the classical period is that discrepancies can be found on practically every issue. Even if Muslim experts agree with Juynboll's readings of the *awa`il* he cites, they will probably give greater weight to sources that they have always held in higher regard.

The Weakest Link

We have seen that *hadith* collection began with the Companions, and that the *Fitnah* that followed Uthman's murder most likely saw the beginnings of *isnad*. The latter was introduced to sift out suspect reports in the face of large-scale invention of false data on the Prophet, as well as other esteemed figures from early Islamic history. As the demand for *isnads* grew, fabricators took to falsifying these as well, and as Juynboll notes: "*isnad* fabrication, as everybody is bound to agree, occurred on as vast a scale as *matn* fabrication."[71] The above-mentioned account of Ibn Sirin indicates that, at first, acceptance of *hadiths* hinged on the sectarian leanings of the informants, for he states that if the person relating the tradition was "from *ahl as-sunnah* (the *sunnah* party) their traditions were accepted, but if they were from *ahl al bida`* (the party of innovators) their reports were not accepted." It is hard to say exactly what two groups this statement has in mind, for it represents a very early use of terms whose meanings evolved over time. The *ahl-as-sunnah* certainly refers to a group involved in *hadith* collection of which Ibn Sirin counted himself a member. If the statement of Ibn Sirin is genuine and its wording accurate, then these are probably the forerunners of the *ahl al hadith* (the *hadith* party), that Juynboll describes as:

---

71. G.H.A. Juynboll, *Muslim Tradition*, Cambridge (1983), p. 4.

A category of people in early Islam who think of their religion as based upon and rooted in a body of religious learning and rituals laid down in the ever-increasing *Hadith*. They should be seen as distinct from, and—at least during the second century A.H.—easily outnumbered by, all those other people who called themselves Muslims, such as the political factions of the Shi`ah and Khawarij, as well as the adherents of a number of other religious political doctrines, e.g. the Qadariyah, Murji`ah, Mu`tazilah, and the followers of the controversial Jahm bin Safwan, to name the most important.[72]

On the other hand, the *ahl al bida* to which the statement refers, "may very well have been those people who had one, or a few, distinct *bida*'s in common and who, as a consequence, were felt by Ibn Sirin to be a danger to society."[73]

Needless to say, party affiliation is not much of a test of a tradition's authenticity, but as *hadith* compilations became more sophisticated, an elaborate system of criticism developed.

This system was based on two premises: (1) the authenticity of a report is best measured by the reliability of the transmitters of the report; and (2) scholars can distinguish authentic from spurious traditions by carefully scrutinizing both their individual transmitters (*rawi*; pl. *ruwat*) and the continuity of their chain of transmission (*sanad*; *isnad*; *silsila*). The rules for evaluating the trustworthiness of a transmitter were borrowed from the procedures and technical vocabulary used to test wit-

---

72. G.H.A. Juynboll, *Studies on the Origins and Uses of Islamic Hadith*, Variorum (1996), V, pp. 111-112.

73. G.H.A. Juynboll, *Studies on the Origins and Uses of Islamic Hadith*, Variorum (1996), III, p. 310.

nesses in legal cases, and a major branch of scholarship, the science of the men (*'ilm al rijal*) emerged. Vast biographical dictionaries were compiled out of the need for evidence by which to establish the reliability or unreliability of transmitters of *hadith*.[74]

Hadith critics took the transmitters probity and strictness in observing ritual duties into consideration.[75] In addition to biographical data, judgements on transmitters' honesty, memory, accuracy, linguistic ability, and mental acuteness regularly appear in the *rijal* literature. Numerous technical terms came into use to describe the merits and shortcomings of transmitters. Descriptions such as *thiqa* (reliable), *adl* (morally upright), *saduq* (veracious), *salih* (pious), *hafiz* (having an excellent memory), *kadhdhab* (mendacious), *mudallas* (someone who tampers with *isnads*), *daif* (weak), *matruk* (abandoned) are some of the most frequently employed designations. It is quite common to find major differences of opinion among the *isnad* critics on the reliability of well-known transmitters, and to find a critic making both favourable and unfavourable statements about a transmitter in a biographical write-up.[76] *Rijal* critics will sometimes specify that *hadiths* that deal with certain themes or come through certain channels cannot be trusted from a particular transmitter, although his other reports can.

---

74. Daniel W. Brown, *Rethinking Tradition in Modern Islamic Thought*, Cambridge (1996), p. 82.

75. Muhammad Zubayr Siddiqi, *Hadith Literature*, Calcutta (1961), pp. 60-61.

76. G.H.A. Juynboll, *Muslim Tradition*, Cambridge (1983), pp.182-183. Suhaib H. Abdul Ghafar, *Criticism of Hadith Among Muslims with Reference to Sunan Ibn Maja* (IFTA: 1984), pp. 77-81.

Although differing views on the reliability of transmitters pervade the *rijal* literature, questioning the trustworthiness of the Companions of the Prophet ultimately became taboo.[77]

> Such tests of reliability and character were applied to each *hadith* transmitter in an *isnad* with the important exception of those in the first generation, the Companions of the Prophet (*Sahaba*). Just as the doctrine of prophetic infallibility (`isma) guarantees that the Prophet is free from error in matters related to revelation, so too the moral integrity of the Companions is assured by the doctrine of their collective moral uprightness (*ta`dil*). According to this doctrine the Companions must be considered free from major sins by virtue of their direct association with the Prophet for "God has declared all of them to be trustworthy. He has revealed their purity and He has chosen [to mention] them in the [very] text of the Qur'an."[78] The Companions are thus excluded from normal scrutiny on theological grounds.[79]

---

77. There are quite a number of authenticated traditions in which Companions describes other Companions as *kadhdhabin* (liars) in relating *hadith*. Sunni scholars hold that *kadhdhab* in these cases only means "being in grave error." Suhaib H. Abdul Ghafar, *Criticism of Hadith Among Muslims with Reference to Sunan Ibn Maja* (IFTA: 1984), pp. 59-63. Also, G.H.A. Juynboll, *Muslim Tradition*, Cambridge (1983), pp. 190-206.

78. This quotation is from Al-Khatib al Baghdadi (d. 463 A.H.), *al Kifaya fi `ilm al-riwaya* (Hyderbad, 1357 A.H.), p. 46. Its translation is taken from Juynboll, *Muslim Tradition*, p. 195. The verses of the Qur'an that are usually cited that are said to establish the collective *ta`dil* of the Companions are 3:110 (i.e. "you are the best of people to be sent forth to mankind") and 2:143 ("thus we have made you a people of the middle way").

79. Daniel W. Brown, *Rethinking Tradition in Modern Islamic Thought*, Cambridge (1996), pp.82-83. For an interesting discussion of this doctrine see Juynboll, *Muslim Tradition*, pp. 190-206.

The biographical data amassed in the *rijal* works, together with the assumption of the collective *ta`dil* of the Companions, are the core elements of *isnad* criticism. Based on these, *Hadith* scholars were able to devise a system of historical criticism that, at least in theory, reduced the evaluation of a tradition's genuineness almost to an algorithm, thus lending it an aura of maximum objectivity. By examining the biographical records of the transmitters of a *hadith*, scholars could determine if each authority in a chain actually had an opportunity to meet and associate with the preceding authority,[80] while also checking each transmitter's reputation for accuracy, memory, religiosity, and honesty. In this way critics were able to grade *hadiths* according to the quality of its *isnad*. Traditions with uninterrupted *isnads* that involve the highest grade of transmitters were designated *sahih* (sound). Reports with continuous chains whose transmitters were felt to be deficient in some respects were called *hasan* (fair), and those whose transmitters were known to be imprecise, inaccurate or careless were labelled *daif* (weak). A *hadith* believed to be spurious or fabricated was designated *mawdu`* (composed). Terminology was also developed that pinpointed defects in the *isnad*. A tradition is *munqati`* (broken) if the *isnad* has a missing link, *mursal* (incomplete) if it is reported from the Prophet by a Successor but does not identify the Companion informant, and *mawquf* (halted) if its *isnad* stops short of reaching the Prophet and thus may appear to represent a statement of a Companion or later authority.

---

80. Al Bukhari (d. 256 A.H./869 C.E.) is said to have included in his *Sahih* only *hadiths* with chains where each narrator explicitly said that he had received the tradition from its authorities. In cases where there was some doubt, he made sure that the authorities were known to have met and associated with each other. Most other critics were content that two persons named consecutively in a chain were contemporaries that could have met. This was the criterion that Muslim bin Hajjaj (d. 261 A.H./874 C.E.) used in compiling his *Sahih*. See Muhammad Zubayr Siddiqui, *Hadith Literature,* Calcutta (1961), pp. 60-61; and John Burton, *An Introduction to the Hadith,* Edinburgh (1994), p. 125.

Hadiths were also classified according to the number of their transmitters during the first three generations. *Mutawatir* (broadly authenticated) *hadiths* were transmitted via so many channels that forgery is believed to be impossible. Very few *hadiths* are in this category. *Mashhur* (well-known) *hadiths*, which are far more numerous, are transmitted by two to four authorities in the first generation and a large number in the next two. *Ahad* traditions are transmitted by a single narrator in the first generation.[81] Before Imam al Shafi`i (d. 204 A.H./819 C.E.), many legal scholars did not accept the last category as a source of Law, but due in part to his defence of their use in his *Risala*, there was little opposition to them after his time.[82]

As much as we have to respect the immensity of the effort to systematize *hadith* evaluation, there are a few concerns that immediately come to mind. We saw that in the beginning stages of *isnad* criticism partisanship was the determining factor in accepting or rejecting traditions. If the narrator of a tradition was affiliated with a particular group, that group was likely to accept his reports, provided that they were not too farfetched, and to reject his reports if his allegiances were elsewhere.[83] But this meant that authentic traditions that were not part of the group outlook could easily be discarded and inauthentic traditions arising within the group were less likely to be seriously questioned. Therefore a key matter that deserves

---

81. And usually one or two transmitters in each of the next two generations.

82. Muhammad ibn Idris al Shafi`i, *Al Risala*, translated by Majid Khadduri, John Hopkins Press (1961), p. 239-284. The *ahad* traditions are held to be superior to *qiyas* (arguments from analogy) by all Sunni schools of Islamic law except the Maliki, which gives priority to *qiyas* over *ahad* traditions.

83. The statement of Ibn Sirin indicates that this was the conduct of the early *ahl al hadith*, but heresiographers also claim that some other groups, most notably the Shiah, acted likewise. There were other political/religious factions, such as the Khawarij and Mutazalih, who were said to have little use for *Hadith*.

investigation is the length of time it took for *isnad* criticism to develop into the highly structured system outlined above.

It is generally agreed that Shu`ba bin al Hajjaj (93 A.H./711 C.E. to 160 A.H./776 C.E.) and Yahya bin Sa`id al Qattan (d. 198 A.H./813 C.E.) were the first critics who systematically examined *isnads* and made trustworthiness of transmitters an essential condition for accepting traditions.[84] Since Shu`ba is supposed to not have become involved in *hadith* collection until he was almost forty, this places the beginning of systematic *rijal* criticism around 130 A.H./747 C.E. If this dating is accurate, then a century elapsed between the beginnings of the *isnad* system and the beginnings of full-fledged *rijal* criticism. This late development of systematic *rijal* investigation makes it difficult to have confidence in its biographical data, which began being collected long after many of the narrators had passed on. To be sure, opinions about transmitters had been shared, mostly orally, before this date, but not in any disciplined and organized way. This may account for the profusion of conflicting judgements on the reliability of transmitters that one finds in the *rijal* literature, as well as a good deal of biographical information that is hard to accept, such as the incredibly advanced ages that a great many transmitters are supposed to have reached in an era when life expectancy was rather short.[85] Hence, *ilm al rijal* is at best an approximate science, and quite a subjective one as well, since "the assessment of persons and *isnads* is not uniform, but varies from scholar to scholar."[86] All things considered, it seems that a major drawback of

---

84. Muhammad Zubayr Siddiqi, *Hadith Literature*, Calcutta (1961), pp. 63-64; G.H.A. Juynboll, Muslim Tradition, Cambridge (1983), p. 20-21.

85. G.H.A. Juynboll, *Muslim Tradition*, Cambridge (1983), pp. 46-48, 61-62. In his article in, *Studies on the First Century of Islamic Society*, Southern Illinois University Press, Edwardsville, 1982, p. 170, Juynboll states: "In a recent study the average age of early Islamic scholars was fixed at 78 lunar years, that is 75 or 76 solar years, when the average lifespan of males in those days in that part of the world was about 50."

86. John Burton, *An Introduction to Hadith*, Edinburgh (1994), p. 124.

classical *Hadith* studies is that judgments on the veracity of one set of data — the *Hadith* reports — are based on a second set of data — the *rijal* reports — that we have no compelling reason to believe is more reliable than the first, quite the opposite.

Another more obvious concern stems from the fact that we know from *rijal* and other *Hadith* related literature that besides *matn* fabrication, *isnad* theft, invention, and tampering had also occurred on an enormous scale, so that the focal point of *hadith* evaluation had also suffered from extensive corruption. Yet if the main evidence of *hadith* criticism had often been manipulated, then we have every right to wonder how well suited was *isnad* criticism to detecting corrupted chains of transmission. If a mendacious *muhaddith* (scholar of *Hadith*) were to attach highly regarded *isnads* to false reports or to "repair" defective chains by inserting respected authorities into appropriate places, could not his *isnads* and the traditions attached to them be deemed acceptable by the standards and methodology of `ilm al rijal. H.A.R. Gibb argues this may not have been as easy as it sounds.

> To Western scholars the technique of *hadith* criticism by the examination of the chain of authorities seems to present some grave defects. A frequent criticism is that it is as easy for forgers to invent an *isnad* as to tamper with or fabricate a text. But this overlooks the difficulty that the forger would have in getting the *isnad* (with his name at the end of it) accepted and passed on by scholars of honest repute. And that the Muslim critics of tradition were generally honest and pious men must be allowed, even if some Muslims have themselves asserted the contrary.[87]

After the generation of Successors, *hadith* collection became by and large a scholarly enterprise, with the great majority of transmit-

87. H. A. R. Gibb, *Mohammedanism*, (London: Oxford University Press, 1969), p. 82.

ters having numerous students who collected their traditions and then passed them on to their students. Gibb's point is that it would be difficult for a student of *Hadith* to attribute false information to his teacher without the teacher's other students detecting and publicizing his deceit.

Gibb's observation is well taken, but while it would be difficult for such forgeries to go undetected, we can imagine circumstances where a fabrication may escape notice of one's peers. For example, if a *muhadith* claimed that he heard a tradition from an authority—or a number of authorities—whom he met in his travels to distant parts of the Islamic world, the local scholars might have no direct knowledge to confirm or deny his assertion. *Isnads* that begin in one locale and then after several links switch to another is quite common in the literature. Another possible scenario is for a traditionist to assert that he had greater or special exposure to a particular authority—for instance, if he was a relative, *mawla* (client), or servant of a transmitter—and had acquired traditions from him that others missed. Here again, if the authority is dead, it is difficult to prove or disprove these assertions. Carelessness on the part of teachers is another frequently mentioned means by which false reports were put into circulation on the authority of respected *muhaddithun*. Some *Hadith* scholars, in particular those with many students, would not always carefully check their pupils' notebooks of traditions they were supposed to have taught them, and yet would provide their students with their *ijaza* (permission) to transmit the material on their authority. Once a scholar signed to the authenticity of *hadith* material he supposedly transmitted, later critics would be hard pressed to challenge it.

When previously unheard-of *hadiths* with ostensibly sound *isnads* were introduced, many scholars may have remained sceptical, but as long as some accredited *muhadithun* gave them credence, the corresponding reports could have acquired a following and ultimately have found their way into respected collections. The key to introducing a successful forgery was not to get all recognized scholars to accept it, but only some to do so, for there are numerous traditions that appear in highly regarded collections, in particular the Six Books,[88] over which there existed strong disagreements for many years. The longer a falsified *hadith* survived its invention, the greater its chances became of becoming recognized as sound. The scholars in the best position to thwart a cleverly crafted forgery belonged to the generation of its creator; later generations were in an increasing weaker position to do so.

Isnad Corruption

Before the institutionalization of *isnad*, mendacity in relating prophetic traditions consisted essentially of producing false reports (*matns*); thereafter *isnad* falsification also became necessary. The easiest way to supply a questionable report with an *isnad* was simply to concoct one going back to the Prophet (or some other esteemed early authority), but if the invented *isnad* had never been heard of, or linked transmitters in the chain could not possibly have met, the forgery would usually be recognized for what it was. A more effective means of providing a suspect *hadith* with a credible *isnad* was to expropriate a highly regarded chain and splice it onto another plausible one that begins with the forger. For example, a certain forger might claim that he heard from his teacher, who heard from his teacher, who heard from D from C from B from A, a report the forger attributes to the Prophet, where the D through A and the forger through his teacher's teacher chains are well known and accepted as legitimate, and where the splicing occurs at the teacher's teacher — D link. As stated above, if the two individuals where the chains are linked could have met, and if the forger's colleagues, especially his teacher's other students, did not object too strongly to the

---

88. The six most respected *Hadith* collections in *Sunni* Islam. These are the collections of al *Bukhari, Muslim, Abu Da`ud, al Tirmidhi, al Nasa`i,* and *Ibn Maja.* Muhammad Zubayr Siddiqi, *Hadith Literature*, Calcutta (1961), pp. 63-64; G.H.A. Juynboll, *Muslim Tradition*, Cambridge (1983), pp. 20-21.

hadith, then the forgery stood a chance of eventually being considered reliable by some respected traditionists.[89]

While the *rijal* literature accuses some traditionists of *isnad* invention and theft, *tadlis* (lit. tampering) is the most frequent allegation made. *Tadlis*, according to the fourth century traditionist, al Hakim al Nisaburi, involved "tampering with *isnads* in order to make them appear more reliable then they are in reality."[90] It consisted either of interpolating the name of a trustworthy transmitter or eliminating the name or names of discreditable transmitters from the *isnad*, or both of these.[91]

It is difficult to pinpoint what prompted some traditionists to "repair" or "improve" *isnads*. The intense rivalry and envy that pervaded the ranks of second century *muhaddithun* may have been a factor. The discovery of *hadiths* with sound *isnads* going back to the Prophet, where previously only versions with imperfect *isnads* were known, could certainly enhance one's reputation as a traditionist, provided the findings are believed to be genuine. Developments in Islamic Law may have also spurred *isnad* tampering.

> By the end of the tenth (fourth Islamic) century, Muslim jurisprudents were divided amongst the Shafi'i, Hanafi, and other schools of law. Two centuries before, however, the principal division among jurisprudents had been that between *ashab al hadith* or traditionalists and *ashab al ra'y*; that is, between proponents of entirely Scriptural authority [the

---

89. This is similar to "*isnad* spread" described below (pp. 234-246), except there the *matn* and *isnad* are both expropriated.

90. G.H.A. Juynboll, *Muslim Tradition*, Cambridge (1983), pp. 179-180.

91. Khaduri gives this definition in his translation of *Al Risala*, John Hopkins Press (1961), p. 240, footnote 4. He cites Ibn Hajar, *Maratib al Mudallisin* (Cairo, 1322/1904), pp. 2-4; I. Goldziher, *Etude sur la Tradition Islamique*, tr. Leon Bercher (Paris, 1952), p. 58; J. Schacht, *Origins of Muhammadan Jurisprudence*, p.37.

Qur'an and traditions] in theology and law and more or less rationalistic jurisprudents. The traditionalists had separated out from the *ashab al ra`y* in the later eighth (second Islamic) century. Traditionalism enjoyed a spectacular triumph when the caliph al Mutawakil rescinded the Inquisition, 237 A.H./853 C.E., and the intellectual descendents of the *ashab al ra`y* were able to win themselves a measure of acceptance only by imitating certain of the forms of the traditionalists. Yet it was a sharp struggle, in the latter eighth (second Islamic) century and through much of the ninth (third Islamic). The form of jurisprudence that finally prevailed was a compromise between the two extremes, regulated by the institution of the guild school of law. ... From the later eighth (second Islamic) century to the beginning of the tenth (fourth Islamic), there raged fierce controversy between those who found their jurisprudence exclusively on *hadith*, *ashab al hadith* or traditionalists, and those who reserved a leading place for common sense, *ashab al ra`y*. The controversy concerned orthodoxy as well as orthopraxy, and on the theological plane continued through most of the Middle Ages.[92]

Such trends and tensions in Islamic jurisprudence are discernible in the differing approaches of the great imams after whom the four Sunni legal *mathahib* (schools) are named. Abu Hanifah (died 150 A.H./767 C.E.) and his students won the reputation of preferring *ra`y* (personal reasoning) to traditions and were said to have made *qiyas* (analogical deduction) the basis of their legal reasoning. This is not to imply that Abu Hanifah ignored *Hadith*, but it does seem that he was "not so much concerned with precedent—from whatever source—as

---

92. Christopher Melchert, *The Formation of the Sunni Schools of Law*, 9th-10th centuries C.E., Lieden (1997), pp. 1-2.

with making *ad hoc* decisions."[93] Imam Malik (died 179 A.H./795 C.E.) tried as far as possible to base his verdicts on the *Sunnah*, which for him did not refer exclusively to the practice of the Prophet, but to the religious customs of Madina. For Malik:

> There was no sense of setting the *sunnah* of the Prophet apart from the *sunnah* of Madina, so that the actions of its knowledgeable people were given even more weight than the behaviour of the Prophet related in *ahad* (single source) *hadiths*. This has always characterized the Maliki viewpoint.[94]

In addition to quoting prophetic *hadiths* with *isnads* of varying quality, Malik also bases his verdicts on the opinions of Companions, Successors and eminent scholars of Medina. Hence, of the *hadith*-items in Malik's *Muwatta*, 822 are *hadiths* of the Prophet, 613 relate acts and judgments of the Companions, and 285 report opinions of the Successors;[95] in addition, Malik frequently offers his own verdicts reached through independent reasoning. Imam al Shafi'i (died 204 A.H.) takes a median position between the *ashab al ra`y* and *ashab al hadith* in his *Risala*. He argues against the view of many of his contemporaries that legal rulings may be derived from opinions reported from the Companions or the Successors. For Shafi`i, law is based on a hierarchy of four sources: the Qur'an, the *Hadith* of the Prophet, arguments from analogy based on either a text in the Qur'an or tradition of the Prophet, and *ijma* (consensus). Concerning the

93. G.H.A. Juynboll, *Muslim Tradition*, Cambridge (1983), pp.118-119. Also, Muhammad ibn Idris al Shafi`i, *Al Risala*, translated by Majid Khadduri, John Hopkins Press (1961), pp. 5-6; Muhammad Zubayr Siddiqi, *Hadith Literature*, Calcutta (1961), p. 63-64; G.H.A. Juynboll, *Muslim Tradition*, Cambridge (1983), p. 198.

94. Malik ibn Anas, *Al Muwatta*, translated by Aishah Abdurrahman Bewley, Kegan Paul International (1989), p.435.

95. Norman Calder, *Studies in Early Muslim Jurisprudence*, Clarendon Press, Oxford (1993), p. 21.

latter, Khadduri writes:

> By *ijma* al Shafi`i does not mean merely the agreement of
> a few scholars of a certain town or locality, as the Hijazi
> and `Iraqi jurists seem to have held, but the majority of
> leading jurists in Muslim lands. He also universalised *ijma* on
> matters of fundamentals to include agreement of the Muslim
> community.[96]

Ahmad bin Hanbal may have offered legal opinions but he
was much more a *muhaddith* (traditionist) than a *faqih* (jurisprudent).
There are many reports in the biographical literature of his distaste
for jurisprudence.[97] Bin Hanbal recognised only the Qur'an and
traditions of the Prophet as genuine roots of Islamic Law.

In the methodologies of these imams we note the growing
demand for *Hadith* of the Prophet, preferably with sound *isnads*, to
support one's legal decisions. Abu Hanifah (died 150 A.H./767 C.E.)
and his early followers based their judgments more on *ra`y* (personal
reasoning) than traditions. Malik (died 179 A.H./795 C.E.) preferred
Prophetic traditions to *hadith* type reports of the Companions and
Successors, although he often based his verdicts on the latter. Al
Shafi`i (died 204 A.H.) argued that non-prophetic traditions should
not be considered a root of law but should only play a supplementary
role, and Ahmad bin Hanbal (died 241 A.H.) felt that only the
Prophet's *Hadith* (in addition, of course, to the Qur'an) are binding.

In this search for motives behind *tadlis*, we may be overlooking
the obvious. As we earlier observed, *hadith* collection began in earnest

---

96. Muhammad ibn Idris al Shafi`i, *Al Risala*, translated by Majid Khadduri,
John Hopkins Press (1961), pp. 31-33.

97. For Ahmad bin Hanbal's hostility towards jurisprudence and the
development of the classical Hanbali school: Christopher Melchert, *The
Formation of the Sunni Schools of Law, 9th-10th Centuries C.E.*, Lieden
(1997), pp. 137-155.

early in the first century A.H. It stands to reason that as more prophetic *Hadith* became available to scholars, the more they would be in demand, since explicit prophetic precedents would naturally carry greater weight than non-prophetic attestation. If a jurist or theologian could support his case with a *hadith* of the Prophet, he would presumably have the edge over an opponent who bases his argument on an opinion of a Companion or Successor, or his own independent reasoning—likewise with regard to the quality of *isnads*. Given the intense rivalry and hostility that prevailed back then— and that continued up until relatively recently—between the different *mathahib* (law schools), we can easily understand that some tradition- ists might have been moved to amend an *isnad* or two to support the positions of their schools.

Though we may speculate on the primary causes of *isnad* tampering, the widespread practice of *tadlis*, so frequently referred to in the *rijal* and other *Hadith* related material, is beyond dispute. The same literature identifies several different forms of *tadlis*. *Ihala* (trans- fer) involves the transfer of traditions from a dubious to a "reliable" *isnad*.[98] *Wasl* or *tawsil* (connecting) refers to making interrupted *isnads* "uninterrupted" by interpolating the names of authorities in chains where there are missing links.[99] *Raf* (raising) consists of raising a tradition to the level of a more prestigious authority, mostly the Prophet, by supplying the necessary links. Through *raf* a tradition that originally reports a statement or act of a Successor could be transformed into a tradition reporting a behavior or saying of a Companion by inserting the name of one of the Prophet's followers at the end of the chain. Similarly, a tradition going back to a Companion—perhaps one that at some earlier time went back to a

98. G.H.A. Juynboll, *Muslim Tradition*, Cambridge (1983), p. 155, note 57.
99. Joynboll points out that *wasl* was not a very common technical term. *Muslim Tradition*, Cambridge (1983), p. 187, note 119.

Successor—could be made into a *hadith* of the Prophet simply by adding his name at the end of the *isnad*.[100]

Ibn Rajab (died 795 A.H./1392 C.E.) provides the following interesting summary:

> The people who are assiduously devoted to worship and whose traditions should be discarded can be divided into two categories. [One group consists of] those whose devotional practices prevent them from memorising *Hadith* properly, so that it becomes marred with fanciful elements; they raise statements of Companions to the level of prophetic sayings (a reference to *raf*) and insert a Companion's name in *isnad*'s lacking this feature (an allusion to *wasl*). [The other group consists of] those who habitually and deliberately fabricate *hadiths*.[101]

Of the three types of *tadlis* just described, *raf* (raising) is the most frequently mentioned in the *rijal* literature, as it appears to have been the most pervasive form of *isnad* tampering.

> Early tradition collections and other early works on the science of tradition, as is well known, abound with reports traced back to the Companions and also Successors, who volunteer solutions to problems presented to them. Even if the ascription of many of these reports is open to doubt, one should not categorically reject their historicity as a whole. Very many of these private opinions remained in the course of time identified and connected with the name of a Companion or Successor, while a great many others—based upon *ra`y* as well as inspired by the example of the Prophet and/or other

100. Ibid pp. 52-55.
101. G.H.A. Juynboll, *Muslim Tradition*, Cambridge (1983), page 187.

Companions or Successors—are found in later collections moulded in the form of prophetic sayings. Witness to this phenomenon are the countless references in the earliest *rijal* works and other sources to people who "raise" a report of a Companion or Successor "to the level" of a prophetic saying. The Arabic terms used are derivatives of the root *RF* .

Names of transmitters from different periods mentioned in connection with *raf* are among innumerable others:

Rufay` bin Mihran Abu 'l-`Aliya (died about 93 A.H./ 711 C.E.), whose traditions occur in all classical collections;

Hasan al Basri (died 110 A.H./728 C.E.)[102];

`Adi bin Thabit (died 116 A.H./734 C.E.), whose traditions occur in all classical collections;

Simak bin Harb (died 123 A.H./740 C.E.), whose *hadiths* occur in five of the Six Books;

`Ali bin Zayd ibn Jud`an (died 129 A.H./746 C.E.), also found in five of the Six Books;

Farqad bin Ya`qub as-Sabakhi (died 131 A.H./748 C.E.), in two of the Six Books;

Aban bin Abi `Ayyash (died 138 A.H./755 C.E.);

Shu`ba bin al Hajjaj (died 160 A.H./766 C.E.), a key figure in Iraqi *Hadith*;

Mabarak bin Fadala (died 166 A.H./782 C.E.), whose traditions are listed in three of the Six Books, and who may be held responsible for "raising" very many sayings and opinions of Hasan al Basri "to the level" of prophetic sayings;

And finally in this shortlist the famous as well as notorious Syrian al Walid bin Muslim (died about 195 A.H./810 C.E.), in whose highly contradictory *tarjama* (biographical write-up)

---

102. Juynboll, *Muslim Tradition*, pp. 49-55, where the author deals with this case extensively.

in Ibn Hajar's *Tahdhib* we read the highest praise as well as the bitterest criticism and also that he was a *raffa`* (one who resorts frequently to *raf*).

Apart from dozens of other transmitters from the classical collections, one can glean the names of hundreds of people accused of the same practice from Ibn Hajar's *Lisan*.[103]

The phenomenon of *raf* is closely associated in Western *Hadith* studies with one of its major conjectures, "the projecting back theory" of J. Schacht. According to Schacht "*isnads* have a tendency to grow backwards," or as Juynboll rephrases it, "*isnads* have a tendency to grow with time in soundness."[104] The theory holds that, as the demand for prophetic traditions grew, non-prophetic reports and prophetic *hadiths* with defective chains were duly provided with sound *isnads* linked to the Prophet. In particular, legal judgments first arrived at by jurists were often later ascribed to the Prophet supported with complete *isnads*. For Schacht, versions of a tradition with defective *isnads* generally represent earlier stages of its evolution than versions of the same tradition with sound *isnads*.

Although it is historically established that the "raising" of reports to prophetic traditions and *isnad* "improvement" were commonplace, this does not prove Schacht's conjecture; for almost all Muslim scholars would challenge the claim that a large number of these deceptions escaped detection and were ultimately deemed *sahih* (sound) by the most respected traditionists. If the *rijal* literature shows nothing else, it shows that Muslim scholars were acutely alert to this problem and thus presumably on top of it. Yet upholders of "*isnads* have a tendency to grow backwards" counter with many illustrations of what they believe are "raised" *hadiths* making their way into the classical collections. G.H.A. Juynboll makes the following argument

103. Juynboll, *Muslim Tradition*, pp. 31-32.

104. J. Schacht, *The Origins of Muhammadan Jurisprudence*, Oxford (1950), p. 5.

concerning the famous Medinese Successor, Sa`id bin al Musayyab.

Sa`id ibn al Musayyab (died 93 A.H./711 C.E.) was known during his lifetime as the greatest expert in *fiqh* (Islamic jurisprudence) matters. Many traditions, later appearing in collections with *isnads* containing his name, can be traced also in other sources as utterances of himself that do not go back to persons older than himself.

E.g. (1) The legal maxim *la talaqa qabla `n-nikah* (i.e., no divorce before [concluding of] the marriage), ascribed to `Ali, Abu Bakr bin `Abd ar-Rahman, `Ubayd Allah bin `Abd Allah bin `Utba, Aban bin `Uthman, `Ali bin Husayn, Sa`id bin Jubayr, al Qasim bin Muhammad, Salim bin Abd Allah, `Ata bin Abi Rabah, `Amir bin Sa`d, Jabir bin Zayd, Nafi bin Jubayr, Muhammad bin Ka`b, Sulayman bin Yasar, Mujahid, al Qasim bin Abd ar-Rahman, `Amr bin Harim, al Sha`bi, `Urwa bin az-Zubayr, Shurayh, Tawus bin Kaysan, Hasan al Basri, `Ikrima as well as Ibn al-Musayyab (see Bukhari, *talaq* 9, = ed. Krehl, III, p.463) is also listed as a prophetic tradition in Ibn Maja, *talaq* 17 (= ed. M.F. `Abd al-Baqi, II, p. 660);

(2) The precept *idha aqbalati 'l-haydatu tarakati 's-salat* (i.e. when [a woman] feels her period has started, she abandons performing *salat*), ascribed to Ibn al Musayyab (Abu Dawud, *tahara* 109, = ed. M.M. `Abd al-Hamid, I, p.76) is found in a slightly different version in a prophetic saying, e.g. Nasa`i, *hayd* 2, = ed. H. M. al-Mas`udi, I, p.181 passim;

(3) The legal maxim *la nikaha illa bi-waliyyin* (i.e. no marriage without a guardian) is listed as a prophetic tradition (Tirmidhi, *nikah*, 14, = ed. M. F. `Abd al Baqi, III, pp. 407ff.) and also as a ruling of various *fuqaha'* among the Successors such as Sa`id, but also Hasan al Basri, Shurayh and Ibrahim an-Nakha`i (ibidem, p. 411);

(4) The legal maxim *al walad li' l-firash* (i.e. the child belongs to the marital bed), allegedly transmitted by Sa'id ibn al Musayyab in the *isnad* between Zuhri and 'Abu Hurayra, is on the other hand, according to a report of the *awa'il genre*, a rule of the pre-Islamic judge Aktham bin Sayfi, cf. E. I. 2, s. v. (Kister) and Ibn Batish, *Ghayat al-wasa'il ila ma'rifat al-awa'il*, I, p.184;

(5) Darimi, *wudu'* 85, (=p. 109) lists a number of precepts concerning the ablutions of the *mustahada* ascribed to Hasan al-Basri and Sa'id bin al-Musayyab. Although many ablution precepts exist traced back to the Prophet, this precept of Sa'id has remained unambiguously traced to him;

(6) In Malik we often find *mursal* traditions and also Sa'id's own statements preceded by the same texts as prophetic sayings, e.g., *salat* 60 and 61, = ed. M. F. 'Abd al-Baqi, pp. 94f. On the whole, precepts formulated by Sa'id are very numerous in the *Muwatta'*.

In al-Khatib al Baghdadi's *Kifaya*, p.404, last few lines, we read a statement in which it is implied that all the *marasil* of Ibn al Musayyab were in the course of time brought into circulation with perfect *isnads* via other people. On p. 405 we find a statement to the contrary.[105]

Juynboll continues:

I maintain that it is Sa'id bin al Musayyab who is to be credited with these legal decisions (which sometimes take the form of maxims) rather than the Prophet or a Companion as mentioned in the *Hadith* collections compiled some hundred and fifty years later. ... The reason why these legal decisions should be considered, in the first instance, as being the products of Sa'id's own juridical insight, rather than as being

---

105. Juynboll, *Muslim Tradition*, pp. 15-16.

traceable back to previous set examples, lies in the mere fact of them being quoted as Sa`id's decisions at all. A legal decision that indeed does go back to the Prophet or one of his Companions simply does not require being put into the mouth of Sa`id as also being a product of the latter's reasoning. The numerous instances where Sa`id is credited with juridical opinions definitely point to one conclusion only. He thought of the solution to the problem in these terms first, before this decision was moulded into a saying attributed to authorities preceding Sa`id. There is indeed no necessity whatsoever for crediting Sa`id with merely having repeated a legal opinion of his predecessors, be they the Prophet or one of his Companions.[106]

Juynboll similarly lists numerous sayings of Hasan al Basri (died 110 A.H./728 C.E.) that he contends later evolved into prophetic traditions that can be found among the Six Books. He offers this evaluation:

> Hasan al Basri has numerous legal decisions and even maxims traced to him which can be found in the explanatory remarks (ta`liqat) Bukhari adds to traditions duly traced back to the Prophet containing in most cases exactly the same wording or brief statements amounting to the same decisions.[107]

In addition, Juynboll provides examples of several other Companions and Successors whose sayings he maintains appear as prophetic *hadiths* in the most respected collections.[108] Moreover, he cautions that those prophetic traditions with no such parallels may still be "raised."

---

106. Ibid p. 16.
107. Ibid pp. 17, 52-55.
108. Ibid pp. 45, 60, 70, 89.

Even if it is maintained that a "prophetic" tradition, because it cannot be found also in the form of a personal opinion ascribed to another authority, has therefore to be accepted as being just that, the fact that there are so many examples of "prophetic" sayings that are traceable to a Companion or a Successor, makes any "prophetic" saying suspect as also belonging to that genre, but whose counterpart simply has not survived in the sources available at present.[109]

Not many Muslim *Hadith* experts have studied Western research in this area, so we cannot yet speak of a concerted Muslim response; nevertheless, we can be sure that most Muslim experts would dispute Schacht's theory. One area over which there would likely be considerable debate is the significance of the evidence cited by Western critics. The problem is that how we read this evidence depends to a large degree on our preconceptions on the efficacy of classical Muslim *hadith* criticism. For Muslims committed to the authenticity of the *Sahih Hadith*, opinions of Companions and Successors that bare resemblance to sound traditions of the Prophet will more than likely be seen as judgments derived from the Prophet' *Sunnah*. Thus Muslims might view the evidence cited by Juynboll in example 1 above as proof that the maxim, "no divorce before [concluding of] the marriage," was a well-established practice among the Companions and the Successors, which the *hadith* in Ibn Maja indicates the Prophet either initiated, or else preceded him and he endorsed. Sa`id's statement in example 2, relieving women from the obligation of five daily prayers during their periods, can also be seen as a juridical ruling based on prophetic precedent. After all, it is not at all farfetched that questions concerning menstruation and prayer were frequently put to the Prophet, especially since other religions in the region had rules addressing this issue. The same could be said of the opinion on marriage without a guardian in example 3, the more so since marriage is the focus of a substantial part of Qur'anic legislation. Concerning

---

109. Ibid p. 72.

example 4, Muslims have much less confidence in the *awa'il* literature than in the authenticated traditions, but even if this maxim has pre-Islamic origins that does not preclude that the Prophet may have affirmed it. Example 5 shows that Sa'id and others gave opinions concerning *wudu'* (washing for prayer) and that the *Hadith* literature also ascribes a number of other statements to the Prophet on this subject. Once again it is hardly surprising that the Prophet as well as these Successors would have provided instruction on this matter. It is also not surprising that many of the Successors would do so without quoting *hadiths*, for ritual washing in the Muslim community has always been passed on by example from one generation to the next, most often without quoting explicit prophetic precedents.[110] The Qur'an too contains instruction on this topic, and no one claims that Sa'id's remarks predated the Scripture's. In example 6, Juynboll points out that Malik's *Muwatta'* contains several sayings of the Prophet that are followed immediately by statements of Sa'id ibn al Musayyab that either say or amount to the same thing. However, it must be kept in mind that when Malik presents a prophetic tradition and follows it with equivalent remarks of Companions and Successors, he is not implying that the former might not be genuine and the latter might be the actual source of the practice; he is indicating that the practice is a genuine *sunnah* of the Prophet and that the corresponding non-prophetic reports corroborate this.[111]

My purpose here is not to invalidate Juynboll's evidence but to contend that it is not conclusive, at least for those who have put their faith in the authenticated traditions. For followers of *Hadith*, if

---

110. I once asked a congregation in a mosque in San Francisco how many had read or heard of a complete description of *wudu'* in the *Hadith literature;* no one had; yet they did explain that they were taught how to perform it without reference to any explanatory traditions.

111. Even when Malik establishes a practice on the authority of a Companion or Successor, he is not claiming that it is not a prophetic *sunnah* but that he knows no Prophetic tradition to support it. See the remark on the Maliki approach in this chapter, p. 220-221.

judgments of early authorities are in agreement with certain authenticated traditions of the Prophet, this is because they are most probably based upon his *Sunnah*; for those who are more sceptical, they may serve as examples of successfully "raised" sayings. In many cases of alleged raising of non-prophetic reports to authenticated prophetic traditions, Muslim scholars can cite other sound *hadiths* with the same *matn* (text) but with completely different *isnads* going back to the Prophet for which there are no parallel reports from which they could have been raised. Critics could counter that the other *isnads* can also be products of various forms of *tadlis* (*isnad* tampering) whose traces have disappeared.

Juynboll asserts that the existence of reports crediting early authorities with juridical opinions that agree with—and are sometimes identical to—sayings of the Prophet, prove that these authorities must have arrived at these decisions first before they were moulded into prophetic traditions. For why indeed cite a Companion's or Successor's verdict when it is based on a saying of the Prophet? Would not it be more natural and efficient to quote the latter, more authoritative source? Juynboll believes there can be only one explanation: for a period of time the statement of the Companion or Successor was the only source for the ruling, which was later transformed into a prophetic tradition. Muslim scholars may not see it this way. Christopher Melchert has thoroughly documented that for many jurists of the first four centuries A.H. the statements of the Companions and Successors played a key role in establishing the Prophet's *Sunnah*.[112] It was felt that these reports were especially useful for determining the *Sunnah* when faced with two conflicting reports from the Prophet both with reputable *isnads*.[113] For example, Abdul Ghafar writes:

---

112. Christopher Melchert, *The Formation of the Sunni Schools of Law, 9th-10th Centuries C.E.*, Lieden (1997).

113. The same information was considered vital to determining which prophetic *sunnahs* were abrogating and abrogated.

Like Malik, he [the famous *muhaddith*, Abu Dawud al Sijistani] preferred *hadith* supported by the practical example of the Companions, as far as the contradictory *ahadith* were concerned. He says under the heading of "Meat acquired by hunting for the *Muhrim* (pilgrim)": "If there are two opposite reports from the Prophet, search should be made to know what his Companions have adopted."[114]

This view of the function of non-prophetic reports is supported by the observation that quite often when a *hadith* of the Prophet has a non-prophetic parallel both can be found in the same collection and frequently quite close to each other. This shows that the collectors in these cases viewed the non-prophetic parallel as complementary and corroborative. It seems quite clear that in such instances the compilers believed that the practices and statements of the Companions and Successors confirmed the various *sunnahs* of the Prophet. Thus once again we see that the same evidence can support two very different interpretations, depending on one's predilections.

We conclude this discussion of *raf* with a clarification regarding Juynboll's assertion that Sa'id bin al Musayyab is to be credited with the above mentioned legal decisions "rather than the Prophet or a Companion as mentioned in the *Hadith* collections compiled some hundred and fifty years later." At first glance it may appear that Juynboll is implying—although this may not be what he intended— that the above cited reports of Sa'id's legal decisions appear in extant compilations that predate the classical collections by a century and a half. If this were true, then this would strengthen the case for the occurrence of *raf* in these examples. However, a quick check of the references provided shows otherwise. In the first five examples, all of the non-prophetic reports are from texts that date from the third

---

114. Suhaib H. Abdul Ghafar, *Criticism of Hadith Among Muslims with Reference to Sunan Ibn Majah* (IFTA: 1984), p. 123, where the author quotes from, Abu Dawud: *Al Sunan*, (Cairo, Taziya Publication), 1:129.

century A.H. or later. In the sixth example both the pronouncements of Saʿid and the corresponding sayings of the Prophet appear in the same source, the *Muwatta* of Imam Malik dating from the middle of the second Islamic century. Therefore Juynboll does not mean to suggest that the rulings he cites of Saʿid appear in extant texts that date back to the first century A.H., but rather, both the statements of Saʿid and the comparable prophetic traditions appear in collections from the same time period, roughly—except for the citations from Malik's *Muwatta*—one hundred and fifty years after Saʿid's demise.[115]

In this section we saw that of all of the various kinds of mendacity associated with *hadith* dissemination, *tadlis* (*isnad* tampering) posed the greatest challenge to the effort of identifying the authentic traditions of the Prophet. This is because through *tadlis* the very evidence—the chain of transmitters—that attests to the genuineness of a report is corrupted, and if done successfully, covers the tracks of the crime. That *tadlis* was widely practiced is well documented, but Muslim scholars would disagree with their Western counterparts on how much this type of forgery escaped detection. The "projecting back theory" of J. Schacht holds that the majority of *sahih* prophetic traditions were originally accounts of other esteemed authorities that were later made into sayings of the Prophet by inserting the names of Successors and Companions into the chains. Schacht believed that as a general rule, the sounder the *isnad*, the later it came into existence. The evidence that Western experts cite to substantiate Schact's theory will not go unchallenged by Muslim scholars, for statements of eminent figures that coincide with traditions of the Prophet can be viewed as being based on his example. While Muslim scholars will have to concede that *raf* (raising of reports to prophetic *hadith*) was prevalent, they would not automatically assume that if a judgment of an early authority agrees with a saying of the Prophet then the latter was derived from the former. In the end, and as to be expected, the overall impression we obtain from reading the *matns*—that is, the

---

115. Imam Malik was born in 90 A.H./708 C.E. and died approximately 167 A.H./783C.E.

degree to which we find the texts of authenticated traditions believ-able—may be the determining factor toward which view we incline. We will return to this issue shortly, but first we present another important theory of J. Schacht that has opened a new avenue of *isnad* criticism.

The Forest Through the Trees

So far we have discussed *matn* fabrication and a variety of forms of *isnad* corruption, including *isnad* invention, expropriation, and *tadlis* (improvement). Another type of deceit that is sometimes mentioned in the *Hadith* literature and that has also been a major area of Western conjecture and investigation is the practice of *isnad proliferation*.[116] Schacht hypothesizes that this type of forgery was as pervasive as he believes "projecting back" was: "Parallel with the improvement and backward growth of *isnads* goes their spread, that is the creation of additional authorities or transmitters for the same doctrine or tradition."[117] Michael Cook elaborates:

> The simplest form of the process is the following. Suppose that you and I are contemporaries, and I learn something from you—an informal event which must be common enough in any scholarly culture. You had it, or say you had it, from your teacher. If I am scrupulously honest, I will transmit it from you from your teacher, leaving posterity with an *isnad* of the form:

---

116. For example, Suhaib H. Abdul Ghafar shows that such accusations were levied against the traditionist Hammad bin al Walid [*Criticism of Hadith Among Muslims with Reference to Sunan Ibn Majah* (IFTA: 1984), pp. 184]. Michael Cook, *Early Muslim Dogma*, Cambridge (1981), pp. 107-116.

117. J. Schacht, *The Origins of Muhammadan Jurisprudence*, Oxford (1950), p. 166.

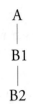

But as it happens, I say to myself that, even if I didn't actually hear it from your teacher, I could have; it goes against the grain to transmit from a mere contemporary. My behavior here is informed by one of the basic values of the system: an elegant *isnad* is a short one. Ideally, one should have a saying direct from the mouth of a sayer; and failing that, the fewer intervening links the better. In the present case, provided your transmission survives independently of mine, posterity finds itself confronted instead with this:

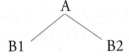

Posterity then believes that it has two independent witnesses for the authenticity of the ascription to A, and thus thinks itself able to rule out fabrication in the generation following.[118]

A second process whereby *isnads* can spread is the following. You transmit a saying of a certain authority from your teacher. Again I like the saying, and wish to transmit it myself without acknowledgement to you. But instead of claiming that I heard it from your teacher, I ascribe it to my own. (Perhaps it

118. For an example see: Michael Cook, *Early Muslim Dogma*, Cambridge (1981), p. 111. The early *muhadithun* were also alert to the phenomenon of *isnad* spread. See, Eerik Dickinson, *The Development of Early Sunnite Hadith Crticism: The Taqdima of Ibn Abi Hatim al Razi*, Brill (2001), pp. 85-90.

is well-known that I never met your teacher, or he carries no weight in the circles I wish to impress, or I consider his politics objectionable.) Again assuming that your transmission survives independently of mine, posterity puts the two *isnads* together and reconstructs the following transmission:

In reality, I (C2) got it from (C1), and my reference to my teacher (B2) is merely a calque on your reference to yours (B1). But posterity is again deceived by the fork in the transmission into thinking that it has independent attestations that A actually said it. The error induced here will normally be a matter of two generations. But again, it could be more. Suppose you are a *Shiʿite* transmitting a saying of Ibn Masʿud's with a string of *Shiʿite* transmitters; I however am a Murjiʾite, and in taking over your tradition substitute a string of transmitters of my own school.[119]

From this description we see that the process of *isnad* proliferation is just another form of *isnad* tampering. Although we find the occasional claim in the *rijal* works that a transmitter is guilty of *hadith* thievery, it is more probable that this form of deception would be described by the more inclusive term *tadlis*. Schacht identified what he believed was the impetus behind the spread of *isnads*: "The spread of *isnads* was intended to meet the objection which used to be made to "isolated" traditions."[120]

---

119. Michael Cook, *Early Muslim Dogma*, Cambridge (1981), pp. 108-110.

120. For Imam al Shafiʿi's argument in favor of *Ahad* traditions: Muhammad ibn Idris al Shafiʿi, *Al Risala*, translated by Majid Khadduri, John Hopkins Press (1961), pp. 239-284.

As we have already seen with other novel Western theories on the evolution of *Hadith* science, this one is also likely to persuade only the already sceptical.

> It becomes a crucial question whether the spread of *isnads* was a process operative on a historically significant scale, or just an ingenious idea of Schacht's. It should be said straight out that the evidence does not lend itself to a conclusive answer to the question; and many of Schacht's own examples of the spread of *isnads* are proof only to the converted. But some store must be set by the fact that the process as outlined is thoroughly in accordance with the character and values of the system; and the pressure of elegance on truth is something entirely familiar to the traditionists themselves.[121]

If we do accept the premise that *isnads* spread appreciably, then we obtain a retort to one of the strongest arguments put forward against the Western outlook that forgery pervades the *Hadith* literature. M. M. al A'zami in his *Studies in Early Hadith Literature* contends that such widespread contamination of the "authenticated" traditions requires, on the part of traditionists, conspiratorial collaboration too extensive to be credible.

> The common feature of a good many traditions in the early part of the second century A. H. is the great number of transmitters who belong to different provinces and countries. We have for example seen in tradition No. 27 some seventy-four students belonging to a dozen different places. It was hardly possible for all these persons to consult each other so as to give a similar form and sense in transmitting a particular tradition. So if a particular tradition is transmitted by so many persons with a similar form and sense, then its genuineness cannot be questioned, while the trustworthiness of the individuals has been vouched for by their contemporaries. ... As it has been shown earlier that the transmitters of a single

---

121. Michael Cook, *Early Muslim Dogma*, Cambridge (1981), p. 111.

tradition, in so many cases, belong to a dozen different countries and thus their meetings and agreement on this sort of fabrication was almost impossible.[122]

As Cook observes, if *isnad* spread had not occurred on a significant scale, then al A'zami's argument is "irrefutable," but if it had, then "al A'zami's argument does not touch us."[123] Whereas it appears that we have arrived here at the crux of Muslim and Western divergence on the integrity of the *Hadith* compilations, and thus what should be the focal point of modern *Hadith* studies, Cook argues that we have in effect reached a dead-end.

> To see the significance of the spread of *isnads* is not to be in a position to remedy it. As already indicated, one of the key features of the phenomenon is a destruction of information which is likely to be irreversible. Schacht's discovery of the spread of *isnads* is in fact a highly ambivalent contribution to knowledge. It can be seen as the foundation of a new method of *isnad*-criticism; and it can be seen as a neat demonstration that such a method cannot be devised. One ignores Schacht at one's peril, but one also follows him at one's peril.[124]

Juynboll is more optimistic about the ability to obtain concrete results through the study of *isnads* and is a leader in this area today. To sketch his method it will be necessary to review some of the terminology he employs. The focus of Juynboll's research is what he terms the *isnad* bundle associated with a given tradition, which is a graphical representation of all known *isnads* that support it. Diagram 1 below is a theoretical *isnad* bundle.[125]

---

122. Muhammad Mustafa al A'zami, *Studies in Early Hadith Literature*, Indianapolis, 1978, pp. 230 and 243.

123. Michael Cook, *Early Muslim Dogma*, Cambridge (1981), p. 116.

124. Ibid p. 116.

125. G. H. A. Juynboll, *Studies in the Origins and Uses of Islamic Hadith*, Variorum (1966), XI, p. 153. For an interesting statistical approach to *isnad* criticism, see Herbert & Berg, *The Development of Exegesis in Early Islam*, Curzon Press (2000).

Diagram 1

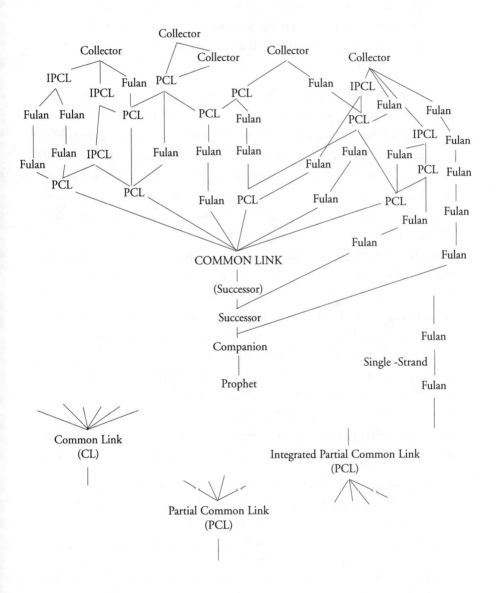

Juynboll bases his analysis of *isnad* bundles on J. Schacht's "common link theory," which he describes as follows:

> The more transmission lines come together in one transmitter, either reaching him or going away from him, the more this transmitter and his transmission have a claim to historicity.

In other words, if many lines of transmission of a *hadith* come together in one person, the greater the likelihood that this person was involved in the circulation of some version of the report that finally reaches us. According to Schacht and Joynboll, the **common link** (cl), the place in the bundle where the *isnad* strands first begin to fan out in different directions, "can on the whole be held responsible not only for the strand back to the Prophet but also for the proliferation of the text (*matn*) of the report or tradition, or in any case for the transmission of that *matn*'s most ancient wording." As Joynboll acknowledges, not all bundles show the cl as clearly as this hypothetical example (Diagram 1), but he states that there are dozens of famous *hadith* with *isnad* bundles that are much more dramatic, with fifteen or more lines extending out from one single common link.[126]

If we move up one level in Figure 1 from the cl, we find six transmitters, labelled partial common links and *fulans*. Juynboll defines a **partial common link** (pcl) as a transmitter who is supplied with a report by one or more masters and passes it on to two or more pupils. He believes that partial common links can reveal much about genuine master-pupil relationships and about the evolution of some traditions.

> The more pupils a transmitter conveys a report to in a certain *isnad* bundle—a fact more often than not corroborated in

---

126. Ibid XI, p. 155. The early scholars of *Hadith* developed methods of criticism that closely resemble Schacht's common link theory. See, Eerik Dickinson, *The Development of Early Sunnite Hadith Criticism*, Brill (2001), pp. 82-85. It should be noted that Cook's description of *isnad* spread (pp. 234-238) undermines the common link theory.

other *isnad* bundles supporting other *matns*—the more the relationship between master and pupils can be considered historically feasible. But there is more to pcls. Juxtaposition and comparison of the various versions of one tradition as they occur in the different collections presented by its *isnad* bundle often enables the researcher to draw certain conclusions as to which pcl can be credited with what alteration to the protoversion. These alterations may be trimmings or embellishments; they may boil down to a paraphrase or enlargement; they may constitute additions to, or abbreviations of, the protoversion. Time and again pcls can be observed, moreover, condensing a historical anecdote into a legal maxim or a juridical opinion, an ethical dictum or a moral adage. In short, next to the cls, pcls have played a crucial role in giving the *hadith* and *akhbar* collections as we know them now their definitive appearance.

Joynboll designates by *fulan* a transmitter in a particular *isnad* bundle who allegedly receives something from only one master and passes it on to only one pupil. The converse of the common link theory is *fulan* transmissions have the weakest claims to historicity. So that while the most credible lines of transmission are of the form cl– pcl– pcl– pcl– pcl– collector, the least credible lines of transmission are those that consist solely of *fulans*, like the right most line of transmission in Diagram 1. The logic here is it simply does not make sense that in a milieu where data on the Prophet was vigorously pursued and disseminated a Successor would pass on a report to only one student, who would share that information with only one of his students, who would share that information with only one of his students, and so on.

In the upper tiers of Figure 1 we find the occasional designation of **inverted partial common link** (ipcl). They are those transmitters who appear to have received a report from more than one master and to have passed it on to one (or relatively few) pupil(s).

Juynboll avers that the *rijal* works report many master/pupil relationships that cannot be trusted:

> [since they turn out] upon closer inspection to be merely an accumulation of master/pupil links exhaustively but uncritically garnered from all the *isnads* in all the collections the author of the *rijal* lexicon uses; in many cases that boils down to all the collections he could lay his hands on. However, very often these transmissions links are not factual, indeed in many cases the transmitters may not even be historical figures, these links being nothing but inventions of later collectors who bring new *isnads* into circulation just to increase the number of *turuq* (transmission paths) via which certain reports are supposed to have reached them. But if a master/pupil relationship turns up time and again in large numbers of *isnad* bundles, and specifically in relationships which are not merely *fulan/fulan* but rather pcl/pcl or pcl/ipcl or even pcl/*fulan*, we are on safe ground when we assume that the relationship is a historically factual one and not an invention of a much later collector with a predilection for masses of invented *turuq*.[127]

These are some of the main concepts and postulates involved in Juynboll's critique of prophetic traditions. Through meticulous analyses of *isnad* bundles incorporating extensive use of classical *Hadith* related sources he comes to numerous conclusions that are at odds with traditional Muslim views, of which I will only list a few. (1) He argues that the famous *mutawatir hadith*, "He who deliberately tells lies about me, will have to seek for himself a place in Hell," is a forgery and thus concludes that *tawatur* is no guarantee for the historicity of a *hadith*'s ascription to the Prophet.[128] (2) Juynboll examines *isnad* bundles of several well known woman-demeaning sayings that appear in canonical collections, among them the problematic *hadith* that asserts that most of the inhabitants of Hell are

---

127. Ibid XI, pp. 156-157.

128. G. H. A. Juynboll, *Muslim Tradition*, pp. 96-133.

women, and identifies what he believes are their real authors, in each case several generations removed from the Prophet's.[129] (3) Juynboll asserts that there are only a few hundred traditions each supported by an *isnad* bundle with a historically tenable line of transmission of the form

$$cl - pcl - pcl - pcl - pcl - collector$$

and that there are thousands upon thousands of traditions whose *isnad* bundles consist almost entirely of *fulans*; he designates these bundles "spiders" (see Diagram 2 below), and, as mentioned above, finds these to have the least credible lines of transmission.[130]

Diagram 2

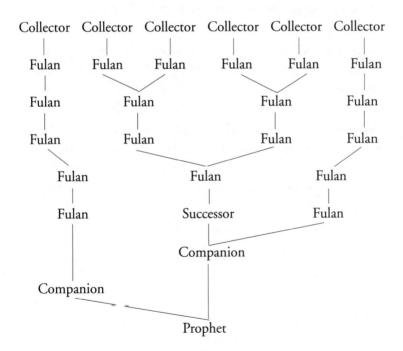

129. G. H. A. Juynboll, *Studies in the Origins and Uses of Islamic Hadith*, Variorum (1966), VI, pp. 343-383.

130. Ibid IX, pp. 215-216.

(4) Juynboll also asserts that almost all of the many bundles he examined, including the non-spiders, shared another unanticipated but clearly identifiable feature: "from the Prophet up to the beginning of the second century A.H. virtually every bundle shows a single strand of transmitters" (Diagram 3 below). Juynboll argues that in these cases the strand must be the construct of the bundle's common link.

> It is namely inconceivable that a remark of the Prophet was transmitted to later generations by one single Companion only, who in his turn passed it on only to one single Successor, who in his turn passed it on only to one single other Successor, etcetera. It is equally inconceivable to visualise an Islamic world of the second century, which as all medieval sources assure us was virtually awash with *hadith* transmission, in which hundreds of separate reports and traditions were passed on by single individuals to single individuals to yet other single individuals to yet other single individuals, and so on. ... In isolated cases it may seem conceivable that a *sahifa* (file) containing traditions and/or reports was passed on by its compiler to a single individual during the first few decades of its existence, but to explain the occurrence of thousand upon thousands of single *isnad* strands by one such isolated case is absurd.[131]

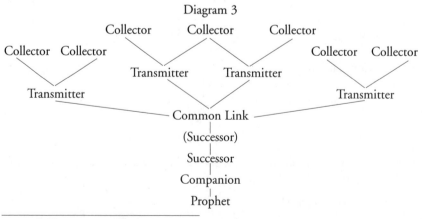

Diagram 3

---

131. Ibid XI, pp. 153-154.

Finally, it should be mentioned that while the assumptions upon which Juynboll bases his investigations seem sound, he himself acknowledges the tentativeness of any conclusions drawn. This is because the traditions and *isnads* we know of today may be only a fraction of those that once existed. Muslim historians report that Ahmad bin Hanbal sifted 30,000 traditions from some 750,000 for his *Musnad* and al Bukhari included in his *Sahih* only 7275 out of 600,000 traditions he critiqued. If these numbers are not gross exaggerations, then this would indicate that there has been a substantial loss of information.

> The sudden availability of a hitherto unpublished source may establish a transmitter as a pcl or ipcl rather than merely a *fulan*, which is good news for the historian or the *isnad* analyst who is on the lookout for positive results. We do not, and I am afraid indeed never will, have all the early *hadith* collections at our disposal. But what allows one to keep going in the present line of research, with this at first sight seemingly contrived terminology, is the conviction that the currently available literature is sufficiently vast to allow one to indulge in some cautious speculation.[132]

Juynboll may feel that the existing *Hadith* literature is sufficiently representative of what once was to allow for some cautious conjecture, but such guarded optimism is unlikely to assure many Muslim scholars. If its chief promoter can promise at best conjectural findings, then Muslim experts will probably not be persuaded to challenge in any significant way the conclusions of classical *hadith* criticism. Yet findings that are at odds with conventional views should not be ignored, for they can turn out to be a prelude to later discoveries that lead to major revision of our viewpoints. Furthermore, if we reject Juynboll's analysis on grounds that too much information has been lost, then this could also undermine our confidence in the findings of the ancient critics, for the more we resort to this defense the more our trust in their critique becomes a matter of faith rather than reason.

---

132. Ibid XI, p. 159.

Whom Do You Trust?

One of the most salient features of the *Hadith* and related literature is the profusion of discrepant information. Scholars dealt with contradictory sayings in a number of ways. The ranking of traditions based mainly on their *isnads* settled many of these conflicts, and subtle exegetics resolved many others. When contradictions between two traditions with equally sound *isnads* could not be reconciled exegetically, scholars would often try to date the traditions—sometimes reasoning quite tendentiously—under the supposition that the later tradition abrogated the earlier.

Yet it is in the *rijal* literature that we find the utmost discord, as conflicting judgments on the reliability of transmitters abound; because of this the evaluation of transmitters and *isnads* becomes by and large a subjective undertaking. Another weak point of classical *isnad* appraisal is that systematic *rijal* criticism upon which it depends did not commence until around 130 A.H./747 C.E., nearly a century after the origins of the *isnad* system. Hence we find ourselves in a serious predicament: the assessment of the reliability of *hadith* reports is based on information that is in nature less reliable than the material we are supposed to judge. This is all the more disconcerting since we have every reason to believe that *tadlis* (*isnad* tampering) occurred on as massive a scale as *matn* fabrication.

Of the various forms of *tadlis* described by *hadith* critics, *raf* (raising) is the most frequently discussed. *Raf* involves "raising" a tradition to the level of a more esteemed authority, most often the Prophet, by supplying the necessary links. Hence by means of *raf* statements of Companions, Successors, and even later authorities were transformed into prophetic traditions. There are numerous examples in the most respected *hadith* collections of sayings of the Prophet for which non-prophetic parallels exist. Although these could represent instances of *raf*, other explanations are possible, so that the question of how successful were the collectors in weeding out "raised" traditions is not so easily answered. Neither is the question of how pervasive was the occurrence of "*isnad* spread," the phenomenon by which a transmitter replaces some links in the *isnad* of a *hadith* with a chain of alternative transmitters linking it to himself.

Juynboll's meticulous study of *isnad* bundles, developed from Schacht's "common link" theory, would indicate that *isnad* invention and corruption was considerable and involved many of the traditions judged authentic by Muslim critics. The approach and assumptions behind Juynboll's investigations of *isnad* bundles are scientific, but the conclusions he reaches are necessarily provisional, since a great amount of data pertaining to traditions and *isnads* may have been lost.

All things considered, our survey of ancient and modern *hadith* investigations has left us in a quandary, as we have found grounds to seriously question the efficacy of ancient Muslim *hadith* criticism, but not enough to either disprove or validate it in general. Maybe we will never be any better off. Perhaps Abdul Ghafar's assessment of modern *Hadith* research is on the mark:

> On the whole it can be safely assumed that a very limited scope of discussion is left for a student of *Hadith* at present on the authenticity of a *hadith* as earlier traditionists have already done an exhaustive study of *Hadith* literature and given findings in detail.[133]

The ancient *muhaddithun* were presumably in the best position to uncover forgery, but we might not share Abdul Ghafar's optimism in their success. For those who suspect the *Hadith* literature, they may infer that we can never know which statements attributed to the Prophet are really his.

For myself, I am not convinced of the pointlessness of contemporary *Hadith* studies. Modern research has produced penetrating

---

133. Suhaib H. Abdul Ghafar, *Criticism of Hadith Among Muslims with Reference to Sunan Ibn Majah* (IFTA: 1984), pp. 247.

insights, raised legitimate questions, and made significant discoveries that challenge traditional conceptions of the history and development of the science. Although much information could have been lost, the impression I get is that there still is a large amount of existing material that needs to be critically examined, and, hopefully, a much greater contribution from modern Muslim scholars awaits us. As for now, given the ambiguousness of the evidence considered thus far, my faith in traditional *hadith* classification necessarily rests on my study of the texts (*matns*) of the traditions.

I have devoted most of my attention to the *Sahihs* of al Bukhari (which I have read twice from cover to cover) and Muslim bin al Hajjaj (which I have read once from start to finish), and have studied portions of the remaining Six Books and Imam Malik's *Muwatta* (which I have read several times). Though many of the authenticated reports seem credible, there are some of which I could not help being suspicious.

E.g. (1) There are a number of well-known Sayings of the Prophet that show much respect for women, but there are several that are rather uncomplimentary.[134] There is the famous tradition that asserts that the majority of the denizens of Hell are women, with some versions explaining that this is on account of their lesser faith and inferior intelligence vis-à-vis men (Bukhari, Muslim, Tirmidhi, Nasa`i). Another oft cited authenticated tradition states that the angels continuously curse a woman who refuses to come to her husband at night until morning, and He who is in Heaven remains angry with her until she satisfies her spouse (Bukhari). A wife's subservience to her husband is enshrined in the *hadith* in which the Prophet asserts that if it were permissible for anyone to prostrate before another person, he would have commanded women to prostrate before their spouses (Muslim).

My intuition is that these traditions reflect predominant attitudes of early Muslim society projected back to the Prophet. There is no

---

134. G. H. A. Juynboll, *Studies in the Origins and Uses of Islamic Hadith*, Variorum (1966), VI, pp. 343-383.

indication in the Qur'an that women are morally or spiritually inferi-
or to men, quite the opposite.[135] The Qur'an never states that women
are inherently of weaker intellect than men, but it does ridicule this
attitude of the ancient Arabs.[136] It even suggests that women excel
in *kayda* (the ability to outwit opponents),[137] a quality it also ascribes
to God. There are some legislative verses from which exegetes tried to
extrapolate a case for female weak-mindedness, such as that which
requires either two male witnesses, or a man and two female witnesses, to a business contract, but this stipulation makes allowances
for the fact that women at that time—and for that matter centuries
thereafter—were generally less knowledgeable in business dealings.[138]

It should also be noted that the Qur'an nowhere insists that
women yield to their husbands' carnal desires irrespective if they feel
up to it; rather it urges husbands to "consort with them [your wives]
in kindness." (4:19) The Qur'an also cannot be said to give husbands
absolute authority over their wives. It does state that its legal pronouncements "in fairness" provide men and women with similar
rights and obligations, and then adds that men have "a degree" over
them, but this is hardly an insistence, as some interpreters hold, on
male supremacy (2:228).

(2) The authenticated traditions contain numerous reports of
the Prophet performing miracles—with God's permission, of course.
Many of theses are similar to ones attributed to Jesus in the New
Testament, such as transforming small quantities of food into enough
to feed a whole host of hungry followers and curing blindness with
his saliva. Although the Qur'an recalls miracles of past prophets in its
narratives, it identifies itself—and perhaps one other supernatural
phenomenon[139]—as the only observable miracle(s) granted to the
Prophet. Moreover, the Qur'an states that the Prophet's opposition

135. *Surahs* 3:195; 9:71; 16:97; 33:35.
136. *Surahs* 43:16-18.
137. *Surahs* 2:28; 33-34.
138. Thus the Qur'an states that the extra female witness is necessary
"so that if one forgets the other will remind her." (2:282)

frequently complained that he produced no other miraculous signs. Yet if the Prophet indeed performed most of the miracles recorded in the *Hadith* literature, then it is a wonder that his opponents consistently complained of a lack of supernatural signs or that the Qur'an did not at least cite more of them in response to pagan objections.

(3) The Qur'an states that the Prophet was recurrently questioned concerning the timing of the Day of Judgement and was repeatedly commanded by God to simply reply, "Knowledge thereof belongs to God alone."[140] In the *Hadith* records, however, the Prophet supplies numerous predictions of events that will herald its coming. Since the Qur'an is so insistent on how the Prophet should respond to these queries, I find it odd that he would offer so many details and hints about the arrival of the Hour.

(4) Numerous traditions concerning the coming of the *Dajjal* (anti-Christ)[141] and of the *Mahdi* (divinely guided one) belong to the most respected collections. Seeing as the Qur'an does not allude to either of these apocalyptic figures, it is hard to believe that the Prophet gave them so much attention.

139. *Surah* 54:1 states: "The Hour drew near and the moon was rent asunder," which most commentators, based on authenticated *hadith* accounts, take as a reference to an incident when the Prophet split the moon in two. But some exegetes believe this verse refers to events on the Day of Judgment, which the Qur'an often relates in the past tense, and some others state that this is an ancient Arabic idiom that means "a matter has become manifest." See Muhammad Ali, *The Holy Qur'an,* Lahore (1963), note 2388.

140. *Surahs* 7:187; 10:48-49; 27:71; 31:34; 32:28; 33;63; 34:29; 36:48; 43:85; 51:12; 67:25-26; 72:25; 79:42-45.

141. As interpreted by the Church, the anti-Christ is a figure to come near the end of time. The New Testament, however, seems to use the word *anti-Christ* as a synonym for Satan and as a general description of anyone who does not follow the teachings of Jesus (1 John 2:18; 4:3; 2 John 0:7). The Church seems to have applied the term *anti-Christ* to "the beast" who, according to the New Testament, is an apocalyptic figure to come with the powers of Satan (Revelations 13:1-3 in which Satan is symbolized as a "dragon"). Some Muslim commentators equate the beast of Revelations to that of *Surah* 27:82.

(5) Some sayings seem almost too good to be true, tailor made, as it were, to settle some major political, jurisprudential, and theological disputes that arose in the first few centuries following the death of the Prophet. We know from their own testimony that the *muhadithun* were on the look out for tendentious *hadiths*, and judging from the *sahih* (authenticated) reports they were largely successful in screening out sectarian traditions produced by factions to which they did not belong, but one wonders if they were as discriminating with regard to traditions that supported their own platforms.

E.g. (A) The issue of political succession after the Prophet's demise gave rise to one of the earliest, bitterest, and most enduring conflicts in Islamic history. Partisans of `Ali believed that the first three political successors to the Prophet (in order: Abu Bakr, 'Umar, and 'Uthman) had usurped Ali's right—many would say "divine right"— to head the community and were known to anathematise these three Companions from the pulpits of their mosques. Likewise, many supporters of the Umayyad dynasty would often curse `Ali from their pulpits. The *ahl al hadith* adopted a more judicious stance; they declared that the rule of each of the first four caliphs was legitimate and that their faith was beyond reproach. The following tradition from Bukhari's *Sahih*, which so succinctly exonerates the first three Caliphs in the precise order of their reigns, certainly sounds like it was invented to refute their detractors.

> On the authority of Abu Musa: The Prophet entered a garden and bade me guard its gate. Then a man came and asked leave to enter. And [the Prophet] said: Let him enter, and announce to him [that he will gain] Paradise.—And lo, it was Abu Bakr. Thereafter another man came and asked leave to enter. And [the Prophet] said: Let him enter, and announce to him [that he will enter] Paradise.—And lo, it was 'Umar. Thereafter another man came and asked leave to enter. And [the Prophet] remained silent for a while; then he said: Let him enter, and

announce to him [that he will gain] Paradise after a calamity that is to befall him.—And lo, it was 'Uthman ibn 'Affan.[142]

(B) As mentioned previously, the doctrine of the collective *ta'dil* of the Companions, which seems to have won near universal acceptance among *hadith* scholars by the fifth Islamic century, holds that the Companions are free of falsehood in transmitting prophetic *hadiths*. In the earlier centuries the veracity of certain Companions was at times challenged.[143] We even find in the *Hadith* corpus instances of Companions distrusting one another.[144] However, no Companion was subject to as much critical scrutiny as Abu Hurayrah.[145] Apparently one point of contention was that he is credited with having transmitted many more traditions than any other Companion, even though he was with the Prophet for just three years.[146] The following two reports from Bukhari have the appearance of unsophisticated attempts at an explanation.

> Abu Hurayrah narrated: The people say that Abu Hurayrah narrates too many narrations, but God knows whether I say the truth or not. They also ask: "Why do the emigrants and the Ansar not narrate as he does?" In fact, my emigrant brothers were busy trading in the markets, and my Ansar

---

142. The translation is by Muhammad Asad, *Sahih al-Bukhari: The Early Years of Islam*, Dar Al-Andalus (1981), pp. 47-48.

143. It is extremely unlikely that the falsified traditions that have come down to us were the fabrications of the Companions appearing in their *isnads*, for the factional disputes that fostered most of their invention did not produce doctrinal planks until after their time.

144. See note 77.

145. G. H. A. Juynboll, *Muslim Tradition*, Cambridge (1983), pp. 192-206.

146. Muhammad Zubayr Siddiqi credits Abu Hurayrah with the transmission of 5374 traditions, more than twice the number of his nearest competitor, 'Abd Allah bin 'Umar. *Hadith Literature*, Calcutta (1961), p. 27.

brothers were busy with their properties. I was a poor man keeping the company of the Messenger of God and was satisfied with what filled my stomach. So I used to be present while they were absent, and I used to remember while they forgot.

Abu Hurayrah narrated: I said to the Messenger of God, "I hear many narrations from you but I forget them." The Messenger of God said, "Spread your *rida'* (cloak)." I did so and then he moved his hands as if filling them with something (and emptied them in my *rida'*) and then said, "Take and wrap this over your body." I did it and after that I never forgot anything.

(C) In the field of jurisprudence we come upon many long-standing disputes in the classical period for which prophetic traditions were ultimately discovered that speak directly to them. For instance, the legitimacy of *ijma'* (consensus) as a source of Islamic Law was much debated during Imam al Shafi'i's time, who defends it in his *Risala*. Yet al Shafi'i, a leader of the *hadith* party, was apparently unaware of the famous statement of the Prophet, "my community will never agree on an error" (al Tirmidhi), which establishes its validity.

Another point of contention among al Shafi'i's colleagues was whether prophetic *sunnahs* on issues unmentioned in the Qur'an are binding. This time, however, al Shafi'i is able to call upon a made-to-order *hadith*.

Narrated Abu Rafi: The Prophet said: 'Let me not find any one of you reclining on his couch and saying when a command reaches him, "I do not know. We shall follow [only] what we find in the Book of God."' (Abu Dawud)

The stoning of married adulterers was also disputed in early Islam, with the opposition objecting that it conflicts with the Qur'anic penalty of flogging (24:2). Its proponents claimed that the Qur'anic punishment is aimed at unmarried adulterers and that the Prophet's *Sunnah* establishes the much harsher punishment for married offenders. Yet this would be an example of the *Sunnah* abrogating the Qur'an, which the majority of scholars could not accept. The following *hadith* rectifies this situation by demonstrating that the "verse of stoning" is in fact a lost part of the Scripture.

> Malik related to me that Yahya ibn Said heard Said ibn al Musayyab say: "When Umar ibn al Khattab came from Mina, he made his camel kneel at al Abtah, and then gathered a pile of small stones and cast his cloak over them and dropped to the ground. Then he raised his hands to the sky and said, 'O Allah! I have become old and my strength has weakened. My flock is scattered. Take me to You with nothing missed out and without having neglected anything.' Then he went to Medina and addressed the people. He said, 'O People! *Sunan* have been laid down for you. Obligations have been laid down for you. You have been left with a clear way unless you lead people astray right and left.' He struck one of his hands on the other and then said, 'Take care lest you destroy the verse of stoning so that one will say, "We do not find two compulsory punishments in the Book of Allah." The Messenger of Allah stoned, so we have stoned. By He in whose hands is my self, had it not been that people would say that Umar ibn al Khattab has added to the Book of Allah, we would have written it in—The full grown man and the full grown woman, stone them absolutely." We have certainly recited that.'"

> Yahya said that he heard Malik say, "As for the words 'The full grown man and the full grown woman' he meant, 'The man and the woman who have been married, stone them absolutely.'" (*Muwatta* of Imam Malik and a shorter version in *Sahih al Bukhari*)

There are numerous examples like these in the tradition literature of seemingly made-to-order *hadiths* that provide unequivocal proof for the correctness of various juridical stances that were taken in long-standing legal debates. If these traditions are genuine, it is surprising that these debates persisted so long—often into the late second and third Islamic centuries—and that these extremely convenient traditions are not cited in earlier works that discuss the topics they address.

(6) The verse-of-stoning *hadith* belongs to a class of traditions that claim the incompleteness of the Qur'an, in the sense that the Scripture as we have it today does not contain all of the verses revealed to the Prophet.[147] Muslim experts considered most of these reports unsound, but a few have infiltrated the authenticated ranks. The two *Sahihs* report Anas as saying:

> There was revealed concerning those slain at Bi'r Ma'una a Qur'anic verse we used to recite until it was retracted later on. The verse was: "Inform our tribe on our behalf that we have met our Lord Who is well pleased with us and we are well pleased. (Bukhari, Muslim).

This and the stoning verse tradition indicate that at least two verses of the Qur'an have been eliminated from the text. Other sound traditions indicate that much larger sections were withdrawn.

> Ubayy asked Zirr, "How many verses do you reckon in *Surah Al Ahzab*?" Zirr replied, "Seventy-two or three." Ubayy declared, "It used to be as long as *Al Baqara* (two hundred eighty six verses), and we used to recite in *Al Ahzab* the stoning verse. Zirr asked what the stoning verse was, and Ubayy recited: "If the *shaykh* and the *shaykha* fornicate, stone them both as an exemplary punishment from God. God is mighty, wise."

147. Richard Burton, *The Sources of Islamic Law, Islamic Theory of Abrogation*, Edinburgh (1990), pp. 43-55, where the author discusses the part such traditions played in the development of the theory of abrogation of Qur'anic verses.

Concerning the ninth *surah* (*al Tawbah*), which consists of one hundred twenty nine verses, Hudhayfah is reported to have remarked: "[Today] you don't recite one fourth of the [original] *surah*."[148]

It is important to recognize that traditional Muslim interpretation does not hold that these absent sections of the Qur'an were simply misplaced or forgotten by the Prophet and his disciples, for the Scripture states that God will protect His Revelation (15:9). Instead, it is believed that God withdrew these verses; that is, He caused them to be lost or forgotten and that this represents another form of divine abrogation of Qur'anic Revelations. Yet this interpretation is strained in the case of the stoning verse, as 'Umar insists that these verses indeed belong to the current text and that he would write them in with his own hand except for fear that people would say that he has added to the Scripture; in other words, in his opinion, these verses were mistakenly omitted from the Qur'an.

Needless to say, my study of the *matns* (texts) of the most respected collections did not assure me of their authenticity. I appreciate and respect the enormity of the effort to sift the genuine from false reports, but there are authenticated traditions that simply do not ring true for me. As I mentioned earlier, my experience of the Qur'an may have left me negatively predisposed toward the reported Sayings of the Prophet. It was for me the most moving, compelling, life-altering experience imaginable; it took me on a journey I could never have anticipated, from one boundary of the religious spectrum to another. The Qur'an, by its sheer irresistible force, made me into a Muslim. And yet, I am embarrassed to admit that in spite of power and profundity of that experience, my reading of the *Hadith* literature caused me at times to second guess it and to wonder if I had been self-deceived. And so I continually replayed it in my mind and steadfastly read the Qur'an each day to check if I had been misled, but each

---

148. Richard Burton, *The Sources of Islamic Law, Islamic Theory of Abrogation*, Edinburgh (1990), pp. 50 and 54.

time I put down the Scripture I was that much more convinced that I had met truth in its pages. The Qur'an kept my faith secure during those first few years after conversion while I navigated the sometimes rough and bewildering currents of *Hadith*. Nonetheless, although my faith is no longer perturbed by my study of the traditions, I still feel the need to come to terms with them.

Approximate Solutions

A comment from a second-generation American Muslim woman:

> The *Hadith*—do you follow them? Some *hadiths* in Sahih Bukhari (so presumably they are correct) still bother me. Why are there so many references to how there are more women than men in Hell, etcetera? There is also the *hadith* that if you follow the five pillars of Islam you will go to Heaven? Isn't this simplistic? I can lie and cheat and still go to Heaven if I do the five rituals?

There are problems for which there are ideal solutions and problems for which there are not. In determining how to interpret and apply specific *hadiths* to one's personal life and lifestyle, sometimes a believer simply must select the best approximate solution. Our search for Qur'anic proof for the obligation to adhere to the Prophet's traditions produced no explicit mandate to do so, however it can be argued that some statements in the Revelation imply it. Assuming that the repeated commands to "Obey God and His Messenger" are directed toward all believers of all times, and acknowledging that the Qur'an is frequently vague as regards its other directives, it would seem highly likely that this linking of submission to God to obedience to the Prophet implies adherence to at least some amount of non-Qur'anic prophetic instruction. Supposing this, the issue then becomes one of extent.

The Companions surely perceived that obedience to the Messenger required heeding all of his teachings and pronouncements, and the early generations of Muslims presumably inherited the same view. Imam al Shafi`i argued that this is the mandatory course for all believers and is accomplished by adhering to the recently pronounced authentic *Sunnah* of the Prophet.

A large segment of jurists in al Shafi`i's time opted for a more cautious approach. In the face of widespread forgery and deceit, especially within the ranks of *ahl al hadith* (the same party that also produced the most concerted effort to separate out the genuine accounts of the Prophet), many felt that only traditions that relate to explicit pronouncements in the Qur'an are authoritative, thus minimizing the amount of religious innovation that could be appended to the religion.

Al Shafi`i also recognized that we cannot be certain of the authenticity of each *sahih hadith*, but he held that juridical judgments based on them, even when the relevant traditions are flawed, are ultimately right, for the scholars who make them have met their obligation to implement God's will to the best of their ability.

> [Legal] knowledge is of various kinds: The first consists of the right decisions in the literal and implied senses, the other, of the right answer in the literal sense only. The right decisions [in the literal and implied senses] are those based [either] on God's command or on a *sunnah* of the Apostle related by the public from an [earlier] public. These are two sources by virtue of which the lawful is established as lawful and unlawful as unlawful. This is [knowledge] of which nobody is allowed to be ignorant or doubtful. Secondly, knowledge of the specialists consists of traditions related by a few and known only to scholars, but others are under no obligation to be familiar with it. Such knowledge may either be found among all or a few [of the scholars] related by a reliable transmitter from the Prophet. This is knowledge that is binding on scholars to accept and it constitutes the right decision in the

literal sense such as when we accept [the validity of] the testimony of two witnesses. This is right [only] in the literal sense, because it is possible that [the testimony of] the two witnesses might be false.[149]

Al Shafi`i distinguishes here between being right in the absolute (literal and implied) sense and right in the ultimate (only literal) sense. He frequently cites the obligation to face the *Kabah* in prayer to illustrate the difference. If the *Kabah* is not in view Muslims do their best to estimate its direction. Ordinarily, the worshipper in this situation will not be exactly right in his or her choice of direction, but the prayer is nevertheless valid. In Al Shafi`i's terminology, the choice of direction in this case is right in the literal sense even though it may not be in the implied sense.[150]

Of these two approaches to the *Hadith* literature, both of which go back to the second Islamic century, al Shafi`i's became the standard of Sunni Islam.[151] The alternative viewpoint in time faded away, although today it appears to have a small but growing following among American Muslim youth. Whereas the alternative approach is meant to limit the amount of false information on the Prophet that could affect Muslim beliefs and practices, al Shafi`i's system limits the amount of genuine information that might be disregarded.

In recent times new ways of viewing *Hadith* and *Sunnah* have been advanced that in some measure accept the findings of modern *hadith* criticism while in theory maintaining the authority of the *Sunnah*.[152] Of special note is the approach put forth by the Pakistani scholar Fazlur Rahman in the 1960s. The cornerstone of his scheme

149. Muhammad ibn Idris al Shafi`i, *Al Risala*, translated by Majid Khadduri, John Hopkins Press (1961), p. 111

150. Ibid p. 300, for example.

151. Often referred to by Western scholars as the Muslim orthodoxy. They comprise approximately eighty five percent of the current Muslim world population.

152 Daniel W. Brown's, *Rethinking Tradition in Modern Islamic Thought*, Cambridge, 1996, pp. 100-107.

is a return to what he views as the original notion of *Sunnah*, a term that took on many nuances in the first two Islamic centuries. In addition to the normative behaviors and rulings of the Prophet, it also included the practices and opinions of his most devoted followers, and sometimes to those of highly respected authorities of the next two generations.[153] The *Muwatta* shows that for Imam Malik *sunnah* often signifies the agreed upon practice of the community (although he seems to have in mind the Medinan community). In Abu Hanifa's letter to 'Uthman al Batti *sunnah* is used on several occasions to refer to "the normative way of the early community as a whole."[154] Citing several similar examples Rahman makes the case that before al Shafi'i *sunnah* was "a general umbrella concept rather than filled with absolutely specific content."[155] Brown outlines Rahman's position:

> [*Sunnah*] was never meant to remain static, but to evolve and develop. Consequently, *sunnah* in the second sense represents the community's interpretation, elaboration, and application of Prophetic *sunnah* in specific situations; it is inspired by the Prophetic example and absorbs it, but its specific formulation is the work of Muslims themselves. The Muslim community is itself responsible for creating *sunnah*, based on the spirit of the Prophetic example, and guaranteed by the principle of *ijma'*. *Sunnah* is therefore "coextensive with the *ijma'* of the community" and *sunnah* and *ijma'* are "materially identical."[156]

153. J. Schacht, *The Origins of Muhammadan Jurisprudence*, Oxford (1950), pp.58-81; M. M. Bravmann, *The Spiritual Background of Early Islam, Studies in Ancient Arab Concepts*, Leiden (1972), pp. 123-198; G. H. A. Juynboll, *Studies on the Origins and Uses of Islamic Hadith*, Variorum (1996) V.

154. G. H. A. Juynboll, *Studies on the Origins and Uses of Islamic Hadith*, Variorum (1996) V, p. 104.

155. Fazlur Rahman, *Islamic Methodology in History,* Karachi, 1965, pp. 11-12, cited by Brown in *Rethinking Tradition,* p. 103.

156. Daniel W. Brown's, *Rethinking Tradition in Modern Islamic Thought*, Cambridge, 1996, p. 103. Brown refers the reader to Rahman's, *Islamic Methodology*, pp. 6, 18-19.

Rahman maintains that *sunnah* in this original broader sense precedes *hadith* and that the latter essentially documents the former. He accepts that most early traditions go back not to the Prophet but to later authorities who he claims were occupied with deriving the "living *sunnah*." He also agrees that many traditions are "raised" from non-prophetic reports. Yet none of this undermines Rahman's conception of *sunnah* nor, in his opinion, reduces the importance of *Hadith* as a source of *sunnah*, for "although *Hadith* verbally speaking does not go back to the Prophet, its spirit certainly does, and *Hadith* is largely the situational interpretation and formulation of the Prophetic model or spirit."[157]

Therefore, for Rahman, *sunnah* is not fixed, as the traditional definition implies, but a "living and on-going process."[158] But how can contemporary Muslims use *Hadith* to recover this "living *sunnah*"? Brown explains:

> Rahman opposes any sort of formalistic or literalistic applica-
> tion of *hadiths*. What is needed instead is "to study *hadith*
> in situational context—to understand their true functional
> significance to extract the real moral value." The *Hadith*
> must be treated as a "gigantic and monumental commentary
> on the Prophet by the early community." Muslims should
> study the commentary not in order to apply it directly, but
> for clues to the spirit behind it. Viewed in this way, the
> whole of the *Hadith* literature proves its value, for even where
> the specific content of a *hadith* must be rejected (e.g., that
> a Muslim will enter Paradise even if he commits adultery and
> theft), the spirit behind such a tradition (i.e., opposition to
> schism and the need for catholicity in the community) can be
> appreciated.

157. Fazlur Rahman, *Islamic Methodology in History*, Karachi, 1965, p. 80, cited by Brown in *Rethinking Tradition*, p. 104.

158. Fazlur Rahman, *Islamic Methodology in History*, Karachi, 1965, p. 75, cited by Brown in *Rethinking Tradition*, p. 104.

Because no particular tradition is tied to the Prophet with any degree of certainty—at best *Hadith* embody the "spirit" of the Prophet—Rahman is free to accept, reject, or reinterpret traditions without appearing to flout the example of the Prophet. A particular practice or law might well be considered a true outworking of the *Sunnah* in one era or one circumstance, but the same law might be interpreted as dispensable or incompatible with *Sunnah* in another era. *Sunnah* is not fixed, but dynamic; not static, but evolving. Rahman's primary example is the case of *riba* (usury). The spirit behind the prohibition on *riba* clearly does extend back to the Qur'an and to the Prophet. But the particular definition given to *riba* formalized by early generations of Muslims and enshrined in the *Hadith* (i.e., that it represented any amount of interest on certain categories of loans) need not be applied. So long as they abide by the spirit behind the prohibition, Muslims are free to work out the detail of its application for themselves.[159]

Rahman's conception of *Sunnah* and its relationship to *Hadith* has not caught on among modern Muslim thinkers, and it is not likely to as long as they remain confident in the evaluations of classical *hadith* criticism. His approach to *Hadith* and *Sunnah* will most likely appeal only to those who are already sceptical of the traditions but reluctant to disregard them, for he offers them a coherent way to reconcile their doubts about the *Hadith* literature with its traditional role as Islam's second source of guidance after the Qur'an. Rahman's principle achievement is his upholding of the authority of the *Sunnah* and the essentiality of *Hadith* without insisting on the historicity of each prophetic tradition. If future research of the traditions by Muslim scholars tends to support Western *hadith* studies, approaches similar to Rahman's may become popular.

---

159. Brown, *Rethinking Tradition*, pp. 105-106. Quotations are from Rahman, *Islamic Methodology*, pp. 76-77.

Although Fazlur Rahman's views on *Hadith* and *Sunnah* provide a defensible posture against modern criticism, it is doubtful that concerns over authenticity and authority will significantly diminish; in the end it may only shift them from one paradigm to another. For if the traditions are by and large only interpretations of the Prophet's example projected back to him, then they can be safely ignored when they seem inconvenient. A believer will naturally feel bound only by what the Prophet actually said or did; opinions of later authorities simply do not carry the same weight, nor should they.

Rahman's characterization of the traditions as interpretations inspired by the Prophet's example benignly attributed to him is also open to question. The *rijal* and other *Hadith* related literature describe other motivations behind *hadith* fabrication. Political, sectarian, partisan, prejudicial, and self-aggrandising aims were frequently behind *hadith* deception. Most often *hadiths* were manufactured and manipulated to lend prophetic authority to customs, opinions, doctrines, or party planks that were unconnected to his teachings and behaviors. This being the case, the felt need to distinguish the traditions that are genuinely based on the Prophet's *Sunnah* from the forgeries will probably persist even if Rahman's ideas were to gain acceptance.

Each of the three approaches discussed above offer plausible responses to the Qur'an's calls to heed God and His Messenger, but none of them are ideal, or as al Shafi`i might put it, "right in both the implied and literal senses." Because of the way I opened this section, it might be expected that I would now indicate which I believed to be optimal. While I can conceive of advantages to each of them, my attitude and approach to *Hadith* seems to be moving toward an intermediate position, which I discuss in the next question; however, I doubt I will ever arrive at a hard and fast formula.

Questions

Question 1 (from an American Muslim female college student):

Your discussion on <u>Hadith</u> in your first book[160] was very helpful to me. It helped me to break down a lot of barriers to believing in Islam. It forced me to ask questions that I knew I had, but was unwilling to confront. I also like the fact that you raise questions rather than give answers. This was a very good technique for forcing people like me to go and do the investigating on our own. But, at the same time I felt that you do have specific views on the role of <u>Hadith</u>, <u>tafsir</u>,[161] and <u>sirah</u>,[162] particularly since you clearly used them in your first and second books.[163] But because you raised a debate over these sources and then used them without justifying fully why, it made it kind of difficult for me to follow your logic on certain issues. It seemed to me that you used <u>hadiths</u> that in your view agree with the Qur'an. I found this very interesting because I realize that I do not fully grasp it. My questions to you are: What do you use to judge that a <u>hadith</u> is false, if not the criteria of classical <u>Hadith</u> science? What role does reason play in determining which <u>hadiths</u> should be used? Can we use reason to judge <u>hadiths</u> when reason is culturally biased? (I know that you answered this question in your first book, but I am still very unclear about it.)

My discussion of the tradition literature in *Struggling to Surrender* is essentially a defense of traditional *Hadith* science, and, in particular, Imam al Shafi`i's views. I think some readers got the opposite impression because I began by relating my initial disillusionment with the traditions—which was the impetus behind my investigations of them—and because I presented (and critiqued) as best as I could modern Western findings in this area. From the feedback I received on my first book, it became quite clear to me that despite my stated

---

160. Jeffrey Lang, *Struggling to Surrender*, Amana Publications.
161. Qur'anic exegesis.
162. Biography of the Prophet.
163. Jeffrey Lang, *Even Angels Ask*, Amana Publications, 1977

misgivings with the conclusions of Western critics, many readers were surprised by them—having never been exposed to them before—and in fact found them at least somewhat convincing. Apparently many readers' intuition was that traditional *hadith* classification is less than perfect—even though many of them would not admit to such feelings[164]—and the findings of Western critics that I outlined made them more conscious of their doubts and helped to intensify them.

When I wrote my first book, I had no personal system for accepting or rejecting traditions, which is why I did not present one. I for the most part accepted all *sahih* (authenticated) *hadiths*, although I felt it necessary to take into consideration the historical contexts of the Prophet's acts. I thought it important to derive general ethical and spiritual lessons from them, rather than attempt to replicate the cultural and historical specifics they describe or to mimic tangential aspects of the Prophet's example. Since then, my views on the Prophet's traditions has evolved in some measure, and I suspect that it will continue to in the future, especially if I am able to study more of the source material. For this reason the following description of my attitude toward the traditions is not a recommendation but merely an explanation of how I presently deal with them.

With regard to the legal traditions (those that influence Muslim practices), I can certainly relate to the concerns of the jurists of al Shafi`i's time who were reluctant to accept *hadiths* that promote *sunnahs* on matters on which there is no text in the Qur'an, since these could have provided an all too convenient vehicle for appending unwarranted practices and beliefs to the religion. On the other hand, if the Prophet did give instruction not alluded to in the Scripture— and he almost certainly did then I would not want to disregard it. I therefore have adopted a compromise position to regard as authoritative the authenticated legal traditions that seem not to conflict with the Qur'an. Thus I object to the stoning penalty for married

---

164. Apparently many Muslims are taught that it is against Islam to suspect that some *sahih* traditions might not be genuine.

adulterers since I feel it is at variance with the Qur'an (24.2) and because the most decisive evidence in its favor—the "stoning verse" tradition attributed to Umar—implies the Qur'an is incomplete, which again to my mind contradicts the Scripture (15:9).[165] On the other hand, although the Qur'an is silent on men wearing gold jewelry, I choose not to do so, since this is prohibited in *sahih* traditions and it is not at odds with the spirit of the sacred Scripture.

When I say that I recognize the authority of the *sahih* legal traditions that are not at variance with the letter or spirit of the Qur'an, this does not mean that I swear by their authenticity, but rather, I acknowledge their evidentiary value. While I am sure that a good number of these reports are inspired by the Prophet's bona fide example, I am not convinced that all of them are, yet I justify their use on grounds similar to the defenses offered by Imam al Shafi`i and to a lesser extent by Fazlur Rahman. Given the limits of my knowledge of *Hadith* and my wish to respond validly to the Qur'an's calls for obedience to God's Messenger, and seeing as the traditional *hadith* classification is currently the best assessment available, I feel that my abiding by these legal traditions is correct in the "literal sense" as described by al Shafi`i.[166] Similar to Rahman, I also feel that authenticated sayings that do not really go back to the Prophet are nevertheless of value, since they represent interpretations of Islam that go back to the first few generations of Muslims. This latter information, which depicts the customs of the earliest believers, is of particular importance in view of the widespread trend among Muslims to project their interpretations of Islam back to this time period. Frequently, it can be demonstrated that first century believers did not follow the practices advocated. For example, female seclusion is enforced in many Muslim communities in America, even though there are numerous *hadiths*

---

165. Cf. pp. 253-254. Verse 15:9 reads, "We have, without doubt, sent down the Reminder, and We will assuredly guard it."

166. Cf. pp. 254-255 above.

relating events during the later phases of the Prophet's career and the time of first four caliphs that show prominent unrelated Muslim men and women in mixed company. Reports such as these demonstrate that the Prophet could not have ordered the general seclusion of women or that it was generally practiced in the first Islamic century.

My approach to the non-legal traditions—which includes the *sira* (Prophet's biography or historical reports), theological traditions, and *tarhib wa targhib* (inspiring awe and piety) traditions—is less formulaic and more guarded than it is toward the legal *hadith*. This is partly because the former seems to contain many more fanciful and tendentious accounts than the latter. However, the main reason I am more wary of non-legal traditions is that I believe that erroneous reports of this kind can be much more damaging to Islam's image, since they provide cynics and the undecided with more serious grounds to question the validity of Islam and integrity of the Prophet than do the strictly legal traditions. Indeed, most of the American Muslims who have shared with me their doubts about Islam link them to the non-legal *hadith* literature.

I am especially cautious with regard to the theological traditions, as fabricated reports on the Prophet can be damaging enough to the religion's perceived veracity but the harm done by false theological doctrines could be much worse. There is nothing that can injure a person's faith or deter someone in his or her search for truth than unfounded, untrue dogmas. I am aware of the inherent limitations of human speech in expressing realities outside of human experience and that traditions that speak of the nature of God and His doings may be highly allegorical and hence should not be taken literally. Thus I do not expect each theological tradition to be completely coherent from the standpoint of formal logic or consistent with all other revealed affirmations on God. But if a theological tradition seems to me utterly unreasonable or ethically objectionable I allow for the possibility that it may have been misreported—as theological propositions are easily misunderstood—or that it might not be genuine. An example of such a *hadith* is the following severe explanation of fate that to me is irreconcilable with the Qur'an's depictions of an all-merciful, all-just, purposeful Creator.

> The Messenger of God said: God created Adam. Then He stroked his back with His right hand and some of his progeny issued from it. He said, "I created these for Paradise and their deeds will be of the people of Paradise." Then He stroked his back again and brought forth the rest of his progeny from him. He said, "I created these for the Fire and their deeds will be of the people of the Fire." A man asked, "Messenger of God, then of what value are deeds?" The Messenger of God replied, "When God creates a slave for Paradise, He gives him the behavior of the people of Paradise so that he dies on one of the deeds of the people of Paradise and by it He brings him into Paradise. When He creates a slave for the Fire, He gives him the behavior of the people of the Fire so that he dies on one of the deeds of the people of the Fire and by it He brings him into Fire.[167]

There are also historical considerations that support circumspection with regard to the theological traditions. We do not have many religious tracts that date from the first Islamic century, but several theological epistles ascribed to this time period have survived. Among those that have received the most attention of late are the *Sirat Salim bin Dhakwan*, two letters of 'Ibn Ibad to the Caliph 'Abd al Malik, the *Kitab al irja'* of Hasan bin Muhammad, the *Risala fi'l qadar* of Hasan of Basra, the anti-Qadarite epistle of 'Umar bin 'Abd al 'Aziz ('Umar II), and the *Questions* of Hasan bin Muhammad.[168] One of the

---

167. Malik ibn Anas, *Al Muwatta*, translated by Aishah Abdurrahman Bewley, Kegan Paul International (1989), p. 380.

168. Michael Cook, *Early Muslim Dogma*, Cambridge (1981). It should be noted that Cook questions the purported authorships of these epistles.

striking features of these polemical writings is that they rarely if ever cite prophetic *hadiths*, although they abound in Qur'anic citations. For example, the first letter of `Ibn Ibad, the *Kitab al irja'*, the *Risala fi'l Qadar*, and the *Questions* cite no traditions, and the *Sirat Salim* and the epistle of Umar II contain only one and two *hadith*, respectively. The second letter of `Ibn Ibad is in a class by itself in that "it shows a pronounced though not consistent hostility to *hadith*."[169] These early works debate a wide range of topics that include predestination, divine knowledge and its relationship to time, the relationship between faith and works, the uncreatedness of the Qur'an,[170] and the faith status of Muslims who commit major sins. The fact that the epistles reference so very few *hadiths* suggests—but certainly does not prove for the evidence is scant—that many of the numerous traditions that directly bear upon their contents came into existence some time after the first Islamic century.

Muslim historians and heresiographers also report that these great theological controversies sprung from the political turmoil that marred the first century of Islam.[171] The dispute over predestination began with claims by defenders of the Umayad caliphs that their rule was divinely foreordained. Arguments over divine knowledge then grew out of the predestination debate.[172] The same could be said of the conflict over the uncreatededness of the Qur'an, for it was argued that the eternality of the Qur'an proves that the many events referred

---

169. Ibid. p. 56.

170. The dispute was over whether the Qur'an is created by God or is eternal.

171. Michael Cook, *Early Muslim Dogma*, Cambridge (1981)

172. The proponents of predestination often argued that God's foreknowledge of all things implies their being predetermined. Some of their opponents proposed that there are limits to what God foreknows.

to in the Scripture were predestined.[173] Disputes over the relationship between faith and works and the faith status of Muslims who commit major sins arose in connection with the *fitnah* that followed 'Uthman's murder and the claims of the anti-Umayads that they were guilty of major sins. If these political conflicts did incite these debates then they must have been in progress during the time of the Successors. But again, if the Prophet expounded on these topics as frequently and deliberately as *hadith* accounts indicate, then one would think that these controversies would never have gotten off the ground so soon after his demise, or at least would have been nipped in the bud fairly soon after.

Before commenting briefly on the place of reason in *Hadith* studies I thought I should recap my current attitude toward the tradition literature. First, I should point out that I do not totally disregard the non-*sahih* traditions, for I believe that they often contain wisdom that goes back to the beginnings of the Muslim community and sometimes to the Prophet himself, but like almost all Muslims I give much greater weight to the authenticated traditions.[174] If a tradition is judged *sahih*, I then consider its consistency with the Qur'an; if it seems to be opposed to the letter or spirit of the Qur'an, then I do not feel bound by it, but I know of few traditions in this category. If a *sahih* legal tradition appears to satisfy the above criteria, then I abide by it, taking into account the historical context of the report. I am somewhat more guarded with respect to the non-legal traditions, which I feel can do much more harm to an individual's search for truth and which seem to contain many more spurious reports. This is especially the case with the theological traditions. If a non-legal

173. Many supporters of human free will realized that God's knowledge of an event does not imply His forcing it to happen.

174. The *Hadith* literature also contains important historical evidence concerning the early Muslim community and, in particular, on the history of Islamic thought.

tradition has been judged *sahih* and is not in obvious conflict with the Qur'an, but nonetheless seems to be questionable on rational or ethical grounds, then I do not feel constrained by it.[175]

I presume that by "reason" the questioner means critical thinking (i.e. disciplined intellectual criticism that incorporates research and knowledge of historical context while aspiring to impartial judgement). The first thing we need to recognize is that the ancient *muhadithun* viewed their field of study as a science and they subjected the traditions to an intense historical criticism that was far ahead of its time; as such, reason played an integral part in their investigations. Now as the questioner states, our reasoning is often imperfect, operating under many biases—not only cultural, but social, political, sectarian, psychological and so on—and this is precisely why the critical study of *Hadith*—and for that matter all of the Islamic sciences—must never be neglected. In no science—especially one as convoluted and whose source material is as discrepant as *hadith* criticism—can we uncritically accept the findings of any researchers, past or present. Since no generation of scholars is immune from error, the obligation to critically review and reassess past results cannot be ignored. This is clearly the burden of true experts, while the rest of us rely on their effort and integrity, but when their conclusions grate against our reason or sense of right, causing us to feel that adherence to them compromises our commitment to truth and hence to God, then we are obliged to request them to prove their case. Humility and genuineness is requisite here, for when we cannot relate to their explanations we need to distinguish between weakness of argument on their part and inability to comprehend due to lack of knowledge,

---

175. For comparable approaches by highly respected modern Muslim authorities, see Brown's discussion of the ideas of Muhammad 'Abduh, Muhammad al Ghazali, Rashid Rida, Yusuf al Qaradawi, Abu al 'Ala Mawdudi and others in, *Rethinking Tradition in Modern Islamic Thought*, Cambridge, 1996, pp. 108-133. Also, Khaled Abou El Fadl's insightful discussion of *hadith* criticism in *And God Knows the Soldiers*, University Press of America (2001).

learning, or intellectual sophistication on our part. We also need to bear in mind that a weak argument by one scholar does not necessarily disprove his or her claim, as another might defend it better. I therefore view the search for truth as a continual and collective enterprise. While not all believers have the means and ability to devote much of themselves to this effort, the state of scholarship in the American Muslim community is such that we desperately need those who can. We need many more deeply committed researchers trained in modern methods of research and learned in the classical Islamic sciences, so that they can speak to generations of Western educated Muslims who are finding themselves alienated from the discourse of the mosque. We also have to prepare the ground for their reception and the difficult work ahead by promoting tolerance, free inquiry, and free expression within our community. We can begin by listening to our young people, especially to their questions, problems, and reservations with regard to their religion and the community, and then thoughtfully and candidly present and discuss them now; for if we fail to do at least this much, then we can almost guarantee that a large segment of another generation of American Muslim youth will drift from the faith.

Question 2 (one of many questions I received after the Reverand Dr. Jerry Vines's widely publicized declaration at the 2002 Southern Baptist Convention Pastors' Conference that the Prophet was "a demon-possessed pedophile"):

This one is a big stumbling block for me. From my readings and then my discussions with our Imam, I have learned that the Prophet married his wife Aishah when she was six and consummated the marriage when she was nine years old. Some people have tried to explain to me that she was nine when she was married and twelve when they consummated the marriage. However, the <u>hadiths</u> from Bukhari and other sources indicate that the former is more likely. Our Imam also mentioned that most scholars believe that the former is the case.

The only explanation I get when I pose this question is that back in those days it was common practice and that it was all right for men to marry girls at a young age. I am also told that it would be wrong to question the Prophet's actions that took place fourteen hundred years ago based on our culture today. In my humble opinion, this explanation is not really satisfactory. The fact that some practices were common among the pagan Arabs and the Jews and the Christians does not prove that it was the "right thing" to do. I believe that a six year old is still a "baby." A nine year old is still a kid, regardless of whether she has had her first period or not. Studies show that girls go through still some major physical changes for two years after their first period. At nine, or even at twelve, girls are not yet totally developed physically or even emotionally. It might have been alright to marry girls at age six back then, but in my limited understanding and knowledge, I would have expected that the Prophet of God, in his wisdom and mercy, would change this custom instead of reinforcing it with his own marriage to a six year old. I would have expected that the Messenger of God would tell his people that it is wrong to marry a child. I always hear about what a great man the Prophet was, how just, merciful and compassionate he was, but this incident just does not fit that picture. It makes me question its legitimacy.

The question recaps most of what has been said on the Prophet's marriage to Aishah; therefore I can do little more than enlarge on the points it raises. The Muslim biographers offer a number of possible reasons—both practical and mystical—for the Prophet's marriage to Aishah, but I believe that McDonald and Watt are on target when they remark that after the death of the Prophet's first wife, Khadijah:

All of Muhammad's marriages and those he arranged for his daughters were made for political reasons. Abu Bakr was his chief lieutenant and aide, and he is reputed to have had an excellent knowledge of the inner politics of the nomadic tribes; thus, he was able to advise Muhammad in his dealings with those tribes. Muhammad's betrothal to Abu Bakr's daughter Aishah was made despite her tender age in order to cement the relationship between the two men.[176]

Many other Western writers see in the Prophet's marriages evidence of his uncontrolled sexual appetite, but the facts that he was celibate until the age of twenty-five, then for the next twenty-five years was married to only one wife, Khadijah, who was fifteen years his senior and formerly a widow; and that, with the exception of Aishah, all of his other wives were previously married[177] speak against his being prompted primarily by passion to marry Aishah or her co-wives. If carnal desire was his prime impulse, he could have chosen for himself a bevy of young virgins, which was the common male fantasy of the day.

Another point that should be kept in mind is that although the ancient Arabs had excellent verbal memories, their perception of time was markedly imprecise. This is to be expected of a largely illiterate people who possessed no calendar or timepieces, kept no birth or death records, did not commemorate birthdays or personal anniversaries, and seldom engaged in long range planning. Thus in the *Hadith* and biographical literature there are very often significant discrepancies on temporal details, even about major happenings that one would think would be well known. Thus we find differing authorities stating that the Prophet died when he was sixty-five, sixty-three, and sixty.[178] There are some who assert that the Prophet stayed ten years in Mecca after receiving the call and others who claim that he stayed thirteen.[179] Some of the Companions are on record as saying that the Prophet received the call when he was forty, others

176. M. V. McDonald and W.Montgomery Watt, *The History of Al-Tabari*, vol. VII, SUNY Press, 1987, p. xviii.

177. One, Zaynab bint Jahsh, was a divorcee and the rest were widows.

178. 178. Ismail K. Poonawala, *The History of Al-Tabari*, vol. X, SUNY Press, 1990, pp. 206-208.

179. Ibid pp. 206-208.

when he was forty-three.[180] There are differences on who embraced Islam first after Khadijah.[181] There are divergent reports on what was the Prophet's first Revelation, on the night in *Ramadan* he received it, and on the duration of the famous "break in revelation."[182]

Concerning Aishah's life in particular, there are many discrepant reports. The age at which she became betrothed to the Prophet is variously reported as six, seven, and nine.[183] The length of time between the death of Khadijah and the Prophet's betrothal to Aishah is one month according to one authenticated tradition and two years according to another.[184] Based on different reports, different estimates are obtained on the length of time between the betrothal and Aishah's joining the Prophet's household,[185] with three years being the minimum and five years being the maximum. There are

---

180. Ibid pp. 205-208

181. M. V. McDonald and W. Montgomery Watt, *The History of al-Tabari,* vol. VI, SUNY Press, 1987, pp. 80-87.

182. M. V. McDonald and W. Montgomery Watt, *The History of al-Tabari,* vol. VII, SUNY Press, 1988, pp. 67-77.

183. Ibid. p. 7 provides the estimates of six and seven as the age of Aishah's betrothal. Muhammad Asad admits that there is some confusion in the *hadith* literature concerning Aishah's age at the time of her betrothal and her marriage, but he argues that the cumulative evidence in the most authoritative collections argue for her betrothal at six or seven and marriage at nine or ten. He goes on to argue that many women of Arabia mature at extremely young ages. M. Asad, *Sahih Al Bukhari, The Early Years,* Dar Al Andalus, 1981, pp. 198-199.

184. Muhammad Asad, *Sahih Al Bukhari, The Early Years,* Dar Al Andalus, 1981, p. 200. In footnote 4, Asad attempts to reconcile the discrepancy.

185. I use the expression, "joined the Prophet's household," rather than the more common expression, "consummated her marriage," because this is the way Aishah is reported to have described her union with the Prophet in authenticated traditions. It could be that this is a euphemistic equivalent of the latter terminology, but I could not rule out that this was meant to be

(contd. on page 276)

several reports from different authorities that the Prophet's daughter, Fatimah, was about five years older than Aishah and that the former was born during the reconstruction of the Kabah, which occurred approximately five years prior to the Prophet's call. This would place Aishah's birth at around the time of the Prophet's call and her joining the Prophet's household at approximately fourteen or fifteen years old. At the same time there are authenticated reports from Aishah that have her joining the Prophet's household at nine. In another tradition, Aishah recalls being a little girl playing about when the *surah, Al Qamar*, was revealed, which is believed to have been revealed in the fourth year of the call, but this again would put her birth close to the time of the call and make her a teenager at the time of her marriage to the Prophet in Medina. There are some traditions that depict Aishah engaged in childlike play in the early years of her marriage and others that show her relating to her co-wives as an emotional and intellectual peer during this same period.

I am not making a case for or against the authenticity of any of these *hadiths,* but the preponderance in the tradition literature of discrepancies on when important events were supposed to have occurred suggests that recollections of time in those days tended to be very approximate. It is also noteworthy that the *isnads* of the great majority of authenticated traditions have a Companion in the first position who was quite young at the time of the death of the Prophet and a Successor in the second position who was much younger than

Footnote No. 185 (contd. from page 275)

taken literally. I have discovered that until very recently, it was not uncommon in Arabia for a marriage to be consummated quite long after the bride moved into her husband's home. This may explain the Qur'an's stipulation that if a man divorces a wife whom he has not "gone into" she is obliged to return half the marriage dowry he gave her; otherwise she is entitled to keep it all. I have been told that this postponement of consummation allowed the bride sufficient time to become acquainted with the ways of her husband's family and for the couple to grow closer to one another, as dating was not known to this culture (Muslims still strongly disapprove of modern dating practices of today).

the Companion in the first position. Therefore the second link in these *isnads* typically receives the information from the Companion many years after the fact. Again, in a culture where dates are not kept, recollections of when things happened long ago often become very clouded. This is even true today, but it is much easier to verify our recollections in a society where so many events are documented shortly after they occur and where so much emphasis is put on time. My daughter, Sarah, asked me the other day how long it has been since my mother died. I told her that it had been three years, but when I checked my mom's death certificate, I found that she had passed away five years ago. Similarly, my oldest daughter, Jameelah, recently insisted to me that she attained puberty at age nine, but my wife later assured me that this occurred when she was eleven.

The apparent cause for the delay between the time of Aishah's betrothal to the Prophet and her joining his household is that she had not yet reached puberty. I have heard of rare cases of girls having their first period at age nine but based on the above considerations I would estimate that Aishah reached puberty and then entered the Prophet's household somewhat later, perhaps closer to twelve or thirteen.

To some this may still seem too early an age to be engaging in sex, but the fact is that there are many young women today who are choosing to do exactly that outside the bounds of marriage. There were many girls—and boys—in the neighborhood I grew up in back in Bridgeport, Connecticut, who were having sex by this age; some of them starting as young as eleven years old. I had always believed that things were different in the suburbs or in the heartland, but I now live in a small college town in Kansas and find that things are much the same. In my daughter's junior high, there was a discussion group last year for troubled young girls, the majority of whom were pregnant, and some of my children's friends have confided to them that they had abortions when they were in the eighth and ninth grades.[186]

---

186. Our local school board is well aware many junior high school children are having sex and thus the school has mandated sex education to begin in the fifth grade.

In the Prophet's time, it made perfect sense for parents to find husbands for their daughters once they had reached puberty. For one thing, the average life span was very short. Recall that the Prophet's father died before he was born, his mother died when he was six, he outlived all of his children but one, Fatimah, who died at twenty-nine, several months after he did. Since there was a very good chance in those days that you would not see the age of forty and since the infant mortality rate was very high, it was believed to be in the best interest of women and society that they should marry as soon as they were able to have children. It should also be remembered that there was not much else for a post-pubescent female to do. She had no other major goals ahead of her, no high school or college degrees to pursue, or employment for which to prepare. Add to that if she were quite young her extended family and tribe would for the most part raise her children for her, it is understandable that becoming a mother was not seen as requiring a lot of maturity or training.

Through my wife and my travels to the Middle East, I have become well acquainted with several Arab women who married at ages of twelve and thirteen. They appear to me no less happy or psychologically healthy than American women whom I know well, quite the contrary. My wife and I are close friends with a couple from Saudi Arabia who wed when he was twenty-eight and she was thirteen. They have been married for fifteen years and are obviously very happy and in love.

My oldest daughter, when she was fourteen, shared with me an interesting perspective on this matter of adolescent marriages. While we were discussing this topic she suddenly surprised me with: "I wish things were more like that today." She went on to tell me that it was unfair to tell young people to remain celibate until marriage and at the same time discourage them from getting married until they have finished college. She stated that for ten or more years a person's body is telling him or her one thing and the parents are telling another. When I pointed out to her that we don't live in extended families anymore, she said that perhaps we should, that if families were in the past willing to sacrifice privacy and convenience to help young people to marry, then maybe they should again. I am not sure of the feasibility of Jameelah's idea, but she makes a valid point.

As far as the Prophet's supporting an objectionable practice with his marriage to Aishah, based on what I have said above, I am not convinced, given the conditions of his times, of the intrinsic immorality of allowing adolescents to marry. Even in our times, I see nothing inherently immoral in it, although modern conditions make such unions much more difficult to envisage. But since many adolescents can and are currently having sex, I do not see how it would be less moral if they were engaging in it within the bounds and protections of marriage.

Having said this, unlike many Muslims, I do not feel it necessary for the Prophet to have completely transcended his times. I believe that the Prophet was an extraordinarily virtuous, God-conscious man, who in many ways was certainly ahead of his time, but not one whose worldview was independent of his time and environment. I do not think it realistic to expect that the Prophet would figure into his personal decisions what society would be like fifteen hundred years hence, or how subjective morals would evolve. I believe that when Muslims study his life example for moral and spiritual guidance they should not ignore the historical contexts of his doings.

Question 3 (concerning the fact that the Prophet had more wives than the maximum allowed other believers; this is frequently highlighted at Evangelical websites on Islam. Interestingly, I received more questions on this from foreign born Muslims than from native born Muslims):

In the Qur'an, the Prophet is given permission to marry as many women as he wants. The believers are allowed to marry up to four, and no more. In my critical and questioning mind, I keep on thinking, "That is really convenient!" Can you tell me why this was the case?

And if you fear that you cannot deal justly with the orphans, marry such women as seem good to you, two, or three, or four; but if you fear that you will not be equitable, then only one, or that which your right hands possess; so it is likelier that you will not be partial. (4:3)

O Prophet, We have made lawful to you your wives whom you have given their dowries, and those whom your right hand possesses from the captives of war that God has bestowed on you, and the daughters of your paternal uncle and the daughters of your maternal aunts, and the daughters of your maternal uncle and the daughters of your maternal aunts who fled with you, and a believing woman, if she gives herself to the Prophet and if the Prophet desires to marry her—an exemption for you, but not for the [rest of] the believers—We are aware of what We ordained for them concerning their wives and those whom their right hands possess—that you may be free from blame, for God is Forgiving, Merciful. (33:50)

It is not allowed for you to take wives after this, nor to change them for other wives, even if their beauty were to please you greatly, only those whom your right hand possesses. And God is ever watchful over all things. (33:52)

The Qur'an does not elaborate on the reasons for these Revelations and while it and the tradition literature provide some clues, any explanation I offer can only be speculative. I came to believe in God and the Qur'an through an experience that was unaffected by this detail of the Scripture; yet when I read these verses now I do so as a believer, which leaves me knowing that I could never fully grasp the divine wisdom behind them. I say this to make it plain that I do not presume to "know" the answer to this question, but I will do my best to make sense of it. Since the verses concern the Prophet's wives, a review of his marriages is in order.

In a society that did not esteem sexual restraint—especially in men—and where loose men and women filled the streets, Muhammad stayed celibate until age twenty-five, at which time he married Khadijah, who was fifteen years his senior and his only wife until she died twenty-five years later. After the death of Khadijah and a period of mourning, the Prophet married Saudah, a woman in her forties, whose husband—also a convert—had recently died. Around this time Muhammed also became betrothed to Aishah bint Abu Bakr, daughter of his closest friend and first lieutenant, but she would not join his household until about four years later.[187]

Then followed the flight to Medina and the beginning of an eight-year period of intermittent warfare with the Quraysh and its allies. The years of conflict saw many Muslims fall in battle and it devolved upon the Prophet and the surviving Companions to take in their families (4:3). When Hafsah, the daughter of Umar ibn al Khattab, lost her husband at the Battle of Badr, the Prophet took her hand in marriage and as a result established family ties with one of his most important followers. In the next year, the Prophet wedded Zainab bint Khuzaimah, who lost her spouse in the Battle of Uhud. She died a few months after her marriage to the Prophet at age thirty in the third year of the *Hijrah*. A year later he married Umm Salamah, whose husband died from wounds sustained at the same battle. In the fourth or fifth year of the Hijrah the Prophet married Zaynab bint Jahsh under circumstances already discussed.[188] Sometime later he also wed Umm Habibah, an early convert to Islam who fled to Abbyssinia with her husband, Ubaid Allah, who there became a Christian and later died. Through this marriage the Prophet disarmed Abu Sufyan, Umm Habibah's father, who was a leader of the Quraysh and an invet-

---

187. In Arabia, marriage often occurred in two steps: the first being the formal commitment that amounted to a betrothal and the second being the finalization of the marriage with the bride moving into the groom's home.

188. Question 10, Chapter 1.

erate foe of Islam. During years six and seven of the Hijrah, the Prophet married three widows—Juwairiyah, Maimunah and Saffiyah—of his enemies, which in each case was a step toward pacification and union with their respective tribes.[189]

The above verses are listed in their order of Revelation. It is commonly understood that 4:3 limits the number of wives a man can have at one time to four; that 33:50 grants the Prophet special permission not to observe this limit; and that 33:52 prohibits him from marrying any other women, and thus establishes the composition of the Prophet's household through the remainder of his mission. The task of exegesis would be greatly aided by a detailed time line of the Revelation of these passages; however, tradition does not provide much information and, as is so often the case, much of what it does provide is conflicting.

There is near unanimity that 4:3 was revealed shortly after the Battle of Uhud in 3 A. H., but there is disagreement on when the remaining two verses were revealed. Many commentators believe that the Revelation of 33:52 occurred shortly after 33:50. But even though they are separated by only one verse in the text, their content would seem to indicate that the time lapse between them was considerable, otherwise the Prophet was first allowed to take more wives and then immediately told he could not. This ostensible contradiction is usually resolved by explaining that 33:50 does not allow the Prophet to marry more women but rather permits him not to divorce the excess number of wives. Nonetheless, the proposition that these two verses appeared at approximately the same time creates other problems. For in order for the Prophet not to have violated 33:52, we must assume that it was revealed after his last marriage in 7 A. H., but this would mean that for several years he had more wives than 4:3 allows without having obtained the exemption of 33:50.

---

189. The Prophet's marriage to Juwairiyah led to the emancipation of hundreds of captives of her tribe, the Banu Mastaliq.

All of these problems can be eliminated if the premise that 33:52 occurred shortly after 33:50 is dropped. If this is done, then a more obvious time line is forced upon us. Like many *surahs*, the thirty third (*Al Ahzab*) was revealed in small segments at various times, yet almost all authorities agree that most of it was revealed after *Surah* 4 (*Al Nisa*), and place the majority of its revelation in the fifth year of the Hijrah. Now at no point prior to the Prophet's marriage to Zainab bint Jahsh—whose marriage to him is mentioned in 33:37—did he have more than four wives at one time, since Zainab bint Khuzaimah had passed on before he married Umm Salamah. Since it is highly unlikely that the Prophet acquired more wives than the four that 4:3 allows before obtaining the exemption provided him in 33:50, we can safely assume that 33:50 was revealed on the same occasion as 33:37, or sometime shortly before. After receiving the permission of 33:50 the Prophet went on to marry five more women, starting with Zainab bint Jahsh, until he was prohibited in 7 A.H. by 33:52 from marrying any more women or from supplanting any of his current wives by others. In sum, the Prophet had four wives in accordance with 4:3 until 33:50 permitted him to acquire more; after this he married five more women, making a total of nine current wives; then came 33:52, which prohibited the Prophet from marrying any other women.

This chronology leads us to two considerations: What was the purpose of the exception of 33:50? And, what was the reason for the prohibition of 33:52 approximately two years later? On the first question we can rule out that the main intent of 33:50 was to indulge the Prophet's fondness for women. If this were the case, then why prevent the Prophet from acquiring more wives with the revelation of 33:52? The Prophet's selection of spouses after the revelation of 33:50 confirms this view. Recall that Zaynab bint Jahsh was a divorcee and that the remaining four women were all widows, some of them with children. Moreover, Zaynab and Umm Habibah were in their mid thirties and Maymunah was fifty-one at the times of their weddings to the Prophet, which was considered much passed their prime in their day.[190] Thus if the object of 33:50 was to provide the Prophet with women to satisfy his physical wants, then he did not make the most of the opportunity, since a man of his position could easily have acquired a large harem of beautiful young virgins, as did many other powerful Middle-Eastern men both before and after his time.

A review of the Prophet's last five marriages suggests that the chief purpose for the exception in 33:50 was to afford the Prophet an age-old and exceedingly effective diplomatic tool. We have already discussed some of the social, moral, and legal implications of the Prophet's marriage to Zaynab.[191] We have also pointed out that his marriages to Juwairiyah, Maimunah, and Saffiyah—widows of enemies—was a time-honoured way of making peace and alliances with one's opponents. Yet the Prophet's union with Umm Habibah may have had the greatest political impact of his last five marriages. It is important to recognize that Umm Habibah's father, Abu Sufyan, was the leader of Quraysh, and that after the Prophet's marriage to his daughter, no further attacks were mounted by his tribe against the Muslims; instead, all remaining conflicts between the Muslims and the Quraysh over the next few years were resolved through diplomacy; in particular, it was Abu Sufyan who personally negotiated the peaceful capitulation of Mecca in the eighth year of the Hijrah.[192]

The thesis that the primary purpose of 33:50 is to avail the Prophet of an important political device fits well with the circum-

---

190. I consulted F. H. Malik's, *Wives of the Prophet*, Taj Company, 1986, for the ages of the Prophet's wives at the times of their marriages to him. It should be kept in mind that such chronological details are usually very rough estimates.

191. Question 10, Chapter 1

192. Although these marriages may have been first and foremost politically motivated, this does not preclude that the Prophet found these women appealing on a more personal level. In my opinion, out of fairness to the women and to ensure the success of the marriages, this was most probably the case.

stances of his last five marriages and also accounts for the barring of the Prophet from marrying additional wives in 33:52, since this verse was revealed when war had come to an end and such acts of diplomacy were no longer necessary. Tradition ascribes other significances to this verse that are compatible with the above interpretation, but I have limited myself here to addressing the concerns of the question.

Question 4 (from a male convert, concerning the *hijab*,[193] about which, unsurprisingly, I received many questions from American women):

I am an American convert to Islam, married to a Muslim woman from Jordan. My wife does not cover her hair but believes that Islam obliges her to do so, and she hopes for the day when she'll summon the strength to do it. I, however, am not convinced. The arguments made by Muhammad Asad, Murad Hoffman, and others for interpretation of the Qur'an's injunctions on modest dress in accordance with prevailing custom and standards of modesty make sense to me. It seemed that in <u>Struggling to Surrender</u> you supported the traditional view, while in <u>Even Angels Ask</u> you urged the American Muslim community to put less pressure on women to adhere to strict traditional dress codes. I was wondering where you now stand on the issue of appropriate dress for Muslim women. Do you still believe that ideally they should dress traditionally?

I thought I had avoided espousing any policy on Muslim women's dress in my two earlier books, but rather outlined some of the common arguments for and against reinterpretation in modern times, while highlighting what I felt are some of their strengths and weaknesses. I did not commit myself to either view as I was not convinced that either one is untenable. I did state that although the great majority of Muslim women do not dress traditionally, most of them uphold the established code, and I opined that this was not going to change anytime soon. I'm not so sure about the last point

---

193. *hijab*: the headscarf worn by Muslim women

anymore—at least in America—but I still feel that persuasive cases can be made both for the conventional code and for reinterpretation in light of changed circumstances. Due to the large volume of email I have received on this matter, I thought I should again present as best I could both sides of the debate, beginning with the traditional view.

The Qur'an contains no explicit prescriptions on modest dress for men, but it has three direct statements with regard to women, cited below in the passages in which they occur.

> And say to the believing men that they should restrain something of their gaze and to guard their private parts: that will make for greater purity. Truly, God is aware of all that they do. And say to the believing women that they should restrain something of their gaze and guard their private parts, and that they should not display their adornments (*zinat*) except what is unavoidable (*zahara*) thereof; hence, let them draw their head-coverings (*khumur*) over their breasts, and not to reveal their adornments (*zinat*) except to their husbands, their fathers, their husband's fathers, their sons, their husbands' sons, their brothers or their brothers' sons, or their sisters' sons, or their women, or those whom their right hands possess (i.e. your slaves), or male attendants who are beyond sexual desire, or children who are as yet unaware of women's nakedness. And let them not strike their feet so as to draw attention to their adornments (*zinat*). And turn unto God together, O believers, in order that you may succeed. (24:30-31)

> O you who believe! Let those whom your right hands possess (i.e. your slaves), and those who have not reached puberty ask your permission at three times (before they come into your presence): Before the morning (*fajr*) prayer, and when you lay aside your garments for the noonday heat, and after the late-night (`isha*) prayer: three times of undress for you. Beyond these neither you nor they will incur any sin if they

move about you, attending to one another. Thus God makes clear the revelations for you. God is knowing, wise. And when the children among you reach puberty let them ask leave even as those before them used to ask leave. Thus God makes clear the revelations for you. God is knowing, wise. And women advanced in years who do not desire sexual intercourse, incur no sin if they discard their garments, provided they do not make a wanton display of adornments (*zinat*). But to refrain is better for them. And God is hearing, knowing. (24: 58-60)

And those who malign believing men and believing women undeservedly, they bear the guilt of slander and a flagrant sin. O Prophet! Tell your wives and daughters, and the believing women to draw something of their cloaks (*jalabib*) close around them (when they go out). That will be better so that they will be recognized and not annoyed. But God is ever forgiving, merciful. If the hypocrites, and those in whose hearts is a disease, and those who stir up sedition in the city do not cease, We verily shall urge you on against them, then they will be your neighbors in it but a little while. (33:58-60)

Muhammad Asad in his *The Message of the Qur'an* recalls that the customary attire of the Arab tribal woman before Islam consisted of an ornamental head covering that hung down her back and showed her hair in the front, a long tunic with a wide opening in the front allowing her breasts to be seen, a skirt tied at the waist, and assorted jewelry, such as necklaces, rings, earrings, arm and ankle bracelets.[194] This style persisted among some of the Bedouin in the Arabian Peninsula until modern times and was photographed by European travelers early last century.[195] The Qur'an's instruction to the believing

---

194. Muhammad Asad, *The Message of the Qur'an*, pp. 22-23, note 87 and pp. 538-539, note 38.
195. Wilfred Thesinger, *Arabian Sands* (New York: E. P. Dutton & Co., 1959), p. 192.

women to draw their head coverings (*khimar*, plural *khumur*) over their bosoms (24:31) and to draw something of their outer garments over themselves (33:59) when in public provided, with minimum inconvenience, a modest manner of dress for believing women.

Muslim jurists would later elaborate strict guidelines for female dress, requiring loose fitting clothing that does not delineate a woman's figure and that allows only her face, hands, and feet to show. The earliest debate on appropriate lady's attire—traced back to the time of the Companions and Successors—centered on whether a woman was also obliged to cover her face.[196] The majority opinion held otherwise, but the issue is still contested in some parts of the Muslim world.

Interestingly, there are not many authenticated traditions that detail proper feminine attire. The collections of Bukhari and Muslim contain no such traditions,[197] and the less esteemed compilations add little to what is stated in the Qur'an. The following oft cited tradition is explicit, but Muslim scholars have classified it *daif* (weak).

> `Aishah narrated that her sister `Asma once came to the Prophet clad in transparent clothes that revealed her body. The Prophet averted his gaze and told her: "Asma, when a women begins to menstruate, nothing should be seen of her except this and this, and he pointed to his face and hands.[198]

---

196. Yusuf al Qaradawi, *The Lawful and Prohibited in Islam*, American Trust Publications, pp. 155-159. Many early Muslim scholars felt that a female Muslim slave did not need to cover her hair. See Khaled Abou El Fadl, *And God Knows the Soldiers*, University Press of America (2001), pp. 121-138.

197. Except perhaps for the *hadith* reports concerning the slander of A'ishah, which some scholars argue establishes that Muslim women should cover their faces. For an interesting article that discusses some of the problems with this interpretation see: Ahmad Shafaat, *Chastity and Hijab in the Teachings of Prophets Muhammad and Jesus*, www.islamicperspectives.com/Chastity1.htm (1999).

198. From the collection of Abu Daoud.

Yet the lack of a *hadith* that explicitly define Muslim women's dress does not necessarily imply the traditional code does not go back to the time of the Prophet; on the contrary, it might indicate that there was never any major disagreement on this topic, apart from differences of opinion on the need for a woman's face to be veiled. In other words, the absence of controversy on this issue supports the view that the traditional code, modulo some later elaboration, was a well-established *sunnah* handed down en masse from generation to generation.

It would probably be vain to try to disprove the historicity of the traditional code but an argument for reinterpretation in view of changed circumstances does not require it. Instead, a case needs to be made that the injunctions on women's dress are, as Muhammad Asad and others have argued, "time-bound" —that is, conditioned by prevailing customs or circumstances. This is not always an easy case to make. It has to be argued that the pronouncements refer to features of seventh century Arabian culture that are time and place specific and whose imposition today would be either contrary or superfluous to the ostensible aims of the commands.

Most Muslims would denounce such an attempt on grounds that divine commandments are not open to reinterpretation but must be followed verbatim and in line with how the earliest Muslims understood them, but even the most conservative believers will probably concede that at least some of the original responses to divine ordinances require adjustment. Take, for example, the command to make adequate preparations for war:

> Make ready for them all you can of force and horses tethered to strike terror into the enemies of God and your enemies, and others besides whom you may not know, but God knows them. Whatsoever you spend in the cause of God shall be repaid to you in full and you will not be wronged. (8:60)

No modern Muslim military commander would insist on accumulating horses before doing battle, even though this was certainly the original understanding. Instead, almost all commentators interpret that preparation for war requires acquisition of the best weaponry available, both to facilitate victory and to provide a military deterrent ("to strike terror into enemies...you may not know").

The verse (24:29) that immediately precedes the passage instructing believing women to draw their *khumur* over their chests provides instruction that makes sense in ancient nomadic environs but might need qualification today.

> O you who believe! Do not enter houses other than your own without first announcing your presence and invoking peace upon those in them. That is better for you, that you may be heedful. And if you find no one therein, do not enter until permission has been given. And if you are asked to go away, go away, for it is purer for you. And God knows what you do. (It is) no sin for you to enter uninhabited houses which serve some use for you. And God knows what you reveal or conceal (24:27-29).

In this day and age it may not be advisable, if only from the standpoint of safety, to allow individuals to make use of abandoned or unoccupied homes.

For almost all Muslims the strongest proof that believing women need to wear *hijab* is the command in 24:30 to "draw their *khumur* over their breasts" which explicitly refers to the head cover. Advocates of amendment to the traditional code can counter that references in Qur'anic commands to features of seventh century Arabian culture do not necessarily imply that the features must be universalized. For example, the reference in 8:60 to gathering horses does not make this a permanent part of Muslim military preparations. Similarly, the many references to slavery and concubinage in Scriptural legislation do not mean that these must be enduring Islamic institutions.[199] And though the Qur'an makes no explicit mention of men's clothing, there are various rules in authenticated traditions that refer to male attire, like the following that speaks of the *izar* (waist sheet) worn by men at that time.

> Narrated Abu Hurairah that the Messenger of God said, "God will not look on the Day of Resurrection at a person who drags his *izar* (behind him) out of pride and arrogance."

> Narrated Abdullah bin Umar: the Messenger of God said, "God will not look on the Day of Resurrection at a person who drags his *izar* (behind him) out of pride." Abu Bakr said, "One side of my *izar* slacks down unless I get very cautious about it." The Messenger of God said, "But you do not do that with pride."

There are modern day believers who insist Muslim males are required to wear styles similar to those worn by the seventh century Arabs, but they are very few.

For revisionists, the pronouncements on women's dress have certain features that suggest they are time-bound formulations not meant to be taken as injunctions (*ahkam*, plural of *hukm*) "in the general, timeless sense of this term, but rather, a moral guideline to be observed against the ever changing background of time and social environment."[200] As already pointed out, women of the Prophet's time wore a long tunic with a wide opening in front, leaving their breasts exposed. Undoubtedly, the focus of 24:31 is on covering the breasts, although the *zinat* (ornaments) of which this verse and 24:60 speak

---

199. For an interesting argument against the legitimacy of concubinage in Islam see, Muhammad Ali, *The Religion of Islam*, Lahore (1990), pp. 488-495.

200. Muhammad Asad, *The Message of the Quran*, p. 651.

may certainly include other feminine attractions. Proponents of modification of the traditional code point out that a literal interpretation of 24:31 would permit a woman's adornments, and hence her breasts in particular, to be seen by "their fathers, their husband's fathers, their sons, their husbands' sons, their brothers or their brothers' sons, or their sisters' sons, or their women, or those whom their right hands possess (i.e. their slaves), or male attendants who are beyond sexual desire, or children who are as yet unaware of women's nakedness." Likewise, a literal reading of 24:60 would allow women advanced in years to appear in a state of relative undress ("to discard their [outer] garments") in the presence of anybody, provided they do not intend a showy display of their adornments, although the Qur'an recommends, "to refrain is better for them." Of course, most Muslims today would not promote a literal application of these allowances, since they run against current social norms. Yet in a primitive tribal society that has just made significant modifications in dress, these concessions allowing women to appear, by today's standards, "naked" in the situations enumerated are certainly appropriate. However, the fact that most modern Muslims would be uncomfortable with a literal response to these permissions underscores that they, and by extension the pronouncements that contain them, are conditioned by the prevailing customs and mores of the Qur'an's initial hearers. Revisionists also cite the references in these commands to slaves, the Prophet's wives and daughters, the traditional afternoon siesta ("when you lay aside your garments for the noonday heat"), and garments (e.g. *khumur, jilabib*) particular to the Prophet's contemporaries as further indications of their contextual character.

The case for reinterpretation of the above directives has its strengths but it also raises concerns. If the purpose of the commands on women's dress is not to establish a permanent code, but instead to promote modesty in keeping with contemporary standards, then the Qur'an could certainly have acomplished this more efficiently by merely instructing Muslim women to dress modestly. From the standpoint of Islamic thought this is not a minor objection, for Muslims have long recognized the *ijaz* of the Qur'an—its inimitable economy and eloquence of expression—and the interpretation offered by proponents of revision of the code would appear to contradict it. Yet revisionists could argue that while the Qur'an communicates to future generations, it first speaks to the immediate needs of the Prophet's generation, and then through their experience to all others. From this perspective the Qur'an's commandments were definitely meant to be taken literally in the milieu it originally addressed, and were absolutely necessary to bring about that society's reform and make it a suitable vehicle for Islam, but at the same time the legislation is also meant to provide explicit, practical models to be generalized to diverse contexts, and in this latter sense all of the Qur'an's pronouncements—including those on slavery, concubines, the Prophet's personal life, war preparations, and women's dress—have relevance today, even though some specifics of them need not be replicated.

Another obvious complaint against the revisionist approach is that it can be used to undermine almost any Qur'anic ordinance, that by exaggerating the differences between our times and the Prophet's, any divine decree can be watered down to make it fit current trends and morals. Revisionists will protest that their purpose is not to weaken any divine commandments but to distinguish those features of them that are distinctive to the seventh century Arabs and superfluous to achieving their apparent aims today. Traditionalists can counter that whereas the Qur'an establishes a code of women's dress to hinder sexual exploitation, the revisionist call for an interpretive code conditioned by current mores provides no code at all; i.e. a moral code that adjusts to fluctuations in morals is ineffectual. Furthermore, an argument can be made that Arabian pre-Islamic standards of feminine modesty were even more lax than that of most modern Western societies; nevertheless the Qur'an obligated the Prophet's female followers to make significant adjustments in dress. Thus if the Qur'an required these changes in a more permissive environment, then on what grounds can we say they would be too extreme or superfluous today? Supporters of reinterpretation may contend that the style of dress required by the Qur'an was not unknown to the ancient Arabs, that when the Qur'an says appropriately dressed women "will be recognized [as chaste] and not annoyed" it shows this was the public attire of women of propriety. Of course, defenders of the traditional code can rebut that the traditional code is certainly not unknown to contemporary Muslims.

Even though it is possible to go on listing more arguments and counterarguments, I will stop here, for my purpose is to highlight some of the major points of the debate.

Question 5 (Not many Muslim-Christian dialogues have led to conversion from the Muslim side, but it often leads to serious soul-searching.):

I have a couple of questions, or rather concerns. Occasionally I have doubts about Islam. When my iman (faith) is strong, it is the best feeling in the world. It is like I'm on a high for days at a time. Unfortunately, I do not feel this way most of the time and I would basically like you to assist me with some of my questions.

First, I get confused when Christians make claims that they have such "peace of mind" from knowing that God loves them and they love God. It makes me think that maybe all God wants from us is to believe in Him. I guess this makes sense to me because the vast majority of humanity does not believe, let alone pray five times a day, fast, and so on. Thus perhaps God would be content with just having us believe in Him. From this point of view, all the works that go along with faith are not so important; and in Islam, as you know, works play an important role.

My doubts also stem from things that Christians say, such as, "It is too difficult to get to Heaven in Islam, and there is no peace of mind and comfort in the Muslim faith." They point to a hadith in which Omar bin al Khattab, a person who was guaranteed Heaven, says that he would not feel safe from Hell even if he had one foot in Heaven.

What's more, none of the Christian doctrines seem impossible to me (e.g. the Trinity, original sin, the crucifixion). I have heard the Muslim arguments against them, but the doctrines still do not seem irrational to me. I guess my logic is: if God can do anything, then why couldn't He have a son? It more or less seems to me to be our word against theirs.

Christians also make me question the integrity of Prophet Muhammad. They point out that he had many wives, fought in wars, owned slaves, taught women to seek permission from their husbands on many matters (e.g. before voluntary fasting), allowed the killing of people who didn't pray or who left the religion, whereas Jesus did none of these things. Although these things have wisdom from an Islamic point of view, the Christian concept of love and peace also makes sense to me to some degree.

Incidentally, I am a practicing Muslim and, despite how it may appear in this letter, I do not walk around doubting Islam all the time. Deep down I know that Islam is the truth. I do, however, need to deal with these issues that have been plaguing me for some time, so that I can move on and achieve a true state of Islam, which is my only goal. The reason I e-mailed you is because this stuff would be embarrassing to talk about with anyone in my community.

Many young American Muslims report similar conversations with Christians, where the same ideas—Christian belief in a God of love and the insufficiency of good works toward attaining redemption, Muslim uncertainty versus Christian certainty of salvation, the concept that God could do anything and hence could be both God and man, the alleged dissoluteness of the Prophet—are advanced by the latter. These themes are part and parcel of Evangelical proselytising strategy towards Muslims, so I assume that it is Christians of this persuasion that are involved here. I say this so that the Muslim reader understands that not all Christians would take this line of attack when discussing their religion. It is also important to realize that the above outline of Evangelical tactics is not representative of

Christian theological thought in general or contemporary historical research on the Prophet, but rather simplistic, albeit carefully crafted formulations aimed at the man or woman in the street.

Each of the great monotheistic religions teaches that God is a loving Creator; at the same time each has also warned of severe suffering in the afterlife for those who refuse to submit to Him. Thus in each tradition you have had those who have emphasized divine love and others divine threat (in the Christian tradition this is often called the "fire and brimstone" message). In Islamic history the first trend has been most represented by the Sufi tradition, which put great emphasis on the experience of divine love and intimacy. Poetry has been a major medium for expressing Sufi spirituality, where one often finds the relationship between the believer and God described as that between the "lover and beloved" and which expresses in highly passionate language the attainment of union with God through mystical experience. This very alluring message has helped make Sufism the chief vehicle for the spread of Islam throughout most of Africa and Asia, but it has lost much of its appeal today among Western educated Muslims who are more habituated to rational than mystical thought.

The predominant trend among contemporary Muslims stresses adherence to the *Shariah* (Islamic Law), and hence right and wrong behavior and their attendant consequences in the afterlife, rather than the believer's personal relationship with God. In the twenty plus years since my conversion I have observed that most of my coreligionist focus much more on divine punishment for lapses in following the *Shariah* than the promise of reward for doing good, so much so that one can easily form the impression that God in Islam is anxiously waiting to chastise Muslims for the slightest infractions. Hence it is not surprising that some might perceive that it is "too difficult to get to Heaven in Islam and there is no peace of mind and comfort in the Muslim faith." This is unfortunate since there is so much in Islam's textual sources to suggest the contrary.

The principle source of Muslim perception of God is the abundant references in the Scripture to His attributes, what the Qur'an terms God's "most beautiful names." In his, *Concordance of the Qur'an*,[201] Kassis renders in English (see below) most of the titles and adjectives applied to God in the Scripture, together with some of their different shades of meaning. His list is not exhaustive. Other Qur'an scholars have obtained longer lists and other possible meanings in English could have been added, as it is hard to do justice to the Arabic original.

Divine Names and Attributes:

Able (*qadira*); Absolute (*samad*); One Who Answers (*ajaaba*); Aware (*khabeer*); Beneficent (*rahmaan*); Benign (*barr*); Bestower (*wahhaab*); Blameless (*haasha*); Bountiful (*akrama, tawl*); Clement (`*afoow, haleem, ra'oof*); Compassionate (*raheem*); Compeller (*jabbaar*); Creator (*badee`, bara'a, fatara, khalaqa, khallaq*); Deliverer (*fattaah*); Disposer (*wakeel*); Embracing (*wasi`a*); Eternal (*qayyoom, samad*); Everlasting (*qayyoom*); Everlasting Refuge (*samad*); Evident (*dhahara*); Exalted (*ta`aal'a*); the Exalter (*rafee`*); Faithful (*aamana*); Fashioner (*sawwara*); First (*awwal*); Forgiver (*ghaffaar, ghafuur*); Gatherer (*jama`a*); Generous (*kareem*); Gentle (*lateef, ra'oof*); Giver (*wahhaab*); Glorious (`*adheem, akrama, majeed*); God (*Allah, ilaah*); Gracious (*lateef, rahmaan*); Grateful (*shakara*); Great (*kabeer*); Guardian (*hafeedh, wakeel, waleey*); Guide (*had'a*); He (*huwa*); Hearing (*samee`*); High (`*aleey*); Holy (*quddoos*); Honorable (*akrama*); Informed (*khabeer*); Inheritor (*waritha*); Inward (*batana*); Irresistible (*jabbaar*); Most Just Judge (*hakama*); Kind (*lateef, ra'oof*); King (*malik, maleek*); Knower (`*aleem, `alima, khabeer*); Last (*aakhir*); Laudable (*hameed*); Light (*nuur*); Living (*hayy*); Lord (*rabb*); Loving (*wadood*); Majestic (*jalaal, takabbara*); Master of the

201. Kassis, Hanna, E., *A Concordance of the Qur'an*, University of California Press, 1983.

Kingdom(*malaka*); Merciful (*rahmaan*); Mighty (`azeez, `adheem*); Omnipotent (*iqtadara, qadeer, qahara, qahhaar*); One (*ahad, waahid*); Originator (*fatara*); Outward (*dhahara*); Overseer (*aqaata*); Pardoner (`afoow*); Peaceable (*salaam*); Powerful (*qadira, qadeer, aqaata*); Praiseworthy (*hameed*); Preserver (*haymana*); Protector (*mawl'a, wala', waleey*); Provider (*razzaaq*); Quickener (*ahyaa*); Reckoner (*haseeb*); Sagacious (*khabeer*); Seeing (*baseer*); Shaper (*sawwara*); Splendid (*akrama*); Strong (*qaweey*); Sublime (*takabbara*); Subtle (*lateef*); Sufficient (*ghaneey, istaghn'a, kaf'a*); Superb (*takabbara*); Sure (*mateen*); Tender (*lateef*); Thankful (*shakara, shakoor*); True (*haqq*); Trustee (*wakeel*), one who Turns towards others (*tawwaab*); Watcher (*raqeeb*); Wise (*hakeem*); Witness (*shaheed*).

Even a cursory glance at the divine attributes would show that the Muslim image of God should be of an infinitely kind and merciful Creator. This is particularly apparent when we consider the frequency of their occurrences in the text, for after *Allah* (the God) and *Rabb* (Lord, the Sustainer) which occur approximately 2700 and 900 times, respectively, the most frequently occurring names are associated with God's attributes of mercy, compassion and forgiveness, and thus the purest manifestations of love. God is called *al-Rahmaan* (the Merciful) 170 times, *al-Raheem* (the Compassionate) 227 times, *al-Ghaffaar* (the Forgiving) and *al-Ghaffoor* (the Forgiving) a total of 97 times.

The Qur'an's "most beautiful names" imply intense divine involvement in the human venture. Names like the Merciful, the Compassionate, the Forgiving, the Giving, the Loving, the Sustainer, and so forth, reveal a God that creates men and women in order to relate to them on a deeply personal level, on a more intimate level than any other creatures known to humankind, not out of a psychological or emotional need, but because this is the very essence of His nature. Therefore we find the relationship between the sincere believer and God consistently characterized as a bond of love. God loves the good-doers (2:195; 3:134, 3:148, 5:13, 5:93), the repentant

(2:222), those that purify themselves (2:222; 9:108), the God-conscious (3:76; 9:4; 9:7), the patient (3:146), those that put their trust in Him (3:159), the just (5:42; 49:9; 60:8), and those who fight in His cause (61:4); and they in turn love God (2:165, 3:31, 5:54).

This bond of love between God and the believer is also portrayed in many *hadith*. The following are a few examples.

> Narrated Abdullah ibn Yazid al Khatami: The Prophet used to say in his supplications, "O Allah, provide me with your love and the love of those whose love will benefit me with you." (From the collection of Tirmidhi)

> Narrated Abu Hurayra: the Messenger of Allah said, "If Allah loves one of his servants, He says to Jibril, 'I love so-and-so, so love him.' So Jibril loves him and then calls out to the inhabitants of heaven, 'Allah loves so-and-so, so love him,' and the people of heaven love him, and then acceptance is placed in the Earth for him." (From al Bukhari's *Sahih*)

> The Prophet said that Allah said: "My servant does not draw closer to Me with anything more loved by Me than the religious duties I have enjoined on him, and my servant continues to draw near to Me with supererogatory works so that I shall love him. And when I love him I become the hearing with which he hears, the seeing with which he sees, the hand with which he strikes and the foot with which he walks. Were he to ask of Me, I will surely give it to him, and were he to ask Me for refuge, I will surely grant it to him." (From al Bukhari's *Sahih*)

> Narrated Abu Hurayrah: The Prophet said, "Allah says, 'I am as my servant thinks I am and I am with him if he remembers Me. If he remembers Me in himself, I too, remember him in Myself; and if he remembers Me in a group of people, I remember him in a group that is better; and if he draws

nearer to Me by a span, I draw nearer to him by a cubit; and if he draws nearer to Me by a cubit, I come nearer to him by two outstretched arms; and if he comes to Me walking, I go to him running.'" (From al Bukhari's *Sahih*)

As to be expected, the Qur'an and *Hadith* threaten Islam's opponents with perdition, but they also continually reassure sincere believers that Paradise awaits them. Virtually every time the Qur'an threatens the unbelievers with damnation it balances it with promises of Paradise for the faithful. The Qur'an informs the believers that as long as they have faith in God and avoid the more heinous sins and abominations they will enter Paradise in the next life.[202] It also asserts that God forgives all sins except idolatry (4:48), that we should never despair of God's mercy or forgiveness (39:53), that God accepts repentance and forgives all sins (42:25), and that only the truly wicked will suffer in Hell (19:68-72). In the *Sahih of al-Bukhari* the Prophet informs his Companions, to their astonishment, that even believing adulterers and drunkards will ultimately enter Heaven. Yet Islam's sacred Scripture goes still further in this regard as it states several times that sincere believers in God of other faiths will also enter Heaven.

Truly, those who believe and those who are Jews, and the Christians, and the Sabians—who believe in God and the last Day and do righteous deeds—shall have their reward with their Lord; and no fear need they have, and neither shall they grieve. (2:62)[203]

Muhammad Asad comments that this inclusiveness distinguishes Islam from other monotheistic religions:

The above passage—which recurs in the Qur'an several times—lays down a fundamental doctrine in Islam. With a

---

202. C.f. 4:31; 42:36-37; 53:32 and chapter 1, pp. 114-118.

203. Also, 5:69, 22:17. The Sabians seem to have been a monotheistic group that existed in Arabia during the Prophet's time.

breadth of vision unparalleled in any other religious faith, the idea of "salvation" is here made conditional upon three elements only: belief in God, belief in the Day of Judgement, and righteous action in life.[204]

It should also be noted that there are passages in the Qur'an and authenticated traditions that suggest that no one will abide in Hell forever.[205]

It is therefore hard to see on what real basis one can argue that it is too difficult to get to Heaven in Islam. It certainly cannot be too difficult for Muslims to avoid major transgressions like murder, torture, rape, idolatry, and adultery, and even in such cases the way to sincere repentance is not closed. A religion that even includes outsiders in its vision of salvation and suggests that no one will suffer endlessly in the next life cannot be said to make Paradise too difficult to attain. A single pious utterance of one of the Prophet's most devout followers does not prove the opposite; all Umar's statement demonstrates is that he was a very God-conscious, humble man. His point seems to have been that we should never become complacent about our relationship with God—the single most important relationship in our lives—since self-surrender to Him is a lifelong commitment. The history of religion is replete with individuals who expressed more radical views, like the many Christian ascetics and monks who spent their lives chastising themselves for fear their penance might not offset their sins.

On the other extreme we have the claim of some Christians that they, unlike Muslims, are "guaranteed" Heaven. A "guarantee" is a formal promise by one individual, in this case God, to take responsibility for the debts or obligations of another individual, in this case

---

204. Muhammad Asad, *The Message of the Qur'an*, Gibraltar (1980), p. 14, note 50.

205. Ibn Abi al `Izz, *Commentary on the Creed of At-Tahawi*, translated by Muhammad `Abdul-Haqq Ansari, Al Imam Muhammad ibn Sa`ud Islamic University, Riyadh (2000), pp. 387-388.

the Christian, if that individual fails to meet them. I cannot speak for Christians that make this assertion, but they certainly cannot mean that they are assured of salvation regardless of how they live their lives. They cannot mean that they have a blank check to indulge in wrong-doing and that they will go to Heaven irrespective of what sins they may commit. A concept like this would seem to make a mockery of religion and render the concepts of divine justice and divine purpose meaningless. History has known avowed Christians who committed abominable acts;[206] did they too possess "peace of mind," certain of God's love and salvation? If they did, then the peace of mind was of dubious value.

A New Testament writer teaches that faith without good deeds is dead (James 2:17), and another writes that God judges each person according to that person's deeds (1 Peter 1:17). The "peace that passes understanding" (Philippians 4:7) that Christians speak of should be the peace given by the Gospel's message of hope for all those who submit to God (Ephesians 2:17-18). The peace that Christ has given, says the New Testament, is to guide us in the choices we make, for it is for this peace that God has called us together into one *ummah* (Colossians 3:15).

As the question asserts, in Islam both faith and works augment each other and play an integral part in our spiritual development. Faith should inspire us to do good, which should increase our capacity to receive and experience God's most beautiful names, which should strengthen our faith, which should intensify our desire to do

---

206. Many of the Nazis who slaughtered millions of civilians during World War II were Christians (in that they were of the Christian religion); many of the Crusaders who massacred unarmed Muslim men, women, and children in the name of God were devoted Christians; the Spanish inquisitors who tortured and murdered non-Christians were committed Christians; the white soldiers who brought about the genocide of native American peoples in North and South America—often accompanied by missionaries—were Christians; and so were the armies of Charlemagne who eagerly slaughtered tens of thousands of pagan Anglo Saxons.

good, and so on, each an increasing function of the other. Through both faith and works we grow in the attributes that have God as their infinite source and in our ability to know Him and to relate to Him through love.

On the concept that God can do anything, Muslims would add one caveat: God can do anything as long as it is not impossible in itself. For examples, one and the same thing existing and not existing at one time, or a set being simultaneously empty and non-empty. The impossible in itself is not a "thing" in the sense of an existent or possible existent, it is actually a "nothing"; it is an absurdity. From the Muslim viewpoint, the notion that Jesus is fully both God and man is also impossible in itself, for if God were a man then He would be at one and the same time finite and infinite, mortal and immortal, transcendent and bound by creation, omniscient and lacking in knowledge, independent and dependent, without beginning and created, et cetera. Now one can eliminate these contradictions by claiming that some of these attributes are not essential to either God or to man and thereby eliminate comparisons, but only at the risk of trivializing both concepts.

Throughout history the character of the Prophet has been much maligned by Western writers. When done by Christians, Muslims have been at a tactical disadvantage, because their faith does not allow them to deride other prophets or possible prophets. Jesus is a revered prophet in Islam, and Muslims are prohibited from speaking disrespectfully of him, and thus from scouring the New Testament for details upon which they could put a bad spin. Therefore, when Christians defame the Prophet, Muslims cannot respond in kind, but must confine themselves to refuting the accusations. As to the concerns mentioned above, it would take many more pages to do them justice; therefore I will respond in brief and refer the reader to other sources for more thorough discussion.

The Prophet indeed had multiple wives, as did many of the Old Testament prophets and early Christian church leaders. Throughout most of history, polygamy was seen as a morally acceptable institution, for in a plural marriage, unlike adulterous unions, men took public financial responsibility for the women with whom they had relations and the children they fathered. While the Qur'an suggests that under normal circumstances monogamy is preferable,[207] it also demonstrates that there are some societal problems to which polygamy provides a remedy, like when there is a dramatic increase in widows with children and not enough single men to wed them.[208] Several of the Prophet's marriages were to widows of fallen comrades and some were to forge key political alliances. Thus McDonald and Watt remark that after the death of the Prophet's first wife, Khadijah, "all of Muhammad's marriages and those he arranged for his daughters were made for political reasons."[209]

It is also true that the Prophet fought a war. After he and his Companions suffered thirteen years of harassment, discrimination, torture, confiscation of property, forced deprivation, murder and exile, they retaliated against their persecutors. The Qur'an describes the circumstances.

> To those against whom war has been wrongfully made, permission [to fight] has been granted, and truly God has the power to defend them—those who have been driven from their homelands against all right for no reason than their saying, "Our Lord is God." For if God had not enabled people to defend themselves against one another, all monasteries and churches and synagogues and mosques, in which

---

207. Jeffrey Lang, *Struggling to Surrender*, Amana, Beltsville (2000), pp. 163-164.

208. This was the crisis addressed in the Qur'an (4:3).

209. M. V. McDonald and Montgomery Watt, *The History of al-Tabari*, vol. VII, SUNY Press, 1987, p. xviii. Also, cf. question 2 of this chapter and, Jeffrey Lang, *Struggling to Surrender*, Amana Publications, Beltsville (2000), pp. 162-165.

God's name is abundantly extolled, would surely have been destroyed (22:39-40).

And what ails you that you will not fight in the cause of the utterly helpless men, women and children who are crying, "O our Lord, lead us forth out of this land whose people are oppressors, and raise for us, out of your grace, a protector, and raise for us, out of your grace, one who will defend us." (4:75)

Fight in God's cause those who wage war against you, but do not commit aggression, for truly God does not love aggressors. (2:191)

Will you not fight a people who broke their solemn pledges, and purposed to drive out the Messenger and attacked you first? (9:13)[210]

In these and other verses the Qur'an repeatedly describes the self-defensive nature of the Muslim involvement in the conflict. In the end, after eight years of intermittent hostility that saw less than three hundred combined casualties on both sides and some brilliant political negotiation by the Prophet, he marched unopposed into Mecca, granted amnesty to his former oppressors, and consolidated most of Arabia under his rule.[211]

The Prophet did acquire a number of slaves. The best known of these was Zaid ibn Harithah whom his first wife Khadijah gave him before the advent of Revelation; Muhammad immediately manumitted and adopted him as a son.[212] The Prophet was also given Mariyah

---

210. Cf. 2:193, 4:191, 8:61.

211. Also see, Jeff Lang, *Even Angels Ask*, Amana, Beltsville (1997), pp. 116-136, and, *Struggling to Surrender*, Amana, Beltsville (2000), pp. 183-190.

212. Muhammad Husayn Haykal, *The Life of Muhammad,* trans. by Isma`il al Faruqi, American Trust (1976), p. 69.

the Copt and her sister Sirin as gifts of the Coptic Archbishop of Egypt around 7 A.H. The Prophet freed and married Sirin to the Companion Hassan ibn Thabit and received Mariyah into his household. The sources disagree on whether Mariyah became a full-fledged wife of the Prophet or stayed a concubine, but the majority opinion seems to be that she and her sister became Muslims before arriving in Medina and that Muhammad then married her.[213] The case of the Jewess, Rayhanah bint Zaid, is also unclear. According to some, she eventually accepted the Prophet's marriage proposals; according to others, she preferred to remain a slave. The historians also mentioned some twenty or more slaves that the Prophet acquired, many through purchase, and then freed.[214]

Slavery was practiced in virtually every culture in the seventh century. In pre-Islamic Arabia slaves were usually obtained through raids by stronger tribes on weaker ones. The Qur'an outlawed acquiring slaves in this way, allowing only captives taken in legitimate warfare to become slaves.

> It is not for any prophet to have captives until he has battled hard in the land. You desire the lure of this world and God desires [for you] the Hereafter. (8:67)

Muhammad Ali explains, "War prisoners were distributed among the various Muslim families because no arrangements for their maintenance by the state existed at the time."[215] When the enemy is finally subdued the Qur'an recommends the release of prisoners either as an act of kindness or for ransom.

---

213. Ibid p. 366. Also, *The History of al Tabari*, volume VIII, trans by Michael Fishburn, SUNY Press, 1997, p. 131.

214. *The History of al-Tabari*, volume IX, trans. by Ismail K. Poonawala, SUNY Press, 1990, pp. 142-147.

215. Muhammad Ali, *Religion of Islam*, Lahore (1990), p. 435.

So when you meet in battle those who disbelieve, smite the necks; then when you have overcome them, make them prisoners, and afterwards set them free as a favor or for ransom until war lays down its burdens. (47:4)[216]

In addition, the Qur'an enjoins kindness to slaves,[217] the manumission of slaves as an act of benevolence and expiation for a number of common sins,[218] and provides slaves with legal avenues to obtain their freedom (24:33).[219] Although it would be impractical and unsafe to handle war prisoners in this way today, the condition of Muslim captives during the Prophet's time was in many ways preferable to that of modern POWs. Because of the need to manage prisoners of war, slavery could not be abolished at the time of Revelation.[220] Yet the Qur'an comes closer to promoting its elimination than any other ancient Scripture,[221] and thus the eventual eradication of

216. In the battle of Hunain, six thousand prisoners of the Hawazin tribe were taken, and they were set free as an act of charity. One hundred families of Banu Mustaliq were taken captive in the battle of Muraisi` and then set free without ransom. Seventy prisoners were taken in the battle of Badr, and in only this case was ransom paid for their release. Several paid their ransom by teaching some of the illiterate Muslims how to read. Ibid p. 434.

217. *Surahs* 4:36, 9:60, 24:58.

218. *Surahs* 2:177, 4:92, 5:89, 18:3, 58:3, 90:13.

219. Bernard Lewis, *Race and Slavery in the Middle East*, Oxford (1990), p. 6.

220.The enslavement of enemy prisoners of war also encouraged the enemy not to maltreat enslaved Muslims.

221. In particular, the Bible speaks positively of slavery in many passages, for example: "Slaves, obey your earthly masters with respect and fear, and with sincerity of heart, just as you obey Christ" (Ephesians 6: 5). "Slaves, obey your masters in everything; and do it, not only when their eye is on you and to win their favor, but with sincerity of heart and reverence for the Lord" (Colossians 3:11). "Masters, provide your slaves with what is right and fair, because you know you also have a master in heaven" (Colossians 4:1).

(contd. on page 308)

slavery is in accord with the spirit of the Revelation.[222]

On the death penalty for apostasy, the questioner may be confusing judgments of Muslim jurists with the traditions of the Prophet. The evidence traditionally cited from the authenticated *hadith* to justify execution for a mere change of faith argues more strongly for such a punishment only in cases of aiding and abetting an enemy of the state, i.e. high treason.[223]

Finally, classical Islamic Law does indeed require a woman to seek her husband's permission to perform a voluntary fast.[224] To the best of my knowledge, the ruling is supported by a single authenticated *hadith* on the authority of Abu Hurairah: "A woman is not to fast for one day while her husband is present except with his permission,

---

Footnote 221 (contd. from page 307)

"Teach slaves to be subject to their masters in everything, to try to please them, not to talk back to them" (Titus 2:9). "Slaves, submit yourselves to your masters with all respect, not only to those who are good and considerate, but also those who are harsh. They promise them freedom, while they themselves are slaves of depravity—for a man is a slave to whatever has mastered him" (1Peter 2:18-19).

222. Ironically, slavery was recently revived in parts of Sudan and Afghanistan.

223. The Qur'an mentions apostasy thirteen times but never specifies execution or any other punitive action against the apostate. The Scripture also refers to two historic and unpunished cases of apostasy during the Medinan period. The only authenticated case of the Prophet punishing apostates involves the party of the tribe of 'Ukul, who accepted Islam, committed murder and then apostatized, while there are a number of authenticated traditions in which the Prophet let apostates go unpunished. Jeffrey Lang, *Struggling to Surrender*, Amana, Beltsville (2000), pp. 195-199. Also, Muhammad Ali, *Religion of Islam*, Lahore (1990), pp. 437-443, and, Mohamed S. El-Awa, *Punishment in Islamic Law* (Indianapolis: American Trust Publications), pp. 49-68.

224. Sayyid Sabiq, *Fiqh us-Sunnah*, as-Zakah, and as-Siyam, Islamic Printing & Publishing Co., Cairo, pp. 123-124.

unless it is during *Ramadan*."[225] The jurists viewed marriage rather austerely as essentially a legal agreement wherein a wife makes herself available to her husband sexually in exchange for full maintenance; as long as she does this, she has fulfilled her end of the bargain. Thus classical Islamic law does not require a wife to do housework or tend to her children. There are many other *hadiths* of varying grades of authenticity that stress a wife should submit to her husband's sexual need on demand.[226] There are also others that empasize a husband's obligations toward his wife.

I do not wish to leave the impression that I believe there are no women-debasing traditions or those that give husbands near complete authority over their wives. There are a number of such *hadiths* that have been rated *sahih* (authentic) and very many more that were not.[227] Female inferiority was assumed in almost all cultures until very recently[228] and the ancient Islamic was no exception. When one looks to Muslim scholarly writings from this era on the nature of women one invariably find opinions, interpretations and attitudes that now seem utterly misogynistic. Hence statements about women in *Hadith* that today would immediately invite suspicion might have seemed quite acceptable to many of the ancient *muhadithun* (traditionists). Given the biases of the time, it would not be surprising that many women-demeaning views would had found their way into even the most respected *Hadith* collections.

---

225. It appears in the collections of al-Bukhari and Ahmed. Another version, on the authority of Abu Sa'id al Khudri, appears in the *Sunan of Abu Dawud*, but it may have been judged suspect.

226. Cf. comment 14, chapter 3.

227. Cf. Chapter 2, pp. 242-243 and 248-249.

228. For example, in the New Testament we have the following statements: "But I want you to understand that the head of every man is Christ, the head of a woman is her husband, and the head of Christ is God" (1 Corinthians 11:3). "A man ought not to cover his head since he is the image and glory of God; but the woman is the glory of man. (For man was not

(contd. on page 310)

Question 6 (Like so many of the questions in this book, this one, from a woman in her twenties, shows that many American Muslim young people are surveying Western research on Islam):

Whenever non-Muslims imply that the Prophet was influenced by Judaism or Christianity and that he borrowed from these religions to "make up" Islam, Muslims say that the Prophet was not in touch with the Jews or the Christians. They say that the Prophet did not come into contact with the Jews until after the <u>Hijrah</u> (exile to Medinah). Could the Prophet not have come in contact with Jews and Christians during his travels for trade? Even if he did not, could he not have met Jewish and Christian traders that visited Mecca, or Meccans that came to know about Judaism and Christianity through their travels? My imam told me "no." He says that at that time the Arabs were very good at keeping travel logs: who went where, when and so on and so forth. In your book, <u>Struggling to Surrender</u>, you mention this briefly and say that the detail with which the Prophet talked about these two religions would indicate that he had to have studied them extensively and that there are some key differences between some of the stories told in the Qur'an and the Bible. Could you elaborate on this topic?

I feel that there are many aspects of the Qur'an that resist explanation if one assumes that it was the Prophet's invention, but because I found other features of the Scripture more perplexing then

---

Footnote No. 228 (contd. from page 309)

made from woman, but woman from man. Neither was man created for woman, but woman for man" (1 Corinthians 11:7-9). "As in all the churches of the saints, the women should keep silence in the churches. For they are not permitted to speak, but should be subordinate, as even the law says. If there is anything they desire to know, let them ask their husbands at home. For it is shameful for a woman to speak in church" (1 Corinthians 14:35). "Let a woman learn in silence with all submissiveness. I permit no woman to teach or to have authority over men; she is to keep silent. For Adam was formed first, then Eve; and Adam was not deceived and became a transgressor (1 Timothy 2:11-14).

its parallels with stories found in the Judeo-Christian tradition, I left only a brief observation regarding this. For the same reason I will only attempt to quickly explain the point I was trying to make in *Struggling to Surrender*.[229]

The Qur'an does not portray itself as a Revelation of a new religion. It states that from every people God chose at least one prophet at some time in their history and that all of them preached the same fundamental theme of the need for self-surrender to Him.[230] It contains examples of peoples to which prophets were repeatedly sent because the divine message they communicated would ultimately become ignored, distorted, or forgotten. The Qur'an also presents the Prophet's mission as corrective and restorative; that the Revelation he communicated confirms the fundamental truths contained in other sacred books and corrects key errors.[231] Accordingly, the Qur'an frequently recounts tales of former prophets, many of them familiar to the Judeo-Christian tradition and some of them alien to it, always demonstrating the essential unity of their missions, while sometimes pointing out where their messages were corrupted.

The Qur'an assumes that its initial audience is already somewhat acquainted with the prophets and other personalities it mentions, although it sometimes indicates that parts of its narratives are unknown to them. It is not surprising that the pagan Arabs would have heroes in common with the relatively few Jewish and Christian tribes scattered about the Peninsula; they shared legends and odes during the annual trade fairs and they recognized a common ancestry through the prophet Abraham. It is therefore likely that through centuries of cultural exchange they adopted with modifications each other's folklore. The Arab traders also had contact with the larger Jewish and Christian presence beyond the Peninsula. Hence the

---

229. *Struggling to Surrender*, Amana, 2000, pp. 201-202.

230. *Surahs* 10:47; 13:7; 16:36; 35:24.

231. *Surahs* 2:91; 6:92; 35:31.

imam's assertion that the Prophet before the migration to Medina had never met Jews, Christians, or pagans who had contact with either, is almost certainly inaccurate. The ancient biographers report that the cousin of his first wife Khadijah, Waraqah ibn Nawfal, was a convert to Christianity.[232] There are also reports that in his youth and as a young man the Prophet accompanied a number of caravans to Syria where he must have at least briefly met Christians and Jews, and a few accounts relate an early passing encounter with a Christian monk named Buhairah.[233]

While the pre-Islamic Arabs were not ignorant of the personages mentioned in the Qur'an, this does not mean that they were well informed about them or had more than a fleeting interest in them. The poetry that has come down to us, although scant, contains virtually no mention of these personalities. The fact that, during the first two centuries after the Hijrah, Muslim scholars had to continually search outside of the Arabian Peninsula for Jewish and Christian sources (termed *Isra'iliyat* in Arabic) to enlarge on the Qur'an's accounts indicates that during Muhammad's lifetime the people of Arabia—including its small Jewish and Christian population—had very limited exposure to the literary corpus of either faith. This also shows that the Prophet left little commentary on the Qur'an's stories, suggesting that his knowledge of them was not much more than what is presented in the Scripture; of course, if the Prophet's source was divine Revelation, then this is what might be expected.

Orientalists in the nineteenth and through much of the twentieth centuries, working under the assumption that the Prophet was an impostor, charged him with plagiarism, citing parallels to Qur'anic accounts in the Bible, Talmudic commentaries, apocryphal books,

---

232. Muhammad Husayn Haykal, *The Life of Muhammad*, trans. by Isma'il al Faruqi, North American Trust Publications (1976), pp. 52, 67, 70, 77, 78, 84, 90.

233. For example, ibid p. 54.

and ancient Jewish and Christian letters and poetry.[234] The large number and wide range of sources they cite and the inaccessibility of many of them—especially to a non-Jewish, non-Christian Arab with no formal education, or even for that matter to a modern, educated, Jewish, or Christian layman—suggests that if the Prophet did plagiarise, then he must have devoted lengthy and concentrated study to Jewish and Christian tradition under the tutelage of genuine masters. This I believe explains why almost all orientalists assumed that the Prophet must have had a teacher or teachers of considerable learning. They found support for this hypothesis in the verse that speaks of the opposition's accusation that "a man teaches him," to which the Qur'an responds, "the language of him they incline towards is unintelligible, while this is pure and clean Arabic" (16:103). This seems to be an allusion to the apparent crudity and ineptness of the alleged teacher, suggesting to many Muslim commentators that he must have been a non-Arab.

Various names have been suggested as to the identity of the person to whom the Prophet's opponents referred, mostly foreign Christian slaves who converted to Islam and were subsequently cruelly tortured but yet held to their faith. Obviously, none of these could serve as the hypothetical erudite informer, as their lowly station would not afford them the opportunity to obtain a higher education and is very unlikely that they would willingly endure persecution for a cause they knew to be false. Some orientalists surmised that Salman the Persian had taught Muhammad, but this is impossible since he did not come until after the Hijrah. The most popular candidate for orientalists is the monk Buhairah whom Muhammad, while still a

---

234. Abraham I. Katsh, *Judaism and the Koran* (A.S. Barnes and Company, New York, 1962); Abraham I. Katz, *Judaism in Islam*, (New York: Sepler-Hermon Press, 1980); Erwin I. J. Rosenthal, *Judaism and Islam*, (London: Published by Thomas Yoseloff, 1961). For research of this kind by a Muslim author: Jerald F. Dirks, *The Cross and the Crescent* (Amana Publications, Beltsville, MD, 2001).

boy, met briefly on his journey to Syria with his uncle Abu Talib, but 16:103 shows that the Prophet's opponents referred to a local man, not to mention that such a short meeting would not provide sufficient time to absorb a large body of knowledge.

The gist of all this is that although the Prophet's adversaries surmised that while in Mecca he must have had a teacher, it seems that they were unable to identify a suitable candidate. The Prophet's chief opposition was his own tribe, and if he had at some time undertaken extensive study under a genuine scholar, his kinsmen would had to have known of it. Yet there is no evidence in any historical source that his enemies made such a claim, and the Islamic sources are remarkably transparent with regard to the accusations of the Prophet's enemies. It also should be remembered that the Prophet obtained an extremely devoted following from among his tribesmen, which would have been very difficult to do if they had been aware of his extended studies.

Verse 16:103 may be better understood in light of other claims made by the Quraysh against the Prophet. They claimed that the Qur'an is the creation of someone possessed or out of his mind (7:184; 15:6; 23:70; 34:8; 37:36; 44:14; 52:29; 68:5-6; 68:51; 81:22), or that the Prophet just invented it on his own (10:37; 11:13; 11:35; 16:101; 21:5; 32:3; 34:8; 34:43; 42:24; 46:8). All of these are recorded in Meccan *surahs* and are fairly evenly distributed throughout the Meccan period. *Surah* 16:103 is believed by many commentators to be the last of them. These show that the Prophet's enemies from his tribe devised several strategies to discredit the Qur'an, especially just before his emigration to Medinah, when by then he had gained a significant following and the Quraysh became more desperate to extinguish his movement. From the chronology of the Revelations it appears that early on the opposition mainly took the insanity or spiritual-possession line of attack (34:8; 52:29; 68:5-6; 68:51; 81:22). In the middle and late Meccan stages of the Prophet's career, the insanity explanation is still resorted to but now the claim that the Prophet concocted the Qur'an on his own becomes popular

(10:37; 11:13; 11:35; 21:5; 32:3; 42:24; 46:8). It seems that finally it had become apparent that both of these explanations were no longer credible. The allegation contained in 16:103 may represent a last ditch effort after previous failed attempts. Taken together these accusations emerge as varied and vain attempts—grabs at straws so to speak—to account for a phenomenon for which the Quraish could not offer a convincing explanation.

The last part of the question asks about differences between some of the stories told in the Qur'an and ancient Judeo-Christian texts. A lengthy comparison is required to do justice to this topic, since in almost every case of parallel accounts there are important, sometimes subtle variations that often significantly affect the purport of the tales. But once again, in the interest of brevity, I will keep to a few short illustrations.

The most salient case of divergent Qur'anic and Judeo-Christian parallels is the stories of the first man and woman in Genesis and the Qur'an.[235] The longer, more detailed Biblical account is an interwoven story made from two different traditions, while the Qur'an distributes the story throughout the text. The Qur'an specifies that God created mankind to be His representatives on earth (2:30); the Genesis account explains that God created mankind to have dominion over the earth's creatures and plants (Genesis 1:26-30) and to till and keep the Garden of Eden (Genesis 2:15). The Biblical version has a vague reference to God's creating humanity in His image; the Qur'an is more explicit in that God breathed something of His spirit into them (32:7-9, 15:28-29). The angels question the creation of man in the Qur'an (2:30) but not in Genesis. In the Qur'an God uses Adam's ability to name things to demonstrate his potential superiority over the angels (2:31-33) in response to their objection in 2:30; the Genesis account mentions that Adam can name things but does not

---

235. *Surahs* 2:30-39; 7:19-25; 15:27-48; 20:120-124; 32:7-9; and Genesis, chapters 1-3.

seem to attach any particular significance to it (Genesis 2:19-20). Genesis has Eve made from Adam's rib (Genesis 2:21-24); the Qur'an is silent on the mode of her creation. In Genesis, Satan is symbolized as a serpent (Genesis 3:3); the Qur'an informs that he is of the Jinn (18:50), a creature made of smokeless fire (15:27). In Genesis, the tree forbidden to the first couple is referred to as the "tree of the knowledge of good and evil" (Genesis 2:15); in the Qur'an, Satan deceives the couple, telling them that the tree is the "tree of immortality and a kingdom that never decays" (7:20-22, 20:120), but the Scripture assigns to the tree no special qualities. In the Biblical version, God appears to be furious at the couple's transgression and punishes them with earthly life (Genesis 3:8-19); in the Qur'an the couple's error is called a "slip" for which they are immediately forgiven, with God then promising them that they have nothing to fear if they follow divine guidance (2:36-38; 20:122). The Genesis account has a cherubim and a fiery sword protect the "tree of life" from man (Genesis 3:22); the Qur'anic story does not mention this. There are other dissimilarities between the Biblical and Qur'anic versions, but these are some of the most obvious.[236]

Even a cursory glance at instances of Qur'anic and Biblical parallels display marked dissimilarities. The Bible accuses Solomon of idol worship in his old age (1 Kings 11:4), but the Qur'an exonerates him of such charges (2:102). In the New Testament Jesus is crucified and dies, while the Qur'an asserts, "they [the Jews] did not kill him nor crucify him" (4:157) but God revealed to Jesus, "I will cause you to die and raise you to myself and cleanse you of those who disbelieve" (3:55). In the Biblical version of the story of Noah, the entire world is flooded (Genesis 7: 23), but the Qur'anic version refers only to the people of Noah (25:37). In the story of Moses, the Qur'an states that God saved Pharoah's body to be a sign for later generations

---

236. See chapter 1 for an interpretation of the story of the first couple in the Qur'an.

(10:90-92), a detail not contained in the Biblical narrative. In the Bible, Lot's wife turns into a pillar of salt when she looks back at Sodom and Gomor'rah (Genesis 19:24), but the Qur'an simply states that she chooses to remain behind in the doomed cities (7:83).

There are many more examples of divergence between parallel narratives and an in depth study and contrast of their effects on the meanings they convey would be of great interest. However, I think it is quite clear that the Qur'an does much more than recount Judeo-Christian stories. Instead it revises them to reveal original meanings consistent with and supportive of its primary message of the human need for *Islam* (self-surrender to God). Hence, in order for Muhammad to be the Qur'an's author, he would not only have had to have been exposed to a enormous amount of Jewish and Christian scholarship, he must also have had the time and skill to rework the material into a coherent whole, apparently without those closest to him being aware of it. Unless of course his followers all cooperated in a great hoax, but again it is inconceivable that they would suffer persecution, exile, loss of family, property, and life to participate in a tremendous lie. Another possibility is the Prophet hid his work on the Qur'an from his disciples, but then he would have had to have composed and edited most of the text in his head.

Chapter Three

WHERE HAVE ALL THE CHILDREN GONE?

*S*ohail and I had many opportunities to talk the two days I was
in town. We spoke on the long drive from the airport to the
*hotel, the two times we ate breakfast together, and the several rides he
gave me to my lectures and meetings with Muslim community leaders. We
talked about many things: the weather, our careers, the Islamic communities in which we live, college basketball, the economy, politics, and our
families. Our discussions were the kind of pleasant, not too personal, not
too serious dialogue that typically occurs between new acquaintances.
But as we started for the airport on the afternoon I was to leave,
Sohail was pensive and hardly uttered a word. My lecture that morning,
"The Disillusionment of American Muslim Youth," was on the inability
of so many of the second generation to relate to their parents' faith. When
I asked Sohail if he was all right, he responded with the customary
"Al-hamdu-lillah" and returned to his thoughts.*

*After several more minutes of silence, during which I tried to figure
out what I had done to offend him, Sohail glanced at me and said, "I used
to be very close to my kids," and then began a long explanation. He spoke
about how they had always been model Muslim children and how they
had been very active in their mosque. They were part of every community function, regularly attended the Sunday Islamic School, helped out in
the mosque cafeteria before the Sunday brunch, and went to Islamic youth
conferences. He talked about his love for them. He said that when he used
to pick up his son from junior high, the boy would come running to his
waiting arms and he would hug him and kiss his head. Of course, his
ninth grade friends poked fun at this daily display of affection, but his son
just ignored them. Sohail could not look at me as he spoke about his*

daughter, and he kept pausing to collect himself. He said how pure and strikingly beautiful she was, that she looked like an angel in her <u>hijab</u>, that the other parents marvelled at her beauty, and that so many friends hoped to match her with their boys. He said that for him the sun rose and set upon her, and the best moments in his life were when she sat on his lap with her arms around his neck.

As the reader can guess, things began to change. When his son was in high school, Sohail found a pack of cigarettes in his jacket one day. He confronted him and was told that it belonged to one of the kids at school. A short time later Sohail proved he was lying. He felt so deeply betrayed. "How could my son lie to me?" he exclaimed. But he soon found that there would be many more to come. He imposed severe restrictions and their relationship became strained, but at least his bond with his daughter stayed strong.

But then she went away to college. Gradually she became distant, began questioning Islam more and more, and too often would not answer the phone when he called her at night. She said she couldn't come home during spring break, so Sohail drove to the university to find out what was wrong. It turns out she had fallen for a non-Muslim boy whom she met in class and had moved in with him. Sohail was devastated. He said he called her every deplorable name in the book, words he wouldn't say to the vilest streetwalker. "How can she have done this to me?" he cried. He hasn't spoken to her since, despite her many attempts to call him.

As for his son, he finished high school several years ago. Sohail frequently gets calls from the police to come down to the station to pick him up, after they find him drunk and passed out in various places around town. One night he discovered his boy sitting on the back porch with a table knife in his hands. When he asked him what he was planning to do with it, he told his father he was contemplating suicide. Sohail went to the kitchen and then came out and handed his son a sharper knife. "If you're going to do it, then at least do it right," he told him, and then walked back in the house. "How can my children betray me?" Sohail pleaded. "I can't even talk to them! I can't even look at them! What should I do?"

What is the largest group of Muslims in America? If you attend most Friday congregational prayers or go to one of the many Islamic conferences held throughout the year, you would probably conclude that the overwhelming majority of America's Muslims are immigrants, mostly middle-aged and older, but this is off the mark. It has been estimated that there are between three and eight million Muslims residing in the United States. To simplify things we'll take five million as a median estimate. Estimates also vary widely as to the number of American converts to Islam, but one million is the most frequently mentioned figure, and this could be low, since most of the Nation of Islam, whose membership at its height in the 1960's was about one million, have come over to mainstream Islam, and there has been slow but steady conversion from all sectors of society over the last three decades. Almost all Muslim children residing in America were born here and Muslim families tend to have more children than the national average, so three per family seems like a reasonable estimate. Hence, about sixty percent of American Muslims, around three million, are born in the United States to Muslim parents. If we add this number of non-first generation Muslims to the number of estimated American converts, we obtain that approximately four million of America's five million Muslims, about eighty percent, were born in this country. Yet if four fifths of the Muslims in America are citizens by birth, then we need to ask where are they? For they are conspicuously absent from the nation's mosques and Islamic gatherings.

Back in 1982, the year I converted to Islam, whenever and wherever I attended a Muslim religious meeting, it would be comprised almost entirely of immigrants around my age and visiting foreign students. More than twenty years have passed but things are much the same today. The audience at Muslim community gatherings is still mostly immigrants close to my age and older, visiting foreign students, and sometimes a sprinkling of converts. Although America has seen in the last half century a large, sustained Muslim immigration, and Muslims have registered more than a thousand mosques and

Islamic centers, have created dozens of K-12 schools, and have founded several national political organizations and lobbies, the largest group of Muslims in America is markedly underrepresented at community gatherings and in community institutions. Many of the Muslim foreign students who descended onto American college campuses since the fifties have become U.S. citizens and residents, and by now have children in their teens, twenties, thirties and even forties, but these descendents of the first generation and the over one million converts are as a group keeping apart from America's mosques, Islamic centers and other Muslim organizations. From this most critical indicator of Islam's progress in the United States, we cannot be at all confident that the religion is now rooted in America or that it ultimately will be.

It appears that without continued reinforcement from abroad, many Islamic institutions in the United States will eventually shut down and many of the descendents of Muslim immigrants and converts, having had practically no connection to the Islamic community, will disavow the religion of their forefathers. Until recently, substantial curtailment of Muslim immigration, which had been steady, seemed a remote possibility, but September 11, 2001, may have changed all that. Reports from mosques on college campuses around the country indicate that the population of Muslim foreign students is already decreasing and there is talk in the United States of placing a moratorium on immigration from Islamic countries. Another major terrorist attack or two on the U.S.—and there is every reason to expect there are more to come—and the Muslim immigrant and Muslim foreign student population in America could ultimately, in effect, dry up.

So why do so many non-immigrant Muslims, whose participation in the community is so urgently needed, steer clear of America's mosques and Islamic centers? The usual explanation is that the surrounding society tempts them from the religion. Peer pressure, the media's demonization of Islam, the pull of pop culture, rabid

consumerism, deep-rooted anti-Muslim prejudice, and the exploitation and promotion of sex, combine to draw too many youth and
converts away. While all religions in America complain of some of the
deleterious influences of modern Western culture, most Muslims
would affirm that Islam stands most firmly against them and that it is
therefore not surprising that this group, that is most vulnerable to the
allurements and pressures of the surrounding society, should have a
high ratio of disengagement from the Islamic community. Indeed,
even though American Buddhists and Hindus fit more easily into the
American landscape, a very large segment of their second generation
have drifted from the parental faith.

The surrounding culture may make it at times difficult to be
Muslim, but the roots of non-immigrant avoidance of the community surely go beyond external pressures. Islam continues to draw more
converts than any other faith in America, despite the negative public-
ity, prejudice and other above mentioned societal influences. A large
number of Americans, fully mindful of all these factors, continue to
embrace Islam. It just doesn't make sense that after emotionally and
psychologically overcoming these hurdles to become Muslim they
would so easily and in such large numbers cave in to them. It is also
understandable that in a society dominated by alternative world-views
and lifestyles young persons would come to question their faith and
some would leave it aside as a matter of mere convenience, but it is
nevertheless peculiar that a religion that attracts the fervent devotion
of so many youth in the traditional Muslim world, who very often
become activists at considerable personal risk, can garner only negli-
gible involvement from children of Muslim immigrants.

Rather than look outside the Islamic community for causes of the
non-immigrant exodus, and rather than ascribe it to insurmountable
cultural forces, Muslim leaders and thinkers are obliged to look intro-
spectively to discern if the community can do more to reach this
potential bridge to the future. Yet the problems we are discussing are
of the heart and mind, and we cannot hope for an effective diagnosis

without the patient's cooperation. If the affected refuse to complain or we refuse to hear them, then we are unlikely to discover a remedy.

This is currently the biggest obstruction to treating the malaise of the missing eighty percent, because for too long their queries and objections have been quelled by derision, intimidation, browbeating and dogmatism. When young people share with me their doubts about certain aspects of Muslim tradition, I ask them why they don't discuss their problems with their parents, and the reply I consistently get is that the latter would fly into a rage. Muslim converts and young people also complain that their mosques and Islamic centers are of no help. Doubt or reservation about traditional views are commonly met with pronouncements like, "but this is Islam," "but that is not Islam," or, "but if you don't accept this, then you're not a Muslim." Books and speeches on contentious issues are often filled with charges of infidelity and threats of damnation for opposing positions. Muslims who seriously question the scholarly legacy or widely held interpretations or customs are dismissed and anathematized as "modernists," "Westernized," "rationalists," or "dangerous."[1] Most speeches at Islamic meetings and conferences are essentially sermons. It is rare that a speaker seriously critiques a conventional view. Admittedly, this might be too much to expect at gatherings that are akin to the revival meetings in Evangelical Christianity, whose principle aim is to awaken religious fervor and inculcate the tradition, but then where are the youth and converts to turn for a thorough, scientific, dispassionate discussion of the questions over which they agonize? For this group, who by and large are college educated, the most obvious repository of such in-depth critical analysis and research is the university, and there is much to be found there on the issues that trouble them, but it is almost entirely the work of non-Muslims and

---

1. It is important to note that many Muslim liberals are equally dogmatic and intolerant of contending views, but their numbers are small, they by and large stay away from American Islamic institutions, and converts and descendents of immigrants have little access to them.

has its own inherent biases. At any rate, if the Islamic community is to effectively respond to the concerns of the absent eighty percent, then facilitating communication is the first order of business, but given the community's reputation for extreme traditionalism, this is a very tall order.

Several years ago, I was invited to a Muslim youth camp located about two and a half hours from Lawrence, Kansas. I participated in two sessions. In the first I gave a short talk, and in the second I was supposed to have a dialogue with the campers, who ranged in age from ten to sixteen. This audience was younger than the group I had in mind and came from very devout families that strongly urged them to attend. Yet I was interested to know if even these boys and girls wrestled with misgivings about their faith. So in the dialogue session, I asked the children if they were ever troubled by questions about their religion. No one responded. I then tried giving some examples. I asked if gender segregation was practiced in their local communities, and if it was, did they ever question it, either to themselves or others. No response. I asked if they ever wondered why a Muslim man could have four wives and a Muslim woman only one husband. No response. I asked if they ever wondered why they could not date like their non-Muslim friends. Total silence. Did they ever wonder why they couldn't celebrate Christmas? Nothing. Why do Muslim women have to dress traditionally but not Muslim men? No response. After several more unanswered questions, I reversed roles and asked them how they would respond if someone asked them each of these questions. As I went through the list, each question produced one or two volunteers who responded very much along traditional lines, exactly as I would expect an imam at a *masjid* to reply. After each answer I asked the audience if they were satisfied with the responses. No problem. So I left the camp that afternoon a little surprised, but at the same time pleased that this admittedly special group of Muslim children was secure in their faith. But when I arrived home more than two hours latter, I no sooner got in the door when I received a phone call from Aminah Assilmi, one of the camp counselors and also an American convert, informing me that the children wanted me to come back to the camp that night to discuss, with Aminah and me alone, some of the questions with which they were struggling. I told Aminah I could not come back that night—the last night of the camp—but I asked her why they kept so quiet when I begged them for their input and why they seemed so satisfied with the standard answers. She said the children felt intimidated discussing things in front of the several community leaders who were also in the audience.

Not all my efforts to reach the great absent majority have been so unsuccessful. For several years after my conversion, the number of converts with whom I had regular contact was few, and the only second generation Muslims I spoke with about Islam were my children. This changed with the publication of my first book, *Struggling to Surrender*, in 1994. I suddenly started receiving letters, telephone calls and email from converts all over the world. Then, when *Even Angels Ask* came out in 1997, email from young American Muslims came pouring in. I also began getting email, letters and telephone calls from Muslim parents seeking advice on how to deal with their straying children and from non-Muslims investigating Islam. These conversations inspired this book and some of the questions and comments that were put to me are distributed throughout the text.

I make no claims that the young adults and converts who made the effort to contact me are a representative sample. The disillusioned American-born Muslims who shared with me their problems still have enough attachment to Islam to fret about it, while Muslim leaders—especially Muslim youth leaders—throughout the country tell me that most of the missing majority are extremely apathetic. It should be emphasized that parents who have no connection to the mosque are the biggest cause of second generation disinterest in Islam. Many adults in traditional Muslim countries also shun the mosque, yet their children normally "absorb" Islam from the culture. In America, however, if parents are not mosque-connected, it is very difficult for their children to develop any real attachment to the religion. Yet the American-born Muslims who write or call me are mainly from mosque-connected families or are converts struggling to hold onto their faith. Even though they may be somewhat unrepresentative of the missing eighty percent, it stands to reason that most of the latter would experience similar problems if they too had greater contact with the Islamic community.

So What's Your Problem?

Muslim leaders should not blankly ascribe the dearth of non-immigrant participation in the community to societal pressures alone, but this is undoubtedly a factor. For non-immigrant Muslims, America is the only homeland they know, and we should assume that as a rule they will adopt many of the prevailing values and customs of their country. Some Muslim parents do their best to insulate their children from the larger society—they may disallow them to have non-Muslim friends, forbid them to watch television or to use the internet unsupervised, prohibit them from listening to radio or buying CDs, and send them to Islamic schools or opt for home schooling—but those who are able to do this are relatively few. Not many communities have full-time Islamic schools and keeping your child in cultural isolation takes a sizeable commitment of time and effort. Moreover, most Muslims parents feel integration into the larger society is necessary for their children's general welfare and that with prudent child rearing they can effectively steer them away from America's undesirable habits without going to such extremes. Hence, barring the few exceptions that have been successfully isolated from the surrounding culture, most native-born Muslims have a discernible American outlook. So it is really not correct to think of the missing eighty percent as being lured from their faith into the American mainstream, for they are already assimilated into their nation's societal landscape and are continually weighing the larger culture and the Muslim subculture against each other. This explains the frequently heard plea from native born Muslims for the separation of religion and culture; since they are not grounded in traditional Muslim society, they naturally want to embrace only those religious beliefs and practices that can be shown to be fundamental to Islam. Therefore, it's not surprising that most of their religious queries derive from a clash of cultures.

In the following discussion of some of the concerns and doubts native born Muslims have shared with me, I consider four major but intersecting perspectives: those of non-immigrant Muslim women, African American converts, descendents of immigrants, and finally, converts in general.

A Woman's Place

At the top of the list of indigene Muslim complaints against the Islamic community is the treatment it accords women, and chief among grievances in this area is the practice of gender segregation. It is one of the biggest impediments to Islam's acceptance in the West and one of the prime causes of disaffection of non-immigrant Muslims. Protests that women are discouraged from attending congregational prayers, are placed in separate rooms away from the main prayer hall, and segregated from men at community gatherings are commonplace. In the United States, where women have had to fight long and hard against gender discrimination, the notion that they should be kept in sexual isolation is abhorrent. What's more, group segregation in any form stirs up memories in America of its own dark history of bigotry and has become synonymous with prejudice and oppression. As one African American lady convert put it, "My people just recently won the right to eat in restaurants with everyone else and to ride in the fronts of busses, now they tell me that I have to stay in the backroom of the mosque!"

A common rationalization for female seclusion is that it deters promiscuity, an aspect of American culture that many Muslims see as rampantly out of control. The fear is that if the sexes are allowed to interact in mosques and at community events, licentiousness, with all its attendant destructive consequences to family and society, will pervade the community. The ancient legal maxim, "Whatever leads to the *haram* (unlawful) is *haram*," is often invoked to prove the necessity of female seclusion. This legal formula, which might at first seem reasonable, can, because it is so open-ended, lead to the most strait-jacketing legislation. If public mixing of the sexes is *haram* because it might lead to promiscuity, then should not women be prevented from leaving their homes except when absolutely necessary, since venturing from their houses might lead to inadvertent mixing? Conservative Muslim scholars have argued this point. The same maxim has been used to argue that a woman should not be granted a driver's license, for if her car were to breakdown when she is alone, a man who arrives on the scene might refuse to help her unless she submit to his sexual demands.

The cogency of arguments like these hinges on how far Muslims are willing to restrict personal freedom to reduce the possibility of transgression and the extent to which they are willing to overlook possible negative side effects. If the United States, for example, were to suddenly ban female driving, it would be necessary, in order to avert social and financial disaster, to import chauffeurs—about 1 per household—to transport women and children when male drivers in the family are occupied.[2] The drivers would also have to be paid low enough wages—lower than the current minimum wage—to make chauffeurs affordable to the average family. Of course, the influx of some fifty million poorly paid male workers would create its own major problems and risks.

Given the Qur'an's persistent condemnation of religious invention and the sanctification of mere tradition, the main issue for Muslims regarding the enforcement of their customs on the American

---

2. This is what is currently done in Saudi Arabia

Islamic scene is not their potential social repercussions but whether or not they are essential to Islam. This is a critical matter in the sacred scripture, for the idealization of opinion, preference, or custom could seriously impede the search for truth.

> Say: Have you considered what provision God has sent down for you, and how you made some of it *haram* (unlawful) and *halal* (lawful)? Say: Has God indeed permitted you, or do you invent a lie concerning God? (10:59)

> And say not, for any false thing your tongues put forth: "This is *halal* (lawful) and this is *haram* (unlawful)", so that you invent a lie against God. (16:116)

It is thus crucial that Muslims in America continually reassess their traditions to distinguish those that are and are not fundamental to the religion. Those deemed non-essential and detrimental to the progress of Islam in America should be dispensed with, or at the very least, accommodations should be made for those who choose not to follow them, but most importantly, they should not be presented as compulsory, for they could become for homegrown Muslims unnecessary sources of doubt, and for non-Muslims, deterrents to exploring Islam as a religious option.[3] However, sifting out inessential beliefs and customs is not always a cut and dry process. Most Muslim traditions are "religious" in the sense that they are piously motivated and could be provided a religious rationale that links them by a series of assumptions, implications, and conclusions to the Qur'an or Sayings of the Prophet. The prohibition of female drivers is a prime example: adultery is clearly prohibited by the Qur'an and Prophetic traditions; there is a possibility—however slight—that a female driver could be put in a position where she can be sexually compromised; thus there should be a ban on female driving. But a religious *justification* for a practice is not enough to prove it *essential*

---

3. For further discussion on this topic see pp. 364-373 of this chapter.

to the faith; the evidence, premises and inferences it is built upon need to be critically examined, and counter-evidence, counter-arguments and counter-considerations need to be considered and weighed. The debate over female seclusion may help to illustrate this point.

I know of no direct textual support for female seclusion (i.e. a verse of the Qur'an or authenticated *hadith* that explicitly forbids Muslim men and women to interact) and the indirect evidence is not overwhelming. Qur'an 33:53 is universally cited as proof that gender segregation is obligatory on Muslims. The relevant passage reads:

> O you who believe, enter not the houses of the Prophet unless permission is given to you for a meal, not waiting for its cooking to be finished. But when you are invited, enter, and when you have taken food, disperse—not seeking to listen to talk. Surely this gives the Prophet trouble, but he forbears from you, but God does not forbear from the truth. And when you ask them for any necessities, ask of them from behind a curtain. This is purer for your hearts and their hearts.

The verse instructs the Companions, male and female, not to barge into the Prophet's wives' apartments unannounced, as had been the habit of some of them. The ancient commentators report that a few embarrassing moments occasioned its revelation. It then tells the Companions that when they have a genuine need to speak to a wife of the Prophet, they should remain outside of her apartment and address her while leaving the curtain at the entrance closed. Advocates of female seclusion also cite *hadiths* in which the Prophet's wives converse with various Companions as described in the passage.

The argument that 33:53 instituted the general practice of female seclusion is not unassailable. First, it is not clear that it is enforcing the type of strict segregation that is practiced in many mosques today, even with respect to the Prophet's wives. It may only be protecting his family and him from awkward situations by assuring them of some level of privacy. At this stage in the Prophet's mission there were regularly swarms of people in the courtyard, just outside his family's living quarters, many of them newly converted, uncouth Bedouin. Second, the tone of the Qur'an does not suggest a general precept. The same *surah* contains several regulations that apply specifically and exclusively to the Prophet and his wives, who are described in the Scripture as "not like any other women" (33:32). Third, there is abundant evidence in the *Hadith* compilations that the seclusion of women was not generally practiced in early Islamic history. There are accounts of the Prophet and his Companions going to unrelated (*non-mahram*) women to have lice removed from their hair during the Farewell Pilgrimage,[4] of women from outside the Prophet's family eating from the same dish as the Prophet,[5] of the wife of a Companion serving his male guests,[6] of the Prophet sitting with a married couple and conversing with the woman about the dream from which he had just awoke,[7] of two male Companions visiting a lady Companion and their mourning the Prophet's recent demise.[8] There are numerous reports of Muslim women participating in battles, where they would fight, supply the archers with arrows, carry food and water to the troops, and treat the injured.[9] A well-known account reports that a

---

4. *Sahih al Bukhari*, trans. Muhammad Muhsin Khan, vol. 2, "*The Book of Hajj*" (26), *Hadith* no. 782, and "*The Book of Jihad*" (52), *Hadith* no. 47.

5. Ibid 65:10. Khalid ibn al Walid and the Prophet's wife Maymuna (also Khalid's aunt) were present, both of whom became Muslims after the revelation of 33:53 cited above, which argues against the notion that 33:53 imposed the general practice of female seclusion. The incident is said to have occurred in Maymuna's apartment.

6. Ibid 62:78.

7. Ibid 74:11.

8. Quoted from *Sahih Muslim* by Imam Nawawi, *Riyad al Salihin*, trans. Muhammad Zafrullah Khan.

9. Zakarya Kandhlwi, *The Teachings of Islam*, Idara Ishaat-e-Diniyat, New Delhi, pp. 161-180.

woman argued with 'Umar in the mosque during his caliphate about limiting the amount of the marriage dowry.[10] Moreover, Imam Malik states in his *Muwatta*, written towards the end of the second Islamic century, that he sees no problem with a woman sitting in mixed company as long as she is accompanied by a male relative, for example, a father or uncle.[11] Imam Malik bases his opinion on the *sunnah* of Medinah, the well established local practice going back to the time of the Prophet.[12]

All evidence suggests that female seclusion was not as a rule enforced in the time of the Prophet; this being the case, there is certainly no warrant for its imposition at American Muslim gatherings. Not only does it place an unnecessary burden on the community but it also sets up a huge impediment to many sincere seekers of faith. I'm not saying that Muslims should embrace the promiscuous intermixing and dating so popular in the West—those of us who grew up here know that it really does too often lead to extramarital sex— but common involvement in community endeavors is critical to the health and growth of the American Islamic community.

---

10. *Tafsir* of Ibn Kathir

11. Malik ibn Anas, *Al Muwatta*, trans. by Aisha A. Beuley, Kegan Paul (1989), p. 393.

12. It deserves mention that towards the end of *Surah al Nur*, a large part of which deals with mutual relations of the sexes and with ethical rules to be observed in the context of this relationship, the Qur'an adds this rejection of manmade taboos regarding dining in mixed company: "There is no blame on the blind, nor on the lame, nor on the sick, nor on yourselves, that you eat in your own houses, or your fathers' houses, or your mothers' houses, or your brothers' houses, or your sisters' houses, or your paternal uncles' houses, or your paternal aunts' houses, or your maternal uncles' houses, or your maternal aunts' houses, or [those] whereof you possess the keys, or your friends' [houses]. It is no sin in you to eat together or separately. So when you enter houses, greet your people with a salutation from God, blessed and goodly. Thus does God make clear to you the messages so that perhaps you will use your reason" (24:61).

In the Hands of a Woman

Female seclusion is alien to American history but like most other cultures the near exclusion of women from positions of power is not. That began to change toward the middle of the last century, although when I was young there were still very few women in leadership positions. Female politicians, professors, doctors, judges, bank presidents, chief executives, police officers, and the like were rarely seen. Today, there are many more women in authority positions, although they are still underrepresented, but America has become much more comfortable with the concept. This is especially true of most American converts to Islam, who tend to be liberal (at least prior to conversion), and second generation Muslims, who are taught in school since day one that there is no career in which women cannot succeed. This leads to another source of disillusionment among many Muslims born in America, for the religious leadership in most Islamic centers is opposed to women being in positions of authority. In such communities women are debarred from serving on boards of directors or executive committees. In many mosques women are not allowed to vote in elections or on community referendums.[13]

Once again, direct evidence in support of the conservative stance is scant. The debate most often focuses on a single, albeit highly regarded, *hadith* from the collection of al Bukhari:

> Abu Bakrah narrated: Allah provided me with considerable benefit during the Battle of the Camel with one word. When news reached the Prophet that the Persians had appointed

---

13. In the early centuries Muslim scholars disagreed on whether women can serve as leaders. Some scholars prohibited women from all public office. Abu Hanifah opined that women could serve as public officials, in particular as judges in cases in which her testimony is admissible. Ibn Hazm, citing the *hadith* of Abu Bakrah, held that women could occupy any public office except the head of state. Ibn Jarir al Tabari permitted women to serve as head of state. Imam Malik is reported to have adopted the same position.

Khosrau's daughter as their ruler, he said: "A nation which places its affairs in the hands of a woman shall not prosper."[14]

Abu Bakrah, the only source for this saying, was the freedman of the Prophet who joined Islam under the promise of manumission at the siege of Ta'if in 8 A.H./629 C.E. The Battle of the Camel was fought in 36 A.H./656 C.E. between forces led by Aishah, the Prophet's youngest wife, and those led by 'Ali, the Prophet's cousin and son-in-law. Abu Bakrah, who fought on Aishah's side, states that he drew comfort from this recollection during the battle, presumably when it became clear to him that Aishah would be defeated. Khosrau, the emperor of Persia, was deposed and executed in 6 A.H. after the Byzantines vanquished his armies. In the chaos of the next three years, at least ten different individuals ascended the throne of the tottering empire. His daughter was put on the throne in approximately 8 A.H., the first time in history that Persia had a female ruler. Her government collapsed just over a year later.

Just about all Muslim scholars accept this *hadith*, although there has been some recent questioning of its authenticity. The tight fit of the historical details of the narration (Abu Bakrah converts in 8 A.H., Khosrau's daughter comes to power the same year, the Prophet had predicted the collapse of Persia which caused the Companions to question him on this development), together with the fact that the narrator is not at all a prominent Companion, lends supports to the supposition that the *hadith* is grounded in a genuine incident. Nevertheless, it seems that some error must have occurred at some stage in the circulation of this report.

The assertion, "a nation which places its affairs in the hands of a woman shall not prosper," is universal in nature; that is, it is an affirmation of a fact unconditioned by considerations of time or place. It does not say, "from this point forward in history, a nation which…" or "this nation which …." It asserts that any nation, of any time or

---

14. From the collection of al Bukhari.

place, which places its affairs in a woman's hands, will not succeed. The reason why I question the accuracy of the transmission is that the Qur'an itself provides an obvious counterexample. It portrays the Queen of Sheba as a wise, judicious, and powerful ruler whose people attain great material success under her rule and are led by her to renounce idol worship and to embrace Solomon's monotheistic creed. At no point does the Qur'an suggest that the Queen abdicated her throne to Solomon or anyone else, or that the Israelites under Solomon took control of Sheba. Thus by every worldly and spiritual measure her people achieved success under her leadership.

Some might object that the Qur'an supersedes earlier Revelations, but we are not speaking here of laws. The purported universal statement of the Prophet concerning female headship of a nation and the Qur'an's portrayal of the Queen of Sheba are presented as truths. A law can abrogate another law, but a fact cannot revoke another fact. If two purported truths contradict each other then at least one of them must be incorrect. Therefore, assuming that the Qur'an is not errant in its portrayal of the Queen of Sheba and the Prophet was not mistaken about female heads of state, we must conclude that a mistake was made in the transmission of this report.

Inaccuracies in the transmission of *hadiths* were a well-known phenomenon to the ancient *hadith* scientists. They acknowledge that in the early stages of transmission narrators sometimes related what they understood the Prophet to have said rather than report verbatim. This accounts for the variations often found in *hadiths* that recount the same incident. Even the Companions are reported to have corrected each other on what they thought they heard from the Prophet. I am not suggesting that the mere possibility of inaccurate transmission is grounds for dismissing a *hadith*, but when a report conflicts with the Quran or a proven fact, then we must allow for errors in transmission, especially if we believe it traces back to a real happening. Hence in the *hadith* of Abu Bakrah some mistake must have occurred at some stage. The actual incident may have gone something like this: the Companions came to the Prophet informing him that the Persians had placed their affairs in a woman's hands, to which he responded, "They will not be successful." At some stage in the transmission a slight confusion may have produced the above account. Of course, this is just speculation and is not central to this discussion. The most important conclusion to be drawn is that the *hadith* disapproving of female leaders must be flawed and hence ought not be used as evidence against female leadership.

Sometimes It's Hard to Be a Woman

> The believers, men and women, are protectors of one another (9:71).

> The Prophet is reported to have said: "the believers are like a single body, when one of them hurts the whole body suffers."[15]

On the day I became a Muslim, I was sure that the choice I had just made placed in jeopardy all the human relationships that had real meaning for me. Joining Islam in the United States shortly after the Iranian hostage crisis and shortly before the bombing of the marine barracks in Lebanon was like committing cultural treason. When my family and friends initially reacted with shock and disapproval, I became sure that lonely days lay ahead. So I sought strength in prayer and began attending the ritual prayers at the mosque to learn how to perform them in accordance with my new faith. It was there that I discovered I had entered a worldwide fraternity bound by a mutual love and caring I had not seen elsewhere except in very close-knit families.

---

15. From the collections of al Bukhari and Muslim.

Muslims refer to each other as "brothers" and "sisters," and many of those I met do much to honor this usage. When members of the community become sick, suffer the loss of loved ones, or fall on hard times, groups of believers come to visit to offer comfort and assistance. Likewise, when there is a birth, graduation, or marriage in the Islamic community, it is celebrated by all, very often with a dinner at the mosque. These ties of brotherhood reach to all corners of the globe, for the divisions of nationhood have much less significance for Muslims than they do for others. When Muslims anywhere suffer injustice, oppression, or attack, believers the world over feel anguish and victimization, and when one of their own succeeds, regardless of his or her origins, Muslims far and wide revel in their achievement.

Even with my conversion, I did not expect to be readily accepted into the Muslim fraternity, since I was ignorant of their traditions and came from a people who have been their perennial adversaries. I assumed that I would be received with a measure of standoffishness, or even suspicion. But if some were aloof, they were very few, and were completely overshadowed by the amazing outpouring of warmth and kindness that welcomed me into the fold. The Muslims of San Francisco overwhelmed me with their hospitality and affection. During the two years before I married, I was invited out to dinner almost every night. The brothers offered me loans, gave me gifts, turned out in mass to help me move, introduced me to their female relatives in hopes that I would marry into their families, offered to take me at their expense to the Pilgrimage or to visit their families back home. I felt like I had been adopted into this gigantic clan. When I would meet many Muslims for the first time they would embrace me like I was their long lost brother.

The kind of reception I received is not at all exceptional; numerous American converts I have met report the same. They tell of how they became virtual celebrities in their mosques and the incredible compassion and largesse they were shown. They speak of the wonderful camaraderie they enjoy with their fellow believers and the great ends to which their brothers go to help them learn the religion. They talk of how the mosque has become for them a home, a place of acceptance, a safe haven from the tensions of living as a Muslim in the West.

Yet not all American Muslims have experienced the kind of communal acceptance and warmth I just described. Though the mosque is for many Muslim men a place of comfort and comradeship, a great many American Muslim women, especially the non-immigrants, see it as the opposite.[16] One of the biggest complaints I hear from native-born Muslim women is that the mosque culture in the Unites States is hopelessly misogynist. Female seclusion and the exclusion of women from positions of influence are seen as evidence of this, but more often personal experiences of demeaning treatment are cited. I have received countless accounts of rude and degrading behavior toward women by "those religious" Muslim men. I've been told of women being yelled at by unfamiliar males for not dressing properly, for praying in the main prayer hall of the mosque, for not entering or exiting the mosque through the proper "women's entrance," and numerous other supposed infractions. I have heard many reports of non-Muslim women venturing to the mosque to learn about Islam, only to be driven away from the religion by coarse rebuffs. Many women object that the mosque is considered male territory and that female participation at mosque functions is usually either not contemplated, or worse, prohibited. On most campuses, *Ramadan* can provide a month long reminder that the mosque is male territory. University Islamic centers typically provide *iftar* meals throughout the fast, and though word gets out to the male students that their attendance is much appreciated, little or no effort is made to inform or encourage the female Muslim students.

Male converts usually get a fair share of respect in their communities, but the female converts often perceive themselves as among its

16. Many African American Muslims have found immigrant mosques to be somewhat less receptive. Cf. pp. 343-347 below.

least esteemed. Although they are more numerous and, from what I have seen, hold more tenaciously to their faith and make greater effort to participate in Islamic activities than male converts, many of them lament that they end up marginalized, disregarded, or scorned in their communities. They also protest that their motives for embracing Islam are sometimes suspected. This might be true of converts in general, but many times I have been told by Muslims that American women come to Islam primarily to find or keep Muslim husbands.

Islam and culture has become so enmeshed in traditional Muslim societies that converts can feel a good deal of pressure to conform to Middle Eastern customs and mores, but this demands much more adjustment on the part of American women than men, for the women's culture of traditional Islamic societies and the women's culture of America are much farther apart than the men's cultures of the two societies. Moreover, almost all immigrant or visiting Muslim men living in the United States and Canada are Western educated and thus more familiar and comfortable with the surrounding society than their female counterparts. The greater lengths American female converts need to go to in order to assimilate into the women's culture of the mosque may contribute to feelings of discomfort or rejection.

Middle-Eastern society tries much harder to guard the chastity of females than males. A young man's flirtations are frowned on but often tolerated, but even the slightest hint of a woman's romantic interest can bring terrible shame on her and her family. In contrast, since the sixties, sexual morality in America has become increasingly lax, with men and women today feeling more or less equally unrestrained. Thanks in large part to the media, Muslims around the world are acutely conscious of this, and the stereotype of licentious, scantily clad females, shamelessly flaunting their sexuality permeates the Muslim image of American women. On several occasions Muslim men looking to get married told me that they were reluctant to marry American converts since they believed hardly any of them are virgins.

This is not to say that these young men believed that female prose-lytes tend to be immoral after conversion, but it is indicative of the pervasiveness of the negative stereotype. At any rate, regardless of past misdeeds, a convert's slate is supposed to be considered clean once they enter the faith, and Muslims on the whole seem to respect this, but I have heard of and observed a few occasions when prejudices of this kind surfaced. I recall one incident, in particular, when I lived in San Francisco. Several female converts, who had been taking Arabic lessons from the imam at a local mosque, complained to the board of directors that the spiritual leader had made numerous sexual advances toward them on different occasions. No women, including the complainants, were allowed to attend the hearing that considered the accusations, but several of the imam's supporters defended him on grounds that his accusers were by background nothing more than "whores" and "prostitutes," even though this type of slander is considered among the ten major sins of Islam. Although I have witnessed only a few instances where the stereotype of the salacious American woman was extended to converts, a fair number of them have reported to me incidents where their lack of virtue was insinuated, more often than not by foreign or immigrant Muslim women! Several second generation young ladies have told me that Muslim women from overseas also sometimes question their virtue, most often in the form of interrogatives like, "Do you have a boyfriend?" or, "Do you date?" even though in traditional Muslim cultures such questions are considered extremely insulting. Now, I have no idea how pervasive these attitudes are toward native-born Muslim women, nor how many American Muslim women perceive this prejudice, either rightly or wrongly, but where it does exist or is felt, it can indeed make them feel unwelcome in the mosque culture.

The potential for prejudice and division exists in any ethnically and culturally mixed society and is seldom one-sided; and both at times surface in the Muslim men's community, but it is common knowledge that the women's is much more socially stratified. Part of the reason for this might go back to the fact that the men's community of most mosques has had greater exposure to Western education and culture than the women's, giving the men considerably more shared experience and common ground to foster interaction and cooperation. In contrast to the men, the women in mosques where gender segregation is enforced normally have quite limited contact with the surrounding society, making them less capable of transcending the parameters of their native culture when dealing with each other. Thus the language of instruction and general communication in the men's meetings at the mosque I attend is always English, but at the women's gatherings it is almost always Arabic. If the women's programs were in English, the majority of the ladies in attendance would not understand what is said.

The above gender related deterrents to homegrown participation in the American Islamic community epitomize the larger crisis of faith and culture that confronts Muslim youth and converts. The extent to which this crisis exists in any local Muslim community naturally depends on how much its mosque culture is at odds with the surrounding culture. To be sure, there are Muslim beliefs and practices that do not accord with American customs and values, and that cannot be dispensed with without fundamentally compromising Islam. Yet even if Islam can never be brought into line with contemporary American culture, Muslims should not uphold or create cultural barriers where none need exist. This is one of the most important implications of the Qur'an's forbiddance of associating manmade constructs with God, for when this is done truth is obscured and religious thought and practice is unnecessarily constrained. Just as it would be wrong for Muslims to discard what their faith clearly requires, they also must not demand in God's name that for which there is no unequivocal warrant. We will return to this topic shortly.

Spontaneous Generation

For the last week, I have been utterly speechless and spell-bound by the graciousness I see displayed all around me by people of all colors . . . You may be shocked by these words coming from me. But on this pilgrimage, what I have seen, and experienced, has forced me to rearrange much of my thought patterns previously held, and to toss aside some of my previous conclusions . . . Perhaps if white Americans could accept the Oneness of God, then perhaps, too, they could accept in reality the Oneness of Man—and cease to measure and hinder and harm others in terms of their "differences" in color . . . Each hour in the Holy Land [Arabia] enables me to have greater spiritual insights into what is happening in America between black and white.

– Malcolm X [17]

All believers are but brothers. So make peace between your brothers, and remain conscious of God, so that you may receive mercy (49:10).

O mankind! We created you from a male and female, and made you into nations and tribes, that you may come to know one another. Truly the most noble of you in the sight of God is the one who is most benevolent (toward others). And God is knowing, aware (49:13).

In *Even Angels Ask* I wrote of the first time I spoke publicly about my conversion to Islam. It was at a Friday night meeting of the Muslim Student Association of the University California Davis. Since I had no idea I would be called to the microphone that evening, I was

---

17. Quoted by Charris Waddy, *The Muslim Mind* (London: Longman, n.d.), pp. 113-116.

totally unprepared. I don't remember a lot of what I said, but I recall briefly linking together what I thought were several key episodes in my life on the road to discovering Islam. I ended the talk by recounting a conversation I had with the imam of the mosque at University of San Francisco just before my conversion.[18] The program was brought to a close shortly after I finished my speech, and as I stood up to leave the entire audience of three hundred or so young men converged on me. They greeted me with hugs, handshakes, and kisses on my cheeks and head. Many of them had tears in their eyes. Everywhere I looked hands were outstretched towards me; many just wanted to touch me for a moment or pat me on the back. I was told again and again how great I was, how sinless I now was, how much God must have loved me, and how much better a believer I was than Muslims by birth. Even though I was in a hurry to get home, it took me over an hour to reach the door of the mosque, which was only about forty feet from the microphone. When I finally made it to the parking lot, my pockets were so stuffed with scraps of paper on which were written the names and phone numbers of members of the audience that I must of looked like the scarecrow in the *Wizard of Oz*.

Several of the students, whom I had never met before, offered to drive me home to my apartment in San Francisco. On the way they talked excitedly about my conversion. They spoke in earnest about the conversion of America to Islam. At one point one of them exclaimed, "I would love to take you back with me to Kuwait and put you on television. If only the people there could see this young, white, blonde-haired, blue-eyed American who became Muslim! To the people there, seeing you would be like watching angels come down from the clouds!"

I related most of this in *Even Angels Ask*, but I failed to mention that my talk that night followed another one, by a young, African American, undergraduate student from UC Berkley, who also spoke

---

18. I was an assistant professor at USF at that time. See, Jeff Lang, *Struggling to Surrender*, Amana Publications, 1994, pp. 13-14.

about his recent conversion to Islam. And while members of the audience also greeted him and shook his hand when the program was over, he received nowhere near the reception I did, and had no trouble quickly making his way through the crowd and out the door.

At the time, I very much appreciated my instant celebrity, but the less enthusiastic reaction to the African American convert, together with the statement about my complexion, eyes and hair color, made me wonder if the community I entered was infected with racial bigotry, despite it being so racially diverse. Twenty-two years later, I still wonder about this, for although I have observed patterns of behavior that could be construed as racist, other plausible explanations could be given and I have witnessed much that contradicts this assumption. For the sake of brevity, I will consider this issue only as it relates to African American Muslims.

Muslims definitely appear to draw more inspiration from the conversion of a white rather than black American, but I have often been told that this is because converts of European origin are still a rarity in the community and they are ethnically from Islam's perennial nemesis. A few immigrant and foreign Muslims have admitted to me that they are somewhat wary of African American Muslims, but not because of their race, but because they think they might be members of the heterodox Nation of Islam, which now represents only a small fraction of the black American Muslim community. On the telling question, "Would you mind if your son or daughter married an African American Muslim?" responses have been about evenly divided. When I substitute "Caucasian American" for "African American" the answers have been around three to one in favor. Some families state that they would be disappointed if their children were to marry outside of their ethnic background regardless of the spouse's color. In my community in Lawrence, Kansas, I have found that almost everyone knows by name the three Caucasian Americans that regularly attend the Friday prayer, but almost no one knows the three African Americans that attend it regularly.

On the positive side, since becoming a Muslim, I have never heard a single racial slur or joke uttered against anyone, Muslim or non-Muslim, of black African ancestry. I have also never seen anyone in any way discouraged from participating in a community activity based on race or nationality. It should also be noted that a fair number of African Americans have risen to positions of leadership in predominantly immigrant Islamic institutions and some have become national leaders.

From these and other considerations it is my opinion that, on the one hand, for whatever reason, white Americans ordinarily get preferential treatment over black Americans in the American Islamic community, although ironically, black Americans are much closer to the community norm in complexion. On the other hand, there are no clear signs I have seen of hatred, fear, or mistrust of African Americans from their brethren in faith. Hence, if there is prejudice toward black Americans in the Islamic community it does not seem to manifest itself in the kind of deep, racial bigotry that has existed in the United States. Yet the greater esteem conferred on white American Muslims is not innocuous, for it is terribly insensitive to the African American struggle for equality and justice and an insult to the great and courageous contribution that black American Muslims have made to the establishment and growth of Islam in America.

During the civil rights era hundreds of thousands of African Americans, already scorned because of their color, chose to become Muslims, and by so doing now became doubly loathed because of their identification with a despised foreign people and religion. Although most of these brothers and sisters originally embraced the unorthodox teachings of Elijah Muhammad, the great majority of them wholeheartedly turned to mainstream Islam upon discovering it. This almost spontaneous generation of an authentic Islamic movement in America took place with virtually no assistance from Muslims abroad and long before Caucasians began accepting Islam in any significant numbers.

I have often been told that I am making too much of the unequal treatment in the community of Caucasian and African Americans and by raising this issue I am actually fostering the racial division I am trying to prevent. I readily concede that the disparity is not grounded in deep-seated racial aversion, but the harm that is done is not to be gauged by the perceptions of those who display the bias but rather by the sentiments of those who feel affronted by it, and allowing it to go unchecked is all the more liable to produce increased resentment. With growing frequency I am hearing from black American brothers and sisters that the Muslim immigrants are bigoted, not just because of the favoritism shown whites, but also because of their unwillingness to work in partnership with African American Muslim groups.

Here again, I feel this disinclination on the part of immigrants has much more to do with culture than racial bias. African American Islamic institutions developed with little foreign influence and hence did not acquire some features found in traditional Muslim culture, features that were viewed by African American Muslims as religiously unnecessary. As to be expected, these same institutions possess a certain African American texture. Many immigrants regard the non-observance of certain cultural conventions and the unfamiliar feel of the social ambience at black American Muslim gatherings as shortcomings in the latter's adherence to Islam. This hesitancy about the legitimacy of African American Islam causes many immigrants to keep their distance from the African American Muslim community.

Between Two Worlds

It is easy for Muslim activists to develop tunnel vision regarding the progress and problems of Muslims in America. Recently, I was talking to one of the leaders of the Islamic Society of Greater Kansas City—who is also a close friend—about the success the ISGKC has had in attracting the second generation to the mosque. I was at first impressed with the results: there are now about twenty young women and ten young men who regularly attend Friday prayers and participate in community activities. I then asked what is the average attendance at Friday prayers. He estimated about 350 men and 250 women, which we both agreed would represent about 400 families. Since the average American Muslim family has three plus children, we concluded that there must be around 1200 second generation youth with at least one parent regularly attending the ISGKC mosque. In other words, of the families *connected* to the mosque only about 2.5 percent of their children frequent it. So what at first appeared to be a hopeful indicator of second generation involvement in the ISGKC, turns out upon closer examination to be a rather telling sign of youth apathy. Yet the situation appears bleaker when we figure in the Muslim families in the area who are not mosque-connected. Based on estimates of the Muslim population in the Kansas City area and Eid celebration attendance, my friend and I deduced that around twenty percent of Muslim families that live in the ISGKC locality have a member that regularly attends its Friday prayer services. From this it follows that only about one half of one percent (1 in 200) of the second generation that lives in the vicinity of this mosque frequent it.

The young Muslims who contact me are not apathetic about Islam. The greater part of them come from religious, mosque-connected families for whom Islam is the focus of their lives, but by the time they reach me the belief they knew as children and the security and comfort it once provided has begun to erode. Many admit that they are afraid of losing their faith. Most seek relief from questions and doubts that gnaw at them. I often feel unequal to the task and advise getting in touch with others whom I feel are better qualified. Sometimes I leave their messages in my inbox for several weeks, while I deliberate on how best to reply. Many times I feel these young adults need not so much answers as they do someone to listen to and assure them it is all right to have doubts. Sometimes I think a simple, "I don't know," from someone considered secure in faith is more comforting than a formulaic, traditional "answer" that really does not speak to all of the concerns behind the question.

In addition to being put off by certain practices that are viewed as essentially cultural, young people often tell of being caught in an intellectual divide between the mosque and mainstream cultures. While the mosque culture stresses the vital importance of following tradition, the surrounding society admires innovation. The mosque culture presses for strict conformance to community norms; the surrounding society lauds individualism. The mosque culture values the eternal and immutable; the outside culture teaches relativism and urges adaptation. The mosque culture preaches adherence to the judgments of ancient authorities; the mainstream expects probing, objective critique of past and present scholarship. The mosque culture substantially restricts free speech and thought; the surrounding culture goes to great lengths to safeguard them.

Americans do not expect religion to have the same parameters of discourse and thought as society at large, which is partly the rationale for the separation of church and state, but for many Muslim American youth the problem is one of degree. It is the seeming dichotomy between mosque and mainstream thinking that has many American Muslim youth uninterested and unresponsive to Islamic community discourse. It is also difficult for the mosque establishment to tolerate the approach and perspective of Muslim young people who question established beliefs and practices. When the second generation challenges the tradition, they do so in a recognizably American way, which is viewed by the mosque establishment as "un-Islamic" and outside the bounds of acceptable Muslim thought. What we then end up with is a seemingly unbridgeable generation and culture gap, where each side dismisses the other's thought and point of view as out of place. In the words of the warden in the film classic, *Cool Hand Luke*: "What we have here is a [very serious] failure to communicate."

The communication rift leaves the second generation with nowhere to turn within the Islamic community to confront their uncertainties and misgivings regarding the daunting tradition they are expected to inherit and pass on. Instead, they are left to grapple with their reservations about classical Muslim theology, or the trustworthiness of *Hadith* literature, or the relevance of traditional Islamic law and practice on their own. Or else they could look outside the community for answers. There are the multitudinous anti-Islam websites that can be quickly accessed on the Internet. Although these will normally be recognized for the propaganda instruments they are, even so they may help to deepen already existing skepticism. And then there is always the university, an obvious place to turn for a generation whose parents had so firmly stressed the indispensability of a college education. There they could learn of the most modern approaches to studying religious traditions. They can learn of historical and textual criticism and observe their application in the fields of Islamic and Middle-Eastern studies. There is nothing inherently sinister about modern research methods and they can shed substantial light on the evolution of Islamic thought, but non-Muslim lecturers currently teach most courses on Islam, and though they may strive for fairness and objectivity, they are nevertheless, by definition, at least somewhat skeptically inclined. This is not to say that in the search for truth and objectivity an outsider's point of view is not of value, but the perspective of the faithful cannot be disregarded. Fortunately, more universities are recruiting Muslim faculty to teach courses on Islam. Yet even if their university studies help some Muslim students acquire a more confident faith, chances are they would still feel uncomfortable in the mosque, probably even more so, since they will have resolved their issues by adopting a modern academic outlook.

Still, the fact is, only a small percentage of disillusioned Muslim youth will invest the time and effort to seriously research Islam. Most will simply turn away when they strongly sense that something is not right with the mosque culture. This does not mean they will necessarily renounce Islam; they may continue to believe in the existence of God and to identify themselves as Muslim, but they will have really no other connection to the religion and almost nothing in their conduct or thinking that would distinguish them as believers.

One would think that the second generation exodus from the Islamic community would be the main concern right now of the American Muslim establishment, but this is apparently not so. American Muslim leaders and scholars almost never discuss the issue in public. Devout Muslim parents who have witnessed the disaffection of their own children prefer not to talk about it due to embarrassment. Most communities have devised no strategies or programs to reach these estranged young men and women. In short, the community is in major denial.

The problem is complex and I make no claim to have a solution. In fact, I doubt there is a clear-cut remedy; that there is some series of concrete steps that if the community were to implement them the second generation would immediately start thronging to the mosque. A key difficulty is just gaining access to the disaffected among the second generation. It is not like they are hanging around the mosque, struggling to make a place for themselves in the community; nearly all of them have long given up on the mosque and have dismissed it as an irrelevant depository of their parent's cultural baggage. The older these descendents of immigrants become the less chance there is of reaching them. Once they finish school and start having families— quite often with non-Muslim spouses—and busy themselves with their careers and raising children, they generally become fully assimilated into American life, far removed from the mosque culture.

It is considerably easier to establish contact with American Muslim youth who are in college, especially since there are Muslim Student Association branches at almost every university throughout the country, whose members will likely encounter American students of Muslim descent in classes and around campus. The problem here, however, is that the membership of the MSAs are for the most part visiting foreign students and the cultural divergence that exists between the surrounding society and immigrant mosques tends to be even greater with respect to MSA run mosques. When I ask second generation students why they don't join the MSA or attend the campus mosque, they tell me the students there are "way too extreme." Even second generation students who are devout and involved in other organizations that promote Muslim causes around the world shun the mosque as too "conservative" or "traditional." At a number of universities, innovative Muslim students have addressed this situation by forming organizations and discussion groups specifically for descendents of immigrants and converts and that are not affiliated with the MSA or the local mosque. The idea behind these American Muslim discussion groups is to provide these students with a non-intimidating environment where they can learn more about Islam and freely explore any questions they may have. The underlying philosophy is that if these young people will not come to the mosque, then at least provide a venue where they can keep in touch with their religion and some fellow believers. Hopefully, they will gain the confidence and desire to contribute their effort and perspective to the development of the American Muslim community.

Yet the reality is that if the Muslim community waits until the second generation finishes high school before attempting to get them involved in the mosque, then they certainly will see very little success. If the descendents of Muslims in America are to develop feelings of belonging and attachment to the mosque, then they need to be regular participants in community activities throughout their child and young adult years, for unlike Muslim children from overseas, there is no chance of them absorbing Islam from the surrounding culture. Yet if their time in the mosque is mostly unpleasant, then it can end up being counterproductive, providing these young people with even more reason to abandon the community at first opportunity. It is therefore crucial that the mosque be a family friendly environment, where Muslim parents and children can take part in community functions together, as families. At present this is not the atmosphere at most *masjids* in America.

I was driving my daughters and our neighbor's little girl to school some years ago, when their friend began talking about her experience at church the previous Sunday. She spoke with great joy of how she, her mommy and daddy sat together in church, listened to the sermon, sang hymns and prayed together. She talked about how forward she looked to going to church each week with her family. At one point she innocently asked my daughters where they went to church. My oldest daughter, Jameelah, who was seven or eight at the time, glumly responded, "My daddy goes to the mosque." Her answer was followed by a period of silence. Their friend then asked, "Do your mom and dad have different religions?"

I had taken my daughters to the mosque almost every night up till then and although they were the only females in attendance, I had assumed that they had developed the feeling that the mosque was as much their place of worship as it was mine. But somehow, all by themselves, they had come to view the mosque as mainly for men. When I later asked them how they got that idea, they said they could just tell that's the way it is. When I pressed them for an explanation, they mentioned that Muslim ladies almost never go to the mosque and that when they do go they don't pray in the main prayer area.

The older my daughters became, the less they wanted to go with me to the mosque. They began to feel that many of the men did not want them there and they were uncomfortable praying by themselves in the "ladies' area" upstairs. By the time they entered junior high, they stopped accompanying me to the prayers. Today they dismiss the local mosque culture as "ridiculous," "primitive," and "weird." I recently asked my two oldest daughters if they intend to become more involved in the mosque when they get older or when they have children someday; they said not unless its customs and atmosphere were to change dramatically and it became a family environment. Many American Muslim parents inform me that their children, boys and girls, have similar attitudes. Many report that their daughters and sons say they "hate the mosque" and that they have no interest whatsoever in attending it.

This is an extremely serious matter as far as the future of Islam in America is concerned. If the mosque remains a principally male as opposed to family friendly institution, then the community should anticipate continued mass second and later generation departure from the community. Given the gravity of the situation, mosque-connected Muslims need to carefully examine whether Islam demands that it stay this way. If it really does, then the status quo in the mosque will have to be maintained regardless of the number of American Muslims who steer clear of if it. If, however, there is room within the religion to make the mosque more family friendly and this is avoided, then the mosque establishment may have to assume primary responsibility for misleading millions of potential Muslims away from the religion.[19]

America's Muslims would also be greatly served if the mosque were to become the intellectual hub of the community—as it was in early Islamic history—where believers, young people in particular, are encouraged to explore, discuss and debate religious questions without fear of censure or reprisal. The mosque should support the formation of youth discussion groups and provide ample opportunity for young people to air their concerns at community forums. It is also important to have second generation representation on the board of directors. These steps may help to improve understanding and communication between the immigrant and second generations. It should also accustom the latter to community involvement. Of course, all of this will require much greater respect for freedom of expression and difference of opinion than right now exists in most communities.

There is also a growing need within the American Muslim community for homegrown, mosque-connected, academically trained

---

19. Interestingly, back in the late 1980's and early 1990's, I visited the Prophet's mosque in Medina and the great Mosque in Mecca numerous times, and families there sat together in mixed company until the time of prayer when the men and women each went to separate sections to pray. This has been the established custom in these two most sacred places of worship in Islam going back to ancient times.

scholars of Islam. At the present time, most of the community's intellectual leaders, although well-educated, have had no higher education in Islamic or Middle Eastern studies, or in related fields. In addition to contributing a much-needed Muslim perspective in areas of research long dominated by non-Muslims, these academics would be well positioned to assist the second generation with their doubts and problems. Most of the second generation is university educated and have been exposed to research in the social and religious sciences. They have become accustomed to their modes of thought and expression and methodologies. Unless Muslim scholars can communicate to the second generation in a way that speaks to their educational background, they will have a difficult time reaching the disaffected. The bulk of questions I have received from Muslim American youth have to do with the separation of religion and culture, in which they seek to distinguish between Muslim practices and ideas that are essential to Islam and those that are time or place bound adaptations or interpretations. American Muslim scholars, trained in history, anthropology, and religious studies, who apply their expertise to the study of the classical Islamic sciences, can be of particular help here. Similarly, scholars of law, economics, political science and psychology could help Muslim youth discover effective religious responses to contemporary issues and to develop a vision of future directions to pursue.

In America today, most Muslim specialists in Islamic studies keep away from their local mosques and vice versa. Their mutual rejection is unfortunate and just one more sign of the malaise that pervades the community. Once again, hopes may have to be pinned on the next generation to create a community of greater openness and tolerance that will enlist the diverse talents and perspectives of the believers. This leaves the community, however, in an obvious catch-22: in order to bring the second generation into the community definite changes need to take place, but right now it seems that these changes have no chance of occurring until the second generation takes over the community.

Neither Here Nor There

> The Prophet said: You should help your brother whether he is wronged or doing wrong. If he is wronged, defend him, and if he is doing wrong, prevent him.[20]

I have met many converts who are perfectly at home in the mosque culture, who fully embrace its attitudes, customs, and social behaviors, and zealously defend them as the embodiment of "true Islam," but they are not in the majority. At least half of the American converts I have known ultimately apostatized and the greater part of those that haven't keep away from the community today. Of the four categories of native Muslims discussed in this chapter, I left converts in general for last because those who feel distant from the mosque have voiced most of the concerns listed above and thus there is no need to rehearse them at length here. Suffice to say, the apparent patriarchalism of Muslim culture, the unequal status in the community of Caucasian and African American converts, the intellectual and social divide between the mosque and surrounding society are problematic for very many Americans who embrace Islam. So we will complete this section by listing a few other often mentioned but perhaps less serious frustrations. It should be kept in mind that there is a large amount of Muslim tradition that converts generally respect and appreciate, but the focus in this section is on features of the mosque culture that may be discouraging them from community participation.

Numerous converts have expressed dismay over the ethnic and national factionalism they feel is enervating the Islamic community. As already pointed out, the preferential treatment accorded white Americans over black Americans who enter the faith, although unacceptable and divisive, stems more from the phenomena of European colonialism, the current dominance of Western civilization, and erroneous suppositions about the Nation of Islam, than in race-based hatred, but there are many other currents of ethnic and national

---

20. From the collections of al Bukhari and Muslim.

prejudice that divide Muslims in America. Converts cite the inter-ethnic and cross national frictions that at times surface in their communities, the racial slurs they overhear, and the ethnic mosques that exist in larger cities and the lack of cooperation—and frequently contentions—between them as evidence that the much touted "brotherhood" of believers is only skin deep. Yet in a population so culturally diverse it would be surprising if there were no such tensions, but since the religion is so squarely founded on the concept of broth-erhood, any noticeable factionalism can seem unduly high. While this may be disillusioning to some converts who idealistically expect most Muslims to live up to Islam's call to fraternal love, there are hopeful signs for the future. The longer immigrants reside here, the more they seem to respect and interrelate with believers of other backgrounds, and ethnic prejudice among the second generation, brought up in a society that preaches tolerance and the acceptance of diversity, should be greatly diminished.

Another problem that may resolve itself, especially if indigene par-ticipation in the community grows, is the identity crisis so many con-verts report going through. Proselytes naturally rely on experienced believers to teach them the new faith, which at present means they almost always receive it from Muslim immigrants. The strong ten-dency on the part of the latter to equate religion with its cultural forms in the motherland can cause converts to adopt behaviors and views that are not religiously necessary and alien to their normal temperament. In their desire to win acceptance in the mosque culture, many converts try to recreate themselves according to community norms, and to such an extent that they suppress their conscience and reason. Many converts describe going through a kind of cultural and mental schizophrenia, where they take on the mannerisms and attitudes (political, social, etc.) of peoples of the Middle East when among Muslims and return to their American personality in other situations.[21] Fortunately, almost all converts survive this stage with no

21. For more on this see the author's, *Even Angels Ask*, Amana publications, 1997, pp. 191-212.

lasting harm and many newcomers to other faiths go through personality crises of one form of another—thus the aphorism: "there is no faith like that of the newly converted." These days the percentage of newcomers to Islam who experience this crisis seems to be on the decline, perhaps thanks to the counsel of other converts who have already been through it.

Lack of introspection and awareness of its own double standards is another complaint converts frequently raise against the Islamic community. As former outsiders they are conceivably more sensitive to this. They mention that Muslims rightfully expect all the rights and privileges that come with full citizenship in the United States, but many of the community's leaders equivocate on whether they would defend the full citizenship of non-believers if Muslims were politically dominant? A recurring critique is that the community is quick to condemn injustices committed by non-Muslims but are reluctant to acknowledge or denounce blatant wrongs committed by coreligionists. Not too long ago the Grand Mufti of Saudi Arabia declared, "The Jews are the scum of the earth, the rats of humanity, and the descendents of apes and swine." This racist generalization by a high profile Muslim religious authority was widely reported in America, but no condemnation was heard from the country's Islamic community. One convert wrote to me, "Where are the Adam Shapiro's,[22] Stanley Cohen's,[23] and Rachel Corrie's[24] in our community? Where are the Muslims who defend the rights of non-Muslims and decry the wrongs of our people?" According to the Qur'an, they should not be difficult to find:

---

22. A Jewish American peace activist who works with Palestinians in struggling against the occupation. As a result, death threats were made against his family.

23. A Jewish American attorney who sued the Israeli government on behalf of Palestinian Americans for war crimes

24. A volunteer with the Palestinian-led International Solidarity Movement. She was killed attempting to prevent the Israeli military from destroying Palestinian civilian homes.

O you who believe, be upholders of justice, bearers of witness before God, even though it be against yourselves or your parents or close relatives, or whether it concerns the rich or poor. And God has better right over them both. Therefore do not follow your passions, lest you swerve (4:135).

O you who believe, be upright before God, bearers of witness with justice, and let not your enmity for a people incite you not to act equitably. Be just; that is nearer to God-consciousness (5:8).

Some converts report that feelings of aloneness set in after conversion. During the question and answer period following a recent lecture, a woman in the audience stated that since her conversion to Islam she has felt like a person without a community. She explained that on the one hand she felt disconnected from the society she grew up in, and on the other, she felt isolated within the Muslim community. She added that when she questions various practices at her mosque she feels even less accepted there. She then asked me how long it normally takes for a convert to feel at home in the community and would it be better for her to stop questioning things that do not seem right to her.

Several of the converts that wrote to me describe feeling estranged from both the surrounding culture and the mosque culture. They explain that relations with family, friends, and co-workers have not been quite the same and that Islam has brought about lifestyle and attitude changes that take them out of the mainstream. While most converts understand and accept that this is a price that may have to be paid, they are ordinarily reluctant to surrender to rules and beliefs only vaguely linked to Islam. Adjusting to any new culture has its difficulties, but with respect to the mosque this problem might be eased if, as repeatedly emphasized, the community would effort to divest itself of customs that are unessential to the religion. As long as the mosque culture remains firmly devoted to its more questionable traditions and as long as converts doubt the essentiality of them, the latter will probably continue to feel out of place in the mosque culture.

It would surely be nice to feel at one with your fellow believers, and for those who feel dislocated from all that is familiar to have a haven of support in their religious community, but faith must and will be put to the test, and the sense of aloneness many converts experience can help them to develop singular reliance on God. It also provides an opportunity to practice a key aspect of genuine brotherhood: namely, sticking with your brothers and sisters even when the relationship is not easy. Nevertheless, converts should not stop challenging what they suspect are moot practices and dogmas. The critical probing that caused them to question their prior beliefs and helped lead them to Islam should not be tossed aside once they enter the community; otherwise, they could easily end up trading one set of falsehoods for another. Moreover, converts are ideally positioned to assist in the task of liberating the religion from centuries of burdensome and enervating accretions—a project widely seen by Muslim thinkers as of vital importance—for they combine in themselves an outsiders perspective with an insiders love of faith. However, they cannot do this if they shrink from intellectual confrontation. There are always some in every mosque who would prefer them to simply acquiesce to convention and serve as yes men and women for Muslim tradition, and the pressure to do this can be enormous, but converts must remember that their self-surrender is to God, not the community.

Divided We Fall

The Prophet said: "A person is not a believer until he loves for his brother [and sister] what he loves for himself."[25]

It is not permissible for a believer to avoid his brother for more than three days, so that when they meet they turn away from each other. The better of them is the first to greet the other.[26]

And hold fast, all together, to the rope of Allah and do not be divided among yourselves. Remember Allah's favor to you when you were enemies, then he united your hearts so that by his favor you became brothers. And you were on the brink of an abyss of fire and then He saved you from it. Thus Allah makes clear to you His revelations, so that you might be guided. And there should arise from among you a party who invite to righteousness, enjoin good and forbid evil; these are they who are successful. And be not like those who became divided and disputed after clear arguments had come to them. And for them is grievous chastisement. (3:103-106)

The need for greater Muslim unity is a recurring theme at Islamic conferences in the United States, where what is usually meant is that immigrant Muslims need to rise above national and ethnic partisanship and come together in brotherhood and mutual cooperation. I do not mean to minimize the issue of ethnocentrism in the community but it seems nowhere near as virulent as the ethnic prejudice I witnessed all around me growing up in Bridgeport, Connecticut. More importantly, whatever distancing there is between various immigrant groups pales in comparison to the problem of the estrangement of American-born Muslims from the mosque culture.

---

25. From the collections of Al Bukhari and Muslim.
26. From the collections of Al Bukhari, Muslim and Abu Dawud.

Any program for Muslim unity that does not address non-immigrant alienation is irrelevant to the future of Muslims in the United States. Before offering a few suggestions on what might be done to foster an effective and meaningful unity, it might be useful to review some of the main concerns of native-born Muslims who keep apart from the mosque.

The biggest issue for homegrown Muslims, irrespective of sex, is the treatment of women in the mosque culture, which many view as terribly demeaning. The practice of female seclusion is especially troublesome. Other common complaints are that women are discouraged from attending congregational prayers, have no independent voice in the community, are denied leadership positions, and are barred from positions on boards of directors and executive committees. Female converts tell of being devalued, marginalized and humiliated in their faith communities. Many protest that they are treated like less than second-class citizens in the mosque even though they are in their own country.

The perceived disparity between mosque and mainstream thought is another core issue for a large segment of the second generation. The Muslim community is viewed by many as stressing extreme traditionalism, conformism, and authoritarianism, and as severely restricting speech and thought. The larger society is seen as valuing rationalism, individualism, innovation, critical research, and as zealously defending free speech. Most of the main concerns of the second generation are not open for discussion in the mosque. Many of these young people are skeptical of the efficacy of classical *hadith* criticism. Many feel that traditional Muslim theology, at least as it is presented in the mosque, fails to cogently address the theological paradoxes that are so central to western thought and which they frequently encounter in conversations with non-Muslims. Many lack confidence in and fail to see the relevance of much of traditional Islamic law. A revival of the classical Islamic disciplines, incorporating modern research methods, is called for on grounds that no science can unquestioningly rely on the findings of earlier generations. Mosque establishments by and large oppose any suggestions along these lines. Compounding this rather serious communication failure is the mosque culture's apparent denial that the large-scale exodus of the second generation from the community is a matter of concern.

Sadly, the segment of the American Muslim community that has been most active in reaching out to estranged Muslim youth and converts and appears to be making some progress in this direction has been largely disregarded by the rest of the community. Although the reasons for the immigrant avoidance of their black American brothers and sisters—and their favoritism of white American Muslims—may have more to do with cultural factors than true racism, if left unchecked it could ultimately produce genuine racial tensions in the community. Because the predominantly black American mosques are indigenous institutions, one finds in most of them a strong focus on accepting only those traditional Muslim beliefs and practices that can be proved mandated by the religion. Thus here again, the African American community has led the way in the quest to separate religion from culture, and it is therefore not surprising that many non-black converts and many children of Muslim immigrants are more comfortable in the African American *masjids*.

The concerns just listed do not belong exclusively to any one subgroup of native Muslims, although some experience them more acutely than others, and very many immigrants share them as well, especially those that have been living in America for some time. However, there are two troublesome experiences that only converts have so far communicated to me. The first is what one convert in a phone call characterized as the "poster boy (or girl) syndrome," where out of a desire to secure acceptance in the Muslim community proselytes feel it necessary to recreate themselves according to community expectations, adopting culturally founded attitudes and behaviors that are alien to their upbringing and former personality and only tenuously linked to Islam. The realization of this "loss of self"[27] is often the first stage toward eventual apostasy. Another difficulty many converts experience is the feeling of not belonging to any community, where they feel dislocated from the societal mainstream and yet not fully accepted into the Muslim community, often because they are unable to accept that some deeply ingrained Muslim traditions are in reality "Islamic." Clearly, these two conditions are opposite sides of the same coin. One is caused by blindly surrendering to questionable Muslim beliefs and customs, while the other results from refusing to do so. The first problem might be avoided and the second somewhat moderated if the convert continually keeps in mind that Islam requires self-surrender to God alone, even when this puts him or her at odds with the local Muslim establishment.

In *Even Angels Ask* I suggested that, barring divine intervention, the immediate future of the American Muslim community appears bleak. I felt that in order to prevent a mass exodus from the community of the second and later generations and in order to avoid sectarian schism in what would be left of the community, several fundamental changes needed to occur in the mosque culture. I did not expect then, nor do I now, that the recommended transformations would take place in time to appreciably forestall these happenings. Nevertheless, it would be irresponsible of me not to try to restate the case for them.

We begin with what I believe is a rather self-evident proposition:

Proposition 1: The greater the number of practices and beliefs that we claim are essential to Islam, the fewer the number of people who will consider Islam as a religious option.

---

27. On this topic, I recommend: J. Lynn Jones, *Believing as Ourselves*, Amana Publications, Beltsville, 2002.

For example, all Muslims would agree that belief in only one God is fundamental to Islam and not every American will be able to accept this. So we can represent the subset of Americans who will by the diagram below.

Subset 1: Those who will accept the oneness of God.

All Muslims will also agree that belief in Muhammad's prophet-hood is essential to Islam. Now the segment of Americans who will accept this together with the oneness of God is obviously a subset of subset 1 above. We represent this by a smaller oval inside the oval representing subset 1.

Subset 2: Those who will accept the oneness of God and Muhammad's prophethood.

An essential Muslim practice is the five daily prayers. When we add this to our list of essential beliefs and practices, the collection of individuals who will accept each of these is a subset of subset 2 above. So we can depict this population by an oval (subset 3) sitting inside the oval representing subset 2.

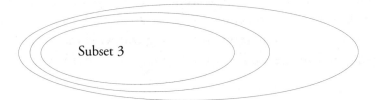

Subset 3

If we then add the fast of *Ramadan* (subset 4), then the payment of *Zakat* (subset 5), then the performance of the pilgrimage (subset 6), then the prohibitions of alcohol (subset 7), gambling (subset 8), pork (subset 9), and fornication (subset 10), the population of those who will accept all of these beliefs and practices continually shrinks.

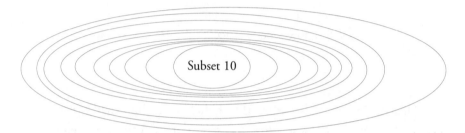

For nearly all Muslims this list of what is essential to Islam is not nearly complete and as more items are added to it the subset of Americans—including converts, potential converts, and second generation—who will accept all of its terms will become increasingly small. This is unavoidable and Muslims should not omit anything from the list that is truly essential to Islam, regardless of how many might become dissuaded from considering it as a faith option. If some belief or behavior is definitely demanded by the religion, then it should not be compromised. Yet, on the other hand, Muslims must also be very careful not to insist on the essentiality of something that may not be so, for when this is done it places unnecessary obstructions between individuals and Islam with the truth becoming needlessly obscured for them. As much as Muslims should not want to neglect a religious fundamental, they should be equally on guard not to drive people from the religion with claims that something not required is "Islam" or "Islamic." This is of critical importance in the Qur'an, for when we claim that something is demanded by the religion without clear warrant, we are in reality associating with God that which is not of God, and in the words of the Scripture we "invent a lie against God."

Say: Have you considered what provision God has sent down for you, and how you made some of it *haram* (unlawful) and *halal* (lawful)? Say: Has God indeed permitted you, or do you invent a lie concerning God? (10:59)

And say not, for any false thing your tongues put forth: "This is *halal* (lawful) and this is *haram* (unlawful)," so that you invent a lie against God. (16:116)

In *surah at-Tawbah* the Jews and Christians are reproached for taking "their rabbis and monks for their lords beside God" (9:31) and a well-known *hadith* in al Tirmidhi's compilation explains that they did this by blindly following their clergy in what they declared to be lawful and unlawful[28]. *Surah Yunus* provides this dire warning to those who do the same:

Say: Do you see what God has sent down to you for sustenance (*rizq*), and then you make some of it *haram* and *halal*? Say: Has God commanded you or do you invent a lie against God? And what think those who invent a lie against God of the Day of Resurrection? Behold, God is bountiful to men but most of them are ungrateful. (10:59-60)

In his commentary on the Qur'an, Muhammad Asad remarks:

In accordance with the doctrine that everything which has not been expressly forbidden by the Qur'an or the explicit teachings of the Prophet is eo ipso lawful, this verse takes

---

28. The *hadith* in al Tirmidhi (Tr. 44:9) states that when this verse was revealed, Adi ibn Hatim, a convert from Christianity, asked the Prophet as to the significance of this verse, for, he said, "We did not worship our doctors of law and monks." The Prophet replied, "Was it not that the people considered lawful what their priests declared to be lawful, though it was forbidden by God?" When Hatim replied in the affirmative, the Prophet said that that was what the verse meant.

a clear-cut stand against all arbitrary prohibitions invented by man or artificially "deduced" from the Qur'an or Prophet's *Sunnah*.[29]

As the Qur'an repeatedly shows, the sacralization of tradition is the most common means by which man-made policies, which may or may not have been appropriate in a particular historical and cultural context, become associated with religion and universalized; typically, when confronted with the fact that revelation does not endorse the practice, the blameworthy stubbornly give preference to tradition.

> O mankind, eat of that which is lawful and wholesome in the earth, and follow not the footsteps of Satan. Truly, he is to you an avowed enemy. He enjoins upon you only the evil and the foul, and that you should say of God that of which you have no knowledge. When it is said to them, 'Follow what God revealed', they say, 'We follow that wherein we found our fathers.' What! Even though their fathers were devoid of wisdom and guidance (2:168-170).

When I converted to Islam over twenty years ago, it seemed that almost every Muslim I met was only too eager to lecture me on some idiosyncrasy they considered integral to the faith. I was skeptical of a good deal of what I was told, but at the time I had no way of knowing for sure of its veracity. On various occasions I was informed that I had to wear Middle Eastern clothing, that I must not listen to music, that I must make all supplications in Arabic, that I must not whistle, that I must eat with my hands and not use utensils, that I should not have a television, that I should not wear a tie, that I must work to overthrow the American government when the opportunity arises, that a woman cannot leave her house without her husband's

---

29. Muhammad Asad, *The Message of the Qur'an*, Dar Al Andalus, Gibraltar (1980).

permission, that women cannot vote, that women cannot work outside their homes, that a woman cannot obtain a driver's license, that democracy is forbidden, that I must change my name to an Arabic one, that targeting civilians is permissible in *jihad*, that it is worse for a women to commit adultery than a man, and countless other do's and don'ts supported by unconvincing and slanted proofs. If my faith back then had not been derived from the Qur'an and I had taken some of these claims as true expressions of Islam, I am almost certain I would have left the religion. Although it is not too difficult for well informed Muslims to argue the weakness of many of these claims, many newcomers or potential newcomers to the faith are not going to invest the time, effort and study required to investigate all that is preached to them in the name of Islam; most will simply obtain a negative—or perhaps a more negative—impression of the Muslim religion and dismiss it as patently ludicrous. It really doesn't take very much, especially given the deep-seated prejudice toward Islam that prevails in America, to reawaken or confirm someone's doubts about Islam.

Fortunately, not many Muslims in America would promote these positions today, for the greatest part of them are citizens and permanent residents, who are now long removed from the cultures that spawned these ideas and consequently less able to relate to the impulses behind them. Yet even though there has been a natural filtering out of gratuitous claims made on behalf of the religion, most Islamic institutions in America still hold fast to some exceedingly questionable practices that are driving away native Muslims and non-Muslim seekers of faith in herds. Even if by imposing them they were repelling only a handful of potential believers, it would still be a dreadful wrong from the standpoint of the Qur'an, but the fact is it may be causing massive defection from the community.

Take again, for example, the practice of female seclusion, still enforced at many Muslim gatherings throughout the country. There is no general proclamation in either the Quran or authenticated *hadiths* ordering the community to implement it, while at the same time there is ample evidence that shows it was not uniformly practiced at any stage of the Prophet's mission or during the time of his Companions.[30] Although various rationalizations for gender segregation are often given, they cannot alter the fact that there is no explicit evidence that the Prophet imposed it on his followers, and there is much concrete evidence to the contrary. Absent such proof, the custom of gender separation cannot be said to be essential to Islam. Yet if this is the correct, then the single greatest barrier to homegrown participation in the community and one of the primary deterrents to non-Muslims seekers of faith is being imposed unnecessarily. Meanwhile, hundreds of thousands are being lost to the community and very many of these to the religion.

The imposition of unnecessary traditions in America's mosque culture is discouraging a huge number of native Muslims from community involvement and leading many of them to distrust their religion, but it also causes division among the mosque-connected, for the more believers conflict on what is essential to the religion, the more factionalized they will become. In some cities, nearby mosques refuse to have anything to do with each other because of disagreements over peripheral issues. Legitimate differences of opinion or interpretation can bring about mutual anathematisation. I know American Muslims who completely discount ISNA because of the method they use for establishing the beginning of *Ramadan*. When I lived in California I heard of a *masjid* in the Midwest that was infamously dubbed "the *kafir* (disbeliever) mosque." What were the violations that earned them the excoriation? During the congregational prayer, women stood on the left side and men on the right side of the main prayer hall, separated by a three foot divider running down the center of the room; some of the female teachers in the Sunday Islamic school did not wear head coverings; families sat in mixed company at community get-togethers; women occupied posi-

---

30. Cf. this chapter pp. 331-334.

tions on the center's board and were among the imam's office staff. Throughout Islamic history, disagreements over moot theological or legal perspectives sometimes led to schism and civil war, most often because one side or both idealized their stance. Sectarian division may be in the offing for American Muslims for similar reasons.

The need to critically re-evaluate what is essential to Islam cannot be overstated. The severity of the Qur'an's warnings in this regard, the existence of numerous Prophetic reports prohibiting it,[31] the massive disaffiliation of American born Muslims from the community due to the confusion of religion and culture, and the inherent divisiveness in ascribing divine authority to judgments and interpretations for which there is at most vague and indirect support in the textual sources, should make this a top priority of American Muslims who seek an effective and broad based unity. Needless to say, this reassessment of community traditions calls for homegrown academic scholars trained in this type of research. It also needs an intellectual environment that promotes dialogue and free speech and that doesn't shy away from controversy, which in and of itself could foster unity, as persons are more inclined to remain part of an association in which their perspective can be heard, just as people tend to avoid an organization that proscribes their point of view. Then again, heterogeneity and consensus do not ordinarily correlate. Greater inclusiveness implies greater diversity of views, which could produce more disagreements, which could increase the likelihood of fragmentation. This is why it is absolutely vital that the mosques in America promote democracy. In a democratic system participants agree to majority decision-making in return for being able to freely and equally participate in the decision making process. That is, participants accept majority rule because they are guaranteed full rights to campaign for their perspective.

---

31. I have in mind here the *hadiths* that denounce *bidah* (innovation) in Islam. For example, *Riyadh as-Salihin* of Imam Nawawi, translation by Muhammad Zafrulla Khan, Curzon Press, 1975, *Hadith* 158, 170, 171.

However, it is not necessary that every conflict of views be put to a vote, for the tyranny of the majority can also be divisive. Members who consistently find themselves in the minority and have to continually yield to policies they disagree with can become frustrated, causing them to disengage. For this reason the first impulse of the community in matters where there are tenable differences of opinion should be toward compromise, tolerance, understanding, and accommodation. Returning again to the issue of female seclusion, if some in the mosque prefer not to sit with members of the opposite sex while others wish to sit with their families at community gatherings, then if at all possible each option should be provided: an area for men only, one for women only, and one where families can gather together.

It is also important for those who are disenchanted with the mosque to keep up attendance and to stand their ground, for we can't expect alternative points of view to become accepted if hardly anyone promotes them. Our community in Lawrence recently held a referendum on its new constitution, discussing and then voting on each article. I met several individuals in the days that followed who did not attend the vote but complained of certain provisions in the constitution, explaining to me that the mentality reflected in them is precisely the reason why they shun the mosque. I informed them that the troubling articles they mentioned were hotly contested and were decided in two cases by one vote and in the remaining cases by less than four. From what I have seen, minority perspectives generally come to dominate a mosque because of apathy on the part of others. As the American experience has repeatedly demonstrated, there is community strength in diversity; nevertheless, many have had to fight hard for inclusion in the system.

Finally, we should not forget that brotherhood is the foundation of Islam's social system. When the Qur'an says to "hold fast to the rope of Allah and do not separate" (3:103), the image suggests that this takes strong determination and effort. Brotherhood has less to do with mutual affection than with refusing to repudiate those with whom we differ. Thus the famous *hadith* states, "It is not permissible for a believer to avoid his brother (or sister) for more than three days, so that when they meet they turn away from each other."[32] The Muslim tendency to disassociate from fellow believers over differences of opinion on moot issues or because of perceived lapses in observance runs counter to this principle, and only serves to further enervate a community that is already under considerable strain. Such divergence is inevitable in a population so diverse as it struggles to adapt to unfamiliar surroundings but it must not be allowed to hinder mutual cooperation and support on the multitude of issues critical to all Muslims in America.

Faith, Reason, and the Future

The tone of this chapter and much of this book has not been upbeat, but the loss of large numbers of American-born Muslims to the community is hardly cause for celebration. I do not speak here of an impending crisis but of one already in progress. A large number of America's Muslims are reaching retirement and their children, now middle-aged, are scarcely to be found in the nation's mosques and other Islamic venues. Much the same can be said of the converts of the last half-century, who are greatly underrepresented at community events. The scant attendance of the younger members of these two groups indicates that the efforts made so far to address the problem have been either ineffective or too small in scope. In predominantly Muslim societies, avoidance of religious institutions rarely leads to abandoning Islam altogether, since the faith can be absorbed from the surrounding culture, but in America it often does, and even if some of those cut off from the community remain nominal Muslims, the chances that their children will identify with the religion are slim. Of course, I'm aware that God could raise up a Muslim people when and wherever He chooses without the assistance of other believers, as the

---

32. From the collections of al Bukhari, Muslim and Abu Dawud.

African American Muslim experience has strikingly demonstrated, but this does not relieve America's believers of the obligation to do all they can to reach disengaged native Muslims with the message God has entrusted them, for He has charged us to "save yourselves and your families from a fire whose fuel is men and stones." (66:6)[33]

Tradition and religion are interfused in Muslim lands, where tradition is so entrenched, all-inclusive, sanctified, and intimidating, that no one but the most reckless would openly discount it, as it would bring the utmost disgrace upon oneself and one's family. Even those Muslims who seriously question their faith will admit it only to a few trusted associates and feign conviction otherwise. But America is a non-traditional society; it is a great pot where foreign traditions are melted away into a heady brew called "freedom." In pursuit of individual liberty traditions can be discarded here with the backing of society, and so much more so as regards Islam, the very mention of which evokes trepidation and perplexity among the citizenry. Freedom in America implies, in particular, intellectual freedom, the inalienable right to doubt, and Islam is openly scrutinized and called into question every day now in the United States in myriad ways. If only by osmosis, Muslims who grow up here will acquire a questioning attitude toward their religion. To be sure, tradition will not keep many non-immigrant Muslims in the fold. Love of family might be a sufficiently strong tie for some, but in America's youth culture most are willing to put that to the test in the struggle for autonomy.

Faith is of the heart and mind, but the mind is the door to dislodging it. If homegrown Muslims are drifting from the religion then this is ultimately an intellectual problem, a clash between faith and reason. If it were another religion or another country I might think that strong appeals to tradition, spirituality, or sentiment might effectively offset doubt. This seems to be the method of the fairly

---

33. Stones represent the idols worshipped by the polytheists of Arabia at that time and in a larger sense could stand for all false objects of worship.

successful Christian Evangelical movement and some young Muslims in America are turning toward Sufism in quest of mystical corroboration. Yet for too many of the Muslims born in America there are simply too many reasons—worldly, rational, ethical and spiritual—to question the religion, too many holes in the dike, too many things "Islamic" that don't ring true, to even remotely consider such an approach, and even if they did the chances are it would work for only a few. The unfortunate reality is that most of the disillusioned second generation and converts have long given up on the mosque culture as the place to turn for answers to their problems, religious or otherwise; if anything, they feel that the mosque is a source of them. For many, it is not non-Muslim misinformation that poisons their attitude towards the mosque; but rather, they cannot relate to the mosque culture, which is seen as alien, anachronistic and unreasonable. If the American mosque culture hopes to reach these estranged descendants and converts, or to at least impede the flight of even more of their younger counterparts, then a critical and thorough re-examination of traditional Muslim thought and practice is vital, not only to distinguish the truly essential in the religion, but also to better understand and convey the judgments, interpretations, and insights of past scholars that may not be essential but nevertheless legitimate and perhaps appropriate today. The goal should not be to filter out the strictly essential and then completely discard all the rest, but to build on past efforts. The better grasp Muslims have of the thought processes, influences and motivations of former scholars, the better they will be able to gauge how much room there is for interpretation and adaptation.

Yet, realistically speaking, who is going to perform this in-depth critique of traditional Muslim thought, and is there any chance that the religious establishment would take it into consideration? I will begin with the second concern, which requires a digression into mainstream Muslim views on the use of reason in Islam.

Many of the ancient Muslim philosophers believed that true faith could be attained through reason alone. Even though reason played a key role in my conversion, I do not subscribe to this view. God's immense orchestration of our spiritual evolutions is too complex to dissect into component elements, so that we can ever confidently distinguish which of intuition, divine inspiration, reason, emotion, or conscience were in play at any given moment. Yet I have no doubt that reason was integral to my own progress toward Islam. Although I did not know where I was heading, I believe I continually relied on it like a sensor to steer me away from blind alleys and pitfalls. It was integral to my choice to leave the religion of my childhood and to become an atheist. Provoked by the terror and brutality I saw around me, I came to the same questions that led so many others to disbelieve: Why would a perfect God create such an imperfect world? Why would He create so criminal and violent a creature as man? Why did He not just make us angels in Heaven? Why does He subject us to temptation? Why did He create us to suffer?

Reason was also at the forefront of the next dozen years of inquiry into other faiths. And it was in large part intellectual curiosity that urged me to open the Qur'an for the first time. When I read the thirtieth verse of *Surah al Baqarah,*

> Behold, your Lord said to the angels, "I will create a vicegerent on earth." They said: "Will you put therein one who will spread corruption and shed blood? While we celebrate your praises and glorify you?" And He said: "I know what you do not know."

I was rationally and emotionally hooked. The question that had directed my life was now staring right at me and no way was I going to back off. The reading turned out to be more than academic, but reason was central to the experience. As the Qur'an gradually picked apart my arguments against the existence of God, the great barricade I had built between myself and Him began to come down, so that I became increasingly open to the possibility of God. And the more I came to question my atheism, the more I came to experience the presence of an overpowering mercy, that burst through and overwhelmed whatever residual resistance I could muster, and resurrected a soul I thought I had done away with years ago. And so, finally, I cried, and held tight to the infinite embrace, and let in, for the first time in a very, very, long time, as far back as I could remember, love.

So it is true that it was not reason alone that led me to self-surrender, but it was definitely at the heart of the process. And this is how I see the relationship between faith and reason; I see the latter as compatible with and at the service of the former. Reason is a corrective that assists in the search for truth; it is a God-given faculty that helps us avoid and correct errors. I understand that this is not the prevailing view in the West, but I was certain that it would be prevalent among Muslims.

From my reading of the Qur'an I had assumed that the community I was about to enter would lay great emphasis on investigating faith issues rationally. The several Muslims I had met until then were not particularly lucid when discussing Islam, but they were still fairly young and obviously limited in their religious learning. I was certain that when I met more learned Muslims they would impress me with their logic, objectivity, and philosophic manner.

Maybe neophytes always idealize their new communities, but it was not long before I realized I could not have been more wrong. Since my conversion, almost every Muslim with whom I spoke seriously about religious questions, regardless of their level of expertise, exhibited a deep-seated apprehension about analyzing faith perceptions rationally.[34] It is not just that Muslims tend to be very resistant

---

34. I should mention that I have not observed this so much among the Shiah Muslims, who comprise about fifteen percent of believers worldwide. Although I personally find Sunni dogma to be more reasonable than Shiah dogma (in most matters where they conflict), the Shiah Muslims I have met do not seem to have the same mistrust of reason. The divergent attitudes might be rooted in the intellectual rift (which we discuss below) that occurred in Sunni Islam.

to questioning established religious views—although I naively expected otherwise, this is an almost universal religious impulse—but rather, they display a definite uneasiness with and sometimes a disdain for rational deliberation on religious propositions per se. Just the mention of certain words associated with the rational disciplines, like "philosophy," "theology," "logic," even "reason," in a religious discussion can elicit concern. On a number of occasions I have heard the opinions of various Muslim intellectuals discounted on grounds that they are "just philosophers" or "thinkers," as if these are pejorative terms. Just recently, a devout Muslim cautioned me, "Brother, you don't read philosophy books, do you? You should really stay away from them."

From my first entry into the community, I have found my coreligionists to be very leery of dialectics, even in defense of the religion. I recall the first time I tried to give a three-part talk at the mosque on the objections I once had to the concept of God and the answers I then found through reading the Qur'an. A large part of the audience was up in arms after I finished presenting the objections and demanded that I not be allowed to continue, because, according to their understanding, to even think about such issues is *haram*. Many of the young Muslims who write me about their doubts apologize for bringing them up, stating that they believe it is *haram* to have them in the first place.

A few years after my conversion, I had a long argument with one of the local leaders about the treatment of the women in our community. When I seemed to be getting the better of the debate, he shouted, "There is no reasoning in Islam! We will look it up in the *tafsir* (Qur'an commentary)!" As if that particular interpretation, which anyway ended up not supporting his case, was the final word on the matter.

My persistence in questioning community norms has frequently evoked consternation. A Middle-Eastern surgeon succinctly expressed what many others seem to feel: "Brother, it is good that reason led you to Islam, but now that you are a Muslim you should follow what the scholars say." I responded that if I were to do that I might be exchanging one form of ignorance for another; not to mention that if I adopted that attitude earlier I would still be a Roman Catholic.

These last two incidents exemplify the prevailing attitude toward the use of reason when approaching faith questions. Muslims do make rational arguments for established positions; in fact, they practically revel in it. They will cite the Qur'an, the *Hadith* literature, scholarly opinion, contemporary research articles in various disciplines, statistics, and any other evidence they feel supports their stance, and will argue inductively, deductively, analogically, syllogistically, and so forth to prove their point. It is only when the very same methods seem to throw doubt on an established opinion that reasoning becomes illegitimate. When your evidence and arguments appear to invalidate a convention, then you have "gone too far" in the use of reason. Moreover, even though both sides employ the same methods of argument, this is frequently denied: those who defend convention most often insist that they are strictly adhering to the Qur'an and *Sunnah* and that their opposition is guilty of rationalism.

Many times I have lectured on the importance the Qur'an attaches to the exercise of reason in the pursuit of faith and without fail Muslims in attendance will inquire as to where we should draw the line in our utilization of reason. In the early days I had no idea what line they were talking about, so I answered that I do not think there is a "line," other than that between reasoning well and reasoning badly. "Well, what if I don't understand something in the Qur'an, like why we have to pray or fast or abstain from pork or alcohol?" will be the typical reply. My usual response is that wisdom can be found in all of these, but in any event, just because a person does not understand something, the misunderstanding does not disprove the teaching. A lot of people cannot understand calculus, but it does not invalidate this area of mathematics. If a person is going to disbelieve in something on grounds that he merely does not comprehend it, then he is reasoning badly. On the other hand, if there is strong evidence against the necessity of a conventional Muslim practice or belief, then calling it into question is a good exercise of reason. Yet this is where many Muslims "draw the line" between faith and reason: reason is permissible as long as it is does not challenge convention.

So where does this pervasive mistrust of rational thought come from in a faith community whose Scripture lays so much emphasis on the use of reason? A likely place to look for the root of a collective anxiety such as this one, which does not appear to derive from the Qur'an, is in the religious-political conflicts that marked the formative period of Islamic thought.[35] Among the numerous factions that existed in the early centuries A.H., there were two that ultimately rose to prominence and came to have strong, contending stances on the role of reason in Islam. One was known as the *ahl al hadith* (the *hadith* party), who were later to become known as the *ahl al hadith wa al sunnah* (the *hadith* and *sunnah* party) and as the *ahl al sunnah wa al jama`a* (the party of the *sunnah* and the community).[36] The other was the *ahl al kalam* (the disputation party), who were forerunners of the Mu`tazilah. The Arabic word *kalam* ordinarily means "speech", but it also carries the technical connotation of "rational, philosophical or speculative theology". Thus, the classification, *ahl al kalam*, stands for those who engage in these studies.

35. W. Montgomery Watt, *The Formative Period of Islamic Thought*, Oneworld Publications, Rockport, 1998, pp. 279-318; W. Montgomery Watt, *Islamic Philosophy and Theology*, Edinburgh University Press, 1962, G.H.A. Juynboll, *Studies on the First Century of Islamic Society*, Southern Illinois University Press, Edwardsville, 1982; H.A. Wolfson, *The Philosophy of the Kalam*, Harvard Press, Cambridge, 1976; A.J. Arberry, *Revelation and Reason in Islam*, George Allen and Unwin Ltd, London, 1957, A.S. Tritton, *Muslim Theology*, Hyperion Press, Westport, 1981; Fazlur Rahman, *Islam*, University of Chicago Press, 1966.

36. Often referred to as the Sunni Muslims. The term "the community" is apparently self-defining and represents those Muslims whom this group considers not to have deviated from the Qur'an and teachings of the Prophet.

Much of the theological deliberation of the early *mutakallimun* (practitioners of *kalam*) was related to practical politics. Questions concerning free will and predestination came to the fore in response to the Umayyad defense that their rule was divinely predetermined, from which arose additional questions, such as whether the Quran, the word of God, was created or uncreated. The *Khawarij* assertion that only they were true Muslims, raised questions concerning true belief, the relationship between faith and works, and the faith status of Muslims who commit major sins.

Interfaith polemics also influenced Islamic theology. The great conquests that began shortly after the death of the Prophet brought vast territories under Islamic rule that were home to many different religious communities with great scholarly traditions and centers of learning. The Arabs were not disposed toward forced conversion of the subjected peoples, so that conversion proceeded very gradually, which kept Muslims in the minority for a long period in the provinces. The contacts between Muslims and non-Muslims often led to polemical arguments, which also stimulated various areas of theological reflection. These interfaith dialogues frequently took the form of public debates that were sometimes presided over by high government officials, including the caliph himself.

In the second century A.H., the *ahl al kalam* merged into another school of thought known as the Mu'tazilah, founded by Wasil ibn Ata, a disciple of the famous Successor, al Hasan al Basri.[37] Their chief aim was to give a rationally coherent account of Islamic beliefs by achieving a synthesis between faith and reason. "Reason," however, included the accepted sciences of the time, most notably that of the Greeks, whose works were now being translated into Arabic at the urging of the government. This led the Mu'tazilah to introduce non-

---

37. W. Montgomery Watt, *The Formative Period of Islamic Thought*, Oneworld Publications, Rockport, 1998, pp. 209-217, challenges this widely accepted ascription.

Qur'anic concepts into their theology, mostly taken from Greek science and philosophy.[38]

The extent to which *kalam* was affected by the internal politics of early Islam, interfaith dialogue, or Hellenistic thought is difficult to determine, even with regard to individual principles. The *ahl al kalam*'s argument that God, being supremely just, could not hold humans accountable for actions over which they had no control, which would rule out predestination, may have also been employed against the Christian concept of original sin in interfaith dialogues. Similarly, their insistence that the Qur'an was created, may not only have derived from their stance on human free will, but could have figured prominently in arguments with Christians about Christ as the Word of God. If the Qur'an is the eternal divine Word revealed as Scripture, Christians could argue, then why could Jesus not be the eternal Word revealed in the form of an authentic man?

To further safeguard the unity of God, the Mu`tazilah denied that the divine attributes were distinct entities, equating them instead with God's essence. They felt that the existence of distinct, eternal, divine attributes admitted plurality into the Godhead. In their opinion, when we say God is "living," "knowing," "powerful," and "eternal," we are simply reaffirming God's essence. Their position, in effect, reduces the attributes to mere alternative designations or synonyms for the divine essence. Here again, fear of confusion with the Christian doctrine of the Trinity may have been behind this dogma, or perhaps the fear that acceptance of the divine attributes would "mean admitting an attribute of speech and ultimately an uncreated Qur'an."[39]

---

38. On the influence of Greek philosophy on Mutazilism and Islamic theology in general, see, H. A. Wolfson, *The Philosophy of the Kalam*, Harvard University Press, Cambridge, 1976, pp. 64-66, 373-376, 410-433, 466-517.

39. W. Montgomery Watt, *The Formative Period of Islamic Thought*, Oneworld Publications, Rockport, 1998, p. 246.

The Mu`tazilite positions just outlined are considered heresies in Sunni Islam, but there was a time when Mu`tazilism was the official state religion of the Islamic Empire. Explanations for their rise and fall are somewhat lacking in the historical writings but what they do tell us suggests some possibilities. During Umayyad rule many of the *ahl al kalam* were "among the intellectual cadres of the opposition movements."[40] Their refutations of predestination undermined the regime's principal claim to legitimacy and cleared the way theologically for the Abbasid revolution. Gratitude and/or prior affiliation during Umayyad times might explain their ascendancy under the Abbasids.[41] At the very least the early Abbasids must have been sympathetic to their theology. Also, appreciation of their superior dialectical skills, often demonstrated before the court in religious debates, may have been a factor. In any case, the Mutazilah reached the summit of political influence when in 827 (213 A.H.) the Caliph al Ma`mun declared their creed the state religion. In 833 (219 A.H.), the year of his death, al Ma`mun issued another edict, whereby a kind of inquisition, known as the *Mihnah*, was instituted, which continued during the reigns of al Mu`tasm, al Wathik, and late into the second year of the reign of al Mutawakkil (847/ 233 A.H). During the *Mihnah*, judges and other prominent persons were required to publicly declare their assent to the doctrine of the creatededness of the Quran. Some agreed immediately, some eventually yielded under the threat of torture and death, and a few, among them Ahmed bin Hanbal, resolutely refused. The latter were imprisoned and treated severely.

---

40. *Studies on the First Century of Islamic Society*, Edited by G.H.A. Juynboll, Southern Illinois University Press, 1982, p. 123.

41. However, their political ascent was apparently uneven. Some of the Mutazilah were against the Abbasids and the Caliph Harun ar-Rashid put Mutazilah theologians in prison, perhaps "because this sect was growing too uppish." A.S. Tritton, *Muslim Theology*, Hyperion Press, Westport, 1981, p. 61.

Nasr Hamed Abu Zeid suggests that the *Mihnah* might be yet another example of religion being put to the service of politics.

> Was the Abassid Caliph al Ma`moun in his determined enforcement of the Quran-is-created doctrine acting out of intellectual conviction? Or was he trying to consolidate his rule by finding an excuse to punish the Hanbalis who had earlier staged an insurrection against his Baghdad-based military chiefs? Baghdad at this time was under the control of a group of corrupt military chieftains who extracted protection money from the inhabitants, particularly the rich. Records of the inquisition-style courts set up by al Ma`moun to force the creed of the Mu`tazzilah on the public show that the defendants were the same *ulema* accused of rebelling against the Baghdad chieftains.[42]

Considering the scope and duration of the *Mihnah*, it seems more probable that al Ma`moun and his two immediate successors had larger aims, namely, keeping the *ahl al hadith* movement, which was growing in numbers and influence among the populace, in check.

Professor Abu Zaid's question regarding al Ma`moun's initiation of the *Mihnah* can also be asked concerning al-Mutawakkil's ending it: Were his reasons more religious or political? The fact that it took him almost two years suggests that he was not immediately bothered by the persecution of the *ahl al hadith* or the dogma that the Qur'an is created. It is also hard to subscribe to him pious motives when throughout his reign "the caliph was a notorious tippler, sensual and ruthless, hardly an exemplar of God's vicegerency on earth."[43]

Moreover, the state of the caliphate was sufficiently unstable when al Mutawakkil came to power to warrant a sudden and dramatic reversal of policy. An inflated bureaucracy, profligate government

---

42. Al-Ahram Weekly, pp. 12-18, 2002, Issue No. 603

43. Abu Ja`far Muhammad ibn Jarir al Tabari, *Ta'rikh al Rusul wa'l Muluk*, translated by Joel L. Kraemer, SUNY Press, 1989, p. xxi.

spending, and diminishing revenues produced economic mayhem. Major revolts erupted in both the center of the empire and distant provinces during the period of al Wathiq and al Mutawakkil. During the latter's rule, wars at the periphery of the empire—in Upper and Lower Egypt, Adharbayjan, Armenia and Asia Minor—spread out of control. Meanwhile the caliphate had to contend with serious internal threat from the Turkish military. Al Mu`tasim, al Mutawakkil's father, founded Samarra and made it his new capital "to avoid the perennial clashes and friction between the Turkish troops and the Baghdad populace."[44] The strategy to isolate the Turkish soldiery in Sammara only served to enhance their growing consolidation and power, which al Mutawakkil tried to break after assuming office by removing officials, confiscating property, and executing powerful notables. This may have also been the motive behind his unsuccessful attempt to re-establish his capital in Damascus. In the end, the Turkish military proved too strong and al Mutawakkil was assassinated by Turkish officers with the aid of his son within the precincts of his own palace.

Given the precariousness of al Mutawakkil's reign, with so much to contend with from so many sources, it would have been an eminently wise and uncostly political move to simply reverse a government policy that had become very unpopular and to align with a movement with mass appeal, which, by the way, held no small resentment toward the Turkish military.[45] Although we cannot be sure whether al Mutawakkil's change of policy, which now made Sunni Islam in effect the state religion, was motivated principally by piety or political calculation, we can be forgiven for leaning toward the second possibility. One thing, however, seems certain: al Mutawakkil's

---

44. Ibid p.xi.

45. The *Mihnah* must have reached the height of public resentment just before al Mutawakkil assumed the throne, when his successor and brother, al Wathiq, made confession of the Mutazilite creed a condition of ransoming Muslim captives in the hands of the Byzantines. Ibid pp. 38-44.

rescission of the *Mihnah* was not an impulse, but instead the initial step of a well thought-out, multifaceted agenda; for upon its repeal, he began to issue and aggressively pursue numerous pro-Sunni policies. In addition to replacing the Mutazilites in office, banning discussion of their creed, and imprisoning and torturing some of its leaders and confiscating their property, he also campaigned violently against the Shiah[46] and re-imposed numerous discriminatory laws against the non-Muslim population that had long fallen into disuse.[47]

---

46. This included having the tomb of al Husayn bin `Ali destroyed, together with the residences and palaces surrounding it. He ordered that the site of his grave be ploughed, sown and irrigated, and that any visitors to it be threatened with prison. According to Ya`qubi, al Mutawakkil also had `Ali bin Muhammad bin `Ali al Rida bin Musa bin Ja`far, the tenth imam of the Shi`ites, brought from Medina to Baghdad and then to Samarra, where he was kept under virtual house arrest. According to Ya`qubi, al Mutawakkil summoned him from Medina due to popular support there for his cause. Ibid pp. 110-111 and p. 76, including note 264.

47. Al Tabari explains, "Al Mutawakkil ordered that the Christians and all other *Dhimmis* (non-Muslims) must wear yellow hoods and *zunnar* (non-decorative) belts, ride on saddles with wooden stirrups, affix two pommels at the rear of the saddles, and place two buttons to the caps of those who wore them, which were to be of a different color from the cap worn by Muslims. [They must] put two patches on their slaves' outer garment, that one of the patches to be in the front of his chest and the other on his back, and that each patch be four finger spans in diameter and yellow. [Those *Dhimmis*] who wore a turban should wear one whose color is yellow. The [*Dhimmi*] women who went out and showed themselves in public should only appear in a yellow wrap. Al Mutawakkil also ordered that their slaves wear *zunnar* belts and prohibited them from wearing a decorative variety. In addition he ordered that their renovated places of worship be destroyed, and that one-tenth of their residences be seized. If the location was sufficiently spacious, it was to be turned into a mosque. If it was not suitable for a mosque, it was to be [destroyed and] the area made an open tract of land. And he ordered that wooden images of devils be nailed to the doors of their houses in order to distinguish between their houses and those of the

(contd. on page 387)

Even if al Mutawakkil's life ended in a coup, the alignment of the caliphate with the *ahl al hadith* seems to have been a sound move politically. Succeeding caliphs followed the same policy, albeit somewhat less aggressively, and though the years between the murder of Mutawakkil in 248 A.H. and the ascension of al Mu'tamid in 257 A.H. are "probably to be regarded as a renewal of the old struggle" between the Mu'tazilah and the *ahl al hadith*, the reign of al Mu'tamid saw a successful reinstatement of caliphal power that continued under his two successors.[48] Thereafter, the caliphate went into a steep decline, yet Sunni Islam was now firmly established as the religion of the empire, so much so that "even other elements in the population seem to have accepted the fact that state and society would be essentially Sunnite."[49] The ascendancy of the *ahl al hadith* meant that the Mutazilite's would be permanently anathematised and discriminated against until they gradually faded away.[50] The two edicts

Footnote No. 47 (contd. from page 386)

Muslims. Al Mutawakkil prohibited the employment of *Dhimmis* in government bureaus and in official functions, in which their authority would be exercised over Muslims. He prohibited their children from studying in Muslim elementary schools or being taught by Muslims. And he prohibited their displaying of crosses on their Palm Sundays and holding religious processions. In addition, he ordered that their graves be made level with the ground so as not to resemble the graves of Muslims" Ibid. pp. 89-94. Four years after imposing these sanctions, al Mutawaakil added on a few more: the *Dhimmis* were required to affix two yellow sleeves to their outer cloaks and they had to restrict their mounts to mules and donkeys.

48. W. Montgomery Watt, *The Formative Period of Islamic Thought*, Oneworld Publications, Rockport, 1998, p. 254.

49. Ibid p. 254.

50. *Kalaam*, in forms that defended orthodoxy, continued in Sunni Islam. W. Montgomery Watt, *The Formative Period of Islamic Thought*, Oneworld Publications, Rockport, 1998, pp. 279-318; Eric. L. Ormsby, *Theodicy in Islamic Thought*, Princeton University Press, 1984; pp. 166-204; *Ibn Taymiyyah Expounds on Islam*; compiled and translated by Muhammad 'Abdul Haqq Ansari, Imam Muhammad Ibn Saud University, 2000

of al Ma`moun that had made Mutazilism the state creed and initiated the *Mihnah* undoubtedly accelerated their decline. As is often the case, a religious party that becomes affiliated with a regime the masses view as corrupt and oppressive and colludes in its persecution of a popular resistance movement deprives itself of credibility and ensures its own demise when the political tide shifts.

Most modern Muslims know very little about the Mutazilah, other than that they were a heretical sect that vanished long ago, but reverberations of that bitter struggle for religious dominance are still discernible in the community today in its widespread aversion to rational inquiry, particularly when it challenges traditional thought or practice. Most of the points that were debated are either forgotten or have lost their relevance but the distrust of reason endures. But can it not be argued that the example of the Mutazilah attests to the dangers that reason poses to faith? Did not reason cause them to deny the reality of the divine attributes or to assert that God's knowledge is limited to universals?

Regardless of how one views Mu`tazilite doctrines, it is inaccurate to say that reason produced them, for reason, rightly applied, has very limited reach. Whether reason yields truth or falsity depends on the premises assumed and the correctness of one's logic. If our assumptions are true then accurate reasoning can only derive other truths. Whatever errors occurred in Mutazilite thought, they are the result of either false assumptions or faulty arguments, which Sunni critics like al Ash`ari, al Ghazali, Ibn Taymiyyah and many others have argued. The fact that these scholars were able to effectively critique Mutazilite theology demonstrates that reason is not the danger but rather the failure to use it to reappraise our sciences and systems of thought; for if the *ummah* had accepted Mutazilism as truth and permanently forbade its critical review, then Muslim faith today would be based on falsehood, waiting to be exposed. In other words, the problem would have been that a "line" between faith and reason was in fact drawn and that critique of convention was prohibited on grounds it would have been "going too far."

For Muslims, the ultimate arbiter on whether or not reason is potentially detrimental to faith should be the Qur'an and as discussed in chapter one the scripture displays no reserve about its use.[51] In fact, it repeatedly admonishes that religion becomes corrupted and people stray from faith because they fail to use their reason or because they reason incorrectly—their logic and arguments are flawed.[52] In the Qur'an, critical reasoning exposes falsehood and illuminates truth, whereas people reject faith because instead of thinking critically they prefer to follow conjecture,[53] their desires[54] or tradition (i.e. the ways of their fathers).[55] It is unnecessary to rehearse what I wrote on this in the first chapter, except to say that the fact the Qur'an begins the story of man by posing the most important theological question in human history, that is at the heart of the great modern crisis of faith and reason, shows how unperturbed the Scripture is about the prospect of approaching matters of faith rationally; not to mention that the first aspect of human nature the Scripture highlights in response to this seeming paradox is human intellect.[56]

Today, Muslims are dumbfounded at the state of the *ummah*, certain that they must have failed to adhere to some central aspect of

---

51. See chapter one, pp. 63-70 for discussion, citations, and references.

52. *Surahs* 2:44; 2:73; 2:76; 2:171; 2:242; 3:65; 5:58; 6:32; 6:151; 7:169; 8:22; 10:16; 11:51; 12:2; 12:109; 21:67; 23:80; 24:61; 28:60; 29:63; 36:62; 36:68; 37:138; 39:43; 40:67; 43:3; 49:4; 57:17; 59:14.

53. *Surahs* 4:157; 6:116; 6:148; 10:36; 10:66; 43:20; 45:32; 53:23; 53:28.

54. *Surahs* 2:111; 2:145; 4:119; 5:77; 6:119; 13:37; 19:59; 28:50; 30:29; 47:14; 47:16; 54:3; 57:14.

55. *Surahs* 2:170; 5:104; 6:148; 7:28; 7:70; 7:173; 10:78; 11:109; 11:62; 11:87; 14:10; 16:35; 21:53-54; 23:24; 26:74; 28:36; 31:21; 34:43; 37:69-70; 43:22-24.

56. I must admit that there is very little emphasis in the *Hadith* literature on the importance of reason in the attainment of faith, and there is even a somewhat antirational thread in the *Hadith* literature, which probably is reflective of the Mutazilah vs. *ahl al hadith* conflict.

God's Revelation, thus accounting for their weakness and inferiority vis-à-vis the rest of the world. How did a people who once led the world in science, technology, and military prowess, and were trustees of God's ultimate Revelation, fall into such an abject state? Typical explanations are that too many Muslims are remiss in their ritual duties, or fail to fully implement Islamic Law, or stray from the Prophet's *Sunnah*, or are ruled by tyrants. I do not discount these possibilities, but I believe that the refusal to critically reappraise the massive legacy of scholarship and custom that has been passed down is the crux of the problem. I feel that Muslims have intellectually paralysed themselves, by making the tremendous body of thought they inherited into a kind of intellectual preserve, an asylum of ideas that must not be disturbed and where troublesome realities are walled out. I feel that the greatest crisis affecting Muslims today is a crisis of thought, a refusal to think critically about what Islam really demands. This rejection of reason in favor of convention, which is indeed opposed to the Qur'an, has debilitated and stagnated the community, and in America, has caused native-born Muslims to discount the country's Islamic institutions as irrelevant to their reality. In my second book,[57] I urged Muslim immigrants and converts to critically reappraise conventional Muslim thought and practice, but I wrote that almost ten years ago and I now realize, as I suspected then, that this was hoping for too much. The children of that generation are now at or reaching adulthood, and most of them shun the mosque, but it does not take a legion of dedicated individuals to radically change the course of history, and there is now a small but notable core of young American Muslim activists acutely alert to the problems confronting this community and earnestly seeking solutions to them.

---

57. *Even Angels Ask*, Amana Publications, Beltsville, 1997.

Illustrations of Conflict

The following questions and comments I have received serve as an indication of the needs and complications existing in the American Muslim community. I offer them publicly in an appeal for all Muslims to come together in aiding and comforting one another and especially those struggling for answers and solutions to very real and personal concerns.

Question 1 (from a female American Muslim convert concerning the *hijab* (headscarf) worn by Muslim women.):

I converted to Islam several years ago and I am really struggling with the hijab. I believe in it and could see that wearing it could be both liberating and faith strengthening for many Muslim women. I greatly admire their courage. I tried wearing it for about a year but unfortunately found it absolutely painful. The angry looks I got from people, the way I was often treated like a foreigner who could not speak English, the harassment my children had to endure in and out of school, the loss of self-esteem I felt and the attendant weight gain I experienced were more than I could handle. Throughout all this I continued to pray for strength, but I just became more and more depressed. After I stopped covering I began to feel better again about myself, but I realize this is indicative of the weakness of my faith. I have also lost most of my friends among the ladies in the Muslim community. I guess I'm writing to you for advice. Do you think I should start wearing hijab again?

From your question, it appears that you are not asking me to weigh the various arguments put forth by Muslims for and against the traditional female dress code. Both sides make some good points (Chapter 2, Question 4) and if we were living in a predominantly Muslim society this would be a societal issue that would need to be discussed and debated openly, for it would probably lead to the enactment of laws on public decency that everyone would be required to follow. In the United States, however, this is a personal choice a Muslim woman faces that has little effect on the mores of society at large.

It seems to me that you're already convinced that Muslim women are required to cover their hair, so I'm going to approach your question from that angle. Your message indicates that wearing *hijab* has been extremely difficult for you. I am not a woman, but I can only imagine that in this country it cannot be at all easy, especially for American converts, since the society will be much more lenient in their reaction toward foreign women than toward Americans by birth, especially since September 11, 2001.

Although my wife is not an American, she finally, after several years, stopped covering her hair following a frightening episode. One day back in 1992, a crazed, drunk bigot trapped my wife in her car in a supermarket parking lot after a car chase through the streets of East Lawrence. He screamed threats, curses, and racist epithets at her while he wildly banged his fists on the hood and windows of her car. This went on according to her for several minutes. People were in the area watching but no one came to my wife's aid. She sat through it crying, begging God to let her see her children and husband again.[58] That incident was the last straw in a long series of unfortunate happenings, which I prefer not to enumerate.

I am uncomfortable giving people this type of advice (I never advised my own wife which way I thought she should go with the headscarf), but if you find it too hard and too painful, you might consider not covering your hair and putting this issue on the shelf for now. Due to our minority status, there are a fair number of religious regulations that Muslims cannot effectively implement in the US. For some American Muslim ladies wearing traditional Muslim dress can be so painful that it may actually hurt their faith more than help it; it really depends on the individual. If you found it a burden greater than

---

58. For Muslim women in similar circumstances I suggest driving to a police station or fire station, if possible.

you can bear (2:286), that does not invariably make you a lesser Muslim. Many a believing man and woman who self-righteously and obstinately insist on the *hijab* for Muslim ladies in America would never have had the courage to critically examine the religion they were born into (together with the many unnecessary cultural accretions that go with it), and then publicly reject it as you have. True conversion, especially when the religion is in the extreme minority stage, takes a profound act of faith. Concerning one of the Companions who leaked information to his family in Mecca of an impending Muslim advance, the Prophet told the Companions who wanted to kill him to leave him alone, for he said, "Who's to say that God may not have forgiven him the rest of his sins for having participated in the Battle of Badr."[59] Those who participated in the Battle of Badr were always given the highest respect because they chose Islam at great risk when their whole society was headed in the opposite direction.

I don't know if any of what I wrote here is of help to you. I may not be answering you in the way you would have wished. But my advice to you is to work on other aspects of your faith until you feel strong enough to try the headscarf again.

In addition to this advice, an American Muslim woman might develop her own *sunnah* by experimenting with different types of scarves and different ways of tying them. Aside from the traditional *hijab*, there are short and long scarves; triangular, square, and rectangular scarves; solid colors and vibrant prints. In the summer, a scarf can be more comfortable being tied behind the head and held in place with clips (the spring kind, not clasps). A stylish scarf with a modest dress or tunic with pants (for examples) can make a woman identify with the American human-scape while setting her apart as a modest and sophisticated Muslim lady.

---

59. The report concerns Hatib bin Balta`ah. Versions of it appear in the collections of Bukhari and Abu Dawud. A version also appears in *The History of al-Tabari*, Vol. 8, translated by Michael Fishbein, SUNY Press, 1997, pp. 166-168.

Question 2 (from a writer seeking to enlighten me on various defects of my religion. The tenor of most of the messages I receive from non-Muslims who have read my books or have seen my lectures is friendly, sympathetic and/or genuinely curious, but occasionally I receive a message like the following. The arguments presented in these kinds of correspondences can be found on almost every Evangelical website on Islam, and were part and parcel of early Western anti-Muslim polemic, and were periodically countered by Muslim scholars. Judging from my email, these archaic criticisms are causing concern to many web-surfing second generation Muslims. I have discussed some of them in other places and some can be addressed very briefly; for these I refer the reader to the footnotes. I respond to the remaining claims in the text below.):

> *It was a great pleasure to attend your lecture last evening at Kansas-State University and learn about your life and your trip from atheism to Islam. It was really sad to hear about your childhood and how having an alcoholic father affected your life, until you found the Qur'an on your desk one day. You explained how when you read the Qur'an you found the answers to your questions, such as, "Why does God allow so much violence and suffering in the world?" You mentioned that because you were able to find convincing answers to your rational objections you made the assumption that God must have revealed this Scripture, and you based your faith on that assumption.*[60]
>
> *Did you ever consider the possibility that this document could have been written by a very clever man?*[61] *I am sure that you know that Muhammed could not read or write, and he was using Waraqa ibn Nafal to write the Revelation for him. But did you know that after ibn Nafal*

---

60. This is an understandable over-simplification. See chapter 1, pp. 118-126.

61. Cf. Chapter 1, pp. 33-35.

died the Revelation from Allah to Muhammed completely stopped?[62] Isn't it stranger that this document is not written in any chronological order, and the way the <u>surahs</u> where put in order is by size?[63]

I have read the Qur'an too, but my background is completely different than yours. I had a loving father, and a wonderful mother, a true mother Theresa. We did not suffer as much as you did. My hard working father was always there for us. He taught us what is right from wrong, and taught us to be good people in the real sense. I lived in the Middle East about two thirds of my life. I know about Muslims and Islam more than you'll ever know. But when I read the Qur'an I found it to be extremely materialistic, and could not believe that God would come up with such a document with so many mistakes in mathematics, history, and science. Below are some examples.

1. In the inheritance law (4:11-12 and 4:176), when a man dies leaving three daughters, parents and a wife, his property will be divided between them with 2/3 going to the daughters, 1/3 going to the parents and 1/8 going to the wife. This will add up to 1 and 1/8!

2. God took six days to create the earth and heavens in 7:54 and eight days in 41:9-12.

---

62. Waraqa ibn Nafal is reported to have died in the second or third year of the Prophet's mission when at most a handful of very short revelations had been received. Most of the historians report that only 96:1-6 had been revealed before Waraqa's demise. The Prophet continued to receive revelations until just before his death at least twenty years after Waraqa's. See: *The Encyclopedia of Islam*, New Edition, Vol. XI, Brill (2000) pp. 142-143, where Ibn Hadjar, Isaba, Cairo (1977), X, p. 304, is cited.

63. It is not clear how this is supposed to prove the fraudulence of the Qur'an. The *surahs* are only roughly of decreasing length. On the order of the *surahs* see, *Even Angels Ask*, Amana Publications, Beltsville (2000), pp. 139-143, and, *Struggling to Surrender*, Amana Publications, Beltsville (2000), pp. 66-67. On the absence of chronology in the Qur'an see, *Even Angels Ask*, Amana Publications, Beltsville (2000), pp. 13-14, and this publication, chapter 1, question 1.

3. A day with Allah is 1,000 human years in 22:47 and 50,000 human years in 70:4.

4. The Qur'an states that the calf worshipped by the Israelites was molded by the Samaritans, during the time of Moses (20:85-87). The Samaritans did not exist until about 700 BC which was several hundred years after Moses time.

5. The Qur'an mentions that Mary was the sister of Aaron, and that the Gospel existed during the time of Moses (7:157).

6. According to 67:3-5 and 71:15-16 there are seven heavens and the stars are in the lower heaven and the moon is in the midst of the seven heavens.

7. In 18:86 the Qur'an says that the sun sets in a muddy spring!!

8. The Qur'an also says that everything was created in pairs (51:49). We know that this is not true in many creatures such as bacteria, fungi, and even some plants.

These were just a few examples of many, many other passages that I had problems with. Below are some others that I object to on moral grounds.

9. When I read it I found that it encourages Muslims to hate other people who are not Muslims. I don't believe that God would want us to be that way. In 9:123 the English Qur'an says, "Fight those of the disbelievers...." The Arabic Qur'an's word for "fight" is "Katello" which comes from "kattal" which means "kill." Is that the kind of society that we would like to have? You mentioned last evening that you found the word "knowledge" in the Qur'an some 846 times. Let me ask you, have you counted how many times the word "kill" or its lighter English version "fight" was mentioned in the Qur'an?

10. You also talked about the importance the Qur'an assigns to "intellect" and "choice" in spiritual growth, and I honestly found a great lack of both when I read it. The Qur'an (9:5) says, "Then when the sacred months have passed, slay the idolaters wherever you find them, and take them (captives), and besiege them, and prepare for them each ambush. But if they repent and establish worship and pay the poor-due, then leave their way free." Here the Qur'an tells Muslims that they are free to convert non-Muslims by force and brutality, and if unsuccessful in doing so, then they are free to kill them. I am not sure if I can see the "choice" here as much as you do.

11. Allah promises Muslims who die in "jihad" that they will be awarded by going to a paradise were they can have sex with seventy-two houris (beautiful young virgin women with wide eyes), drink wine, and eat good food, and so on. First, would the Muslim have to ditch his wife first and then get the seventy-two houris? I wonder sometimes if there is a place in this paradise for good wives and mothers. Second, the Qur'an says that wine is the handiwork of the devil. How would Allah serve the handiwork of the devil in his heaven?

12. Finally, let me say that I believe it takes a strong man to admit that God exists after being an atheist for a long time, but I believe that it takes a much stronger man to find the true God. I know that you have established a great status in the society being a Western Muslim, and you have written books about Islam, among many things going for you after becoming a Muslim. But is it worth your eternal life?

For convenience I will remind the reader of each claim before giving my response.

1. In the inheritance law (4:11-12 and 4:176), when a man dies leaving two daughters, parents and a wife, his property will be divided between them with 2/3 going to the daughters, 1/3 going to the parents and 1/8 going to the wife. This will add up to 1 and 1/8!

The passages cited could indeed be confounding as they tersely sketch an array of inheritance cases, and hence they can be—and have been—interpreted in a variety of ways. The above dilemma is to be found in countless classical texts on Islamic law where different interpretive solutions are offered. The verses state:

God enjoins you concerning your children: for the male the equivalent of the portion of two females, but if there be more than two females (and no males), than theirs is two-thirds of the inheritance, and if there be (only) one female then (to her) the half. And for his parents a sixth of the inheritance, if he has a child; but if he has no child and his parents are his only heirs, then to his mother belongs a third; but if he has brothers (or sisters) then to his mother belongs the sixth, after any legacy he may have bequeathed, or debt (has been paid). Your parents or your children: You know not which of them is nearer unto you in benefit. It is an injunction from God. Truly, God is Knower, Wise.

And unto you belongs a half of that which your wives leave if they have no child; but if they have a child then unto you the fourth of that which they leave, after any legacy they may have bequeathed, or debt (they may have contracted has been paid). And unto them belongs the fourth of that which you leave if you have no child, but if you have a child then the eighth of that which you leave, after any legacy you may have bequeathed, or debt (you may have contracted has been paid). And if a man or woman having no descendents, leaves property to be inherited and he (or she) has a brother or sister, then for each of these is the sixth, but if they are more than that, then they shall share in the third after any legacy that may have been bequeathed or debt (contracted), not injuring others (4:11-12).

They ask you for a pronouncement. Say: God has pronounced for you concerning the person who has no descendents (and no parents). If a man dies childless and he has only a sister, hers is half the inheritance, and he shall be her heir if she dies childless. And if there be two sisters, then theirs are two-thirds of the inheritance; and if there be brethren, men and women, unto the male is the equivalent of the share of two females. God expounds to you so that you do not err. God is knower of all things (4:176).

In addition to these two passages we only have a single broad principle traced to the Prophet: "Give the fixed portions to those who are entitled to them, and what remains should go to the nearest male" (Al Bukhari's *Sahih*).

In his, *The Religion of Islam*, Muhammad Ali provides a straight-forward formula for calculating inheritance portions that is consistent with the above verses and *hadith* and easily handles all possible cases that may arise. Ali's interpretation is based on the plausible assumption that the opening command in 4:11 concerning the children shares lays down a general formula that is applied to what remains of the deceased parent's estate after, sequentially, payment of debts, execution of the will,[64] and then fixed shares for parents and spouse as defined in 4:11-12. He then shows that under this assumption and with the verses and *hadith* cited all possible cases, including those that vexed many ancient jurists, can be handled in a simple and equitable manner. At the end of his discussion, he provides the following recapitulation.[65]

Briefly, the inheritance law as laid down in the Qur'an is this. After the payments of debts and execution of the will, if any, the shares of the parents and husband or wife shall be first taken out; after that the rest of the property shall go to the

---

64. One is allowed to bequeath up to one-third of one's estate after debts have been paid.

65. For details see, Muhammad Ali, *The Religion of Islam*, Ahmadiyya Anjuman Isha`at Islam (Lahore), 1990, pp. 518-523.

children, the son having double the portion of the daughter; if there are no children and there are brothers and sisters, one sixth if there is only one brother or sister, and one third if there more than one, shall go to them; if the deceased leaves neither children nor parents, the whole of the property, after the husband's or the wife's share has been taken out, shall go to the brothers and sisters; if there is a single female, daughter or sister, she shall take one-half the property, a single brother following the same rule, and if there are two or more daughter or sisters they shall take two-thirds, the residue going to the nearest male relative according to the tradition; if a person entitled to inheritance is dead but leaves behind offspring, that offspring shall take his or her place, if the father or mother is dead, the grandfather or grandmother shall take his or her place; all brothers and sisters, whether uterine or consanguine or full, shall be treated equally; if there are no brothers or sisters, the nearest relatives after them, such as father's brothers or father's sisters, shall take their place.

If we apply this scheme to the case in question—a man is survived by his parents, a wife and two daughters—then after payment of debts and any bequests,[66] the parents are each given a sixth, his wife is given an eighth, and then his daughters are given two-thirds of the residue with the remaining one-third of the residue going to the nearest male relative. We obtain a mathematical inconsistency in this case only if we impose upon these ordinances an interpretation that forces a contradiction. Muhammad Ali's is not the only possible inheritance scheme that is in harmony with the Qur'an and avoids mathematical contradictions, but in addition to being fair it is certainly the most straightforward.[67]

---

66. One is allowed to bequeath up to one-third of one's estate after debts have been paid.

67. Muhammad Ali, *The Religion of Islam*, Ahmadiyya Anjuman Isha`at Islam (Lahore), 1990, pp. 519-525.

2. God took six days to create the earth and heavens in 7:54 and eight days in 41:9-12.

> Truly, your Lord is God, who has created the heavens and earth in six days...(7:54).

> Say: Do you indeed disbelieve in Him who created the earth in two days, and do you set up equals to Him. He is the Lord of the Worlds. And He set in it mountains standing firm, and He blessed therein and ordained therein its sustenance in four days, alike for (all) seekers. Furthermore, (*thumma*) He turned to the heaven when it was smoke and said to it and the earth: "Come both of you, willingly or unwillingly!" They said: "We come willingly." So He ordained them seven heavens in two days, and imparted to each heaven its function. And we adorned the lower heaven with lights and made them secure. That is the decree of the Mighty, the Knowing (41: 9-12).

This is another example of manufacturing a contradiction by imposing an unnecessary interpretation on the text. First it should be noted that "the word *yaum*, commonly translated as "day" is used in Arabic to denote any period, whether extremely long ("aeon") or extremely short ("moment"): its application to an earthly "day" of twenty-four hours is only one of its many connotations."[68] Hence, immediately after mentioning that God created the heavens and earth in six days in 32:4, the Qur'an states that "in the end all shall ascend to Him on a day (the Day of Judgement) whereof the measure is a thousand years of your reckoning" (32:5); and 70:4 states that "the angels and Spirit ascend to Him in a day whereof the measure is 50,000 years."

---

68. Muhammad Asad, *The Message of the Qur'an*, Dar Al-Andalus, Gibraltar (1980), p. 211, note 43.

We should also note that the word *thumma*, translated as "furthermore," could also mean "moreover" or "then." Therefore if we render *thumma* as "then" we obtain that the earth was created first, and then the heavens, but if we render *thumma* as "furthermore" or "moreover," then, as Maurice Bucaille explains:

> It may be a simple reference to events juxtaposed without any intention of bringing in the notion of the one following the other. However this may be, the periods of the creation of the Heavens may just as easily coincide with the two periods of the Earth's creation. ...There does not appear to be any contradiction between the passage quoted here and the concept of the formation of the world in six stages that is to be found in other texts in the Qur'an.[69]

3. A day with Allah is 1,000 human years in 22: 47 and 50,000 human years in 70:4.

As just mentioned, the Arabic *yaum* is used to denote any period of time, as 22:47 and 70:4 illustrate. It should also be observed that in each of the cases cited *yaum* refers to different events.

4. The Qur'an states that the Samaritan molded the calf worshipped by the Israelites, during the time of Moses (20: 85-87). The Samaritans did not exist until about 700 BC which was several hundred years after Moses time.

The passage in question reads:

> He said: Surely We have tried your people in your absence, and the *samiri*[70] has led them astray. So Moses returned to his people angry, sorrowing. He said: O my people, did not your Lord promise you a goodly promise? Did the promised time,

---

69. Maurice Bucaille, *The Bible, The Qur'an and Science*, Seghers (Paris, 1977), pp. 134-137.

70. The Arabic spelling is *sin aleph mim ra ya*.

then, seem long to you, or did you wish that displeasure from your Lord should come upon you, so that you broke (your) promise to me? They said: We broke not the promise to you of our own accord, but we were made to bear the burdens of the ornaments of the people, then we cast them away, and thus did the *samiri* suggest (20: 85-87).

Aside from having some phonetic resemblance with the word "Samaritan," there is no reason to assume that the Arabic *as-samiri* refers to a member of the ancient Jewish sect. Muslim exegetes offered different explanations. Muhammad Asad explains:

The designation *as-samari* is undoubtedly an adjectival noun denoting the person's descent or origin. According to one of the explanations advanced by Tabari and Zamakhshari, it signifies "a man of the Jewish clan of the *Samirah*", i.e., the ethnic and religious group designated in later times as the Samaritans (a small remnant of whom is still living in Nablus, in Palestine). Since that sect as such did not yet exist at the time of Moses, it is possible that—as Ibn `Abbas maintained (Razi)—the person in question was one of the many Egyptians who had been converted to the faith of Moses and joined the Israelites on their exodus from Egypt: in which case the designation *samiri* might be connected with the ancient Egyptian *shemer*, "a foreigner" or "stranger." This surmise is strengthened by his introduction of the worship of the golden calf, undoubtedly an echo of the Egyptian cult of Apis. In any case, it is not impossible that the latter-day Samaritans descended—or were reputed to descend—from this personality, whether of Hebrew or of Egyptian origin; this might partly explain the persistent antagonism between them and the rest of the Israelite community.[71]

71. Muhammad Asad, *The Message of the Qur'an*, Dar Al-Andalus, Gibraltar (1980), p. 479, note 70.

Moreover, Yuseph Ali adds:

If the Egyptian origin of the root is not accepted, we have a Hebrew origin in *shomer*, "a guard", "watchman", or "sentinel"; allied to the Arabic *samara, yasmuru*, to keep awake by night, to converse by night; *samir*, one who keeps awake by night. The *samiri* may have been a watchman, in fact or by nickname.[72]

5. The Qur'an mentions that Mary was the sister of Aaron, and that the Gospel existed during the time of Moses (7:157).

Almost all orientalist have cited 19:28, where Mary's kinsmen address her as "sister of Aaron," as a blatant anachronism. The duplicity of this criticism is apparent to anyone familiar with the New Testament, where Mary's cousin Elizabeth is called a "daughter of Aaron."[73] In Semitic cultures and among Muslims and Arabs to this day, such expressions as "daughter," "brother," "sister," "uncle," "aunt," and "son" are very often used figuratively to connote friendship, respect, descent, or familial associations. Muslims refer to each other as "brothers" or "sisters." A younger person often addresses an older person as "aunt" or "uncle." A descendant of someone may be referred to as his or her "son" or "daughter." Figurative expressions like "son of Adam," "son of David," and "children of Israel" appear regularly in the Bible.

The expression "sister of Aaron" in 19:28 is all the more appropriate if we accept that Elizabeth is a "daughter of Aaron"—a direct descendent of Aaron. Since Mary in the New Testament is Elizabeth's cousin, Mary would be only a "sister of Aaron"—since she was related by blood to the patriarch but not a direct descendent.

The Qur'an says absolutely nothing about the Gospel existing during the time of Moses. Surah 7:157 states that followers of the Prophet can find his coming foretold in the Torah and the Gospel.

---

72. 'Abdullah Yusuf 'Ali, *The Meaning of The Holy Qur'an*, Amana Publications, Beltsville (1966), p. 782, footnote 2608.

73. Luke 1:5-36.

Many Muslim commentators believe that Old Testament prophecies (e.g. Deut. 18:15-18) of a prophet to come who shall be like Moses and New Testament predictions of the coming of another messenger after Jesus (e.g. Matt. 13:31; Matt. 21:33-44, Mark 12:1-11, Luke 20: 9-18, John 1:22, John 14:16, John 14:26) refer to Prophet Muhammad.

6. *According to 67:3-5 and 71:15-16 there are seven heavens and the stars are in the lower heaven and the moon is in the midst of the seven heavens.*

> Who has created seven heavens (*samawat*) in harmony. You can see no fault in the Beneficent's creation; then look again: Can you see any rifts? Then look again and again, your sight will return unto you weakened and made dim. And verily We have beautified the nearest heaven (*sama'*) with lamps, and We make them missiles for the satans, and for them We have prepared the doom of flame (67: 3-5).

> Do you not see how God has created seven heavens (*samawat*) in harmony? And has made the moon in them (*fi-hinna*) a light (*nur*), and made the sun a lamp (*siraj*) (71:15-16).

It is not clear exactly what point the questioner is trying to make but from his interpretations of key words it seems that he feels the Qur'an indicates that the stars are in the nearest heaven and the moon is in a more distant heaven. The Qur'an does not spell out exactly what are the seven heavens, or what is the lowest heaven, or what are the lamps spoken of in 67:5, and because of this, Muslim commentators disagree in their interpretations of these. Yet all scholars would accept the following definition.

> The noun *sama'* denotes, primarily, "something that is above [another thing]", and is used—mostly in its plural form

samawat—to describe (a) the visible skies (as well as, occasionally, the clouds), (b) the cosmic space in which the stars, the solar systems (including our own) and the galaxies pursue their course, and (c) the abstract concept of forces emanating from God (since He is, in the metonymical sense of the word, "above" all that exists).[74]

The majority of exegetes believe the lowest heaven is the cosmic system described in (b) and thus contains the moon along with the planets, sun, stars, and the rest. Yet even if we accept this interpretation it leads to no contradiction between the passages cited above. For if the moon exists in the lowest heaven—or for that matter, any of the heavens—then it exists in one of the heavens, and hence would exist "in them" (*fi-hinna*) as described in 71:16.

7. In 18:86 the Qur'an says that the sun sets in a muddy spring![75]

8. The Qur'an also says that everything was created in pairs (51:49). We know that this is not true in many creatures such as bacteria, fungi and even some plants.

And of all things We have created pairs so that you may be mindful. (51:49)

Since the verse states that of *all things* God has created pairs, I assume that this refers to a universal aspect of creation that goes

74. Muhammad Asad, *The Message of the Qur'an*, Dar Al-Andalus, Gibraltar (1980), p. 356, note 4.

75. See Chapter 1, question 1, for my discussion on this verse. For other explanations: `Abdallah Yusuf `Ali, *The Meaning of the Holy Qur'an*, Amana Publications, Beltsville (1996), p. 732, note 2430; Muhammad Ali, *The Holy Qur'an*, with English Translation and Commentary, Ahmadiyya Anjuman Isha`at Islam (Lahore), 1990, notes 1518 and 1519, p. 588; Muhammad Asad, *The Message of the Qur'an*, Dar Al-Andalus, Gibraltar (1980), p. 452, note 85.

beyond just living things, or the phenomenon of reproduction to which the questioner presumably alludes. There are passages that many modern commentators believe refer to vegetable, animal, and human reproduction,[76] but all commentaries I have found on 51:49, past and present, agree that the Qur'an is alluding here to "the polarity evident in all creation, both animate and inanimate, which expresses itself in the existence of antithetic yet complementary forces."[77] Yusuf Ali conveys the common view:

> All things are in pairs: sex in plants and animals, by which one individual is complimentary to another; in the subtle forces of nature, Day and Night, positive and negative electricity, forces of attraction and repulsion: and numerous other opposites, each fulfilling its purpose, and contributing to Allah's Universe: and in the moral and spiritual world, Love and Aversion, Mercy and Justice, Striving and Rest, and so on— all fulfilling their functions according to the Artistry and wonderful Purpose of Allah. Everything has its counterpart, or pair, or complement. Allah alone is One, with none like Him, or needed to complement Him.[78]

Thus 51:49 turns out to be in conflict with modern science only if we accept the questioner's particular elucidation.

9. When I read it I found that it encourages Muslims to hate other people who are not Muslims. I don't believe that God would want us to be that way. In 9:123 the English Qur'an says: "Fight those of the disbelievers...." The Arabic Qur'an's word for "fight" is "Katello" which comes

---

76. Maurice Bucaille, *The Bible, The Qur'an and Science*, Seghers (Paris, 1977), pp. 188-191, 198-210.

77. Muhammad Asad, *The Message of the Qur'an*, Dar Al-Andalus, Gibraltar (1980), p. 676, note 18.

78. `Abdallah Yusuf `Ali, *The Meaning of the Holy Qur'an*, Amana Publications, Beltsville (1996), p. 1363, note 5025.

from "kattal" which means "kill." Is that the kind of society that we would like to have? You mentioned last evening that you found that the word "knowledge" in the Qur'an occurs some 846 times. Let me ask you, have you counted how many times the word "kill" or its lighter English version "fight" was mentioned in the Qur'an?

I wrote at some length in my two previous books on the Qur'an's pronouncements on warfare, which pretty well covers the concerns raised in this and the next question. To do justice to this topic I would have to rehearse most of what I wrote in *Struggling...* and *...Angels...*,[79] but for the sake of brevity I will concentrate on the stated complaints.

The questioner asserts that when he read the Qur'an he "found that it encourages Muslims to hate other people who are not Muslims." The Qur'an does prohibit friendship with non-believers (3:28, 3:118, 60:1-2), and, in particular, with Jews and Christians (5:51), but only "such of them as are actively hostile towards believers."[80] Hence 3:28 tells Muslims not to take the disbelievers for friends in preference to the believers,[81] yet later in the same *surah* the Qur'an repeats the command with this description of the unbelievers to be shunned:

> [Those] who would spare no pains to ruin you; they love
> to see you in distress. Vehement hatred has already appeared
> from out of their mouths, but that which their hearts conceal
> is greater still. We have made plain for you the revelations if
> you will use your reason (3:118).

79. *Strugglimg to Surrender*, Amana Publications, Beltsville, 2000, pp. 183-190; *Even Angels Ask*, Amana Publications, Beltsville, pp. 116-136.

80. Muhammad Asad, *The Message of the Qur'an*, Dar Al-Andalus, Gibraltar (1980), p. 855, note 3.

81. The Muslims were at war with the disbelievers of Mecca when this verse was revealed.

Similarly 5:51 instructs the believers not to take the Jews and Christians for friends, but a few verses later adds this qualification:

> O you who believe. Choose not for friends those who mock and make a sport of your religion, from among those who were given the Book before you and the disbelievers; and remain conscious of God if you are believers. And when you call to prayer, they mock at it and make a jest of it—because they are a people who do not use their reason (5:57).

Finally, verse 60:1-2, revealed in 8 A.H. towards the end of the Prophet's mission, describes the disbelievers who should not be befriended as those who "have driven the Prophet and yourselves away because you believe in God, your Lord," and, "if they could overcome you, will be your enemies, and will stretch out their hand and tongues towards you with evil: for they desire that you disbelieve." However, here again, the Qur'an elucidates in the same passage that friendly relations between Muslims and non-Muslims, as such, is not prohibited.

> As for those who do not fight against you because of religion, and neither drive you forth from your homes, God does not forbid you to show them kindness and to deal equitably with them. Truly God loves those who act equitably. God only forbids you to turn in friendship towards those who fight against you because of religion and drive you forth from your homes, or help in driving you forth. Whoever makes friends of them—such are wrongdoers (60:8-9).

Therefore, each time the Qur'an proscribes friendship with non-Muslims, it clarifies that this is directed against only those of them who are openly hostile to the believers and their faith.

The questioner cites 9:123 apparently to show that the Qur'an encourages unprovoked aggression. The verse reads:

O you who believe, fight those of the disbelievers who are nearby, and let them find harshness in you. And know that God is with the God-conscious (9:123).

The *surah* in which it appears deals with issues of war and peace, placing special emphasis on peace treaties and how to respond to those who violate them. Enemy tribes frequently made treaties of mutual alliance with the Muslims, only to violate them again and again when it suited them. After years of such treachery the Qur'an declared these truces annulled, with two clear exceptions: one in the case of those tribes who had remained true to their obligations (9:4, 9:7) and the second in the case of any idolater who sought protection from the Muslims. The latter were to be conducted "to his place of safety" (i.e. to a safe place of his choice) and not molested (9:6). All references in this *surah* to fighting idolaters, including 9:123 cited above, relate to this context.

It so happens that the Arabic words *qital* ("fighting") and *qatala* ("to fight") are associated with Muslim behaviour a total of 41 times in the Qur'an, which is not much considering that the revelation covers several years of warfare.

10. You also talked about the importance the Qur'an assigns to "intellect" and "choice" in spiritual growth, and I honestly found a great lack of both when I read it. The Qur'an (9:5) says, "Then when the sacred months have passed, slay the idolaters wherever ye find them, and take them (captives), and besiege them, and prepare for them each ambush. But if they repent and establish worship and pay the poor-due, then leave their way free." Here the Qur'an tells Muslims that they are free to convert non-Muslims by force and brutality, and if unsuccessful in doing so, then they are free to kill them. I am not sure if I can see the "choice" here as much as you do.

This verse is by far the preferred quote of those—whether they be opponents of Islam or militant Muslim extremists—who wish to prove that the Qur'an promotes military aggression or conversion by the sword. But to make this argument numerous statements must be discounted that unequivocally allow fighting only in defense of self or victims of tyranny and oppression.

> To those against whom war has been wrongfully made, permission [to fight] has been granted, and truly God has the power to defend them—those who have been driven from their homelands against all right for no reason than their saying, "Our Lord is God." For if God had not enabled people to defend themselves against one another, all monasteries and churches and synagogues and mosques, in which God's name is abundantly extolled, would surely have been destroyed (22:39-40).

> And what ails you that you will not fight in the cause of the utterly helpless men, women and children who are crying, "O our Lord, lead us forth out of this land whose people are oppressors, and raise for us, out of your grace, a protector, and raise for us, out of your grace, one who will defend us" (4:75).

> Fight in God's cause those who wage war against you, but do not commit aggression, for truly God does not love aggressors. And slay them wherever you catch them, and turn them out from where they turned you out; for sedition is worse then killing . . . But if they cease, God is Ever-forgiving, Most Merciful (2:190-192).

> And fight them until there is no more persecution, and religion is for God. But if they desist, then let there be no hostility except against the oppressors (2:193).

> There shall be no compulsion in matters of faith; the right way is henceforth distinct from error (2:256).

Others you will find that wish to be secure from you and secure from their own people. Every time they are sent back to temptation, they succumb to it. If they do not let you be, and do not offer you peace, and do not stay their hands, seize them and slay them whenever you come upon them: and it is against these that We have empowered you (4:91)

But if the enemy inclines toward peace, incline you also to it, and trust in God: for He is the One that hears and knows (8:61).

As already stated, 9:5 concerns idolaters who broke their treaty obligations through acts of aggression, as 9:4; 9:7; and 9:13 make plain.

[Fight them] excepting those of the idolaters with whom you have a treaty, and who have not failed you in anything and have not supported anyone against you; so fulfil their treaty to the end of their term (9:4).

How can there be a treaty with God and His Messenger for the idolaters except those with whom you made a treaty at the Sacred Mosque? So long as they are true to you, be true to them. Truly God loves the God-conscious (9:7).

Will you not fight a people who broke their solemn pledges, and purposed to drive out the Messenger and attacked you first? (9:13).

Nonetheless, the exception in 9:5, that states that Muslims should leave alone those idolaters who violate their treaties but then later accept Islam, could be construed to promote forced conversion, at least in this special case. Yet the verse that follows it proves this conclusion is unwarranted. Verse 9:6 states:

And if any of the idolaters seek your protection, then protect him so that he may hear the word of God; and afterward convey him to a place of safety. That is because they are a people who do not know (9:6).

Therefore, if idolaters break their treaties the Muslims should fight them unless: (1) they should become Muslims, or (2) seek the protection of the Muslims, in which case they should be escorted to a place of safety agreeable to them. If it had been the intention of the Qur'an to force these idol worshippers to convert, the second alternative would not have been offered. The first alternative just reiterates in this context a well-established Islamic principle: if an enemy unbeliever accepts Islam then he or she becomes a full-fledged member of the Muslim community with all the associated rights and privileges, and must not be subject to retribution. Hence 9:11 reminds the believers:

But if they repent and establish prayer and pay the poor-due, they are your brethren in faith. And we make the messages clear for a people who know (9:11).

Under normal circumstances a mere profession of faith would provide acceptance in the Muslim community, but since these passages are dealing with those who repeatedly broke their word, a stronger show of commitment is required: the establishment of regular prayer and observance of the poor-due.

11. Allah promises Muslims who die in "jihad" that they will be awarded by going to a paradise were they can have sex with seventy-two houris (beautiful young virgin women with wide eyes), drink wine, and eat good food, and so on. First, would the Muslim have to ditch his wife first and then get the seventy-two houris? I wonder sometimes if there is a place in this paradise for good wives and mothers. Second, the Koran says that wine is the handiwork of the devil. How would Allah serve the handiwork of the devil in his heaven?

On the allegorical nature of the Qur'an's depictions of realities beyond human experience, including Heaven and Hell, I refer the reader to question 3 of chapter 1.[82] To debate allegorical passages seems to me a puerile exercise, but for the sake of accuracy I wish to correct a few points: the Qur'an does not mention the seventy-two houris promised to martyrs—this is mentioned in a *hadith* in the collections of Tirmidhi and Ibn Majah; the Qur'an states that the "wine" in paradise is not intoxicating (37:47; 52:23; 56:19); and it categorically states that righteous women will go to Heaven.

Finally, I should mention that the same kinds of arguments the questioner attempts to make against the Qur'an have been made against the Bible with much greater force and effect by Western scholars. Since the questioner apparently believes in the divine Revelation of his own Scripture, he either does not know of this scholarship, or his criteria for judging the Bible and the Qur'an are different.

Question 3 (part of a lengthy conversation I had with a young immigrant Muslim women who struggles to find peace of mind and spirit in her inherited faith; this struggle is a frequently mentioned frustration of many young Muslim Americans):

I think that in my last e-mail I mentioned to you that the more I study Islam and the more I learn about it, the less I feel connected to God. I am sure that this sounds strange to you since you have come to know God through Islam. But the fact is that the more I go through the do's and don't's of our faith, the further away I feel from God. For example, for about four months or so, I was extremely religious about my prayers: five times a day, on time and all of that stuff. Well, not even once in my prayers did I feel God's presence or any sense of peace. I would pray that He would guide me to the truth and show me His way.

After a while, my prayers started feeling like a burden. I felt like I was doing them because "that is the way it is," or "God commanded us to do

---

82. Also, *Even Angels Ask*, Amana Publications, Beltsville (2000), pp. 9-15.

them." I wanted to get them over with. This just does not feel right to me. Isn't prayer supposed to be our quiet time with God, where we feel a connection rather than resentment and burden and consequently a disconnection and moving away from God? I do not feel that I should be feeling all these negative emotions in my worship to Him. In other words, I felt like a total hypocrite just going through the motions of prayer while resenting the fact that I had to do it.

Then, of course, I started getting angry. I started asking: why does God not want me, why does He not help me, why does He not guide me and help me find the Truth when I try so hard and when I beg for His help? Well, all this anger and resentment ended up in my stopping my prayers (last three to four weeks) and my study of Islam. Plus, I had a couple of conversations with my imam that turned me off. I just feel that every Muslim feels that there is a conspiracy against Islam and all of the Muslims in the world, and that we are always the victims and never the criminals. They also feel that whatever happens to the Muslims, it is really the Jews' fault. I guess I get tired of hearing all of this because we are never willing to admit where we went wrong, we are never willing to admit that we might be wrong.

Well, I really did not want to bore you by going into all of this, but I guess I still have so much energy, anger, and conflict about all of it that it just comes out. So, I ask you, Dr. Lang, why does God not guide some of us when we want to be guided so badly? Why does He not come into our lives when we admit our need for Him and beg Him to come into our hearts?

> God has sent down the most beautiful discourse, a book with repeated allegories, whereat shiver the skins of those who hold their Lord in awe, then their skins and their hearts soften to God's remembrance. That is God's guidance—He guides whom He wishes, and he whom He allows to stray, for him there is no guide. (39:23)

It is very hard to answer a question like this one. It elicits profound feelings of inadequacy and responsibility. How can something so personal, intangible, and mystical be analyzed? The human personality in itself can be mysterious and unfathomable but what about the divine nature and the communion between them? This is not like diagnosing a weight problem and proscribing a diet. God is not subject to our formulations; it is we who are subject to His laws. Also, given the yearning and passion behind the question, almost any response is bound to disappoint, since from the human side the problem is often too deep-rooted to hope for a quick remedy. Spirituality is so enmeshed in individual perceptions of life, self and God, so strongly affected by the traditions and teachings to which we have been exposed and the lives we have led, that a profound reorientation might be necessary. Yet, despite the disclaimer, a plea such as this should not be ignored, even if all we can offer is advice based mostly on experience, because God guides as He chooses, and sometimes He does so through the filter of our limitations.

It is important to try as much as possible to avoid ambiguity in this discussion, for our imagination can set expectations so high that what we long for is rarely if ever attained by anyone. On the other hand, mystical happenings are by definition difficult to define and they vary widely in kind and profundity from one individual to the next. Nevertheless, we must assume that a potential for spirituality is part of human nature and that almost all of us have felt this faculty at least slightly aroused at some time by something. Just as we all have the ability to love other than God, we probably all have the ability to have our spirituality stirred even by non-religious means.

Worshippers who have shared with me their spiritual encounters in prayer differ in their descriptions. As to be expected, their initial depictions seem rooted in their religious backgrounds and educations. All of them report a distinct physical or spiritual sensation but describe it in different words. Some report feeling a kind of encompassing "heaviness" descending over them, others the "descent of angels," some describe being bathed in an invisible "light," some feel a "warmth" radiating from within. Some have feelings of being either "submerged" or "lifted up" by God's "mercy" or "love." Some describe the perception of an intangible "presence." A very common description is of being permeated by a kind of "coolness," and many report shuddering involuntarily and feeling goose bumps. The length of these encounters can be as short as a fraction of a second or as long as an entire prayer (and sometimes beyond that), but most recall moderately short experiences. The intensity of the encounter also varies from mild to very strong. Almost all of those I spoke with state that these experiences are not very frequent. Many say that they are rare. It should also be noted that most of those I interviewed about their prayers reported no such encounters, although many of them are devout. When I asked those who recalled spiritual moments during prayer if they ever had similar episodes outside of worship, many admitted they had on rare occasion somewhat similar experiences, most often when listening to or seeing something particularly moving or beautiful, like an inspirational song, speech or poem, or a breathtaking scene from nature. Most state that the difference between the moments within prayer and those unconnected to worship is that the former often come unexpectedly and with no discernible inspirational stimulus; for example, many report that they were consumed by feelings of shame or repentance when they occurred. From these informal investigations and at the risk of trivializing mystical experiences, I would venture to say that they resemble the moments of numinous awe people in general experience when they are deeply inspired, like when many Americans hear the national anthem beautifully sung or a stirring oration promoting the ideals of universal freedom, brotherhood, and justice; the major differences I can discern—at least from what was conveyed to me—are the spiritual experiences often seem longer and more intense than non-religious moments of inspiration, they happen with greater unpredictability, and most often occur when the worshipper is experiencing profound feelings of humility, remorse, gratitude or love. My personal opinion is that the "spiritual sense" by which we are deeply moved by an emotive song or speech is the same as that by which God communicates His mercy to us in worship, but God knows best.

As mentioned repeatedly in the first chapter, spirituality and growth in goodness go hand in hand. The more we grow in the attributes that emanate from God, the greater becomes our ability to receive and experience His most beautiful names, both in and out of the rituals, and in this life and the next. Worship in Islam is holistic. Self-surrender to God is revealed more by our day-to-day conduct toward others than by our practice of religious rites. This point is made emphatically in *Surah al Ma`un*:

> Have you seen the one who belies religion? That is he who repels the orphan, and does not urge the feeding of the needy. So woe to the praying ones, who are unmindful of their prayer, who would be seen (at worship), yet refuses small kindnesses (107:1-7).

This may also explain why the Qur'an so frequently refers to the obligations of *salat*[83] (prayer) and *zakat*[84] (charity) in tandem,[85] because faith and charitable giving augment each other.

Note too that *salat* and *zakat* are not impromptu supplication and self-sacrifice, both of which are highly valued in Islam, but prescribed and strictly regulated ritual prayer and charity. These are minimal prayer and charitable requirements that should habituate the believer

---

83. The ritual prayer of Islam performed five times daily. It consists of prescribed positions and recitations combined with personal supplications. It is the second pillar of Islam.

84. The annual charity tax in Islam set at 2.5% of one's capital. It is the third pillar of Islam.

85. E.g. 2:43; 2:83; 2:277; 4:162; 5:12; 9:18; 13:22; 19:31; 19:55; 21:73; 22:41; 24:37; 27:3; 31:4; 33:35; 73:20; 98:5.

to both forms of worship, just like regular exercise accustoms an athlete to physical exertion and regular homework habituates a student to learning. Growth in virtue is akin to both of these forms of personal training, for it too takes determination and discipline; it requires pressing on, not just when it feels good or you are inspired to, but even when you are not, or when it is uncomfortable, or when it is certain not to be appreciated by anyone other than God. Moreover, with regular practice of Islam's rituals the desire to serve God usually grows, prompting the worshipper to go beyond what is required, the same way athletes and students typically develop the need to continually "raise the bar" of their performance.

However, it is important to recognize that God does not require perfection before divine intimacy can be experienced.[86] Indeed, the Qur'an states that none of us should claim to be pure (53:32) and it repeatedly shows that even the prophets, God's elect, had weaknesses and failings. Yet one quality in particular softens the heart to reception of divine light and its opposite hardens it. "Successful are the believers, who are humble in their prayers," states the Qur'an (23:1-2). Although it bucks the current trend in American culture, humility is the appropriate bearing of the Muslim;[87] this is because it acknowledges our true standing before God, and truth is crucial to real intimacy in any relationship, but especially in our relationship with God, the source of truth.

I have heard of Muslim converts who turned their lives totally around and abandoned virtually all of their former vices from the day they made their first *shahadah*. Unfortunately, my example was not so inspiring. Mine has been at times a long and difficult struggle toward personal reform. In that critical period following conversion I fought hard against some long-standing bad habits, and suffered my share of setbacks, so that my five daily prayers were filled with tears, remorse,

---

86. Cf. chapter one, pages 112-118.

87. Cf. 2:45; 4:36; 5:54; 6:42-43; 11:23; 17:37; 22:34-35; 22:54; 23:2; 23:76; 31:18; 33:35; 57:16; 57:23.

and pleas for help. I knew with every ounce of my being the reality of my weakness and complete dependence on the mercy of God. Yet it was in this state of acute consciousness of my utter lowliness that I experienced some of my most moving prayers. I don't know why God graced me with those intense spiritual moments back then, but I do know that I prayed with the most genuine humility and contrition, and although my Qur'an recitation was short and clumsy, I spent a long time in *salat* pouring out my heart in repentance.

There have also been lengthy intervals in which I felt no such divine closeness. The first time this happened I fell into a state of prolonged dismay. Why has God withdrawn Himself from me? I thought. I pleaded with Him to let me feel His merciful embrace once again, to let me know the assurance and beauty that used to come so freely. But despite my persistent beseeching my prayers remained non-descript.

Although I endured a period of despondency, I ultimately found solace in a number of considerations. The first was God's assurance in the Qur'an that He is always near, and that He hears and responds to our supplications, even though we are most often oblivious of it.

> And when My servants ask of Me, I am truly near. I heed the call of every caller when he calls on Me. Let them also, with a will, listen to My call and believe in Me, that they may walk in the right way. (2:186)

Another was that while I was not experiencing the intensity I had come to anticipate in my prayers, I was still gaining very much from them. Just the discipline of five daily prayers at appointed times became a source of strength during a period when I was under enormous pressure because of my choice to convert. The prayers also became a spiritual retreat, an opportunity to remove myself for a few minutes from the chaos and stress of temporal pursuits to reorient and remind myself of life's real purpose.

Then there was the verse in the *Surah al Kahf* that tells the

Prophet that the Revelations don't come to him when he wants, but when God decides.

> And say not about anything, truly I will do that tomorrow,[88] [but say] unless God wishes. And remember your Lord when you forget, and say: Perhaps my Lord will guide me unto a nearer way of truth than this (18:23-24).

One of the things I got from this is that while God's Revelations and our prayers are certainly for our benefit, we should remember that one of their basic aims is to inculcate self-surrender to Him and that He is not at our service but we are at His. This changed my outlook on *salat*. I realized that to think of it mainly as a means of obtaining divine assurance and mystical experiences is to conceive of God as serving me and thus undermines their principal function.

Finally, there is the Prophet's well-known break in Revelation, where after his first Revelation—consisting of the first five verses of *Surah al Alaq*—a period elapsed when he received no Revelation at all. The length in the break cannot be established with certainty but estimates put it between six months and three years. It was a time of deepest distress for the Prophet. I often reflected on why God imposed this interruption in Revelation, especially since it caused the Prophet so much anxiety and self-doubt. I found almost no commentary on this, either in the *Hadith*, *sirah*, or *tafsir* literature. Nevertheless, I felt that if God in His wisdom allowed His Messenger to suffer a long and anxious period of perceived separation, then who am I to fret over periods when my prayers were unremarkable. Of course, I would examine myself to try to determine if I had lost focus in my prayers, or had been doing something wrong recently, or had taken steps backwards in faith, and sometimes I felt this was the case and I then tried to correct myself, but I think sometimes God simply

---

88. It is said that the Prophet told his detractors that he would receive a Revelation about one of their questions the next day.

chose to let me be for a while. So I resolved to just continue to grate-
fully perform the Islamic rituals and to work on self-improvement, to
derive the many divine benefits that come from doing so, and to leave
the matter of spiritual encounters in God's hands, where it entirely
belongs anyway. I thought that even if I never had another one
throughout the rest of my life, I would be forever thankful for those I
already had and for everything else God has given me.

And then it was not long before I began to feel God's merciful
embrace again, sometimes in prayer, sometimes in contemplation,
and even sometimes when in the company of others. Even so, my
most intense experiences still belonged to that early stage after conversion. I know it is foolish to try to explain this, but I truly believe
that I would not have made it through that difficult period without
them. Despite my absolute conviction in the Revelation of the Qur'an
and prophethood of Muhammad, I probably would have given up on
faith if it were not for the divine support. It was not that I doubted
Islam, but rather I doubted myself. I did not believe that I could overcome the wrongdoing to which I had become so accustomed, and
many times I felt like fleeing the community instead of remaining a
hypocrite within it, but these moments of divine mercy inspired
me to persevere. In other words, I feel that those moments of divine
tenderness had more to do with God's mercy and my utter weakness
than anything else. I write this because I do not want readers, like the
young lady above, to despair if they do not have spiritual moments in
their prayers. It does not mean that they have lost favor with God.
I know of many devout Muslims who have rarely, or even never,
had such experiences, but have come to know tremendous happiness
and inner peace—a state of inner well-being that grew gradually and
to them indiscernibly through the years—through steadfast commitment to Islam. This said, I will attempt to give somewhat practical
advice to young American Muslims who are disillusioned with their
prayers.

My oldest daughter—she is now seventeen—began complaining

several years back that her experience of prayer was extremely dry and meaningless. She finally stopped praying altogether and despite our urging she would not return to them. After she and I discussed the issue at length I made a few suggestions.

She told me that she had no idea what she was reciting in Arabic, that she felt like a mindless parrot, and that this made the ritual for her completely sterile. I suggested that she try saying the entire prayer in English, including the Qur'an recitation, for a while, and see if she notices a difference. I also told her that in the meantime she should try to learn the meaning of the Arabic recitations, preferably word for word, and that my wife and I would help her with this, so that she might incorporate them back into her prayers with real understanding. I shared with her that in the prayers I perform alone, I often follow my Arabic recitations with my own English translations, and that she might try this someday as well.

She also stated that she found it impossible to stick to the discipline of five prayers daily, that she didn't have the willpower. I mentioned that performing five prayers every day might be too much for her to start with, like the fellow who decides he will get in shape by running ten miles every day and then gives up after the first run because he becomes so badly winded. I suggested that she begin with a more comfortable regimen, such as pray the evening prayer each day or perhaps the afternoon and evening. I recommended that she try to become regular in this, then gradually increase the level when she feels ready.

I mentioned to her that sometimes people are blocked by guilt in their worship, either about things they did in the past and can't forget or things they currently are doing and can't overcome. I said that in this case they should tell God about them in their prayers, and ask Him for His help and forgiveness, and, most importantly, trust that He will help them if they are sincere.

I advised her to make the most of *salat* by using it as an opportunity to express herself to God; to tell Him her fears, hopes, and problems; to ask Him for help and guidance; to pray from her heart. I suggested that this might be why the prayers became monotonous and meaningless to her, because we tend to make them that way by being too formulaic. I advise all my children to speak to God from the heart, even if only a few words, in every prayer.

I also discovered that she had a paralyzing fear of God that she somehow picked up from the Muslim community while she was growing up, and which helped to turn her prayers into an unpleasant standing before what she saw as a terrifying deity. I told her that I thought she needed to reorient her thinking about God; that it might help to remind herself of the many verses of the Qur'an and sayings of the Prophet that emphasize God's forgiveness and compassion, and His not demanding perfection from us. I reminded her that the Qur'an was revealed to a people the majority of whom made war against truth, and so it warns and threatens them, but it also continually reassures those who believe in God and who strive to serve Him. I also said that we all have failings and that she is a good person, and that God says in the Qur'an that only the wicked will suffer in the Hereafter.

Of course, I realize that the advice I gave my daughter is not going to be a cure-all for young people who are not performing their prayers, and I don't offer it as one. I hope that it might encourage others to think creatively on ways to address similar problems. As for my daughter, I left her to herself for a while. I resisted the urge to monitor her progress, because I felt it important that she return to her prayers on her own initiative, for the sake of her relationship with God instead of her relationship with me. About a month later I found her praying one evening when I went to kiss her goodnight. I asked my wife about it and she told me that she had been praying pretty regularly lately. After another month my wife told me that she was now praying all five prayers. A few weeks passed and then I asked her while we were sitting alone one evening if she was getting anything out of her prayers lately and she assured me she was. I do not think my advice played a major part in her return to the prayers—my intuition tells me that this was something very personal between God and her—but as always, God knows best.

Question 4 (from a young man in his mid-thirties and pertaining to verse 34 of *Surah al Nisa'* about wife-beating. Most of those who contact me to discuss religion are second generation American Muslims and converts to Islam, but I also receive a fair amount of mail from American non-Muslims interested in Islam. The biggest issue for the latter, regardless of gender, is the position of women in the Muslim community. The subject of wife beating very frequently comes up. This topic is also one of the most hotly contended these days on the Internet.):

I have been thinking about converting to Islam, but I can't seem to get past some issues. Most of my problems pertain to the treatment of women. At the top of the list is Qur'an 4:34, which instructs husbands to beat their disobedient wives. I'm sorry, but beating your wife for not abiding by your commands—no matter how reasonable they may be—is just flat out wrong. I'm interested to know your take on this?

Question 5 (also about wife-beating and from a convert to Islam in his late twenties):

I was searching the Internet the other day for information on the position of women in Islam. The non-Muslim sites, which quote heavily from Muslim sources, present an appalling picture—so do some of the more conservative Muslim sites. I've noticed that most of the Muslim web pages that defend the status of women in Islam do not discuss the most embarrassing <u>hadiths</u> quoted on Christian sites. I have also come across several Muslim sites that state that "daraba" in 4:34 does not mean "beat" as traditionally understood, but has other more innocuous meanings, such as "separate" or even "make love"! My first reaction was, "What a relief!"

I had always felt the popular defense that says in this verse "daraba" really means, "pat" or "tap with a toothbrush" or "swat with a napkin," is just a whitewash. Although I was at first excited about the possibility that "daraba" may not mean "beat," I then thought maybe this is just another desperate attempt to grab onto anything that might get Islam off the hook. I mean can Muslims have gotten it wrong all these centuries? Rather than ramble on, let me ask a simple question: Do you think there is any merit to this linguistic argument?

> Men are the providers of women with what God has favored some of you over others[89] and with what they expend of their wealth. Thus virtuous women are obedient (*qanitat*), guarding in secret (*lil ghayb*) what God has guarded. And those (women) from whom you fear their antipathy (*nushuz*), exhort them,[90] leave them alone in bed, and beat them (*udribu-hunna*). Then if they give in, then do not seek a way against them. Truly God is ever most high, great. And if you fear a break up between them, then appoint an arbiter from his people and an arbiter from her people; if they both desire making up,[91] God will reconcile them. Truly God is ever exalted, great (4:34-35).

89. The two preceding verses make it clear that inheritance distribution (women generally receive half the share of inheritance prescribed for men (4:11)) is mainly referred to here. They read:

"And do not covet what God *has favored some of you over others.* For men is a share from what they earned and to women a share from what they earned. And ask God of His benevolence, truly God is ever aware of all things. And to every one we have appointed heirs of that which parents and near relatives leave. And as to those whom you pledged your right hand (support?), give them their due. Truly God is ever witness over all things" (4:32-33).

90. The verb *wa`azu* means "to preach," "to appeal to someone's conscience," "to admonish," and "to exhort."

91. I translated *islah* here as "making up." It has many nuances that convey the general idea of "restoration."

Of the Islamic legal issues I have thought about, this one—and I have deliberated on it so often since becoming a Muslim—has been for me the most difficult. Every time I reflect on it, I remember my mother and all she had to endure all those years from my father. I also know how deeply a man's maltreatment of his spouse can scar his children. To tell the truth, I must have missed this verse the first time I read the Qur'an, or maybe the interpreter chose a more obscure phrasing, because I think if I had read the above translation I might have given up on the Scripture then and there. But then again, perhaps not, because 4:34 occurs near the beginning of the text and at that point in my reading I was only concerned with what the Qur'an says about the meaning of life, so I may have just passed over it, since it is not directly related to this issue. After I became convinced of God's existence and the Revelation of the Qur'an, puzzlement with a single verse was not going to shake my conviction, but I nevertheless felt the need to come to terms with it. The reader will have to forgive me if below I appear to be bending over backwards to reconcile this verse with contemporary Western sensibilities. I am sure that many of them grew up in loving, harmonious homes, and by no means would see 4:34 as a blank check for men to strike their wives; most of these will be content to cite the ancient and modern Muslim scholars who maintain that this permit is essentially symbolic. I, however, am haunted by the spectre of a short-tempered, angry brute, who rejects or is unacquainted with this particular opinion, and who takes full advantage of what he sees as his God given right to control his wife through violence. I know what I write here will hardly affect such an attitude, but I do so in empathy with those who have been hounded by the same nightmare.

I will look at this passage from different angles. First, I focus specifically on the translation and some key words in the passage and their possible meanings, leaving aside for the moment external evidence from the *Hadith* literature and scholarly commentary. Then I consider some of the most commonly cited traditions of the Prophet that speak to this topic. Finally, I mention how Muslim jurists have understood 4:34.

I have tried to be as literal as possible in the above translation of 4:34-35. Interpreting the passage is fairly straightforward, but the four transliterated Arabic phrases pose difficulties. The description of virtuous women as "obedient" (*qanitat*) could mean "obedient to God," as made clear by comparison with 33:31, 33:35, and 66:5, or equally, "obedient to their husbands." The former seems preferable since *qanitat* is used to described here "virtuous (or pious) women" (*salihat*) and hence appears to signify a religious quality.

Al ghayb means "absence," "that which is absent," "that which is concealed," "the unseen," "the imperceptible," or "the secret." Most interpreters prefer "guarding in secret" or the near equivalent "guarding the unseen" to "guarding in absence." The last accords with a famous *hadith*,[92] which we'll come to shortly. Either of the first two interpretations is consonant with the overall tenor of 4:34, which attempts to cope with marital discord in private before finally resorting to outside arbitration as described in 4:35.

The lexicons do not have much to say on the noun *nushuz*. Generally it connotes "animosity," "belligerence," "hostility," "antipathy," or "dissonance." Dictionaries also commonly offer the interpretation, "disobedience of a wife toward her husband," when applied to a married woman, and, "brutality of a husband toward his wife," when describing a married man. These latter two marital and gender specific definitions are apparently not pre-Islamic but reflect the influence of Muslim jurisprudence. Later in the same *surah* (4:128) the Qur'an discusses what a woman should do if she fears *nushuz* from her husband, and again we may assume that to the Qur'an's first hearers this had the more general sense of "animosity," "hostility," etcetera.

The verb *daraba*, whose command form *udribu* appears in this verse, is rich in meaning. Lane's discussion of it spans several folios in

---

92. Cf. traditions 2 and 9 below.

his famous lexicon. Among the scores of connotations listed are "to beat," "to strike," "to hit," "to shoot," "to make music," "to separate," "to part," "to impose," "to turn away from," "to leave," "to avoid," "to shun," "to sting," "to disregard," "to ignore," and "to pay no attention to.". Nevertheless, narrowing its meaning in a given instance is not as difficult as it may first seem, because in Arabic verbs acquire various connotations only in combination with specific prepositions. For instance, *daraba* acquires the meaning of "to separate" in combination with *baina*, and the meanings of "to turn away from," "to leave," "to avoid," and "to shun" in combination with *'an*. In the passage in question, *daraba* is not combined with either of these prepositions. Yet Lane points out that the command form of the verb, *udribu*, with or without *'an*, can mean "ignore," "pay no attention to," or "turn away from," as well as "hit," "beat," or "strike."[93] Hence, *udribu-hunna*, could mean, "beat them" or "strike them," or alternatively, "turn them away," "ignore them," or "shun them."

Exegetes have always maintained that 4:34 presents a prioritized series of steps, not to be taken simultaneously. The increasing severity of the successive actions supports this view. Hence, from the above analysis we obtain two possible procedures, depending on the meaning we assign to *udribu*, to be followed by a husband who is fearful of his wife's growing aversion toward him. If we interpret *udribu* to mean "beat," then he should first admonish her. If this yields no positive effect, the husband should then sleep apart from his wife for a while. If this proves unsuccessful, he should beat her, although Muslim scholars insist that the beating should be light. If she remains hateful of him, and he still has hopes of saving the marriage, then 4:35 recommends bringing in family representatives from both sides to help effect reconciliation. This is, of course, a last resort, because when family is brought into a marriage conflict, bitterness toward their

---

93. Edward Lane, *Arabic-English Lexicon*, Fredrick Unger Publishing (1956), page 1779, first column, two-thirds down the page.

respective son or daughter in-law is likely to persist even if their children iron out their differences, which could contribute to further marital discord later on.

If instead of assuming that *udribu* means "beat," we understand it to mean, "turn away from," then everything we said in the previous paragraph applies, accept with regard to the third step. From this perspective, if a husband is troubled by his wife's belligerency toward him, and if exhortation followed by temporary cessation of sexual relations does not instigate reconciliation, then the husband might try completely ignoring his wife for a while. If after this their marriage remains in trouble, family representatives should be brought in. From a purely rational standpoint this alternative interpretation seems preferable to the traditional one, for with regard to the latter it is hard to see how inflicting physical punishment on the wife would lesson her resentment of her husband. If anything, one would think that beating her would accomplish just the opposite. On the other hand, appealing to his wife's conscience, followed by cessation of sexual relations, followed by the silent treatment are progressive nonviolent steps that might salvage the marriage if the wife still has deep-seated affection for her husband. This interpretation of *udribu* also fits with the non-violent character of all the other recommendations, including the fourth step of bringing in family conciliators.

Before turning to the *Hadith* literature for further elucidation, we round out our examination of marital *nushuz* in the Qur'an by briefly considering 4:128.

> And if a woman fears antipathy (*nushuz*) from her husband or desertion (*i`rad*), then there is no blame on them if they settle things peacefully between themselves, for peace is best, but selfishness is ever-present in the soul. And if you do good and are God-conscious, then truly God is ever aware of what you do. (4:128)

And if they separate, God provides for everyone from His abundance. And God is ever unstinting, wise. (4:130)

Note the absence of a series of explicit steps like those in 4:34-35. After mentioning that it is certainly not wrong for a woman in this situation to try to resolve the problem with her spouse peacefully and privately, the Qur'an next discusses separation of the couple. The cautionary phrase, "there is no blame on them," suggests that the wife should exercise due caution in trying to solve this problem privately, because a belligerent husband when confronted presents obvious risks. For this reason the Scripture then moves immediately to separation. Hence if the husband is displaying real enmity toward his wife, she may first try to work things out peacefully, but her interest might be better served by a formal separation, especially if he becomes more antagonistic toward her, or has already, in effect, deserted her. At this point she could seek the help of her family and others to either effect reconciliation, or, if necessary, divorce.

Thus far we have seen that linguistically two interpretations of 4:34-35 are possible; one results in a procedure that includes the possibility of wife beating and the other steers clear of physical violence. All things being equal, I believe that many modern Muslims would prefer the second interpretation, but the case for it diminishes when we factor in the *hadiths* that treat this subject.

The *Hadith* literature contains a fair number of traditions that discuss wife beating. The following (numbered for later reference) are from the most respected compilations.

(1) Narrated Abdullah bin Zama: The Prophet forbade laughing at a person who passes wind, and said, "How does anyone of you beat his wife as he beats his stallion camel and then he embraces (i.e. sleeps with) her?" (al Bukhari).[94]

---

94. Some writers state that a version of this *hadith* appears in *Sahih Muslim*, but I could not find it there.

(2) Jabir ibn Abdullah narrated that on the occasion of the Prophet's Farewell Pilgrimage, the Messenger of God said: Fear God concerning women. Verily you have taken them as a trust of God and intercourse with them has been made lawful to you by God's words. You too have a right over them, that they should not allow anyone onto your bed whom you do not like. And if they do that, then you can beat them but not severely. Their right upon you is that you provide for them food and clothing in a fitting manner (Muslim). [95]

(3) Laqit ibn Sabirah narrated that he said to the Messenger of God: "I have a wife who has something in her tongue (i.e. is insolent). He (the Prophet) said, "Then divorce her." I said, "Messenger of God, she had company with me and I have children from her." He (the Prophet) said, "Then request her (to stop). If there is some good in her, she will do so; and do not beat your wife as you beat your slave-girl" (Abu Dawud).

(4) Narrated Mu`awiyah ibn Haydan: I said, "Messenger of God, how should we approach our wives and how should we leave them?" He replied: "Approach your tilth when and how you will, give her food when you take food, clothe her when you clothe yourself, do not revile her face, and do not beat her" (Abu Dawud).

(5) Narrated Mu`awiyyah al Qushayri: I went to the Messenger of God and asked him: "What do you say about our wives." He replied, "Give them food from what you have for yourself, and clothe them by which you clothe yourself, and do not beat them, and do not revile them" (Abu Dawud).

(6) Narrated Mu`awiyyah al Qushayri: Mu`awiyyah asked, "Messenger of God, what is the right of the wife of one of us over him?" He replied, "That you should give her food when you eat, clothe her when you clothe yourself, do not strike her on the face, do not revile her or separate yourself from her except in the house" (Abu Dawud & Ibn Majah).

---

95. This is part of a much longer narration in *Sahih Muslim*.

(7) Narrated Abdullah ibn Abu Dhubab: Iyas ibn Abdullah ibn Abu Dhubab reported that the Messenger of God said: "Do not beat God's female servants." Then 'Umar came to the Messenger of God and said that the women have become emboldened toward their husbands. So the Prophet gave permission to beat them. Then many women came pouring in to see the family of the Prophet to complain about their husbands. So the Messenger of God said: "Many women have poured in to see Muhammad's family complaining against their husbands. They (masculine plural) are not the best among you" (Abu Dawud).

(8) Narrated Umar ibn al Khattab: The Prophet said: "A man is not to be asked as to why he beat his wife" (Abu Dawud, al Nisa'i, Ibn Majah).

(9) Narrated Amr ibn al Ahwas al Jushami: Amr heard the Prophet say in his farewell address on the eve of his last pilgrimage, after he had glorified and praised God, he cautioned his followers: "Listen! Treat women kindly; they are like prisoners in your hands. Beyond this you do not owe anything to them. Should they be guilty of flagrant misbehavior, you may remove them from your beds and beat them, but do not inflict upon them any severe punishment. Then if they obey you, do not have recourse to anything else against them. Listen! You have rights upon your wives and they have their rights upon you. Your right is that they shall not allow anyone you dislike to trample your bed and that they do not permit those you dislike to enter your home. Their right is that you should treat them well in the matter of food and clothing (al Tirmidhi).

In a search for traditions of the Prophet that deal with wife beating the first thing we notice is their scarcity in the earlier and most respected extant collections. The *Muwatta* of Imam Malik (died 177 A.H./793 C.E.), the earliest compilation to have come down to us, contains no direct sayings of the Prophet of this kind. The *Sahih* of al Bukhari (died 256 A.H./869 C.E.) contains only one such *hadith*, which strongly disapproves of wife beating (tradition 1 above). The *Sahih* of Muslim (died 261 A.H./874 C.E.) contains one saying of the Prophet (tradition 2 above) that treats this topic. In contrast, when we come to the *Sunan* of Abu Dawud (died 275 A.H./888 C.E.), we find six traditions that address the issue of wife beating (traditions 3 through 8 above). In tradition 3 the Prophet forbids a Companion to beat his hostile wife. *Hadiths* 4-6 are slightly different versions of a single saying and probably come from the same authority, there being an apparent uncertainty as to which Mu`awiyyah (al Qushayri or ibn Haydan)[96] actually transmitted it. Taken together these three versions prohibit beating and reviling a wife. In tradition 7 the Prophet first prohibits beating one's wife, then allows it, and then censures those who do it ("They are not the best among you"). Tradition 8 seems to give husbands a free hand in this matter. Tradition 9, which appears in al Tirmidhi's collection, is a variant of tradition 2. It concisely states what came to be the agreed upon legal position. Most classical works that discuss wife beating stipulate that it must not be severe and that it is only allowed in cases of flagrant misbehavior, such as stipulated in this saying and tradition 2.

Not counting variants, the above reports are evenly divided on the issue of wife beating; three disapprove of it and three allow it, although one of the latter (tradition 7) is in the end critical of those who beat their wives (too severely?) and another (traditions 2 and 9) limits the severity of the chastisement and specifies when it is justified. Many of the ancient scholars had an obvious explanation for the disparity: the Prophet originally forbade wife beating, but with the revelation of 34:4 he revised his position. There is even a *hadith* that attests to this:

---

96. Unless of course the two are in fact one and the same and Mu`awiyyah ibn Haydan is from the Qushayri tribe. Ibn Haydan appears as the authority of some forty-two traditions.

A woman complained to the Prophet that her husband slapped her on the face, which was still marked by the slap. At first the Prophet said to her: "Get even with him," but then added: "Wait until I think about it." Later on 4:34 was revealed, after which the Prophet said: "We wanted one thing but God wanted another, and what God wanted is best."[97]

Although this *hadith* provides a neat explanation, Muslim scholars suspect it. Firstly, it is narrated only on the authority of al Hasan al Basri and it is *mursal*.[98] Secondly, it implies that before the revelation of 4:34, the Prophet's exhortations on this matter reflect his personal opinion, which contradicts what came to be the widely held doctrine that all of his *Sunnah* was divinely inspired.

It does not take much ingenuity to reconcile traditions 1-9, the dogma of divine inspiration of the entire prophetic *Sunnah*, and the timing of the revelation of 4:34. The simplest solution is to assume that the Prophet originally forbade wife beating, then later on abrogated this prohibition (tradition 7), all under divine inspiration, and then sometime still later 4:34 was revealed. From this perspective, if we take *udribu* to mean "beat," then 4:34 was always in tune with the current divinely inspired *sunnah*, since it was revealed sometime after the *sunnah* prohibiting wife-beating had been repealed by the *sunnah* permitting it. This was the position taken by Imam al Shafi`i, who cited tradition 7 for evidence.[99]

---

97. Razi, *Al Tafsir al Kabir*, on 4:34.

98. *Mursal* (incomplete) means it is reported from the Prophet by a Successor but does not identify the Companion informant.

99. Razi, *Al Tafsir al Kabir*, on 4:34. Also, on the basis of this tradition, al Shafi`i concluded that hitting one's wife is permissible, but not hitting her is preferable. It seems that traditions 2 and 9 were either unknown to al Shafi`i or else he lacked confidence in them, because he did not cite either one in support of this opinion.

The above traditions come from collections that are highly esteemed in Sunni[100] Islam. The *Sahihs* of al Bukhari and Muslim are the two most respected *Hadith* sources and most Muslims accept without question that the traditions in them are fully accurate. The *Sunans* of Abu Dawud and al Tirmidhi are widely regarded as the third and fourth most authoritative *hadith* compilations, respectively, although they are well known to contain some questionable reports. All the same, I have not been able to find negative comments on any of these traditions on *isnad*-analytic grounds, although that is not to assert that such criticism has not been made; it only means I have been unable to find it.

The *Hadith* scholars normally limited their critique of traditions only to their *isnads*, but an examination of their *matns* (texts) might also provide clues to their authenticity. I believe it could be accepted as a general principle that the more the moral dictates of a *hadith* are ahead of its time, the greater the likelihood they reflect genuine teachings of the Prophet. For if a precept flies in the face of the cultures that produced the first few generations of Muslims, then it is hard to imagine how it could have gained wide acceptance, unless it really did originate with the Prophet. Hence on these grounds alone, we can be confident that the above traditions forbidding wife beating are based on authentic Prophetic instruction. It has to be remembered that women had a lowly rank in the civilizations that came under Muslim rule in the first two Islamic centuries. A wife's position vis-à-vis her husband was similar to that of his children, and quite frequently she was just beyond puberty when she married. From this historical perspective, a woman, emotionally and intellectually, was hardly more than a child, her contribution to society limited to bearing and raising offspring and satisfying men's sexual needs. In this milieu, where a wife was essentially the ward of her husband, it would indeed seem outlandish to forbid men to physically discipline their wives.[101]

---

100. About 85% of the worldwide Muslim population follows Sunni Islam.
101. Gamal A. Badawi, *The Status of Women In Islam*, MSA of US & Canada (1976), pp. 5-10.

Even in pre-Islamic Arabia, where women had more freedom and suffered fewer restrictions than they did in the surrounding more advanced cultures, they were held in very low regard. The Arab patriarchy saw the woman as an inherently irrational, frivolous being, preoccupied with self-beautification and the acquisition of baubles. The Qur'an provides the following disturbing illustrations of this attitude.

> Or has He taken daughters to Himself of what He creates and chosen you to have sons? And when one of them is given news of that of which he sets up a likeness to the Merciful, his face becomes black and full of rage: "What! [Am I to have] one decked with ornaments and unable to make plain speech in disputes?" (43:16-18)

> And they ascribe daughters unto God. Glory be to Him! And for them is what they desire! And when the birth of a daughter is announced to one of them, his face becomes black and he is full of rage, avoiding people because of the evil of the glad tiding he has received. [And he deliberates:] Shall he keep it with contempt or bury it in the dust? Oh, evil is what they decide. (16:57)

Here we are presented two extreme and reciprocal symptoms of a pathological contempt for women: the adoration of an imaginary and unattainable object of male desire, and simultaneous suffocation and devaluation of real womanhood.

The misogyny of the times was also reflected in the very real ways women were treated as male property. Tribes would raid each other to expropriate women as booty. Slave owners forced their slave-girls into prostitution (24:33). A man could acquire an unlimited numbers of wives and concubines. Men harassed and propositioned women in the streets.[102] Apparently, women also viewed themselves in this way, for the many Quranic commands against immodest dress,[103] lewd and

102. *Surahs* 33:59, 24:60.
103. *Surahs* 24:31; 24:58-60; 33:58-60.

lascivious public behavior,[104] and adultery[105] indicate that very many women saw themselves as little more than objects of male sexuality. This objectification of the feminine is starkly exposed in the custom of *zihar*, by which a man divorces his wife while not allowing her to leave his house and marry elsewhere. By merely saying "You are as my mothers back," a husband was able to permanently desert his wife while at the same time confine her to his home. In this way he was able to keep possession of "his women" for whom he had no further use. The practice was apparently so entrenched that the Qur'an had to condemn it twice.

> Those of you who put away their wives by calling them their mothers—they are not your mothers. None are their mothers save those who gave them birth, and they utter indeed a hateful word and a lie. (58:2)

> God has not made for any man two hearts within him, nor has He made your wives whom you desert by *zihar* your mothers…(33:4)

More evidence of ancient Arabia's misogyny could be obtained from the historical sources, but this may be overkill, for a culture that condones the above practices clearly has low regard for women. This brings us back to our earlier assertion that the proscription against wife beating was much at odds with the cultures that came under early Islamic rule, and hence, based on the above principle, increases our conviction that it originated with the Prophet.

But can we not invoke the same principle in support of tradition 7 that censures wife beaters and traditions 2 and 9 that permit only mild wife beating? Would not these be out of synch with the times? Perhaps, but is not the sight of a severely beaten wife always offensive,

---

104. *Surahs* 4:15-16; 24:31.

105. *Surahs* 17:32; 24:2-4; 24:13; 25:68; 60:12.

even to the most woman-denigrating males? A ban on wife thrashing could be accepted as prevention against cruelty but a ban on all physical punishment could be seen as an attack on male authority. The argument here is also less compelling since these traditions seem to back off from a more progressive policy.

It could be true, as tradition 7 explains, that the prohibition of wife beating proved too liberal in seventh century Arabia. If this is really the case, then the modification of the ban might be interpreted as a concession to the primitiveness of the times and the original proscription could then be seen as the ideal to be imposed when conditions permit. Others, however, would insist that, for whatever reason, the Prophet's last word on this subject abrogates his earlier pronouncements. A more skeptical approach might see in these traditions a post-Prophetic accommodation to an unshakable patriarchy that was projected back to the Prophet. A lot depends on the trust given to these remaining traditions. As already mentioned, they are generally considered authentic, but once more we can examine their texts (*matns*) for anything that might stand out.

Until now we have said little about tradition 8, the most difficult for opponents of patriarchalism. This *hadith* is one of the most cited on anti-Islam websites and receives virtually no mention by Muslim writers on the status of women in Islam. It may be that the tradition is not widely accepted but I have found no such assertion. Of all the traditions mentioned above this one can be properly considered an outlier, that is, one whose message diverges markedly from the others. All of the other traditions prohibit, curb or frown on wife beating, but tradition 8, if taken at face value, appears to give the husband a free hand. Due to the exceptional nature of this *hadith* and in consideration of the Qur'an's several exhortations concerned with just and kind treatment of women, I doubt that it represents an authentic teaching of the Prophet.

Traditions 2 and 9 relate the Prophet's admonitions concerning the treatment of women on the occasion of his last pilgrimage. If genuine, then reading *udribu* in 4:34 as "to turn away from" is not tenable. In these accounts the Prophet is undoubtedly commenting on 4:34, and the statement, "and if they do that, you can beat them but not severely," confirms that the command form of *daraba* in this verse means, "beat." But there is reason to question the accuracy of these two reports, in spite of their near universal acceptance. In them the Prophet explicitly states that if a wife invites other men to her spouse's bed, the husband may apply 4:34, with the proviso that any beating must not be severe. Now I assume that, "allow onto your bed," implies having sexual relations of some sort. If this is the case, then we obtain a formula for dealing with a promiscuous wife that is exceedingly lenient, even by today's standards: first admonish her; if she persists, then sleep apart from her for a while; if she still persists, then lightly chastise her; if she finally quits the illicit behavior, then take no further action, otherwise he should seek family arbitration. I suppose that by the above principle we should be doubly inclined to believe that this way of handling a wife's infidelity is Prophetic, accept that it also seems out of synch with the Qur'an; for the Scripture treats adultery as a major sin and prescribes very strict measures to combat it. Thus, all things considered, I doubt the accuracy of these two accounts.

This takes us finally to tradition 7. It appears in al Shafi'i's *Musnad* and in the collections of Abu Da'ud, al Nasa'i, Ibn Majah, al Tabarani, and al Hakim. Al Nawawi grades it *sahih* (authentic) in his *Riyad al Salihin*, as does al Suyuti in his *al Jami' al Saghir*. Its narrator, 'Umar ibn al Khattab, is once again the proponent of stern treatment of women. While his reputation for severity is probably rooted in truth, the great frequency with which 'Umar assumes this role in the *Hadith* literature makes one wonder if he did not become a convenient personage to ascribe harsh views on women. This, however, is not evidence for or against the tradition under discussion. One might question that the Prophet would rebuke men for wife beating just after giving them permission to do it, but he could have been objecting to the cruelty with which some of them did it. On a doctrinal level, several *hadiths* have 'Umar and other highly respected Companions beating their wives, while this tradition appears to exclude them from the community's elite, but again the severity of the chastisement could be at issue here. In sum, the text of tradition 7 contains nothing substantial to cause suspicion.

This examination of the *matns* of these traditions is rather limited, but even a more thoroughgoing critique would probably not produce conclusive results. Undoubtedly, the great majority of believers would still insist on their authenticity regardless of the soundness of the findings. This does not mean that Muslims living in the West must feel at variance with the larger society's condemnation of spouse abuse. Every text on Islamic Law, ancient and modern, states that it is unlawful for a husband to severely beat his wife. Most jurists assert that a man is allowed to chastise his spouse only in cases of flagrant indecency and that even here it is preferable to avoid it. Scholars stipulate that it is not permissible to strike the face, cause any bodily harm, to be harsh or leave any marks. It is not at all a whitewash to state that Islamic scholars oppose any act that would qualify as spouse abuse in contemporary Western law. Of course, on the ideological level, modern feminists will reject the notion that a husband has the right to beat his wife, however lightly, for although it might be only a "symbolic" act, as some modern Muslim writers assert, it is still a symbol of male domination of women.

As for myself, I incline more toward the "turn away from them" over the "beat them" interpretation of *udribu-hunna*. It fits well with the anti-violent nature of the other recommendations of 4:34. Moreover, all but one of the *hadiths* that support the standard interpretation contain statements that seem at odds with the Qur'an. Even the report where the Prophet first prohibits wife beating, then allows it, and then censures some of those that take advantage of the permission seems to me a bit contrived. I concede that centuries of consensus on the meaning of *udrib* in 4:34 argues forcefully against me, but the traditions that categorically forbid striking one's wife could be vestiges of ancient difference of opinion on this topic.

Comment 1 (from an American Muslim high school senior. The doubt and confusion expressed, especially that arising from conflicts between the "magical" side of his parents' beliefs and the critical reasoning stressed in school, is common in this generation.):

If you recall, I had emailed you earlier about problems I was having with my faith. Let me explain myself further.

My parents are conservative, but liberal at the same time. By this I mean they are very much into traditional values, but also a little more lenient than other Muslim parents. So as I grew up, I felt I had the best approach. I was always religious, but always moderate; meaning I would go to the masjid (mosque) frequently, but not every day, and I would not necessarily attend halaqas (discussion groups) very often, but I had no aversion to them and would go occasionally. I felt very sure of myself. This continued into high school, even though I was the only Muslim in an all boys' Catholic school where I was bombarded with Catholic doctrines, beliefs, and reasoning. I never once questioned my belief and I in fact benefited greatly from class discussions. They often increased my faith.

Then in the summer between my sophomore and junior years, I had a lot of free time and I spent a lot of it in the masjid and in Qur'an study classes and Arabic classes. I was in the masjid every day from maghrib [prayer][106] *until isha [prayer],*[107] *involved in some sort of activity. While I enjoyed this time very much and my faith increased, I fear that I became close-minded about religion. I felt like I had found the true religion and that I must shield my mind from views that disagreed with mine, as it would only corrupt my faith. It was with this antagonistic attitude that I took a philosophy class that really messed with my head.*

---

106. The sunset prayer.
107. The evening prayer.

After that summer of intense devotion my approach to Islam became more theoretical and less practical, meaning that I prayed to find deeper fulfilment. But it seems to me now that as I thought I was getting closer to Allah, I was in fact setting myself up for a huge fall. This happened because I forgot the value of free thought and open discussion. I became close-minded. So when I took the philosophy class and my faith was questioned, I didn't respond as I should have, by using reason to support my convictions. Instead I tried to block out questions. This approach caused me to lose my faith even faster. I mean I wanted to believe in Allah, but I couldn't justify such a belief, because my faith had become much more mystical than rational, if you know what I mean.

So this continued for two years. Getting better at times and then worse at others, it never went away. Since last summer, I have tried to use reason to dispel these doubts, but I have yet to be successful. It is just so hard to forget the peace I felt by simply believing. Whenever I would try to reason, I felt like I had to figure all this out right now, because I could die tomorrow and then I would go to Hell for doubting Allah. This approach has not led me to any success, since I was putting an artificial limit on my level of understanding. Until now, I understand the arguments for the existence of Allah and for the supremacy of Islam, but I cannot, no matter how I try, translate that into firm faith. I may feel good for a couple weeks, but sooner or later I fall back into doubt and these doubts have destroyed my life.

If you see me, I seem very religious and confident that my faith is correct, so as a result people look up to me. In this situation I feel that I must have faith because people think I do, but I never really possess the full faith. I may accept that Allah must exist and that the Qur'an is the truth, but still, whenever I read about the unseen things in the Qur'an, my heart seems reluctant to believe. In this situation I am in a total loss about what to do. I may read certain <u>surahs</u> that are said to protect one from <u>shaytan</u> (Satan), or I may pray <u>nafl</u> prayers, but as I'm doing these things, I do not really believe in them, so as a result they have no effect. I may believe in them but this belief is not complete; it wavers. This wavering is not the *simple wavering of <u>iman</u> (faith) that everyone goes through; it is a little bit more complex. I'm constantly on the edge of Islam—sometimes in the fold and sometimes out. This is a very difficult way to live. Maybe since you are a convert you can understand me. I do not understand why when I read in the Qur'an about angels, or <u>jinn</u> (unseen spiritual beings), or the hereafter, or Jesus, I feel reluctant to follow it. Is this because my approach is wrong or because <u>shaytan</u> is dominant over me? Or is this all just something I'm imagining.*

I don't know how to end this "rebellion" against Allah's religion. I mean I have a very religious family, but they have not gone through doubts to the extent I have, so they do not understand me. My parents are of the opinion that I must stop thinking. I do not agree with this. My brothers say keep thinking about these things and they will go away, but it is impossible for me to reason the way I should when my day-to-day health is so directly affected. I just can't contemplate, come to a decision, and change my life. I have been in this situation for so long I don't know how to end these doubts. It sometimes feels like I have lost my passion to seek truth and that I'm just trying to find a way out no matter if I follow truth or falsehood, just so long as I don't suffer anymore, but it is such a complex problem.

When I see converts to Islam, even though I know I have these doubts, I feel like I know more and am better than them, a clearly stupid approach that I am very embarrassed about but one that I can't get rid of. I have always been an extremely nice person who avoids confrontation at all costs. It seems that I don't have the courage to stand up and follow truth, and I am completely lost as to how to get this courage.

I also visited the local imam, who performed a "test" on me to discover if my problems were due to <u>nazar</u> (when someone's jealousy or someone's attention can have an effect on someone else, sort of a form of magic). Being raised in America, I find it very hard to believe in such things. I know the Prophet said things about <u>nazar</u>, so I recognize that it must exist, but I don't know how to have complete assurance that it is real. That I think is the basic problem: I know the Prophet was true, but I can't for *the life of me stick with his teachings. My heart is not satisfied, and I'm not sure if this is due to a problem with my search, or a mystical magical problem, or what? I really don't know. I can't explain why I feel things that are clearly wrong, yet I don't have the courage to say they're wrong and forget them and follow just true and just things. I know this is a rather vague explanation, but I really didn't know to whom to turn, and I figured since you went through a period of doubt, perhaps you could relate.*

Comment 2 (from an American Muslim university student. The greater part of the correspondence I receive from second generation women complain, as in this email, of the treatment of women in the Islamic community.):

I'm not sure if you're already done with your new book but I have some thoughts I wanted to share with you. I'm a second generation American Muslim and I've dealt with my share of Muslims who haven't arrived in the 21st century yet, so I thought I should contribute my views to you, as it might help you in writing your book.

A few days ago, I went to the mosque in my community for iftar.[108] I usually break my fast at home with my family, but they were out of town, so I decided to go to the mosque with some of my friends. We had heard they have daily iftar gatherings, mainly for bachelors (I assumed bachelorettes too!).

The mosque has two levels. A small pink room upstairs is designated the women's prayer room and next to it is the children's room. Also upstairs is the mosque library and multi-purpose room, but both are locked from the sisters' side. The entire downstairs is the men's prayer room. After the call for maghrib,[109] the middle door was still locked from the sisters' side. One sister who is a regular at the iftar gatherings told us it is normal for them to forget about sisters and to not offer us dates to break our fast.

---

108. The meal after sunset during *Ramadan* when Muslims break the fast.
109. The sunset prayer.

Good thing I had a candy bar in my purse. We split that into pieces and broke our fast.

After prayer, we heard one of the brothers come upstairs and unlock the door, so we went into the dining room. Little did we know, but that wasn't how it worked. We weren't allowed in there and had to wait to be served our food by the brothers! We waited and someone asked us how many sisters were present. Eventually, the door cracked opened and a brother handed six plates of food to us through the door crack. I felt like I was a dog being fed its dinner. <u>Subhan-Allah</u>! [110]

All of the sisters are American Muslims and were appalled by this kind of treatment. So we opened the door and told them how we felt about not being able to participate in the actual <u>iftar</u> gathering. This sparked a lot more than we had expected because the sisters let out all of their frustrations with the entire system of the mosque. We told them how the "separate but equal" notion isn't applicable in many instances at the mosque. For example, the infrastructure of the mosque is unfair. If sisters have a question, they cannot ask it because there is no microphone like there is downstairs. We can only hear what is being said and often even that is muffled. On Friday, there was an announcement made asking if people would prefer to change <u>jum`ah</u> [111] *to 1:00 pm or 12:30 pm. The sisters could only hear the brothers voting downstairs. The sisters are not involved in the decision making process. The <u>shura</u>* [112] *does hold a "sister head" position, but that is the only position a female is allowed to have. Sisters only vote for that position, we are not allowed to vote for the imam or any other <u>shura</u> members. I never imagined something like this could happen in America! The <u>shura</u> consists of foreign-born adults who adhere to the "non-Muslims are <u>kafir</u>,* [113] *we should have nothing to do with them" stand. This is very frustrating.*

---

110. An exclamation of surprise: "Glory be to God!"
111. The weekly congregational prayer on Friday.
112. A consultative council.
113. Unbeliever.

I've lived in Iowa my whole life and in Iowa City for ten years. About five years ago, my mosque was taken over by a few <u>Salafis</u>.[114] *Apparently, no brothers can stand up against the leaders' rigid ideology and their imposing this ideology on others. The leadership will not even talk to sisters, so our attempts (such as the one made at <u>iftar</u>) aren't effective. What bothers me the most is how the international sisters treat the American (including second generation) sisters.*

A few weeks ago when some of my friends and I started using the library to study in, they told us to leave. We were told that it is the brothers' library. Not once when we had been there had a brother been present in the library. We explained to them how we should set up a schedule so both can use it, however they wanted us out. They put dead-bolt locks on the library door from the sisters' entrance. The imam and the sister-head have a key, yet the sister-head cannot unlock it without the imam's permission and of course the imam doesn't allow us to study there. What is this — the Taliban where only men receive education? No community can flourish without educated women.

When a sister wanted to start a study circle for American sisters, she was told that there could not be differing views in the mosque. She failed their <u>Salafi</u> exam. Even the <u>Shiahs</u>[115] *were kicked out of the mosque because they were seen as a threat. Instead of having discussions and even debates, they took the cowardly way out and told them they are not welcome at the mosque until they believe what the leadership believes. This is tyranny.*

Last year at the convention, I was Conference Chair and there were a few brothers from the mosque who were saying that we should not be "reversing the roles" and that a brother should be in charge of the

114. The *Salafiyah* is a contemporary Islamic movement that originated in Saudi Arabia, not to be confused with the reform movement in Egypt founded by Muhammad 'Abduh (1849-1905).

115. *Shi'a* is Arabic for "the party," short for "the party of 'Ali," and stands for the branch of Muslims who recognize 'Ali, the prophet's cousin, as his rightful successor.

convention. They even went as far as to tell me that I should take on the babysitting or food committees! However, our MSA consists of open-minded, strong Muslim students. This year I am Program Chair and the entire food committee is filled with brothers; it's not even an issue. I have faith in the new generation of Muslims — those who are strong enough to not let the backwardness (for lack of a better word) of some Muslims get in the way of their faith.

Last year, someone who learned about Islam on her own took shahadah.[116] *She finally got enough courage to go to the mosque and join the Muslim community. She came to the mosque and was unsure of which entrance to use, so she used the main (men's) entrance. She opened the door and found some brothers telling her to leave. They said to her, "All white women come here to find husbands, is that why you are here?"*

I've had issues with the entrance too. Once I used the main entrance (men's) because I had parked right in front of it and didn't want to get my key out from my backpack. It was cold so I didn't want to go all the way around and up the stairs into the sisters' entrance. I'd done this about twenty times before, and it wasn't even prayer time when brothers are around, but this time I opened the door and two brothers are standing there. They were shocked and started making it a big issue. They called me immodest and misjudged my intentions for using that entrance. It's as if I'm expected to completely hide from men so there can be total segregation. This isn't realistic. In the Qur'an, men are commanded to lower their gaze first. And in the next verse women are commanded to lower theirs and not display their beauty. Some of these brothers are used to men-only grocery stores in their countries and so even the sight of a woman, even if she's covered, is enough to shock them. A recently converted sister wanted to talk

116. Designates the Muslim testimony of faith: "There is no god but God and Muhammad is the Messenger of God."

to the imam about her problem. He told her to go into the sisters' room and he stayed in the other room. They were talking through a wall. This is extreme.

When I started wearing hijab, I didn't think it would taint my identity. It was to identify me as a Muslim, yet it seems to label me as a foreigner because the women who do wear it tend to be. It's as if I have to go around proving myself and showing people that I am not one of those women who allow themselves to be oppressed and dominated by men. Yet, I am also not on the other extreme — women who are dominated by men because they have to be sexual objects. It's a very tricky balance that I often can't maintain.

All these problems at the mosque are very upsetting to the American Muslim sisters because we are not used to them. We've grown up in a society where we can speak our minds and are urged to question the rules and authority. We are taught to analyze and ponder, not blindly accept what we are told. In my majors of Pre-law and Religion, I have to be objective and critical. So when we deal with these issues with some of the international brothers who aren't used to sisters like us, it illustrates the clash of cultures. For example, after our concerns at iftar were not taken seriously, we did not just back off. It called for a "revolution." We started going in groups downstairs to pray behind the brothers. We received dirty looks, our shoes were thrown outside, and we were even threatened to be removed physically. However, Allah has given us the right to pray in the same room and so we continue to rebel. It's sad that rebellion is actually the only method that gets through to these people and makes them take us seriously. They call it creating fitna,[117] but that's a cliché. Fitna is a struggle, and the actual struggle here is the sisters' fighting to get back our rights granted to us by Allah.

---

117. Temptation, trial, enticement, sedition, discord, dissension, civil strife.

Comment 3 (forwarded to me from a Muslim women's group from the same university as the young lady's in the previous comment. Second generation Muslim women are beginning to become more organized in their protests against traditional women's roles in the Islamic community.):

Brothers/Sisters and Friends:

We seek to start the New Year with improvements at our mosque and equal rights for everyone. Together we can reform the system and better the community. The following are our main concerns:

1. ELECTIONS ARE NOT HELD ANNUALLY.

The position of imam is not a permanent one at the mosque. Therefore, in the past elections were held yearly to give new people a chance to lead. Now elections are held only when the leadership is pressured to hold them. The last election for the mosque was held in 1999. There are many knowledgeable leaders in our community and they deserve an opportunity to lead their community.

2. WOMEN ARE NOT ALLOWED TO VOTE FOR THE IMAM (if elections are held).

The current leaders do not allow women to cast a vote for the position of imam, leader of the mosque. This has no basis in Islam. Islam actually liberated women and gave them the right to vote.

3. ONLY ONE POSITION ON THE BOARD IS FOR WOMEN.

Women are either not allowed to or are discouraged from participating in the decision making process. For example, a few weeks ago an announcement was made regarding the new Friday prayer time. As the discussions for the time change were taking place downstairs in the men's area, the women sat upstairs in their pink room listening through the speakers. Afterwards a sign-up sheet was posted on the downstairs bulletin board so men could cast their votes. Women played absolutely no role in choosing the new prayer time. Women are often not asked to offer their opinions on such decisions. There is not a microphone upstairs where women can express their opinions, make announcements or even ask questions.

4. THE MUSLIM STUDENTS ASSOCIATION (umbrella organization of the mosque) DOES NOT HOLD ELECTIONS OR INCLUDE WOMEN.

There are nearly 300 Muslim students at the university, yet year after year the same imam appoints the same person as president of the MSA. Similarly, the imam appoints the cabinet. There are many students, brothers and sisters, who are qualified and willing to lead the MSA. These people need to be given a chance. The MSA is not following their own constitution, which clearly states that elections will be held annually.

As usual, the last MSA meeting excluded women. It was held in the downstairs section of the mosque, which is considered to be the men's area. In an announcement, the MSA president only addressed males when he stated something to the effect of, "Brothers, please stay for the MSA meeting, which will be held after jum`ah."

5. AN EXTRA SISTERHEAD WAS APPOINTED WITHOUT ELECTIONS OR DISCUSSION.

One of the sisters refused to work with, or go through, the current sisterhead due to personal tension. Instead of setting aside these problems and working together, the sister who couldn't work with the current sisterhead formed a separate sisters' party through her weekly halaqas.[118] The imam appointed her as sisterhead, even though the first sisterhead had won the most votes in the 1999 election. Now there are two study circles led by the two sisterheads. Only one was fairly elected, even though it was three years ago.

---

118. Literally, "circle"; in this case a study circle.

Recently dead-bolt locks were put on the library doors at the request of the sisterhead after her attempts to keep sisters out of the library failed. Women should have the right to study in the library; it is unfair to have one library in the mosque and call it the brothers' library.

6. SALAFI/WAHABI VIEWS ARE INCORRECTLY CONSIDERED THE VIEWS OF THE MAJORITY.

The imam of our community is openly a Wahabi (AKA Salafi), a rigid interpretation of Islam that the Taliban also adheres to. Such a leader, who is inflexible in his views, is not qualified to be the imam. The women of this mosque deserve to have a leader who can treat us as equals and not only allows for our voices to be heard, but encourages it. The majority of Muslims in this city do not adhere to Wahabism and we need to realize how this rigid interpretation of Islam is far from the tenets of Islam.

Recently, an article posted downstairs in the men's area stated that it is forbidden for Muslim women to wear pants. Muslims immediately dismiss this type of Wahabi ideology. Yet, the article was posted for at least a month and no one challenged it.

On September 12 when some Muslims encouraged the mosque leadership to hold a prayer service for the victims of 9-11, the president of the MSA spoke on their behalf and refused. He felt that it was inappropriate for Muslims to pray for non-Muslims. Even though there were hundreds of Muslims who worked in the WTC, the leadership failed to realize a basic human principle: Muslim or non-Muslim, we are all God's creatures. Most mosques around Iowa and the country held prayer services for the victims of 9-11, our mosque should be no different.

It is important to note that the Muslim Students Association has invited only Wahabi speakers in the past few years. This is because the imam must screen the speaker before he (the speakers have always been male) can be invited. If one gives the suggestion to invite a non-Wahabi speaker, they claim that the speaker is not knowledgeable enough.

Each year, the mosque leadership profusely promotes a trip to the Islamic Assembly of North America (IANA) Conference. Announcements are made, buses are rented, and registration forms are handed out. Yet, they mislead people by not informing them that this is a Wahabi conference. The largest and most popular Islamic conference in this country is the Islamic Society of North America (ISNA) Conference, also held annually in Chicago. The fliers for this conference are never posted and announcements are not made. The annual state conference on Islam is also completely ignored, although every other mosque and MSA in the state not only attends and supports the conference, but helps to organize it.

Recently, an unidentified male at a campus Muslim event verbally harassed a female student. She expressed her concerns and a meeting was held. Although the MSA leadership was willing to help identify the male, they unfairly assessed the situation. They implied that she had gotten herself into the situation and to avoid this in the future, she should only attend events that segregate males and females. This is irrelevant, as the issue was the fact that she was harassed. The male who did this should solely be held responsible, his actions cannot be justified and his victim should not share his blame.

This Is What We Want:

An election committee is formed, consisting of diverse Muslims. A respected individual from another Muslim community in Iowa will oversee this election committee. The election committee will set a date for elections, including but not limited to, these positions: imam, board members (open to both males and females!), MSA president and MSA executive board. The election committee will seek nominations and allow for the community to know who the nominees are, and what their ideas and strengths are, either through handouts, speeches (to both males and females), or another method. Elections will be held and the results will be posted.

It is unbelievable that such antiquated occurrences are taking place in America in the 21st century. Please help us change this situation!

Comment 4 (as this message illustrates, second generation women in Canada are also protesting the status quo):

I have just come back from the most recent controversy. New controversy-old issue. The issue concerns where women will pray. Background info. The mosque in Regina was a former church now used as a mosque. Therefore the design of the mosque is different. Meaning that there is a main prayer hall on the main floor. On the upper floor there are classrooms and other rooms. One of those rooms has been designated as a "Sister's Prayer area." Over the years the sisters have worked hard to have it remain a women's choice as to where a sister would like to pray. However, there are men who want to have the final say on that.

Flash forward to today: Because I am a Lucky City employee I had the day off today. I had been planning for a week to make time to go to jum`ah.*[119] *I was psyched because I haven't been for a while. Around 10:00 this morning a friend phoned and during our conversation I mentioned that I would see her at jum`ah. She proceeded to tell me that she will not go because at the last jum`ah it was announced that, "The sisters will have to pray in the small, upstairs room." The reason was because there were "guests" coming from the university (a teacher and his students from a class on Islam) and that there wouldn't be any room for the sisters. The board of directors decided this. She was so offended that she decided not to go this week. I was so disheartened. I was so looking forward to going to jum`ah and having a spiritual moment. I was also mad. Who gives men the right to tell me where to pray or not to pray? I decided not to go either. At the last minute I changed my mind. I decided that by not going they would win and I would lose. I had planned to go to jum`ah and I have the right to go. So I decided to go and to pray in the main prayer hall. I was nervous. I didn't know what would happen. I arrived during the khutba.[120] *I walked in and entered the main prayer hall. I got some looks*

---

119. The Friday congregational prayer.
120. *Khutba* is Arabic for "a public address." At the Friday congregational prayer it represents the sermon that precedes the prayer.

going in. It's funny because it seems that everyone had his "Sister Radar" on. I sat down and listened to the <u>khutba</u>. After a few minutes, a "brother" in the first row got out of his chair (he has to pray in a chair but has enough strength to come over to admonish me [121]), walked to the back of the prayer hall where I was sitting and over to me.

Brother: "You have to go upstairs."

Me: "I choose to pray here."

Brother: "There is only one of you and you can't pray <u>jum`ah</u> by yourself. You have to go upstairs."

Me: "No. I'm praying down here."

Brother: "The other sisters are upstairs and you have to go upstairs and pray with them."

I think he thought that this would dissuade me and that I would be humbled and march upstairs, but I stayed put.

Me: "Well they can pray down here if they would like."

After a few minutes another brother came up to me.

Second Brother: "Sister, the arrangement has been made this week for the sisters to pray upstairs."

Me: "I'm praying downstairs."

Second Brother: "But it was decided. Just for this week."

Me: "I'm staying here."

I guess he didn't want a fuss, so he left and returned to his seat. The <u>khutba</u> continued and after a few minutes another sister arrived and sat beside me. When the <u>khutba</u> was finished the sister and I prayed together where we had been sitting. After the prayer I noticed the professor from the class. I went and talked to him for a bit.

Me:"Hello. Are you from the U of R?"

Professor:"Yes. I'm so and so and I teach a class on Islam at the university."

---

121. The congregation generally sits on the floor, but if someone has a physical condition that makes it painful to sit on the floor then that person may sit in a chair.

Me: "Did you bring your students?"

Professor: "Yes." He introduces me to his student who is sitting beside him. Count them: two additional people to the prayer hall! "There are also two female students but they are upstairs."

After that I said my <u>salam</u> to the other sister and then proceeded to leave the building. The two brothers who spoke to me in the prayer hall had to say a few more things to me.

Second Brother: "Sister you should have gone upstairs when it was decided. It was announced last week that it would be for this special occasion. For the guests."

Me: "Brother, there were only four additional people and they could be accommodated very easily. I don't appreciate your coming up to me during the <u>khutba</u>. You wrecked my concentration."

Second Brother: "You wrecked our concentration too. You should have gone upstairs."

Me: "Brother, I won't go upstairs to pray. I don't agree with the board's decision. I think they need to discuss it with all the members of the community. I don't appreciate being treated like this when I come to the mosque. I take time from work to come and pray."

Second Brother: "Yes, it is very good that you come and pray."

Blah, Blah, Blah. During this time the Brother who sat in a chair felt that he had to get some parting words in too.

First Brother: "You should have gone upstairs when I told you too. It is the principle. You were only one."

Me: "No, another sister came and joined me."

First Brother: "She came in when she saw you. You should have gone upstairs. She didn't know that all the sisters were upstairs."

Now he's blaming me for corrupting this sister, too. Then he starting saying how I couldn't pray by myself, although I had pointed out that in terms of gender there were two women in the room, and really I was praying with all the community members. I guess my community only consists of women.

Me: "Brother, I won't have this discussion with you unless you have some proof to what you are saying. What are you basing this on?"

First Brother:"Well, I don't have any proof, so I guess we can't have this discussion."

Me: "Right."

I then left and went on my merry way.

Comment 5 (from a Muslim woman from North Africa. I have received a large amount of encouragement from Muslims from overseas. I also get much more critical correspondence from Muslims and have found some very disparaging views on my books and lectures on the Internet. This message expresses a shared—and for me completely unexpected—hope of many of those who contact me from abroad: that the converts to Islam will be in the lead of a critical re-evaluation of Muslim thought and practice. As much as I truly appreciate the supportive sentiments, I believe that any movement in Islamic thought that does not come from the traditional Muslim world will not take hold there.):

I am sure you receive a number of e-mails thanking you for your two books. However, I had to express my gratitude for your effort to help me and all Muslims and non-Muslims alike in understanding our religion better. I was on a business trip last week and had the opportunity to read through your first book and I am currently in the middle of reading your second one. After having to go through my nth security check before boarding a plane since September 11 (I wear the <u>hijab</u> and work as an engineering consultant in the petrochemical industry, so I do a fair bit of travel and get profiled constantly), I needed to read something that will remind me of why this might be my little piece of "jihad" so I can take the aggravation more cheerfully. Your books provided a much needed sanity check at that point.

I would just like to say that I found your thought process very intriguing and your presentation of facts very succinct and informative. Islam is

God's religion and was aimed at all mankind and you are a living proof that a convert can become more knowledgeable about Islam than a born Muslim.[122] *I am a born Muslim and was brought up in an Islamic community in North East Africa, but I also had the advantage of early exposure to Christianity via the Catholic schooling system I attended. Very few people, Christian, Jewish or Muslim, have the benefit of exposure to different religions at an early age or even the benefit of parents who teach them to think before they decide for themselves or judge others ... if they have to ever judge.*

This ability to think outside the box is generally to be expected of people who take big daring steps like conversion. Hence, that strong point in our converts should be capitalized on in developing our Islamic Ummah.[123] *I am afraid most born Muslims are very hesitant when it comes to questioning certain religious tenets, and when they have not thought through an issue carefully before, they are very seldom capable of defending it, if a discussion arises. Moreover, we find it very difficult to put ourselves in others' shoes. I had a very disappointing discussion with a group of very educated born Muslims back in Ramadan. I found myself to be the only one holding the opinion that the concept of faith in God transcends all religions and if we truly believe that God is merciful we can never condemn good people of other religious backgrounds to eternal damnation just because they did not say the shahadah.*[124] *If that group was a representative sample of our Ummah's educated elite, then your books are even more needed among born Muslims, not just converts. It is much harder for born Muslims to walk a mile in others' shoes, yet they expect everyone to be able to see the goodness in Islam with all the stigma*

---

122. This is a very kind sentiment but when I look at some of the careless mistakes I have made in my past lectures and writings I feel quite lacking in knowledge.

123. Arabic for *community*.

124. The testimony of faith by which someone becomes a Muslim: "I testify that there is no god but God and Muhammad is the Messenger of God".

surrounding it and with the very limited unbiased information that the western world receives.

In our current day and age, basic human compassion, tolerance, open-mindedness and informed and confident faith in Allah is our Ummah's hope. May God bless you in your efforts. Please continue to do your share in helping both Muslims and non-Muslims in understanding Islam.

Comment 6 (concerning a young lady who married a non-Muslim. Second generation Muslims marrying outside their faith is becoming more commonplace.):

I read your book, <u>Struggling to Surrender</u>. I found it very interesting and I thought the way you converted to Islam is very touching. My father saw on the back of your book that you are a professor at the University of Kansas, so I did a search and I found your e-mail address. I need your help on a situation with my sister. She had always been very religious and wore <u>hijab</u>, but recently she left Islam. She says she believes in God but not in a particular religion or prophet. I will give you more details below.

My sister was religious all her life and in her second year of college she put on <u>hijab</u>. She joined the MSA[125] and wrote a paper comparing women in Judaism, Christianity and Islam. She gave several <u>khutbas</u>[126] on the topic of women's rights in Islam.

Six months before her graduation as an engineer, she told my mother she had questions about Islam. My mother answered some of her questions and she was satisfied with the answers. Then two weeks before graduation she told my mother that she is no longer a Muslim because she does not understand <u>Qadr</u>[127] and some of the women's issues. My parents invited four scholars in Islam to our house on four different occasions. She sat with each one and they gave her very good answers, but she still did not want to open her heart up to Islam again.

---

125. Muslim Student Association.
126. The Arabic word *khutba* means a lecture, speech, or sermon.
127. *Qadr* here refers to the doctrine of predestination. See Chapter 1, Question 7.

She got a full scholarship to the best graduate school in engineering and my parents were unable to prevent her from accepting it. The college was four hours away. Every time my sister came to visit there would always be arguments about religion. My parents are very religious and they cannot accept her being a disbeliever. After two years my parents decided to disown her. Five months later my parents decided they could not continue on like that and they started a relationship with her again. Over a course of three years my sister received several marriage proposals from Muslim young men, but she would always make excuses. When she came back into the relationship with us, she made conditions that (1) we don't speak with her about religion, and (2) we accept who ever she chooses to marry. My parents agreed to these conditions. Then six months later my sister got a proposal again and refused, so my mom asked her if there was anyone in her life, and she said that there is and started crying. Finally my sister told my mom that an atheist loved her since college, and he asked her to marry him. She turned him down because she didn't want to disappoint her family and he left for Europe. My sister said she tried to find other people, but she can't forget him. So she asked my mom if she could marry him.

My mom said that she is concerned about my other sister and my getting married someday. Even though my sister is not a believer, nobody in the Islamic community knows that. My mom made the condition that if my sister wants to marry this man, then he must take the <u>shahadah</u> and marry her Islamically and talk to an Islamic scholar. He agreed to take the <u>shahadah</u> and marry the Islamic way. My sister says her feelings are very strong and she has known him since college, but he was an atheistic influence on her and probably turned her away from Islam. When she was an undergrad she tried to convince him of Islam but instead he was the one that turned her away from her beliefs.

We first want someone to convince him that there is a God. If he believes in God then the next step is to talk to him about Islam. If he, <u>insha-Allah</u>,[128] were to become a believer, maybe he will be the one to bring

---

128. Arabic for "If God wills."

my sister back into Islam. Would it be possible for you to email him since you were an atheist before Allah led you to Islam? We would really appreciate your help. Thank you for your time. I know my email was pretty long. Please let me know if you would be able to help us.

Response:

I'm very willing to talk to the young man, but it would be best if the initiative came from him. There is no point in having a stranger push Islam on him, it will only make him resist even more. I think your best strategy is to try to first win back your sister. If she returns to Islam, then she could have an influence on her husband; the reverse strategy is much more likely to fail. Toward this end I think it important to keep close relations with your sister and her husband. Invite them to participate in family gatherings, fasting during Ramadan, religious celebrations, and so forth. I do not encourage your family to be pushy with your sister and her spouse, but just give them the opportunity to appreciate in your family's behavior some of the good things in your life that come from the religion. If your sister stays close to her family she might someday feel the need to reconsider her atheism and to explore Islam more deeply.

Incidentally, I think I know some of what your sister has gone through. I too find the dogmas related to *Qadr*, which represent a single trend in Islamic thought that took hundreds of years to crystallize, extremely disappointing. I also find the Muslim community's whitewashing of many of the problems related to the treatment of Muslim women unconvincing. My second book, *Even Angels Ask*, discusses these and other problems. I do not blame your sister or your parents. I sympathize with and feel sad for all concerned. Very many young American Muslim women and their families are going through the same very painful experience. The way the community teaches and applies Islam may work well in traditional Muslim societies, but many young Muslim Americans cannot relate to views that are often strongly culturally influenced, especially after they enter college and are exposed to well defended alternative outlooks.

Now it may be that your parents would prefer to have someone else talk to your sister and her spouse, someone more committed to a more conventional outlook, but I would be very happy to talk to them if they were to contact me.

Comment 7 (expressing grave misgivings about Islam. I have received many similar communications from second generation Muslims. There is nothing shocking in this; very many American young people of every faith go through periods of doubt; but I have been surprised by the large amount of email and letters I've received from second generation atheists of Muslim parentage. It is not that these young persons become atheists that astonishes me—many Americans have done the same—but that they make the effort to contact me to discuss their leaving Islam. It is fascinating that they go out of their way to find someone who they must assume will not champion their decision. Below is an excerpt from a long conversation that took place over several months between a young lady and myself. In her first email she told me that she had stopped believing in God. However, it was not long before she returned, quite on her own, to Islam, albeit with many questions and hesitations. This excerpt is from an email she sent me after her return to faith.):

I would appreciate it if you would continue your discussions with me, particularly on the place of <u>Hadith</u>, <u>seerah</u>,[129] and <u>tafsir</u>[130] and their relationship to understanding the Qur'an. I ask this because you raised a crucial question in your first book that shocked me. You asked, as I recall, something about why do we need textual sources of religious guidance other than the Qur'an. I raised this question to myself when I was probably eighteen. My answer was completely different from yours. The more that I think about it the more I realize that maybe because of the way I answered this question I ended up in the predicament

---

129. The biographical literature on the Prophet.
130. Qur'an commentary.

that I am in now. At that time, I recall asking myself what was the difference between Judaism, Christianity, and Islam. I felt the answer was that not only is our Scripture in its original, unadulterated form, I also felt that unlike the Christians or Jews, we have Hadith. This was significant to me because I felt it did not leave everything to interpretation. The Hadith, in my mind, would lessen the disparities in understanding that result from culturally influenced biases. I would always quote the hadith in which Aisha would say that Prophet Muhammad was the walking Qur'an. To me this meant that not only did he explain the meaning, but also he taught us how to take that meaning and incorporate it into our behavior. It also meant to me that there are certain aspects of human beings that never change. Islam came and gave specific rules for those aspects of our lives. So, this is one of the things that led me to the point I was at a month or so ago, when I felt I could not believe in Islam anymore. I didn't see the Qur'an as a book that made you think, but one that gave rules on how to live, and the Hadith helped to limit the amount of interpretation of the Qur'an.

This one superficial conclusion led me to join a group of people who propagated a form of Islam that stated that every single solution to every problem in life could be strictly derived from the Qur'an and Hadith. This very well suited the type of questions and concerns I had when I first met this group. Actually, I told you a little about my experience with them in my first letter. I think when I met them I had very legitimate concerns and questions, but the solutions I found were easy answers rather than ones of which I was really convinced.

When I was nineteen or so, I started becoming very involved in the Muslim community. I loved Islam very much and was aching to express it. Being around Muslim people was the greatest feeling. There was a sense of peace and unity. But, with this growing sense of peace and unity, I was also becoming aware of the problems of the ummah. All at once I saw on TV the Muslims in Bosnia being killed, I also had a Muslim friend who had just come from Bosnia and it made it even harder for me to understand. I became extremely sensitive to the problems of Palestine, Kashmir, and so on. It seemed to me that every Muslim country was in crisis. We were being killed left and right, taken advantage of. I recall going to an overnight ijtima `[131]` *for women only. I remember saying to one of the speakers almost in tears that we need to get together and unify. We need to get Clinton to see our side of things.*

This response of mine changed shortly thereafter. I no longer saw that we needed Clinton's help, but that since Islam is the truth it has to hold the solution to this and every other problem. And since the kuffar [132] *do not have Islam, we can never rely on them to help us. In fact, I concluded that they are the cause of the problem.*

At precisely this moment in my life I met a group of Muslims that promoted similar ideas to the ones I was developing. This group of Muslims belongs to the group called hizbut tahrir. [133] *I am not going to bash them in any way. Actually, to a large extent I love them very much. They made me have a passion for Islam and to a large extent they are the ones that got me to start thinking about Islam and why it is the truth. They got me to think about those things in a way I had never done before. They were the first people that said to me that you could think about Islam and think about why it is the truth. It was as though they were able to give expression to what was in my soul. They made me believe that my mind had to play a role. If this is the case, you must be wondering why I am in my current place, unsure of what I believe.*

Well, I think it is because they promote a very restricted use of reason. They talk about the role of the mind and how as human beings we can only come to certain universal truths such as the `aqeedah [134] *of Islam. But, beyond that we cannot question. We cannot explain why Allah tells women to wear hijab or why we cannot eat pork. We cannot speculate on why men can have four wives and women only one husband, because these*

---

131. "Gathering" or "get together."
132. Arabic for "unbelievers."
133. Roughly, "the liberation party."
134. Roughly, "the creed" or "articles of faith."

would lead us to give reasons that are limited by our culture and time in history, i.e., tainted by our own biases. They even said that we are not to look at what is inside the Qur'an to come to believe that it is the truth. They said that the reason for this is the Qur'an speaks of al-ghayb,[135] *the unseen, and that we cannot think about those things. So, it is silly to use what is inside the Qur'an as evidence of its truth. We simply need to look at how it was revealed. This is proof enough of its truth. This made sense to me because once again I felt that the only way to lessen the gap between Muslims would be to limit interpretations. This well-intentioned path I took unfortunately led me to suffocation. It is funny, when you described your experience as an atheist of initially feeling free, well, after I decided that I was no longer a Muslim I felt free. I felt like I could finally think, I could determine at least on my own what was right or wrong. Being part of the hizb made me so rigid that I did not even know what was right or wrong. I may be stretching it a little, but I think if someone didn't tell me what to say in the halaqas,*[136] *I would not have known what to say when giving dawah.*[137]

It is even stranger that when I sat in the halaqas, I felt inferior, like I was always wrong, yet when I went to go and talk with people in the ummah[138] *I would be arrogant. I was quick to say that everyone was wrong. Someone I knew in school made a recent observation of me. He said that after a person speaks with me, my response always starts with "but." I no longer listened to others; I felt that the hizb was the only way. I felt that disagreement should be minimal. I created my own disaster. I started realizing this in early October. I started realizing it when I was speaking to my professor, for whom I have complete and utter respect, on the phone. He listened to me complain and blame others for my not being able to understand my Middle Eastern Studies professor. This thoughtful,*

135. Literally, "the unseen," i.e. realities beyond human perception.
136. "Study circles."
137. Calling others to Islam, Muslim witness.
138. Muslim community.

quiet professor of mine said in the gentlest way, "You know, it is the greatest thing in the world to be able to see things from two perspectives." It took me another month to realize that the whole year that I had spent talking with him about Islam—which was not a discussion, but only my speaking—he was silent because he was trying to see my side. Yet not even for a moment did I bother to try to hear his side. I was always convinced that his side was tainted. I felt that the <u>kuffar</u> could never understand Islam unless they became Muslims. Now, that I think about it, this sounds a lot like the Christians who say that you have to have the spirit to believe. And then you ask them how one gets the spirit, they say you have to believe. I used to think that these circular arguments were ones that only Christians made, not Muslims or me. The more that I think about the last few years of my life the more upset I become. The more I realize that it is important to be able to see different sides, to always continue to question. It is funny, for about two months before I wrote to you I refused to talk to Muslims because I was so upset and disgusted. I would only talk to the <u>kuffar</u>. I felt as though not one single Muslim was able to engage my mind, to stimulate my thought. I couldn't believe that being engaged, thinking, growing creatively could possibly be wrong. Yet, every Muslim I knew would say that this is wrong.

I guess what I am trying to tell you is that getting through your books was a rough ride, but I learned a great deal from them. I learned most importantly that I have to continue asking my questions and on top of that pursue them with vigor. <u>Insha'Allah</u>,[139] I will keep doing that. Thank you for everything. I hope that you will not mind keeping in contact with me. There are not many people around me that would give me as much leeway to learn and to question as you did. Thank you very much.

About a week or so ago, I actually told my mom and my sister what I am going through. It was a pretty stupid thing to do because they both reacted with extreme anger and disgust. They have calmed down now and claim that they will try to understand, but in reality they don't and I am

---

139. "God willing."

not even sure if they can understand even if they tried. My sister keeps telling me that I need to see things from the "Islamic perspective" and my mom keeps telling me not to question because it will only confuse me more. So, I am truly grateful to you for not responding to me like that and for telling me to hang in there.

Comment 8 (from a woman in Iowa interested in Islam. It once again illustrates the difficulties that American women have accessing the mosque culture and the suspicions they frequently encounter in the process.):

I wanted to tell you how much I appreciated your lecture at the First Muslim Iowa Conference. I am a non-traditional (read "old") graduate student at Iowa State. My study of Islam started last summer. Although I feel a very strong pull from Islam, I have not yet made the <u>shahadah</u>. One of the reasons is the isolation I feel from this religion; actually I am sure it is cultural. Nevertheless I find myself speaking to a few men at arm's length or searching for information on the Internet.

Your lecture about the missing seventy-five percent [140] *demonstrated to me that what I am feeling is not personal at all. Being female and white and interested in Islam seems to leave suspicion in the minds of the Muslims here. I am not sure but I have the feeling that they think I am using Islam to find a husband. Having heard from you that this is a problem for many females actually made me feel better. I will continue my study of Islam and I hope to maintain contact with the new women friends I made at the conference.*

---

140. In my lecture I explained that the majority of Muslim Americans approximately seventy-five percent of them—were born in the United States, yet only a relative handful of these convert and second generation Muslims are ever seen in mosques and Islamic centers. In the beginning of this chapter I estimate that eighty percent of American born Muslims shun the Islamic community. These estimates are very rough, but the actual percentage is undoubtedly high.

Thank you for taking the time and interest to research and address something that was so personally important for me.

Comment 9 (from a second generation engineering student who converted to Christianity, then left the Church, and now belongs to no religion. A fair number of young people have complained to me of a lack of spirituality in Islam. A big part of the problem is that most of them do not understand Arabic, which is the liturgical language of the religion.[141]):

I just wanted to tell you that I really enjoyed hearing you speak this weekend and I got quite a bit out of the lectures. I don't know if you remember but I had mentioned to you that I don't really believe in anything at all right now.

What I wanted to mention to you, but didn't get to because everyone else as well as myself wanted to talk to you, was why I had come to the point that I did. I remember you briefly mentioning the emotional and spiritual experiences you had while reading the Quran. I've had the same experiences as well but the thing is I had them in Christianity. Islam was always a "dead" faith to me. I mean it was always a set of empty rules and regulations; any type of relationship or comfort from anything tangible was non-existent for me. I know this couldn't have been the case during Muhammad's lifetime, but that's the way it always was, and basically still is for me now.

It would take a very long time for me to explain fully my experiences in Christianity. I had at one point in time accepted Christ, which made my family and Muslim friends totally furious, but had left Christianity after looking into the authenticity of the Bible and the Christian faith. But when I was looking for the truth or constantly asking God for it, I honestly feel like I was being directed to Christ. I honestly felt when I prayed to him, someone was hearing me; it was the most real thing

---

141. Cf. question 3.

I had ever had, even though it was totally intangible. I think you might know what I mean by that last statement.

Anyway, that connection to God I never had before and I just don't have it in Islam. I have been told that this is a test or something like that, but I cannot resolve the fact that in one instance I have a spiritual connection and in the other I don't. So I just quit. The more I searched and pondered, the more I felt I was going crazy. So I just quit. It just seemed pointless. I still have that deep-rooted anger and unsettledness that won't go away. I just try not to think about it.

There is no substitute for a real spiritual connection, no matter how intellectually sound it may be. I assume you believe Islam is the truth, but I just wanted to tell you why I didn't believe in anything. I don't know if the Qur'an says anything about something like this, but if it does please let me know.

Response:

Thank you for your very kind words. I met so many people those two days I can't remember exactly who was who, but I think I remember you.

I am not sure what to say about your or my spiritual experiences. In my lecture, I did not go into detail about mine because they are, as you mentioned, quite impalpable and therefore hard to explain. I lectured almost entirely on the rational aspects of my first reading of the Qur'an because I feel that this is much easier to convey and for others to relate to. The other difficulty is that spiritual experiences are highly subjective; from my observances of Sufi *dhikr* circles and charismatic Christian gatherings, they also seem to be often self-induced.

Since I alluded to my spiritual experiences while reading the Qur'an but did not describe them, and since what I said apparently struck a chord with you, I'll share with you a few particulars about them, but keep in mind that there is no reason to expect that yours would be identical to mine. If your spiritual moments do not share features with mine, that says nothing about their genuineness.

My search began as a mostly rational one, perhaps because I held that if there were a God then He must have endowed us with reason—which I saw as our most powerful faculty—for a purpose. I thought that if God really did exist, then reason should help protect us from following or developing incorrect beliefs about Him. I also felt that a primarily emotional, psychological or spiritual approach to faith is untrustworthy, because I assumed our sentiments are more prone to error than is trained and disciplined reason. My problem had been that reason inevitably conflicted with the faiths I investigated. So my reading of the Qur'an began as a rational exploration, which only later and unexpectedly took on a spiritual side. When I first started to read the Scripture I had no inclination to believe in God. It was not until I had practically no arguments left against the existence of God that I began to have the experiences I mentioned. I must say, however, that I really did not expect or seek a spiritual connection. On the contrary, for some time I resisted the spiritual moments I was having. I tried to shake them off and explain them away. I really did not seek or desire them; they just happened.

I think you are right when you say that spirituality is a vital component of faith. And I can understand how your experience of faith in Islam could have been spiritually barren. This is just my opinion as one who came from outside the faith, but the Muslims appear to me to have almost killed the spiritual message of Islam and the powerful spiritual potential of Islam's rituals by putting so much stress on rules, regulations, punishments, formalities, and politics to the near exclusion of the spiritual and ethical dimension, which is the predominant message of the Qur'an. I have listened to Friday *khutbas* for over twenty years now and almost never hear lectures that relate belief and deeds to spirituality and our relationship with God. If my only source of information about Islam were the Friday *khutbas* and the conversations I've had with Muslims, I think my perception of God in Islam would be of an infinitely jealous power who imposes uncountable ordinances on us solely to test our obedience to Him, and then waits for the slightest infraction to assail us with His punishment. Or maybe I would have come to view Islam as principally a political movement, whose main purpose was to re-establish Muslims as a world superpower so that they can gain revenge for the humiliation and suffering they have known since the downfall of their civilization. What I am trying to say is that if a young American Muslim is going to find a lost or never experienced spirituality in Islam, then he or she might have to go it mostly alone and blaze his or her own trail, away from the preoccupations of the current Islamic community, and should probably begin with the Qur'an, while trying to remain as open-minded as possible, not being too committed to what he or she has been previously taught. Some young people have experienced spirituality through Sufism, but I cannot personally endorse it because I have found it doesn't go well with my personality and way of thinking, but to each his own.

For me, reason is also an essential element of faith. This is not to say that someone cannot be genuinely religious without a coherent personal theology, or for that matter without experiencing spiritual moments, but I believe that if someone feels his or her faith is devoid of spirituality or opposes reason, than something is most likely wrong somewhere and the pursuit of truth should continue. In your case, it seems that you have not found real peace in any of the religions with which you have been acquainted. You were attracted to Christianity and felt that Jesus heard your prayers, but Christianity didn't appeal to you rationally. On the other hand, Islam, as you have learned it, has been a "dead faith" for you. Unfortunately, I don't know you well enough to give you indepth advice. Since you still believe in God, it would make sense to continue seeking His guidance, and perhaps you already are, and it may be that He is guiding you right now, even though it may not seem that way to you. I can only advise you to not give up, for to be without God is too great a loss.

And if My servants ask of Me, I am truly near. I heed the call of every caller when he calls on Me. Let them also, with a will, heed My call and believe in Me, that they may walk in the right way (2:186).

You have been very forthright in sharing your problems with me and I have tried to do the same in my reply. I hope you haven't been offended by anything I've said; it's easy to unintentionally hurt another's feelings when discussing things so intimate. I apologize if I have done that. If you would like to discuss these or any issues further, please don't be shy to email me.

Comment 10 (The majority of American converts to Islam during the last two decades are women, most of whom are college educated and slanted to the left socially and politically. Until now they have displayed stronger commitment and staying power than their male counterparts, which is surprising since most mosques and Islamic centers promote customs and attitudes toward women that collide with Western values. This short email depicts some of the many frustrations of lady converts and the lengths to which they sometimes go to cope with them.):

I apologize for writing, as I know you are swamped. I was very comforted by your first two books as an early convert to Islam seven years ago, as I struggled with our American version of the Islamic religious police. Actually, I only heard of you four years ago at the Unity conference where a speaker mentioned you. I just watched your recent video on raising our children in Islam or keeping them there and I could see your passion almost brought you to tears and twice almost brought me to tears. You absolutely spoke for me about the horrible experiences we have with legalistic, culture bound, rule obsessed and <u>hadith</u>-crazed people. I have been driven out of my local mosque where my attempts to support converts were stymied when the imam's wife, herself an American Taliban-style convert, told people to keep away from me, mainly because I refuse to wear *hijab outside and I go to a Sufi mosque in Philadelphia, one of the few places in our community where I feel accepted and at home. I have several friends, converts, hanging by a thread to Islam and avoiding the community for the same reasons; some of them are going to the church when desperate for joyful non-judgmental spiritual association. The Sufi mosque is over an hour away. Sometimes I have cried and said, "Why did I become a Muslim?" But I feel spirit-led to unite Islam with progressive justice issues, feminist issues, and help my friends and people like me to become Muslims, but still be Americans who look like Americans and are socially and politically active, who are not pressured to show up at work in a jellabiya[142] and kufi,[143] and can be themselves at work and in the community at large. I want that too. I have tried informally to be a convert support system and I am organizing a small retreat for Muslim women converts or dropouts who want that middle path of the essentials of Islam. Your speech made me feel I was doing the right thing and should keep on going. When you said you will be saying the same things until your dying day even if no one listens, I said, "Me too," and I guess I am not so crazy. The Progressive Muslim Network has been a big help to me and this week several in the DC area had their first Friday prayer. We discussed possibly having men and women in the same line on opposite sides of the Mosque during the prayer and rotating khutbas with women leading the prayers and giving them in rotation too. At least these things are up for discussion. Anyway, thank you, thank you, thank you, and please if you have an email list, notify me when your next book comes out.*

Comment 11 (This is really more of a question than a comment, but I lost contact with the sender and was not able to reply to him. Judging from past experience, if the young man and I had embarked on a discussion it probably would have touched on many of the

---

142. A loose, shirt-like garment, commonly worn by males in Egypt.

143. A cap traditionally warn by Middle Eastern Muslim men.

themes presented in chapter one. It is the large volume of messages I've received like this one that led me to include in this book another chapter on the purpose of life. If I have learned nothing else from my communications with Muslim American young people, I have learned that by and large American Islamic institutions are either out of touch or indifferent to their concerns and problems.):

I am suffering from a serious problem. I hope you can find time to respond to my concerns. I believe that there is a power that has created this universe. Muslims know this power as Allah. But, I feel that Allah is not fair. Why does He allow the torture and killing of innocent people in Africa and in Asia? Why does He punish people by strange types of diseases? I feel that if He is good then He is not in control of everything, and that's why we have suffering and crises in this world, for if He is all-powerful, then why is He not good to people? From the Muslim point of view He is both all-powerful and good, which I see as irreconcilable. Then what? Does this make me a non-Muslim?

I often feel that it is better not to take religion so seriously and just do my prayers, fasting and charity as best I could and ignore the rest. I also want to make my goal in life to contribute to the happiness of others as much as possible. But that's it. I don't want to be a deep believer in God, nor do I think He is without shortcomings or that He needs to be continually remembered or worshipped. After all, He did not make things clear even in His last message, the Qur'an. Why should I devote my time to reading more about Him? There are other things to do in life, like taking care of your work and your family. I feel if you keep on thinking about these things, your mind will never be at peace.

Since He gave us the freedom to think, then I do not think He will punish us as long as we do not hurt others. Thus, one does not need to be Muslim to be good or to be saved. Maybe there are some Christians or non-believers who will be saved. But can one be a Muslim who, like me, is without firm belief in God? I'm anxiously awaiting your reply.

Comment 12 (from a long impassioned email I received from a visiting doctoral student from Cyprus. Numerous converts and second generation Muslims have shared with me their doubts about the *Hadith* literature, but it appears that skepticism among Muslim youth about the trustworthiness of this material may be growing worldwide.):

Given the vast corruption of Islamic practice, the Islamic practice— not Islam itself—has to continually renew and purify itself to survive. There is no choice in this, as I see it. And there is no way toward purification and renewal unless we are not afraid to ask hard questions and to be questioned by others. To agree to disagree has to be an accepted principle of social discourse.

There is a lot of <u>shirk</u> in today's Islamic practice, we have to accept that, but few will be willing to even consider the possibility. Dissent is rarely appreciated because unity for the sake of unity is much more cherished than truth. I believe that throughout the many centuries, the real evildoers have injected fabrications into Islamic practice, and after many generations, they have come to be accepted—and, frequently, we see the power of the sword in shaping practices rather than belief. Yet, in general, Muslims do not seem to yearn for a purified Islamic practice or an Islamic practice rooted only in the Book of Allah, but prefer instead volumes upon volumes on what Prophet Muhammad supposedly said or did.

Most Muslims believe that their interpretation of Islam is the only acceptable form of Islam, since they are no longer willing to question practices that have been enshrouded in the "holy protection" of <u>Hadith</u> and <u>Sunnah</u>. I've come to believe that it is time to go back to the Qur'an, from which we have deviated so much in our practices, and take a different, heavily questioning attitude toward <u>Hadith</u> and <u>Sunnah</u>. I believe we have to commit ourselves to the Qur'an as our only source of Islam, as Allah neither needs nor requires any supplement to His Book. In the Qur'an, Allah gives us the guarantee that He will, by Himself, protect the

Qur'an (how one perceives verse 15:9 may differ in breadth and depth, but the essential idea of divine protection of the Qur'an is abundantly clear). As there is no other book that has the same protection, we have no choice but to accept that the Qur'an is sufficient for us.

Islam is ultimately between the individual and Allah, then why must I be dependent on others than Allah to make this or that halal[144] or haram[145]? How is it that the will of the individual is delegated to others, just as prone to error as I am? Is there Qur'anic support for this? I think not. For this reason I cannot accept religious restrictions other than those clearly stated in the Qur'an, because Allah knows what to prohibit and what to allow.

I'd love to see the day when women are welcome in all mosques at all prayer times, regardless of their bodily state, and given half of the praying space, not the back space but either the right or the left side of the prayer area. I come from Cyprus, where I have never seen such seclusion of women as what is practiced in mosques in America. In the Mosque I attend in the United States we have actually regressed. Women used to be allowed to at least pray in the back!

My mom or grandmothers never wore veils or burkas to cover from head to toe in order to be good people. Even verse 24:31 can be understood in different ways. A verse that clearly commands women to cover their chests has been misconstrued to mean that women must cover their head, and so on, even though there is no explicit mention of "head" or "hair" in it.

In many verses, the predicate that a commandment is based upon, the "if", is often disregarded, as in the passage that explains the historical circumstances that made it necessary for the testimony of two women to equal that of one man or the passage that states under what conditions polygamy is allowed. The "if" is never mentioned. The Quran mentions it, but it is never talked about.

---

144. Meaning *lawful.*
145. Meaning *prohibited.*

I know Muslims who do not eat jelly because it contains gelatine, which may come from pig bones, but the Qur'an specifically forbids "the flesh of the pig," not its bones or other parts. There cannot be a better example than this verse (6:146) in showing us that when Allah wants to be specific with a prohibition, He will be. The Qur'an specifically forbids four kinds of meat (5:3, 6:145). If these "divine laws" are based on tradition, then we have to ask upon what is the tradition based? Is it Hadith or Sunnah? If so, then how can some supposed saying and/or practice of the Prophet bring restrictions in addition to those in the Qur'an?

Another issue is washing before prayer. The Qur'an specifically tells us how to do it (5:6). It tells us about tayamun[146] (4:43, 5:5) in case there is no water to wash with. Yet, under the name of Sunnah many, if not most, Muslims feel obliged to do additional things during wudu'[147] and to recite formulaic supplications and so on. And we never ask if the beloved Prophet would add or take away from the commandments of Allah, especially when they are so clearly spelled out in the Qur'an? It matters none to me that there is some hadiths here and there that tell me how the Prophet supposedly washed himself before prayer. I find it easier and one hundred percent trustworthy to read the Qur'an and believe that that is what the Prophet practiced to the letter. Is there a chance, even a slim one, that we are augmenting Allah's word with something else?

I don't think people treat the Qur'an as it should be treated. How can the Word of Allah be equated or supplemented by books written by men about a man? Some go so far as to say that Hadith is Revelation that the Prophet did not put down in the Qur'an. The story of the lost verse that commands killing adulterers by stoning illustrates the dangers of this approach; anything that goes to this extent to impose a corrupt Islam is nothing but an abomination. Many find great wisdom in the supposed practices of Prophet Muhammad, written in Hadith, for which we have

---

146. The use of pure earth to cleans oneself.
147. Ritual ablution.

to have total unwavering trust, equal to the trust we should have in the Qur'an, also with rare regard as to whether he did something as a human (bashar) or whether he did something as a messenger (rasul) and prophet (nabi) of Allah. To me, Hadith books are only historical accounts at best; "at best" because the source of many are shady and come from many generations of later (deemed by the decision of a particular group with strongly vested interests) "truthful" narrators. The argument about "hadith science" is also laughable because it follows the same logic some Bible scholars put forth regarding the authenticity and supposed uncorrupted nature of the Biblical text, the argument being that there was a strong oral tradition at the time that ensures that the stories were transmitted without loss or corruption. The entire argument of traditionalist Islam comes down to this: where do we seek the explanation of what seems to be "unclear" in the Qur'an? To me, there is one and only one direction to turn: to the Word of Allah and only Allah (Allah wa illa Allah) as revealed in His final Scriptural Revelation.

Comment 13 (one of a number of messages from American Muslim immigrants who drifted from their religion but were inspired to renewed interest in Islam through their marriages to devout persons of other faiths. In this young lady's story, note her stress on the importance of reason and logic in her spiritual search. A few of her questions appear elsewhere in the text.):

You do not know me and to be honest, I had not heard about you until a couple of weeks ago. Then, one of my friends at the mosque that I go to told me about your book, Even Angels Ask. So, I bought it and read it. Before I go on to explain why I am contacting you, I would just like to take a minute and tell you that your book has given back to me something that I had lost in my faith; that is, hope. Your book reminded me of the spiritual beauty and meaning of Islam, which I am afraid, is very different from what is taught and practiced by many Muslims today. Your book encouraged me to stay on my spiritual journey to find God.

Now, the reason I am contacting you: I am a born Muslim. I was born and raised in Turkey. My family is not very religious. My father believes in God, but no organized religion, and my mother is a Muslim but not a rigidly practicing one. When I was sixteen years old, I came to the U.S. with a scholarship and ended up going to college and eventually staying here. Now I live in Southern Orange County, California.

I have always had great interest in all religions and especially in understanding Islam. Unfortunately, I did not search hard enough, or perhaps when I did search and asked questions, those that were around to answer did so in the usual, superficial way; i.e., "Some things you should not question," "That is what the Qur'an says," "Well, it was okay back in the Prophet's days." The answers just never made sense and they turned me off. So, over the years, I lost interest in finding the Truth, until I married an American who is a Christian. Meeting him, falling in love with him, and learning more about Christianity through him sparked my interest in God, religion and the truth once again. So, I started searching for God, yet again.

I started going to a mosque and meeting more Muslims. I was looking for someone who was very knowledgeable in Islam that I could discuss and question things with and someone who would not condemn or judge me because of my inquisitive nature. Thank God, the imam was just that person. I asked him if he would mind studying the Qur'an with me. He said that he would make time for that. I have been studying with him for a couple of months now and I really enjoy it. He is a wonderful imam, a gentle, open-minded, kind soul. We have been studying the Qur'an surah by surah.

Yet, I still have some MAJOR questions that he has not been able to answer to my satisfaction. And sometimes these questions are big stumbling blocks for me that can and do cloud my faith. Having read your book and seeing your approach to Islam and some of the questions, I came to think that maybe I could ask you for help. You seem to approach things from a logical and analytical point of view, which really describes the process I am going through to find the Truth. I believe that you might be able to answer some of my questions logically.

As I study Islam and the Qur'an, and as questions arise that my imam cannot answer to my satisfaction, can I please ask for your help? I know that you must have an awfully busy schedule and that this is probably the last thing you have time for: a stranger asking you for some time to answer questions. However, I do believe that you have insight and knowledge that could shed some light into some of the areas I find troubling in Islam, the Qur'an and even the Prophet's life. I would truly appreciate your help in my search for God, but I would also understand if you do not have the time to do this.

Comment 14 (from a young Muslim immigrant struggling to defend his religion. Most Muslim immigrants to America come from countries where it is illegal to disparage Islam. In contrast, their children are often exposed to harsh concerted criticism of their faith. The following is a sample of what they encounter. Below and in the footnotes I briefly comment on some of the points. My purpose here is not to present a defense but to show the kinds of intellectual confrontations Muslim American youth become embroiled in.[148]):

Someone I know is having a debate with someone over women's rights in Islam. They sent this to me illustrating some of the points that are being argued. I'm going to need some help on debating this stuff and looking up stuff. If you can send me what you can, I'd be grateful. So far my best argument is against the source, since I feel that Khomeini does not represent Islam. Also, if you can give me references or URL's that would

---

148. For another more elaborate example of this kind, see the critique by Newton and Rafiqul-Haqq at: debate.domini.org/Newton/womeng.htm.

be very helpful. The brother's opponent sent him the following excerpts from one of Ayatollah Khomeini's books.[149]

Ayatollah Khomeini's Religious Teachings on Marriage, Divorce and Relationships from Khomeini's book, "Tahrirolvasyleh", fourth volume, Darol Elm, Gom, Iran, 1990:[150]

(1) A man can marry a girl younger than nine years of age, even if the girl is still a baby being breastfed.[151] *A man, however, is prohibited from having intercourse with a girl younger than nine, other sexual acts*

---

149. Ayyatollah Khomeini's book, *Tahrir al-Vasileh* ("Commentary on the Vehicle [of Salvation by S. Abul-Hasan Isfahani]") is a commentary on a work of an earlier scholar, S. Abul-Hasan Isfahani, which quotes rulings that go back many centuries. Unfortunately, I have not been able to obtain a copy of the book or an English translation of it to check for accuracy. At most the first three quotations are opinions of Ayatollah Khomeini, the rest of the quotes are verses from the Qur'an (citations 4 and 5) and Sunni *Hadith* collections (citations 6-29). Accept for a few noted exceptions, the *hadiths* do appear in the cited compilations but cannot have been part of a book by Ayatollah Khomeini, since as a Shiite scholar he would not rely on Sunni sources. In all likelihood, the opponent was using different sources available to him to build his case, and not claiming that all are from the same text.

150. It should be born in mind that traditional legal works of this kind attempt to anticipate every imaginable legal problem, no matter how remote or unrealistic. See, for example, the forward to, *A Clarification of Questions, An unabridged translation of Resaleh Towzih al-Masael by Ayatollah Khomeini*, translated by J. Borujerdi, with a forward by M. Fischer and M. Abedi.

151. In traditional Islamic cultures the time between the formal marriage ceremony and cohabitation could be many years. After the formal marriage ceremony, meetings between the couple are as a rule strictly chaperoned until they finally share a household. While the formal marriage ceremony can take place when either or both of the intended are still infants,

(contd. on page 488)

such as foreplay, rubbing, kissing and sodomy is allowed.[152] *A man having intercourse with a girl younger than nine years of age has not committed a crime, but only an infraction, if the girl is not permanently damaged. If the girl, however, is permanently damaged, the man must provide for her all her life. But this girl will not count as one of the man's four permanent wives. He also is not permitted to marry the girl's sister.*[153]

(2) A woman who has contracted a permanent marriage must not go out of the house without her husband's permission; she must remain at his disposal for the fulfilling of any of his desires,[154] *and must not prevent him from having intercourse with her except for a religiously valid reason. If she obeys him in these, the husband must provide her with her food, clothing, lodging, and other necessary appliances, and if he does not do so*

Footnote No. 151 (contd. from page 487)

cohabitation and sexual relations are not allowed until both have attained puberty. Thus in what follows an extremely improbable scenario is discussed, if indeed this quote is accurate, but again this type of abstract casuistry is common to these traditional "handbooks" on legal questions. In some classical treatises marriages between humans and *jinns* are discussed. It should be noted that the demands of modernization have made child marriages as just described an increasingly rare occurrence in Muslim countries.

152. Shiite legal theory allows sodomy between a husband and wife; Sunni law forbids it.

153. As mentioned above, I do not know whether this is a loose paraphrase or close to the actual wording, but quotes 4 and 5 can be found almost word for word in Imam Khomeini's *Resaleh Towzih al-Masael.* See *A Clarification of Questions*, page 318, #2412 and #2413.

154. Legitimate desires (i.e. within the limits of the *Shariah*) are implied here, for immediately after making this statement in the *Resaleh Towzih al-Masael*, Khomeini states: "A man does not have the right to force his wife into servicing the house." See *A Clarification of Questions*, page 318, #2414.

then he is indebted to the woman, whether or not he can afford them.

(3) A woman who refuses herself to her husband is blameworthy, and may not demand from him food, clothing, lodging, or any later sexual relations; however, she retains the right to her dowry.[155]

Comment by opponent: Don't get me wrong, there are lots of positive bits too, but these were the ones that shocked me. Only thing is, Khomeini's words may not be religiously valid, because he was a fanatic who caused civil war in Iran.[156] *Or that's what I've been told by other Muslims, at least. But look at the following verses from the Qur'an.*

(4) Men are in charge of women, because Allah hath made the one of them to excel the other, and because they spend of their property (for the support of women). So good women are obedient, guarding in secret that which Allah hath guarded. As for those from whom you fear rebellion, admonish them and banish them to beds apart; and scourge (beat) them. Then if they obey you, seek not a way against them. Lo! Allah is ever High Exalted, Great (4:34).[157]

Comment by opponent: Well, you see my problem for obvious reasons. But this is not a biggie: I knew about this one for ages.

(5) If any of your women are guilty of lewdness, take the evidence of four (reliable) witnesses from amongst you against them; and if they testify, confine them to houses until death do claim them, or God ordains for them some (other) way. If two men among you are guilty of lewdness, punish them both. If they repent and amend, leave them alone, for God is Oft-returning, Most Merciful (4:15-16).[158]

---

155. Opinions like these (points 1-3) are not at all uncommon among Muslim scholars; the fact that most Muslims living in the West would object to them underscores the need for critical review of all Muslim scholarship, past and present.

156. There was no civil war in Iran under Khomeini's rule, but Iraq attacked Iran and several years of war ensued.

157. For more on this verse, see Question 4 and 5 in this Chapter.

158. See my comment below.

Comment by opponent: I hadn't realized just how deep the double standards went. The following Sayings of Muhammad also seem to give men despotic authority over their wives.

(6) The Prophet said: "If a husband tells his wife to keep carrying a load of stones from a red mountain to a black one, or from a black mountain to a white one, it would be incumbent on her to do so" (Tirmidhi).

(7) The Prophet said: "By Him in whose hands is the life of Muhammad, a woman cannot discharge her duty towards God until she has discharged her duty towards her husband: if she is riding a camel and her husband expresses his desire, she must not refuse"(Ibn Maja`).[159]

(8) The Prophet said: "If a man is in a mood to have sexual intercourse, the wife must go to him immediately even if she is occupied in baking bread" (Tirmidhi).

(9) The Prophet said: "If a husband calls his wife to his bed (i.e. to have sex) and she refuses and causes him to sleep in anger, the angels will curse her until morning" (Bukhari).

(10) The Prophet said: "When a wife vexes her husband, then the houris of Paradise utter curses on her saying, 'May God destroy you, do not annoy your husband, because he is with you only for a short time; he will shortly leave you to come to us in Paradise'" (Tirmidhi).

(11) The Prophet said that a woman's evidence carries half the weight of that of a man because of her inferior intelligence (Bukhari).[160]

(12) The Prophet said: "Beware of the beguilement of the world and women. The first trial of the children of Israel was through women" (Muslim).

(13) The Prophet said: "Misfortune is a part of women, residences and horses" (Mishkat).

---

159. Reported by al Bazzar, the transmitters are said to be *rijal sahih* (reliable narrators), see *Majma' al Zawa'id*, 4/296, and *Sahih al Jami'*.

160. Quotes 11 and 23 are from the same *hadith*.

(14) The Prophet said: "If Eve was not created, no woman would have been dishonest towards her husband" (Bukhari).[161]

Comment of opponent: Of course, then women would not have existed at all in the first place.

(15) The Prophet said: "When a woman dies, if her husband was pleased with her, she goes to Paradise" (Tirmidhi).

(16) The Prophet said: "On the Day of Judgement, a man shall not be asked why he beat his wife" (Abu Dawud).[162]

(17) Women had become bold with their men, and so the Prophet authorised beating them. As a result seventy women, during one evening, gathered at the residence of the Prophet to complain ruefully against their husbands, who they thought, were not good people (Abu Dawud).[163]

(18) The Prophet said: "A woman is forbidden to spend any money without the permission of her husband, and it includes giving food to the needy or feasts to friends" (Abu Dawud, Tirmidhi).[164]

(19) A wife is forbidden to perform extra prayers (nafal) or observe fasting (other than Ramadan) without the permission of her husband (Bukhari).[165]

---

161. The actual wording of this *hadith* is: "If it were not for the children of Israel, meat would never decay, and if it were not for Eve, wives would never betray their husbands." The comment on Eve reflects the Genesis—and not the Qur'anic—story of the first couple in which Eve tempts Adam.

162. It should be mentioned that of the other three *hadiths* in Abu Dawud's collection that mention wife beating, two forbid it and one discourages it.

163. The text actually reads: Iyas ibn Abdullah ibn Abu Dhubab reported that the Messenger of God said: "Do not beat God's female servants." But when 'Umar came to the Messenger of God and said that the women have become emboldened toward their husbands, he gave permission to beat them. Then many women came round the family of the Prophet complaining about their husbands. So the Messenger of God said, "Many women have gone round Muhammad's family complaining against their husbands. They (masculine plural) are not the best among you."

164. Islamic law also does not allow a husband to spend anything of his wife's wealth without her permission; it maintains each partner's financial independence.

165. I only found voluntary fasting mentioned in these reports.

(20) A woman who seeks <u>khula</u> (divorce from her husband) without a just cause shall not enter Paradise (Abu Dawud).

Comment by opponent: On the other hand, a Muslim husband can divorce his wife unilaterally.

(21) A woman in many ways is deprived of the possession of her own body. Even her milk belongs to her husband (Bukhari).[166]

(22) A woman is not a believer if she undertakes a journey that may last three days or longer, unless she is accompanied by her husband, son, father (Bukhari).[167]

(23) The majority of people in hell are women (Bukhari).[168]

(24) The Prophet said: "When a man calls his wife to bed and she refuses, the one who is in heaven (Allah) will be angry with her until the husband is pleased with her (Bukhari and Muslim).

(25) The Prophet said: "Woman has been created from a rib, and will in no way be straightened for you" (Bukhari).[169]

(26) Ibn Ma'sud reported that the Messenger of Allah said, "A woman is like a private part (sex organ). When she goes out (walking) the devil casts a glance at her (in lust)."[170]

---

166. There is no report in Bukhari's collection that can be construed to suggest this.

167. The *hadith* actually reads: "A woman should not go on a two day journey without her husband or a *mahram* (guardian)." Given the dangers associated with travel at that time, this is not surprising.

168. Quotes 11 and 23 are from the same *hadith*.

169. The full text reads: "Treat women kindly, for a women is like a rib, and the most curved portion of a rib is the upper portion, so if you try to straighten it, it will break, but if you leave it as it is, it will remain crooked. So treat women kindly."

170. No source is given. It belongs to al Tirmidhi's collection. A more appropriate interpretation might be: The Prophet said, "A woman is *awrah* (something that should be covered), for when she goes out Satan looks at her."

(27) Ibn Masud reported, "We were fighting with the Messenger of Allah, and our wives were not with us. We asked the Messenger of Allah, 'Should we castrate ourselves?' The Holy Prophet forbade us from that, and then he allowed us muta (temporary) marriage. So, we all married wives for a fixed time for the dowry of a garment."[171]

(28) Abdur Rahman bin Salam reported that the Apostle of Allah said, "You should marry virgins, and verily they are sweeter in tongue, more prolific in wombs, and easily satisfied with little."[172]

(29) Ali reported that the Apostle of Allah said, "There is in Paradise a market wherein there will be no buying or selling, but will consist of men and women. When a man desires a beauty, he will have intercourse with them."[173]

Author's comment:

As I pointed out in several footnotes, some of the quotes are not direct but negatively biased paraphrases. The opponent most probably found them on the Internet. Not only can most of this information be easily found on many of the Evangelical websites that attack Islam, but also on many conservative Muslim websites that discuss the position of women in Islam.

---

171. No source is given. It appears in *Sahih al Bukhari*.

172. No source is given. The *hadith* appears in the collection of al Tirmidhi. The actual wording is: "Marry virgins, for they have the sweetest mouths, the most prolific wombs, and are the most satisfied with little." It also appears in *mursal* form (incomplete *isnad*) in Ibn Majah's compilation. It should be noted that only one of the Prophet's wives, Aishah, was a virgin when they wed.

173. No source is given. The *hadith*, which is to be found in al Tirmidhi's compilation, reads: "In Paradise there is a market in which there is no buying or selling, but only the forms of men and women; and when a person desires a form he enters it." A less salacious interpretation than the opponent's is more likely. The *hadith* seems to suggest that individuals will be able to select their outward appearance in Paradise. Al Tirmidhi states that it is a *gharib* (strange) tradition.

The interpretation of Qur'an 4:15-16 in point 5 is also not quite accurate. A more literal interpretation would be:

And those who are guilty of lewdness (*fahishah*) from among your women, call to witness four of you against them. And if they testify, then confine them (feminine plural) to their houses until death takes them or God appoints for them a way. And those two of you (*alladhani*) who are guilty of it, punish them both. Then if they repent and amend, then let them be. Truly God is relenting, merciful (4:15-16).

The key difference between this and the opponent's rendition is that "two men" are not mentioned but rather the masculine dual (*alladhani*) is used, which in Arabic means "those two" (which can mean either "that women and that man" or "those two men," depending on the context). There is no indication or reason to assume that the two verses are not connected, quite the contrary. Hence a more natural reading of 4:16 would be:

And those two (a woman found guilty of lewdness as discussed in 4:15 and her male partner, or even two men guilty of some form of lewdness) from among you who are guilty of it, punish them both. Then if they repent and improve, then let them be. Truly God is relenting, merciful (4:15-16).

Thus, Muhammad Ali comments:

Though the word *fahishah* is used sometimes as meaning fornication, the context shows that here it is used to signify immoral conduct short of fornication, for the punishment of fornication is given in 24:2. The words of the verse that follows, referring to a similar immoral act with the indefinite nature of punishment support this conclusion, for punishment in the case of an act short of fornication would vary with nature of the crime. Thus women guilty of immoral conduct are curtailed of their liberty. If they mend their ways, or being unmarried they get married, a way is opened for them by Allah, and they regain their liberty; if they do not the curtailment should be extended till they die. ... The crime spoken of in this verse (4:16) is the same as that in the previous verse. The committers are two.[174]

In addition to some of the citations being tendentious rewordings, Muslim *Hadith* critics have also judged several of the traditions suspect. Yet despite the imprecision, there is enough that is considered trustworthy here to make a persuasive case that Islam accords women a distinctly subordinate and submissive role in marriage. Now it can be argued that the Qur'anic regulations and most of the *Hadith* legislation that is often cited in support of this conclusion reflect a particular social-historical context and that within this milieu the position of women was greatly improved. From this perspective this legislation can be seen as a model of gender relations reform that should be emulated, extended and furthered when the natural evolution of society allows. Yet there are two major obstacles to this view: first, some of the prophetic traditions (e.g. some of the *hadiths* cited above) are very hard to square with it, and second, the great majority of Muslim scholars and lay people reject it.

Comment 15 (a poem by an American convert in her twenties from Cedar Rapids, Iowa. It expresses the isolation from both the larger society and the Islamic community that so many converts testify to.):

---

174. Maulana Muhammad Ali, *The Holy Qur'an with English Translation and Commentary*, Lahore (1994), notes 551 and 552. Also see, Muhammad Asad, *The Message of the Qur'an*, Dar al Andalus, Gibraltar (1980), notes 13 and 14.

Torn Between Two Worlds
– Carly Caris

Torn between two worlds
Searching for identity
On a quest for solitude
A place where I can be me.

> I look in the mirror
> But who is staring back at me?
> I feel like an innocent girl
> Who has lost her virginity.

I look at the people
Staring and whispering as I pass by
Calling me a "traitor"
Believing that my faith is a lie.

> I search deep inside my soul
> Questioning the inner me
> Praying for my struggle
> For peace and solidarity.

I muster up the courage
To speak about who I am
Reflecting on where I've been
Proud to take this stand.

> I'm torn between two worlds
> Not fitting into one or the other
> I've adapted to complement both
> Without feeling smothered.

People judge before I speak
They criticize and analyze
Trying to make me weak
"A slave I am not," I cry.

I slowly walk through the doors
Preparing my spirit and soul
Knowing that no matter what they say
I am still completely whole.

I don't fit here, nor do I fit there
I'm somewhere in between
Identity could have been lost
But in the end I have to be me.

Comment 16 (a rap song from an American male convert aged 29. The sentiments expressed are not at all uncommon among native-born Muslims. It is an eruption of frustration and disillusionment with the mosque culture.)

See What You See
Lyrics and phrasing by Kyle William Anders
[Copyright 2003]

When I talk they say I'm disrespecting the Prophet,
but if they'd listen, I'm not even disrespecting Buhkari.
All I'm saying is no matter how long they
try to slice it and dice it, categorize it, I'll say:
There's only one book, one hook that has got me,
protected by God and it sure isn't man-made.
It's like they had the Qur'an and the wisdom inside it,
but they didn't like it or get it, and then they forgot it, but

not before they locked it up with a key that they swallowed.
Corrupted, neglected, and misused its guidance.
And now the rest of us are left with hundreds of years of their
    progress?
Didn't they read it? I mean 'read' was the first word.
If you look at us now, you'd think 'read'
Wasn't in it,
or missing, or deleted, or backspaced,
or the last word,
that they never heard,
'cause they didn't get that far,
when they tossed the book on their shelf or probably the floor.

Okay, so maybe I'm harsh. I'm sure there were some,
a long time ago,
who got it, or some of it, or a little of it, and used it.
But that doesn't mean that we shouldn't, or can't,
or aren't smart enough to expound on the wisdom they found,
combined with the time that has passed
    and the knowledge of now,
but the problem is, it's still locked up away.
Don't you get it? Come on, you know what I'm saying.
Oh yeah, you can read it, but only at home,
or if you read it, make sure you don't say what you got.
Someone will pull out a tradition, shoot you down on the spot,
tell you that's not what you got, that you didn't understand it,
that you need 15 other books to explain it,
written by a guy you don't know, never met, do you get it?
And even if this guy's really smart, he didn't drive a car, or
    program a VCR,
'cause there was none, not yet,
I mean, he had a camel,
and that's not bad, but still-
it just goes to show you, you can't have insight that is right, see,

if you lived anytime past the 13th century.

And still I go back to my main thought that I lost in
my ranting and raving that might have made you quite cross.
Oh my God, did I just do that?
I just used two words in my song, from 'Your Song'
      by Sir Elton John, and he's gay,
but at least he's got Yahya at the end of his name.
And there are worse things than gay, although I don't like it,
but some of you Muslims, if given the chance you would kill him.
And my God, isn't that worse?
This brings me back to my point, that
we rolled up the Qur'an, lit it, and smoked it up as a joint.
I mean, why not?!? The paper was made of hemp,
might as well get some use from it.
And who needs it anyway? Look around,
      no one thinks it's a shame,
'cause we've got 15 gazillion other books in it's name.
But written by who? You guessed it. You know who.
      Yeah, me and you.
Any human on the block, and the last I knew, Muslims thought
that God didn't enter His creation, that He was Allah.
I mean, when I quote God, I quote God - right from the Qur'an.
But we're sayin' the Prophet said this or that as our talk,
or this or that is right, 'cause it's what I was taught.
In Islam we do this, or as Muslims we feel,
sounds like we're speaking for God,
and I can't believe this is real.
I mean the last thing that I would ever want to do,
is stick my foot in my mouth by trying to walk in His shoes.

And don't get me wrong, I mean if the Prophet said it,
      I'd follow it.

But somebody tellin' me "he saids, she saids,"
    I don't buy it, won't swallow it,
and I ask them to produce one single ounce of evidence,
that would prove to me beyond a shadow of doubt,
    that the books in their hand,
weren't made by man, and are divine and they shine,
like the light and the wisdom coming from mine.

The book that is read, the book that is read.
The word Qur'an means, the book that is read.
The book that is read, the book that is read,
Let its knowledge feed your head, before you are dead.

When God said specific, they enforced it as general,
And then they rounded us all up and
    made themselves the Generals.
And when God kept it general, they said specific,
looked in any book no matter how illegitimate.
Filled in all the gaps, they thought God forgot.
Didn't trust His wisdom, didn't trust His word,
took all His stories, made them sound absurd,
or wrong, or stupid, or lose their meaning.
But from their efforts, at least, they got a book signing.
And the rest of us fell for it,
'cause we stopped reading it ourselves.
Started arguing about the unclear,
as we followed our leaders into hell.

And now after a long time our community's been left with a faith,
that's been raped and used up for personal gain.
Left on a corner for waste to be picked up by the mafia,
or terrorists, as we so proudly call them,
as we argue each night in the mosque,
that, "Hmm, suicide bombing might be okay,

if you've got a guy and a bomb who's willing today."
And for a religion that wasn't allowed to have clergy,
Why the hell have we got more priests than Christianity?
We're nodding and bowing, standing and
      kissing this sheik and that sheik.
We aught to have a bake sale of sheiks and get rid of all of 'em.

And what about this word religion,
I thought Islam, oh I mean submission,
was a 'way' or that's at least what our scholars want you to say,
at least to non-Muslims,
but when they come around, preachin' and hollerin',
better put your nose to the ground, this ain't a 'way' – it's religion,
with dogma, excess, and illiterate peasants.
And what you think is wrong,
'less it was a scholar's decision.

The book that is read, the book that is read.
The Word Qur'an means, the book that is read.
The book that is read, the book that is read.
Let its knowledge feed our heads, before we are dead.
Read it many times,
over and over,
march up this uphill climb,
into the hereafter.
Many people want you to think that you're stupid,
that you won't understand it, that it won't speak to ya'.
That you need them to hug, kiss, and bow to
But trust Allah's word, instead of their mouthfuls.
And so, everyone listening, don't listen to me,
just read the Qur'an and see
what You see.
But by read the Qur'an, I mean read the Qur'an,
not every other book that we can't rely on.

Parting Remarks
To the Homegrown American Sisters and Brothers

At present, our community in America, whether or not we are aware of it or acknowledge it, is engulfed in a decisive conflict, and we are taking heavy losses. Mass numbers of descendents of Muslims, converts, and spiritual seekers are forsaking the American Islamic community and many of these will inevitably abandon the religion. The confrontation is of course not military, but rather is occurring on the intellectual plane. On one front our religion is being both subtly and overtly demeaned by the media. On another, anti-Islam websites are assaulting the faith with mostly discarded but now resurrected antiquated orientalist criticisms. On another, an extreme, virulent and irrational interpretation of the faith has assumed, with a good deal of outside support, center stage on the world scene. On another, most mosques in this country impose in the name of Islam traditions and beliefs of questionable necessity that obfuscate the fundamental message of God's last revelation to humanity and that are driving individuals from the faith in droves, and that serve to confirm for too many youth of Muslim parentage and American converts the overriding negative impression of Islam that society seems to hold at large. Instead of seeing a path to spiritual growth, enlightenment and fulfillment, many of these disengaged Muslims start to see a stagnant, retrogressive, patriarchal remnant of a lagging culture, mired in meaningless controversies and hollow, lifeless formalism.

If this is going to be countered, it will require an immense and courageous intellectual effort, and those upon whose shoulders this challenge and duty primarily rests are the second generation and converts who have held fast to their faith despite the many challenges this has presented. It is you, the activist American Muslim youth and converts, though your numbers are small, who have been placed in a pivotal role. Through your American upbringing, you have come to fully know and understand the surrounding society, and through your love and commitment to God and your religion, in a milieu that constantly tests it, you have by nature and necessity become the crucial bridge between your faith and its future in this country. You are in the best position to rationally respond to Islam's detractors and to communicate and demonstrate to your fellow countrymen and women what it really means to be a Muslim. You think their think, talk their talk, and appreciate their confusions and concerns. You are also in the best position to reassess the vast tradition that has come down to us in the name of Islam. It is precisely because you have not been reared in a traditional Muslim culture and because you have been taught since your first day in school to search, question, critique, and analyze that you are the prime candidates to endeavor to separate religion from culture, to distinguish the essential to Islam from time and place bound interpretations. It is you who are best able to understand and communicate to the disaffected Muslim youth. This is your *jihad*, a *jihad* for minds and hearts, a *jihad* of intellect and reason.

So I encourage you to arm yourselves, my younger brothers and sisters, with books, and pens and personal computers, and all the other instruments of learning. And arm yourselves with knowledge of your religious tradition and the works and thoughts of its great minds of the past. But also arm yourselves with modern techniques of critical, analytical, investigative research, so that you can better study and critique past contributions in the Islamic sciences. Learn all you can in your coursework, and especially in such fields as religious studies, history, anthropology, and linguistics. Arm yourselves also, if you have the inclination and aptitude, with advanced degrees in these areas of research so critical to the project of reappraising our community's traditions. And arm yourselves with humility, because it is vital to objectivity, and with courage and perseverance, brothers and sisters, because you will be opposed from without and within the Muslim community. And remember to always pursue the truth, for God is the Truth, and always pray for and trust in His guidance. And so arm yourselves also with steadfast devotion to your Lord, never forgetting that to Him, and Him only, you have surrendered—not to a tradition, or a school of thought, or a local community, or culture, or scholarly legacy—and that your living, striving, sacrifice and dying, all is for Allah.

INDEX

Other Books by
Jeffrey Lang

Also available by

Struggling to Surrender

Some Impressions of
an American Convert
to Islam

ISBN 0-915957-26-4
Sixth Printing
$11.75

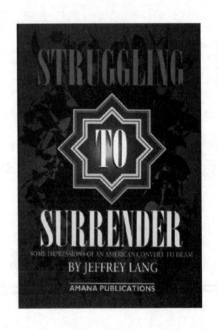

In this book, Professor Lang gives a very personal
account of his search for God when he found out that
his inherited religious beliefs could no longer answer
his questions. A chance encounter led him to Islam.
But now how does he adapt to his new community,
its beliefs and lifestyle?

Jeffrey Lang

Even Angels Ask
A Journey to Islam
in America

Drawing on his personal
experiences as a Muslim,
Professor Lang discusses
conflicts between faith
and reason, obstacles in
converting to Islam,
extremism within some
Muslim communities and
future outlook for
American Muslims.

ISBN 0-915957-67-1
Fourth Printing
$11.75

For more information on these books, please visit
amana-publications.com